Integrating Play Techniques in Comprehensive School Counseling Programs

Integrating Play Techniques in Comprehensive School Counseling Programs

by

Jennifer R. Curry
Louisiana State University

and

Laura J. Fazio-Griffith
Southeastern Louisiana University

Information Age Publishing, Inc.
Charlotte, North Carolina • www.infoagepub.com

Library of Congress Cataloging-in-Publication Data

CIP data for this book can be found on the Library of Congress website http://www.loc.gov/index.html

ISBNs: Paperback: 978-1-62396-304-0
Hardcover: 978-1-62396-305-7
eBook: 978-1-62396-306-4

Printed in the United States of America

CONTENTS

INTRODUCTION TO EDITED BOOK

Jennifer R. Curry and Laura J. Fazio-Griffith

School counselors play a unique role in the mental health of students, families, community stakeholders, and educational systems through delivery of a prevention based, developmental, comprehensive school counseling program. Today's school counseling programs are based on the American School Counselor Association's *National Model* (ASCA, 2012). This model allows school counselors to design, implement and manage school counseling programs that include a guidance curriculum to promote student competence in the areas of personal/social, career, and academic development. However, there are times when students face adjustment difficulties or personal crises and need extra support from their school counselor. Extra support includes referrals to outside agencies (e.g., reporting child abuse), coordination of services with other professionals (i.e., social workers or case managers), and responsive services. Responsive services are a direct service provided by school counselors and include the provision of individual and small group counseling for students demonstrating need.

Because school counselors are responsible for an entire program, it is not possible for them to deliver long-term, therapeutic interventions or to address deep, psychological issues through intense treatment modalities (ASCA, 2012). Specifically, limited responsive services such as short term, brief counseling that targets student adjustment and healthy coping are

Integrating Play Techniques in Comprehensive School Counseling Programs, pp. vii–ix

within the purview of the school counselor's work. In this book, we invited authors to review specific issues that cause student adjustment difficulties and we asked the authors to provide play therapy interventions that are brief in both duration and length to accommodate counseling in the school environment. Examples of student concerns addressed in this book include bullying, parent incarceration, parent military deployment, grief and loss, natural disasters, separation anxiety, family substance abuse, and other issues that impact students' daily functioning at school.

Play therapists, such as Virginia Axline, Garry Landreth, Charles Schafer, Kevin O'Connor, Eliana Gill, Terry Kottman and many others are credited with recognizing the importance of play when counseling children. The foundation of play therapy approaches is rooted in the belief that children naturally communicate and resolve problems through play; as such, play is a natural medium for counseling with children. While we are grateful for the original works of seminal play therapy authors and researchers, in this edited book we have necessarily tailored their work to the school setting. Because schools are a unique environment, counseling practices must be adapted to the practical considerations of school settings and the school day. In this book, the authors explore concerns that children may commonly express in the school environment and provide school counselors with guidelines for implementing play techniques and interventions based on best practice interventions in the school environment.

The chapters of this book are designed with several specific purposes in mind. To begin with, each chapter highlights a specific concern that may compromise student adjustment and, thereby, may create a barrier to student learning. Second, each chapter provides a miniature literature review which serves as a description of the problem or concern (e.g., caregiver substance abuse), how this issue may affect children, and the scope and prevalence of the problem. It is our hope that the information in the literature review may be used by school counselors to inform stakeholders (parents, teachers, administrators) about various problems children experience and the impact of these problems on children's mental health and school functioning. For example, school counselors with students in their schools who have parents being deployed for military combat will find information in the military deployment chapter about the phases of military deployment, common adjustment problems faced by children when parents are deployed, normal adjustment periods, and signs that children are having difficulty adjusting. This information may be useful for a parent workshop or faculty in-service presentation. Third, each chapter highlights an evidenced based play therapy practice for addressing the student concern or problem presented in the chapter and gives a case study example of how to conduct counseling sessions utilizing play therapy interventions within a school environment.

As previously mentioned, the case studies and play practices demonstrated in this book are based on play therapy theory. This book underscores traditional practices and techniques of various play therapy theories (i.e., Adlerian, child centered, reality based, cognitive behavioral, solution focused brief play therapy) and pulls from the work of outstanding play therapy researchers, authors and practitioners (i.e., Garry Landreth, Sue Bratton, Eliana Gil, Athena Drewes, Virginia Axline, Terry Kottman). Our goal is not to denounce classical play therapy approaches, rather, the evidenced-based practices contained in this book orient play therapy to the contemporary school setting within the context of a comprehensive, school counseling program as short-term, brief responsive services.

It is our hope that this book will become a useful guide for school counselors who may have limited play therapy training with a high need for knowledge of how to help children in the most effective, developmentally appropriate ways possible. This book is dedicated to the hard work and devotion of school counselors. More importantly, this book is also dedicated to children who need encouragement, love, and support from competent, school counseling professionals.

CHAPTER 1

INCORPORATING PLAY INTERVENTIONS WITHIN INDIVIDUAL AND SMALL GROUP COUNSELING IN SCHOOLS

Jacqueline M. Swank

School counselors are encouraged to spend 80% of their time providing services to students, their families, and school staff (Gysbers & Henderson, 2000). However, school counselors may struggle with providing quality services to the number of students, families, and staff requiring assistance, due to the large number of students they serve and the additional responsibilities assigned to them beyond providing direct service. The U.S. Department of Education, National Institute for Educational Statistics (n.d.) reported the national average for school counselor to student ratio as being 1:250 for the 2009-2010 school year, while a 1:459 ratio is recommended by the American School Counselor Association (American School Counselor Association [ASCA], 2012). Therefore, a need exists for providing short-term, quality, evidenced-based counseling services in an effective manner within the learning environment.

Integrating Play Techniques in Comprehensive School Counseling Programs, pp. 1–18

Individual and small group counseling are two methods for school counselors to utilize in providing direct services to students. Due to the large number of students assigned to one school counselor, it is essential that school counselors use their time wisely to best meet the needs of their students and other stakeholders. This requires school counselors to employ strategies that will facilitate the development of rapport quickly and allow students to feel safe and comfortable sharing with the school counselor. Additionally, the school counselor's awareness of child development and the integration of appropriate interventions, such as play, are essential components to facilitate an effective school counseling program. Thus, school counselors utilize various strategies within individual and small group counseling to address the needs of students that are influencing their academic and social success in the learning environment.

Vignette 1

Felicia is the only school counselor at an elementary school, which serves 450 students. She is responsible for conducting large group guidance lessons with every classroom, while also facilitating small groups on various topics. Additionally, she is expected to meet individually with students to address their diverse individual needs. Felicia has experienced an increase in students requesting individual time with her and she is uncertain how to meet the needs of each student on an individual basis.

Vignette 2

Samuel is the sixth grade school counselor in a middle school. The school administration and parents are concerned about bullying occurring in the school. Samuel has conducted a series of large group guidance lessons to address the issue with all sixth graders; however, there appears to be a small group of students who are continuously bullying other students. Samuel is wondering if facilitating a small group with these students will be effective.

These two vignettes illustrate the concerns that many school counselors may experience in providing services to students. The focus of this chapter is on the integration of play interventions through individual and small group counseling within the school environment to address various issues experienced by students.

COUNSELING IN SCHOOLS

The ASCA (2012) *National Model* outlines four elements crucial for the development of a comprehensive school counseling program: foundation, delivery system, management system, and accountability. Within the delivery system, there are direct and indirect services. The response services component, within direct services, is designed to "meet students' immediate needs and concerns" (p. 86). School counselors are encouraged to spend 30%-40% of their time at the elementary and middle school levels and 25%-35% of their time at the high school level providing responsive services (Gysbers & Henderson, 2000). Individual and small group counseling are within the responsive services component and is focused on helping students "overcome issues impeding achievement and success" (p. 86). Additionally, counseling services are focused on helping students engage in the problem solving process in a healthy manner. Furthermore, counseling interventions are designed to be short term (ASCA, 2012). Thus, individual and small group counseling are crucial services within the delivery system of the ASCA *National Model*.

In examining the practice of group work, Kulic, Horne, and Dagley (2004) conducted a meta-analysis of 94 research articles focused on prevention groups for children and adolescents and found that 79.8% of the groups took place within the school environment. Additionally, Steen, Bauman, and Smith (2007) surveyed 802 school counselors and found that 87% of them reported conducting groups in schools, with the majority of groups focused on the personal/social domain. The participants reported that the greatest barriers to facilitating groups were time constraints and lack of support from school administrators and teachers.

The issue of missing instructional time might be addressed through creative planning within the school curriculum. Within the high school environment, Riester (2002) recommends adding a lab component to a psychology class, which allows time to focus on interpersonal issues. The lab component may encompass large group discussions and activities, or small group facilitation involving school counselors. Although this recommendation might be useful, psychology is generally offered as an elective within the high school curriculum and is taken within the last two years of high school; therefore additional strategies are needed to address the issue of missing instructional time. Riester also suggests assigning students to study hall sections designed to address specific counseling issues, with the school counselor serving as the study hall leader. The study hall format reduces scheduling problems and may assist with maintaining confidentiality (Riester, 2002).

INDIVIDUAL OR GROUP

When choosing among individual and small group counseling interventions, school counselors are encouraged to be mindful of the developmental considerations of students at elementary, middle, and high school levels. In addition, school counselor may contemplate the topic to be addressed, and practical considerations (e.g., time and space available). Therefore, school counselors reflect upon their knowledge of their student population and the specific school environment when selecting individual and small group counseling interventions.

Small groups provide counselors with the opportunity to work with a group of students at the same time, which addresses the logistical issue of time. Additionally, group counseling supports social development. Students who are having difficulties with interpersonal relationships and social skills may benefit by learning from their peers and modeling, which occurs in a group setting (Yalom, 1995). Within the group, students are also able to develop relationships and relate to each other through shared experiences, supporting group cohesion and universality, which facilitates therapeutic change (Yalom, 1995). The establishment of effective peer relationships is a crucial task in developing social competence (Akos, Hamm, Mack, & Dunaway, 2007). Furthermore, group counseling supports cognitive development by challenging students to consider the perspectives of others and determine whether they will adopt the perspectives into their own processing of an issue (Paisley & Milsom, 2007).

In regards to middle school students, small group counseling is often advantageous because association with peer groups is a natural developmental task for early adolescents. Nevertheless, school counselors must also be mindful that the dynamics of peer groups may also inhibit the success of small groups (Akos et al., 2007). Peer groups provide opportunities for adolescents to give and receive feedback and develop skills and behaviors by learning from each other, which may support healthy growth (e.g., considering others' perspectives, recognizing strengths and areas for improvement) or unhealthy development (e.g., promoting bullying) (Akos et al., 2007). Therefore, school counselors need to be purposeful in selecting group members. Additionally, Bloom (2010) reported that counseling groups may form naturally when a few peers accompany a student to the school counselor's office. The peers report accompanying the identified student with a problem to provide support; however, the school counselor may discover that the entire peer group could benefit from small group counseling. This natural formation of a group can provide support through the established peer group. However, when facilitating any group, the school counselor needs to exhibit strong group facilitation skills (e.g., establishing and maintaining a safe, warm environment, eliciting responses from group members, establishing group rules, modeling, reframing/redirecting) in order to promote positive group interactions and address negative interactions that may occur within the group.

An individual counseling format is more appropriate for some students (e.g., students suffering from a recent trauma). In determining whether to provide individual or small group counseling, the school counselor may consider the feasibility and appropriateness of addressing the issue within an individual versus a group format. Additionally, the school counselor may consider the temperament of the student and the potential benefits and concerns with utilizing individual or small group counseling. Allowing time to meet individually with students may require the counselor to be creative, which may involve brief meetings or "check-ins" with the student. The counselor may also use individual counseling as a stepping stone for students to enter small group. Students may "warm-up" to the counselor during individual sessions and then show an interest in being involved in small group counseling.

Counseling researchers have demonstrated the effectiveness of counseling inventions within the school environment (Webb, Brigman, & Campbell, 2005, Zinck & Littrell, 2000). Webb and colleagues compared the finding of three studies involving small group counseling facilitated by school counselors and found that interventions addressing skills associated with school success can improve academic performance and social interactions. Zinck and Littrell (2000) examined the effectiveness of small group counseling with adolescent girls (N = 35) and found that participants reported progress in meeting goals, a reduction in problem severity, and meaningful changes in their relationships with others.

PLAY INTERVENTIONS

Play is a child's language (Landreth, 2002); and therefore, it is useful in providing counseling to children and adolescents. In providing responsive services within the delivery system of the ASCA *National Model* (2012), play therapy interventions are likely the most developmentally appropriate, especially for elementary school children (Ray, Muro, & Schumann, 2004). School counselors may use a variety of play inventions including unstructured play, art, music, games, drama, and dance. Play interventions empower children and adolescents, assisting them with developing self-confidence, mastery, social skills, problem-solving skills, and healthy coping skills (Drewes, 2006, Packman & Bratton, 2003). Play interventions provided in the school also "help children get ready to profit fully from what teachers have to offer" (Landreth, 2002, p. 148). For young children, play may involve a variety of traditional toys, while play with preadolescents and adolescents may encompass more structure and the integration of a variety of activities, such as expressive arts.

Veach and Gladding (2007) discussed the use of various creative, playful techniques to use with groups of high school students. Listening and reflecting upon music may evoke powerful emotions in adolescents and song writing offers them an opportunity to creatively express themselves. Additionally, school counselors may integrate music with movement, which allows students an opportunity to communicate in a physical, behavioral manner within a safe environment (Veach & Gladding, 2007). Art, drama, and literature may also be integrated within small group counseling to facilitate self-expression and identity development through the use of different media. Furthermore, games are appealing to preadolescents and adolescents and may include sports, video games, and board games. Games may facilitate teamwork, achievement, and reflection upon developmental tasks (Veach & Gladding, 2007). Thus, school counselors can use their own creativity to develop a repertoire of playful activities to use during individual and small group counseling.

The perceptions and usage of play by elementary school counselors ($N = 381$) was examined by Ray, Armstrong, Warren, and Balkin (2005). Ray and colleagues found that 73% of respondents perceived play therapy as an effective intervention for elementary school counselors. However, time constraints and lack of training were barriers identified by participants that limited their use of play therapy in the school. Counseling researchers have also examined the effectiveness of play therapy interventions. Two studies consisting of meta-analyses of play therapy research studies ($N = 94, 93$), showed that play and filial therapy were effective interventions to address children's problems (Bratton, Ray, Rhine, & Jones, 2005; Ray, Bratton, Rhine, & Jones, 2001). In addition, Blanco and Ray (2011) examined the effectiveness of child-centered play therapy (CCPT) with elementary school children ($N = 43$) in the school environment and found that children at-risk for academic failure benefited from CCPT. Furthermore, Packman and Bratton (2003) examined the effectiveness on play and activity group interventions with preadolescents ($N = 24$) diagnosed with learning disabilities who were experiencing behavioral and socialization problems. Packman and Bratton found that preadolescents who participated in the play group counseling sessions demonstrated a decrease in problem behavior. Thus, research findings demonstrate the effectiveness of utilizing play interventions with children and adolescents, supporting the use of play within the school environment.

APPROACH AND TECHNIQUES

The use of play within individual and small group counseling may involve a variety of techniques. The techniques may differ based on the developmental level of the students. Additionally, school counselors may choose techniques grounded within various counseling play therapy theories that are nondirective or directive in nature. Thus, the school counseling environment offers the opportunity for creative integration of play interventions.

Theoretical Premise

Play interventions are integrated within various counseling theories. Therefore, in selecting play interventions to utilize within the school environment, school counselors may first want to consider their counseling theoretical orientation. The counselor may then research play therapy theories to develop a greater understanding of how play is integrated within various counseling theories. A brief overview of a few play therapy theories follows in this section.

A nondirective play therapy approach is nationally known as CCPT. School counselors may find this approach especially useful with young children. CCPT, like person centered counseling (Rogers, 1942), is focused on the relationship. Within CCPT, the counselor provides a variety of play materials that are offered to the child for exploration and expression. Since this is a nondirective approach, counseling does not involve the integration of various play techniques, but instead focuses on tracking and reflecting the child's nonverbal behaviors and verbal responses (Landreth, 2002). School counselors may use CCPT during individual counseling or during small play groups.

The school counselor may also employ more directive play interventions that are grounded within various play therapy theories. Cognitive-behavioral play therapy (CBPT) involves the school counselor embracing the role of an educator to assist students in challenging maladaptive thoughts and behaviors (Knell, 1997). Additionally, the school counselor may embrace a solution-focused or strength-based approach. Within this theoretical premise, school counselors focus individual and small group sessions on identifying and building upon students strengths, instead of focusing on the consequences of problematic behavior. The foundation of solution-focused or strength-based approaches is the principle that focusing on success facilitates positive change (Cooley, 2009).

The school counselor may also employ an Adlerian play therapy approach, which focuses on increasing social interest and skill development

(Kottman, 2001). Thus, the school counselor may integrate play interventions within various theoretical orientations. Throughout this book, multiple theoretical orientations and corresponding techniques are highlighted.

Play Techniques

The integration of play within counseling encompasses a myriad of techniques, including art, music, games, drama, and movement. Individual and small group counseling may also involve unstructured play. In selecting play interventions, the school counselor considers the age and developmental level of the student to identify appropriate techniques. Puppets and dolls are generally appealing to elementary school students, while middle and high school students may have a greater interest in games, drama, art, and music. Various types of art may also be more appealing to different age groups. For example, young children may prefer the bright colors of Play-Doh while older students may prefer clay. Additionally, young students may enjoy finger paint, while older students may find water color, tempera paint, and oil pastels more appealing. However, it is important to remember that these are general considerations and may vary for individual students. The school counselor may decide to have a variety of different materials available to allow individuals the opportunity to select the materials that are most appealing to them. School counselors may find this particularly helpful with older students to communicate being nonjudgmental. The counselor communicates that the students are viewed as older and responsible to handle more challenging materials, while also communicating that it is acceptable to use materials that they used as a young child if this is their preference. Furthermore, obtaining information from the student or group of students about their interests can be useful in planning play interventions to incorporate within individual and small group counseling.

Sample Sessions

This section provides school counselors with examples of integrating play in individual and small group counseling within the school environment. Each sample session is presented with goals, materials needed, a description of the play intervention, and a discussion of considerations. School counselors are encouraged to use the following suggestions as a springboard for enhancing their school counseling interventions.

PLAYFUL EXPRESSION

Theme: Exploration and self-expression
Age: Young children, can be adapted for older children
Modality: Individual or Group

Goals:

- Promote self-regulation, self-confidence, mastery, and problem solving
- Develop interpersonal skills (group play)

Materials:

A variety of play materials within specified categories are needed for CCPT sessions. Landreth (2002) recommends the following categories of toys: (a) real-life toys, (b) acting-out toys that provide aggressive-release, and (c) toys for emotional release and creative expression.

Description:

Designate a play space for the student or group of students. The counselor invites the student(s) into the playroom, offering an opportunity to explore the toys and engage in self-expression. Throughout the session, the counselor focuses on tracking and reflecting. Additionally, the counselor sets limits as needed during the session to provide safety.

Considerations:

In selecting toys to have available to students, it is important to have a variety in each category. However, the school counselor should also be aware of toys that may not be acceptable in the school environment. For example, plastic knives and guns are appropriate to have in a playroom to allow children to express aggression in a safe environment. Nevertheless, the school may prohibit the use of these items.

WHAT DO I DO?

Theme: Problem solving
Age: Elementary School
Modality: Individual or Group

Goals:

- Promote positive interactions with others
- Develop problem-solving skills

Materials:

- Variety of puppets
- White socks
- Markers
- Buttons
- Yarn
- Glue
- Scissors
- Construction paper
- Paper plates
- Craft sticks
- Puppet theater or table and tablecloth

Description:

The school counselor may begin the group by reading a book or showing a video clip that presents a problem or dilemma that is relevant to the group. In reading the book or showing the movie clip, the counselor may choose to only read/show the first part of the book/video that presents the problem and then finish the book/video after the group activity. Alternatively, the school counselor may discuss a problem that she knows group members are experiencing or situations that are relevant for the age group, or ask the students to share problems that they are currently experiencing or have experienced in the past. The students are given the opportunity to discuss the situation and to use problem-solving skills.

Students are then given the opportunity to work together to create skits using puppets that demonstrate healthy ways to solve the problem. Students may use existing puppets, create their own puppets, or use both. The school counselor provides a variety of craft materials to create puppets out of socks or using paper plates with a craft stick as a handle. The children then present their puppet shows and discuss the problem-solving strategies. The group concludes with finishing the book/video and discussing the strategy used by the character(s) to address the problem. The students are also encouraged to use their problem-solving strategies during the week and discuss what happened during the following group session.

Considerations:

This group activity will likely require two sessions. Additionally, depending on the materials used for creating the puppets, the puppets may need time to dry before using them to prevent pieces from falling off. The school counselor may keep the puppets to use during a future group with the students. If the school counselor does not have a puppet theater, a table with a tablecloth can be used as a puppet theater.

THE POSITIVE ME

Theme: Self-esteem
Age: All grade levels
Modality: Individual or Group

Goals:

- Identify positive qualities and strengths about self
- Promote positive self-talk through verbalization of positive attributes
- Foster positive interactions with others

Materials:

- Pictures of celebrities, cartoon characters, etc.
- White heavy paper
- Construction paper
- Markers, crayons, colored pencils
- Magazines
- Buttons
- Feathers
- Glitter
- Yarn
- Glue
- Scissors

Description:

The group begins with asking students to look at pictures of famous individuals, which may include: cartoon characters, celebrities, etc., and to identify what they like about the individual/character (their strengths/positive attributes). Students are encouraged to include a physical description, personality characteristics, hobbies, and to discuss how easy or difficult it was to identify positive qualities among the various individuals/characters. Next, students are asked to reflect upon what they would include in a self-description focusing on their positive attributes and strengths, and are given the opportunity to develop a creative representation of themselves using a variety of creative materials (e.g., collage of words and/or pictures). Then, group members are given the opportunity to share their creative representations with the group and receive positive feedback from group members. The school counselor facilitates a discussion about how it felt to describe the famous people compared to describing oneself. Finally, students are encouraged to keep their projects as a reminder of their strengths and positive attributes. Students may also be encouraged to write their strengths on a sheet of paper or notecard to carry with them to refer to when they are having a difficult day and need encouragement. In follow-up sessions, group members are asked to share how they are using their list of positive attributes to help them when they feel discouraged.

Considerations:

It is important to set ground rules about giving feedback and discuss the importance of supporting each other to promote a positive self-esteem. Additionally, the counselor may choose to provide a fewer number of glue bottles and scissors, etc. then the number of students in the group, which requires the group members to share materials with each other, supporting social skill development and providing another area for discussion. Furthermore, it is important for the counselor to review the magazines prior to using them with the group to ensure the appropriateness of the content, photographs, and advertisements.

GET IT OUT: PART 1

Theme: Self-expression
Age: All grade levels
Modality: Individual or Group

Goals:

- Promote healthy expression of feelings
- Foster healthy ways to cope with stress

Materials:

- Music
- Open space
- Paper
- Markers, crayons, colored pencils

Description:

Students are asked to think about a stressful situation that they are currently experiencing or recently experienced. The school counselor may need to offer some suggestions (e.g., testing) if students are having difficulty thinking of a situation. Students are then asked to draw an outline of their body and color in the areas where they feel stress in their body. The counselor then facilitates a discussion about how stress can affect us physically, in addition to emotionally. After the discussion, the school counselor has students engage in movement exercises to relieve tension and stress in the body. Some exercises involve small parts of the body (i.e., hands or feet), while other exercises involve moving the entire body. The exercises encompass a variety of movement activities involving both slow and fast movement. The counselor allows time between the exercises for students to discuss how their body feels after engaging in the movement activity. The counselor then processes the experience with the students asking them to describe the feelings they experienced during the movement activity, and how they might use this strategy in stressful situations (e.g., shake out their hands and wiggle their fingers and toes when they are not able to move their entire body while sitting in class). Additionally, the counselor may choose to play various types of music (e.g., classical, rap, country), along with recordings of sounds from nature during the movement activities and then process the feelings experienced while hearing various types of music and sound.

Considerations:

The school counselor ensures that there is enough space for students to spread out to engage in the movement activities in a safe manner. Additionally, the counselor may choose to facilitate a meditation activity with the students, in addition to the movement activity, during a follow-up session or in lieu of the movement activity.

GET IT OUT: PART 2

Theme: Self-expression
Age: All grade levels
Modality: Individual or Group

Goals:

- Promote healthy expression of feelings
- Foster healthy ways to cope with stress

Materials:

- Play-Doh
- Clay
- Music
- Paper (optional)
- Pencils, markers, colored pencils, crayons (optional)

Description:

Students are given Play-Doh/clay and allowed to explore the material (e.g., squishing and pounding it). The school counselor may also choose to play music during this time and discuss how the music affects one's mood. The school counselor asks the students to describe the material (e.g., temperature, smell, texture) and the feelings they experience while exploring the material. The counselor may share with the group that the material can be used in a manner similar to using a stress ball to release tension and stress.

Students are then invited to create something out of the clay that evokes stress, frustration, or tension and then share it with the group. After sharing, the student is then invited to change the Play-Doh/clay into something that may help them feel better, or something that symbolizes them feeling better. Through sharing, group members are able to develop a variety of positive strategies to cope with stress and frustration. Students can write or draw pictures of the strategies to help them remember the healthy ways to cope with stress.

Considerations:

Young children may find Play-Doh more appealing because of the bright colors and familiarity with the material, while older children and adolescents may prefer to use clay for this activity. The school counselor may choose to have both available and allow the individual students the opportunity to choose which one they want to use during the group activity.

CASE STUDY

A group of four middle school girls arrived in the school counselor's office to discuss a problem experienced by one of the girls, Sara. The three other girls stated that they were accompanying Sara to provide support in talking with the counselor. Sara was quiet and stood towards the back of the group allowing one of the other girls, Jenisha, to take the lead in talking with the school counselor. Jenisha reported that another group of girls had been saying negative things about Sara. As the conversation unfolded, the school counselor discovered that Jenisha and the other two girls were also experiencing this problem; however, Sara appeared to be struggling with it more than the other girls, as evidenced by her being tearful and withdrawing from the group. Jenisha and the other girls appeared to be more outspoken and were able to talk through this issue. Furthermore, it appeared that Sara was the target of this behavior more frequently than the other girls. During the meeting, Sara sat in the back of the office holding a doll that was sitting on the chair and drawing on some paper she found on a small table in the office. The school counselor attempted to engage Sara in the conversation; however, she was hesitant and simply agreed with what the others said about the problem.

The school counselor asked the four girls if they were interested in meeting with her as a group once a week to discuss the issue. Sara was hesitant; however, she finally agreed to come with some persuasion from the other girls. The counselor planned an eight week small group focused on self-expression, building healthy self-esteem, and coping skills. Having observed Sara exploring the art materials in the office during the initial meeting, the counselor decided to incorporate this into the group. The counselor integrated a variety of art activities within the group sessions to emphasize self-expression and to assist with developing healthy coping skills, including drawing a self-portrait, using the art materials to get out their feelings, and the "positive me" activity previously discussed. The counselor also had a variety of stuffed animals that were more appealing to older students (i.e., beanie babies) available in the room. Additionally, the girls were encouraged to bring in music they enjoy and the counselor facilitated a discussion about the meaning of the lyrics. The counselor also facilitated an activity having the students paint to various types of music and then discussing how the music affects an individual's mood.

During the first three group sessions, Sara remained a quiet participant and often selected a stuffed animal to hold during the session, which appeared to give her comfort. In an effort to build a stronger relationship with Sara, the counselor invited Sara to talk with her individually. Sara stated that she felt more comfortable attending the group and did not want to meet individually with the counselor. The counselor identified that Sara had an interest in music, listening to various genres of music and writing music lyrics, in addition to art. The counselor encouraged Sara to write a song to share with the group. The counselor also used this interest as a focus for the next group session to provide continued encouragement to Sara and also offer the other group members an opportunity to create song lyrics as well. Additionally, the counselor was purposeful in finding opportunities to see Sara in the hallway at school to smile and say "hi" to help connect with her. Sara engaged in the group activity focused on the topic; however, she continued to remain quiet. The following week, Sara returned to group carrying a folder. The counselor noticed the folder and asked about it. Sara shared with the group that she wrote a song about being teased at school and what she was learning from the group to cope with this issue. Jenisha and the other girls encouraged Sara to share the song with the group. With encouragement, Sara shared her story, while being supported by her peers. During the remaining group sessions, Sara opened up more and asked the school counselor if she could come to her office and talk individually. The counselor met with Sara individually and continued to encourage her to write, listen to music, and draw as healthy coping skills. Sara expressed feeling better about herself and having a greater sense of confidence.

SUMMARY

School counselors have a crucial role in addressing the needs of students that influence their academic success. Individual and small group counseling are essential responsive services within the delivery system of the ASCA (2012) *National Model*. School counselors can integrate a variety of play activities within individual and small group counseling at various grade levels. Counseling researchers support the integration of nondirective and directive play interventions within the school environment. Additionally, play interventions are developmentally appropriate for children and adolescents and are also appealing to them. Thus, school counselors are encouraged to be creative in facilitating a myriad of play interventions at the elementary, middle, and high school levels.

REFERENCES

Akos, P., Hamm, J. V., Mack, S. G., & Dunaway, M. (2007). Utilizing the developmental influence of peers in middle school groups. *The Journal for Specialists in Group Work, 32*(1), 51-60. doi:10.1080/01933920600977648

American School Counselor Association. (2012). *The ASCA National Model: A framework for school counseling programs* (3rd ed.). Alexandria, VA: Author.

Blanco, P. J., & Ray. D. C. (2011). Play therapy in elementary schools: A best practice for improving academic achievement. *Journal of Counseling & Development, 89*(2), 235-243. doi:10.1002/j.1556-6678.2011.tb00083.x

Bloom, S. (2010). Learning the language: Strategies for successful group work in schools. *Group, 34*(3), 239-254.

Bratton, S. C., Ray, D., Rhine, T., & Jones, L. (2005). The efficacy of play therapy with children: A meta-analytic review of treatment outcomes. *Professional Psychology Research and Practice, 36*(4), 376-390. doi:10.1037/0735-7028.36.4.376

Cooley, L. (2009). *The power of groups: Solution-focused group counseling in schools.* Thousand Oaks, CA: Corwin.

Drewes, A. A. (2006). Play-based interventions. *Journal of early childhood and infant psychology, 2*, 139-156.

Gysbers, N. C., & Henderson, P. (Eds.). (2000). *Developing and managing your school guidance program* (3rd ed.). Alexandria, VA: American Counseling Association.

Knell, S. M. (1997). Cognitive-behavioral play therapy. In K. O'Connor & L. M. Braverman (Eds.), *Play therapy theory and practice: A comparative presentation* (pp. 79-99). New York, NY: John Wiley & Sons.

Kottman, T. (2001). Adlerian play therapy. *International Journal of Play Therapy, 10*(2), 1-12. doi:10.1037/h0089476

Kulic, K. R., Horne, A. M., & Dagley, J. C. (2004). A comprehensive review of prevention groups for children and adolescents. *Group dynamics: Theory, research, and practice, 8*(2), 139-151. doi:10.1037/1089-2699.8.2.139

Landreth, G. L. (2002). *Play therapy: The art of the relationship* (2nd ed.). New York, NY: Brunner-Routledge.

Packman, J. & Bratton, S. C. (2003). A school-based group play/activity therapy intervention with learning disabled preadolescents exhibiting behavior problems. *International Journal of Play Therapy, 12*(2), 7-29. doi: 10.1037/h0088876

Paisley, P. O., & Milsom, A. (2007). Group work as an essential contribution to transforming school counseling. *The Journal for Specialist in Group Work, 32*(1), 9-17. doi:10.1080/01933920600977465

Ray, D., Bratton, S., Rhine, T., & Jones, L. (2001). The effectiveness of play therapy: Responding to the critics. *International Journal of Play Therapy, 10*(1), 85-108. doi:10.1037/h0089444

Ray, D., Muro, J., & Schumann, B. (2004). Implementing play therapy in the schools: Lessons learned. *International Journal of Play Therapy, 13*(1), 79-100. doi: 10.1037/h0088886

Ray, D. C., Armstrong, S. A., Warren, E. S., & Balkin, R. S. (2005). Play therapy practices among elementary school counselors. *Professional School Counseling, 8*(4) 360-365.

Riester, A. E. (2002). The basics in establishing groups in schools. In Aronson, S., & Scheidlinger, S. (Eds.), *Group treatment of adolescents in context: Outpatient, inpatient, and school* (pp. 175-190). Madison, CT: International Universities.

Rogers, C. R. (1942). *Counseling and psychotherapy: Newer concepts in practice.* Boston, MA: Houghton Mifflin.

Steen, S., Bauman, S., & Smith, J. (2007). Professional school counselors and the practice of group work. *Professional School Counseling, 11*(2), 72-80. doi:10.5330/PSC.n.2010-11.72

U.S. Department of Education, National Institute for Educational Statistics. (*n.d.*). *Publicelementary and secondary school student enrollment and staff from the common core of data: School year 2009-2010.* Retrieved from http://www.schoolcounselor.org/files/Ratios09-10.pdf

Veach, L. J., & Gladding, S. T. (2007). Using creative group techniques in high schools. *The Journal for Specialists in Group Work, 32*(1), 71-81. doi:10.1080/01933920600978570

Webb, L. D., Brigman, G. A., & Campbell, C. (2005). Linking school counselors and student success: A replication of the Student Success Skills approach targeting the academic and social competence of students. *Professional School Counseling, 8*(5), 407-413. doi:

Yalom, I. (1995). *The theory and practice of group psychotherapy* (4th ed.). New York: HarperCollins.

Zinck, K., & Littrell, J. M. (2000). Action research shows group counseling effective with at-risk adolescent girls. *Professional School Counseling, 4*(1), 50-59.

CHAPTER 2

USING PLAY TECHNIQUES TO ADDRESS STUDENT GRIEF AND LOSS

Peggy L. Ceballos & June M. Williams

Vignette 1

Emily (14) is a well-adjusted, popular, outgoing girl. She makes excellent grades, is involved in several student groups as well as dancing and gymnastics. As an only child whose parents divorced when she was three, Emily and her mom, Sara, have been extremely close, spending a great deal of time together, going shopping together, talking about anything and everything, and taking yearly vacations together. Recently, Sara has started dating, and is spending more time with her boyfriend and less and less time with Emily. Emily's teachers have noticed that the normally bubbly, happy Emily has become sullen and angry. Neither the teachers nor the school counselor are aware of what could be causing the changes in Emily's mood.

Integrating Play Techniques in Comprehensive School Counseling Programs, pp. 19–42

Vignette 2

David (5) is a typical kindergartener. He is developmentally on track, and aside from occasional problems with impulsivity, he is well-behaved in the classroom. He is engaged, talkative, and has many friends. A few weeks ago, David, the younger of two boys, became a big brother when his mom gave birth to his little sister. Initially, David was excited to be a big brother; however, lately his behavior is concerning his teachers. He no longer actively participates in class, and occasionally he will be found sitting in the corner sucking his thumb. His teachers' attempts to draw him out do not seem to be working.

We selected the following description of grief to frame this chapter because we believe that it captures the complex, multifaceted nature of grief:

> Grief is an inevitable, never-ending process that results from a permanent or temporary disruption in routine, a separation, or a change in a relationship that may be beyond the person's control. The disruption, change, or separation causes pain and discomfort and impacts the person's thoughts, feelings, and behaviors. Although loss is a universal experience, the causes and manifestations of it are unique to each individual and may change over time. (Fiorini & Mullen, 2006, p. 10)

Often, when grief is mentioned, the assumption is that the grief and loss are associated with a death. However, it is important to recognize that as children and adolescents grow and develop, they experience a multitude of losses along the way. The two vignettes at the beginning of this chapter illustrate two very common situations that children face as their families experience growth and change. Additional examples of common losses that children experience include the loss of a favorite toy, death of a loved one, parental separation (i.e., divorce, deployment, incarceration), moving away from friends or family members, the loss of a pet, changing schools, and the losses that naturally occur at the end of the school year. Children's developmental stages impact the way in which they grieve in these situations. For example, young children who are in the preoperational cognitive stage do not understand abstract concepts and are unable to understand others' reactions to a situation (Piaget, 1977). Children at this developmental stage may lack the cognitive ability to understand that death is permanent and may experience difficulties recognizing how other adults in their lives are also affected by the death of a family member. As a result, at the preoperational stage, children may continue to expect the deceased person to come back and may respond to family members' reactions to the situation as if they are at fault for causing such reactions. In contrast, teenagers who are developmentally at the formal operation stage (Piaget, 1977) are able to engage in abstract thinking and have an increased ability to understand others' reactions to an event. Thus, teenagers are able to understand the permanence of death and can understand that family members' grieve process is not caused by something they did.

Beyond helping children process an immediate loss, a primary goal of grief counseling is to teach children skills they can apply to future grieving experiences. For example, children need to learn how to self-regulate so that they can simultaneously manage the emotional responses to loss while at the same time engaging in their normal, daily activities (e.g., school, sports, hobbies). Similarly, through counseling children can learn to seek support in healthy ways when they are faced with difficult situations. As school counselors, our awareness that all forms of change and loss can deeply affect children will enable us to help them successfully navigate through new situations and transitions as well as work through significant losses including death. Our goals in this chapter are to (1) provide a basic conceptual framework, including an overview of various losses, children's understandings of death and manifestations of grief, and (2) provide a theoretical foundation and practical illustrations regarding the use of play therapy to help children and preadolescents process grief both in individual and group sessions. We would like to clarify at the outset that traumatic grief situations, crisis events, and intensive, ongoing therapy are beyond the scope of this chapter. Additionally, due to limited space in this chapter, the focus is on young children and preadolescents. While play therapy techniques may be incorporated into grief work with adolescents, that topic would require additional attention.

Fiorini and Mullen (2006) provide an excellent overview of various losses that children and adolescents may experience, categorizing them as (a) intangible losses (e.g., trust, safety, security, power, control, attention), (b) losses through death, (c) interpersonal losses (e.g., moving away from friends/family, end of friendships, break-ups), (d) transitional losses (e.g., moving, parental job loss, divorce, military deployment, illness), (e) developmental losses (e.g., physical changes, family changes, school transitions), and (f) tragic and stigmatizing losses (e.g., child abuse, murder, suicide, incarceration of loved one, disasters). According to Goldman (2004), in many cases, multiple losses occur simultaneously, and students may experience secondary losses (e.g., loss of routine, predictability, attention) as a result of a primary loss (e.g., death, divorce, relocation). Students will grieve any significant loss, including those that are not death-related.

Many myths abound regarding children and grief with a primary one being that children do not grieve. Wolfelt (2001) reminds us of a child's capacity to grieve when he stated that "Anyone old enough to love is old enough to grieve" (p. 1). Related to the myth that children do not grieve is Doka's (1989) concept of disenfranchised grief. Disenfranchised grief was defined by Doka as "the grief that persons experience when they incur a loss that is not or cannot be openly acknowledged, publicly mourned or socially supported" (p. 4). Doka proposed four ways in which grief (or grievers) may be disenfranchised: (a) the relationship is not recognized; (b) the loss is not recognized; (c) the griever is not recognized; and (d) certain deaths may be disenfranchised. The reality is that children do grieve; however, they express their grief differently than adults do (Worden, 1991).

In applying the concept of disenfranchised grief to children, Crenshaw (2002) observed that the attachments formed by children are often underestimated by adults and that many nondeath losses experienced by children (e.g., divorce, adoption, foster care, pet loss) are not recognized as losses, thus depriving the child of support and understanding during the grieving process. Children are often not recognized as grievers, often because adults assume that children do not have a cognitive understanding of the loss or because the adult may be attempting to protect the child from the pain of the loss (Crenshaw, 2002). Even if the grief is not disenfranchised, adults often overestimate the child's ability to adjust to the loss and may not recognize that the child is experiencing a grief reaction. Another reality is that children may lose loved ones to a type of stigmatized or disenfranchised death (e.g., suicide, AIDS, murder) or other disenfranchised loss (e.g., parental incarceration). Crenshaw recommended for adults to be honest and developmentally appropriate in explaining circumstances of the death or illness to children. Children have an innate capacity to handle difficult situations, even if these may be painful.

Although many school counselors might be familiar with Elizabeth Kübler-Ross's (1997) stages of death and dying, there are other conceptual frameworks for grief that may be more applicable to practice in school environments. For children who are grieving a death-related loss, Fox (1988) described what she called *good grief*. She proposed that children experience *good grief* when they have worked through four tasks of grief: (a) understanding, (b) grieving, (c) commemorating, and (d) going on. Trozzi (1999) provided an in-depth explanation of these tasks, including many examples demonstrating how children developmentally experience these tasks. She offered adults suggestions regarding how to talk to children about death and help them process their grief.

In order to help children successfully reach Fox's first grieving stage, understanding, it is critical to recognize how children's cognitive development affects how they conceptualize death. However, prior to providing an overview of cognitive developmental stages, readers need to be mindful that although age ranges are typically provided for each cognitive stage, children's level of development rather than age will determine the degree of understanding.

Preschool age children lack the cognitive ability to understand death abstractly (Jimerson & Miller, 2008). During the pre-operational stage of cognitive development (Piaget, 1977) children's thinking is characterized by magical thinking, egocentrism, reversibility, and causality. The egocentrism that defines young children's understanding of the world often results in their believing that something that they did or said resulted in a loved one's death. For example, the day before 5-year old Jenny's 10-year old brother was killed in a car accident, in a fit of anger she yelled at him, "I wish you were dead." Egocentrism and magical thinking resulted in her believing that she somehow caused her brother's death. The concept of causality is similar to magical thinking in that children may attribute events to their thoughts or behaviors. Preschool age children frequently believe that death is temporary and that loved ones who have died are able to come back to life.

Throughout elementary school, children typically develop a better understanding of death. School-age children understand that death happens to older people, but have a more difficult time understanding when it happens to someone young (Webb, 2011). During the elementary school years, children become curious about death (Webb, 2011), and ask questions about the circumstances of the death as well as about some of the physical aspects of dying (Trozzi, 1999). According to Webb (2011), children at this stage of development tend to have difficulty with the causality of death and frequently question whether or not they could have prevented the death. Although children's natural curiosity and inquisitiveness about death is healthy and normal, many adults are unsure of how to honestly answer children's questions, including parents and school counselors.

Once children have an understanding of death that is developmentally appropriate, Fox's (1988) next task if that of grieving. The manner in which children and adolescents manifest grief is closely related to their ability to understanding death and loss. Heath et al. (2008) illustrated that grieving children may experience changes cognitively (e.g., avoidance, denial, distraction), emotionally (e.g., sadness, depression, hypersensitivity), physically (e.g., crying, fighting, regressive behaviors), and socially (e.g., withdrawal, rebellion). As a result of these changes, the child's academic performance is often affected due to an inability to concentrate or focus changes in behavioral and social patterns, and emotional distress. In many cases, a decline in academic performance can be a symptom of underlying grief issues.

A challenge for teachers and school counselors is to know when to intervene with a child who is experiencing grief. Often, a parent or guardian will ask that the child be referred to the school counselor whereas at other times, the teacher may observe behaviors. Goldman (2006) identified several behaviors typical of bereaved children, including (a) withdrawal, (b) restlessness, (c) impulsivity, (d) lack of focus, (e) extreme talkativeness, (f) disorganization, (g) recklessness, and (h) becoming the class clown. While at times these may not necessarily be cause for concern, teachers and school counselors can observe if the behaviors seem to be out of character for the child, if the child is having trouble returning to equilibrium, or if a cluster of these behaviors is occurring simultaneously.

In attempting to understand how children grieve, we find the dual process model (Stroebe & Schut, 1999) particularly helpful. Stroebe and Schut (1999) proposed a grief model that characterizes grief as fluctuating between the loss orientation (focusing on the painful feelings of the loss) and the restoration orientation (dealing with the everyday changes as a result of the loss). Children's grief is very fluid, and their expression of grief may vary from day to day, moment to moment. It is not unusual for a child to be inconsolable in one moment, and shortly thereafter be off playing, seemingly carefree. Expressive play therapy can be helpful in providing opportunities for children to work through the difficult emotions they are experiencing. Simultaneously, children can be encouraged to draw on their strengths and develop new coping skills so that they can appropriately deal with new and different situations.

Once children have worked through some of the difficult feelings related to the loss, the next task is that of commemorating the loved one (Fox, 1988). Often, children are not involved in the rituals (e.g., funerals, wakes) when a loved one dies. Even if they are, they may be only marginally involved. The task of commemorating allows the child an opportunity to remember the person who died. Counselors may use activities such as memory books, memory boxes, memory strings, drawings, and stories to help children find ways to remember their loved one.

According to Fox (1988), the final task for children is that of going on. This task involves a transformation over time in which children learn that the pain of grief subsides and the legacy of their loved one lies within them (Trozzi, 1999). For example, a child may attribute a personality characteristic or talent (e.g., musical ability, athletic ability, sense of humor) to a deceased parent, and may always feel a connection with the parent as a result. A reality for children who experience a significant death-related loss is that they will likely experience the loss in different ways as they grow older. For instance, a child who loses a parent at a very young age may reexperience grief as he or she matures both cognitively and emotionally. Significant events such as graduations, family reunions, births, weddings, and holidays are often reminders of loved ones who have died and may retrigger a grief reaction. These changes in how children experience grief over time are due in part to their cognitive development. As children develop their ability to think abstractly, they are able to process the loss differently.

Landreth (2002) stated "unlike adults, whose natural medium of communication is verbalization, the natural medium of communication for children is play" (p. 9). Thus, the younger the children the more that grief will be reflected in their actions rather than through their words (Crenshaw, 2002). Consequently, play therapy is recognized as a developmentally appropriate therapeutic intervention for children (Bratton, Ray, Rhine, & Jones, 2005). However, because preadolescents are beginning to develop their ability to engage in abstract thought (Piaget, 1977), they have a tendency to fluctuate between verbal and nonverbal communication. While they may view conventional play therapy as juvenile (Ginott, 1994), they may still not be ready to sit down and talk for 50 minutes about their loss. In response, therapeutic interventions that aid to bridge the gap between concrete and abstract thinking are most appropriate (Bratton, Ceballos, & Ferebee, 2009). For example, traditional play therapy that works well with children under the age of 10 can be adapted to the needs of preadolescents through the incorporation of expressive arts—in lieu of toys as a medium for play therapy (Shen & Armstrong, 2008). Additionally, group therapy in particular is recognized as a beneficial therapeutic intervention for bereaved children and adolescents as it helps them form peer support and normalize their feelings (Finn, 2003; Goldman, 2004).

EVIDENCE-BASED APPROACHES

A review of the literature revealed a lack of evidence-based research investigating the effectiveness of play therapy interventions for children experiencing grief and loss. However, trauma-focused cognitive-behavioral therapy (TF-CBT) is recognized as evidence-based treatment and proposed as a plausible intervention for young children experiencing traumatic grief (Cohen & Mannarino, 2011). In a recently published case study, Allen, Oseni, and Allen (2011) combined TF-CBT with parental behavioral training and motivational interviewing to work with an adolescent experiencing traumatic grief. Results indicated a one standard deviation decrease in the client's behavioral problems after treatment. Other researchers in the field have investigated the effects of group interventions on children's grieving process (Goldberg & Harriet, 1998; Huss & Ritchie, 1999; Salloum & Overstreet, 2008; Tonkins & Lambert 1996.

Huss and Ritchie (1999) found that children who participated in a 6 week experimental grief therapy group reported feeling better following treatment while children in the control group continued to experience the same feelings. Similarly, Goldberg and Harriet (1998) noted that grieving children who participated in group therapy reported feeling less lonely after the intervention and parents and teachers of children in treatment reported that children's misbehaviors improved after participating in group. These results echoed Tonkins and Lamberts' (1996) findings that revealed significant decrease in children's externalizing behavioral problems related to grief after participating in group therapy. Externalizing behaviors refer to engaging in actions that "involve conflicts with other people and their expectations for the child" (Achenbach & Rescorla, 2001, p. 24). Externalizing behaviors may include aggressiveness, lack of attention, and hyperactivity. More recently, Salloum and Overstreet (2008) studied the effects of group versus individual grief and trauma therapy for 56 children who reported moderate levels of post-traumatic stress following Hurricane Katrina. Results indicated that children in both types of treatment reported decreased grieving symptoms such as post-traumatic stress, traumatic grief and depression.

While several authors advocate for the use of play therapy to help children overcome grief and loss (Baggerly & Abugideiri, 2010; Crenshaw, 2002; Edgar-Bailey & Kress, 2010; Green & Connolli, 2009; Robson, 2008), a review of literature suggests that evidence-based research needs to be conducted in the field to establish the effectiveness of play therapy with this population. In summary, it appears that TF-CBT can be a viable treatment for children who experience traumatic grief. Furthermore, it appears that group and individual interventions are helpful, as group therapy helps children normalize their experiences with grief.

PROPOSED TREATMENT APPROACHES AND TECHNIQUES

School counselors can use different theoretical approaches when working with grieving children, including cognitive-behavioral play therapy (Edgar-Bailey & Kress, 2010), Jungian play therapy (Green & Connolli, 2009) and child-centered play therapy (Baggerly & Abugideiri, 2010; Robson, 2008). In this chapter, we propose a humanistic approach to play therapy when working with this population. While a humanistic approach is usually associated with long-term therapy, we outline how to work from a person-centered framework within a time limited psycho-educational group play therapy intervention. In order to adapt the interventions to the developmental level of young children and preadolescents, we discuss the use of specific materials associated with both play and creative arts, such as sand-trays and craft materials. Although we focus on preadolescents between the ages of 9 and 13, the proposed play activities can be easily adapted to younger and/or older children.

Theoretical Underpinning of the Play Approach

Within the play therapy field, a humanistic approach is defined as an intervention that views the establishment of a safe and strong therapeutic relationship as essential to facilitate growth and sees the child's inner drive for self-actualization as the motivating force that brings about change (Bratton & Ray, 2002; Landreth, 2002; Shen & Armstrong, 2008). Bratton and Ray (2002) further clarified the self-actualizing force as the child's ability to strive toward growth and maturity and to engage in self-direction, self-regulation, and self-responsibility.

Because in humanistic play therapy, the relationship is pivotal for growth to occur, empathizing with children's and preadolescents' experiences of the grief process is more important than the activity itself. Baggerly and Abugideiri (2010) corroborated this need by explaining that providing empathy to bereaved clients in play therapy is critical for their therapeutic growth. Heath et al. (2008) further recommended that school counselors be emotionally ready to listen empathetically to the intensity of clients' feelings regarding their loss and convey such understanding through reflections of feelings and content.

Central to humanistic play therapy is that the child's experience of the play, not the activity itself, is what is important. Thus, it is critical to balance the use of structured activities and self-directed play. While structured play activities are helpful to facilitate the engagement of clients by reducing anxiety and serving as a way to introduce the topic (Bratton et al., 2009), Evie (1988) cautioned that overstructuring can inhibit the therapeutic process by hindering clients' ability to share individual concerns. Thus, nondirective time provides opportunities to process individual concerns that may not be addressed through the planned activities. In response, we recommend starting with a planned activity to introduce the topic and/or teach the skills needed for that week and allowing the last 15 minutes for nondirective time. In a play therapy group, this transition can be accomplished by telling group members, "We have about 15 minutes left for today's group, and you can decide as a group what you would like to do for the rest of our time together." During nondirective time, school counselors use group therapy skills such as linking members' experiences to bring awareness to members about their feelings, coping skills and similarities/differences with each other.

Since nondirective time allows clients the freedom to express grief within their cultural context, working from a humanistic approach is recognized as being culturally responsive (Flahive & Ray, 2007; Shen & Armstrong, 2008). This is important given that culture is intrinsically related to how children process grief (Baggerly & Abugideiri, 2010). School counselors should also be culturally responsive by being knowledgeable about clients' culture, including grieving rituals associated with the children's religious beliefs. Additionally, materials in the play room should represent clients' culture and planned activities need to be sensitive to the culture of clients.

Group Play Therapy as an Intervention

When planning a play therapy group, school counselors need to carefully select members, be familiar with the unique characteristics and dynamics in therapeutic groups targeting children/teens, and think through the logistics. As a general rule, when working with preadolescents, group members should not be more than 2 years apart in age and should be of the same gender (Kulic, Dagley, & Horne, 2001). School counselors must judge if potential group members are ready to share their experiences, especially when the grief was caused by a traumatic event or when the grief is too recent. Depending on the intensity of the trauma or how recently the loss happened, individual therapy may be needed to strengthen self-concept prior to participating in a group (Bratton & Ferebee, 1999). Strengthening their self-concept can assist children to acquire skills to cognitively process the situation.

The purpose of group therapy with children and teens is similar to that of groups for adults: facilitating learning through group interactions (Yalom, 1995). However, Greenberg (2003) highlighted that adult groups tend to be more cohesive and focused than therapeutic groups for children as adults are more open to express verbally their emotions and engage in confrontation with each other. Thus, children and teens do not tend to process their experiences as in depth as adult clients during group (Bratton et al., 2009) and cohesion is not an essential part of group play therapy with children and teens (Landreth, 2002).

Lastly, school counselors need to address the logistics of conducting a play therapy group in their schools (e.g., meeting times, location, confidentiality). While addressing all of these concerns is beyond the scope of this chapter, we recommend Greenberg's (2003) handbook as it offers specific considerations for conducting groups in school settings, including gaining support from administrators and teachers and addressing confidentiality.

Specific Play Techniques With Description

In this section, we provide descriptions of five media that can be used in a grief and loss play therapy group. The media we propose can be used in many different ways; therefore, although specific ideas are provided, the reader is invited to use the media creatively. Members should be allowed to adapt the activities and carry them out in a way that feels safe to them; thus, it is not about how well they follow instructions or their final creation, but about the process.

Sand-Trays. Kalff (1980, as cited in Carey, 1991) was the first to report on the use of sand-tray as a therapeutic media when working with children/adolescents. Since then, the therapeutic value of sand-tray has been recognized in the literature (Draper, Ritter, & Willingham, 2003; Kestly, 2005) and promoted for use with children, adolescents, and adults (McNally, 2001), primarily because the use of sand-trays allows clients to represent and change their feelings and perceptions as they manipulate the miniatures to create new meaning(s). However, there are some differences in the use of sand-trays according to the client's age and developmental stage. Because the ability to engage in abstract thinking develops with age, the younger the child, the less likely that the child will be able to verbally process the meaning of their creation and relate it to their life circumstances (Boik & Goodwin, 2000). Additionally, elementary aged children will be more likely to engage in sand-play, characterized by a lot of movement, action and spontaneity. This is different from adolescents and adults who may use a sand-tray to represent something specific and then talk about it (Boik & Goodwin, 2000).

Sand-tray can be used individually by having each member create a separate sand-tray to share with other members, or as a group activity wherein each member contributes to cocreating a group sand-tray. Examples of different sand-tray activities that address issues of grief and loss include (a) representing the loss they have experienced (e.g., parents' divorce, loss of a friend), (b) dividing the sand-tray in two parts, with one side representing life before the loss and the other side life after the loss, and (c) representing things and people that can help them through this time. For group sand-trays, the school counselor could have a sand-tray in the middle of the group and instruct the group to: (a) represent feelings regarding losses (e.g., parents' divorce, moving to a new city), (b) represent ways to feel better when feeling sad, angry, fearful, or (c) create a story about the situation (e.g. death, divorce, moving).

Bibliotherapy and Drawing. Because educating children about death and loss is an important part of recovery (Heath et al., 2008), bibliotherapy is often recommended when conducting counseling with bereaved school age youth (Leavy, 2005; Wass, 2003). Heath at al. (2008) offered the following guidelines when selecting books for working with children and teens: (a) the content should be developmentally appropriate; (b) the story has to be culturally sensitive (e.g., religious practices); (c) unique circumstances surrounding the loss or grief as well as clients' individual interests must be taken into account; (d) concepts such as death must be explained in a way that is logical, consistent, and accurate; (e) the story does not always have to be about a death-related loss, (f) the characters must portray feelings associated with grief as well as healthy coping skills, and (g) the ending should exemplify support, comfort, and hope. A list of recommended books for different age groups can be found in Heath et al.

Bibliotherapy can be used in conjunction with drawings. The use of media such as paper, markers, paints, and crayons, provides a non-verbal means for clients to express themselves (Hagood, 2000). Chesley, Gillet, and Wagner (2008) proposed that drawing allows children to represent their problems while providing them the opportunity to reconstruct their views. Malchiodi (2002) suggested that the use of drawings with grieving children allows them to identify feelings and make sense of the loss through sensory means.

Examples of different drawing activities that can be used after reading books about death and loss include (a) asking clients to draw what the characters were feeling and then have a conversation about how similar and/or different their feelings are compared to the characters in the story; (b) talking about the coping mechanisms the characters in the story used and then directing group members to use a large piece of paper to create a mural that represents ways to deal with their own feelings about loss (e.g., what helps them when they are feeling sad/angry/etc.); (c) processing how the characters in the story remembered or adjusted to their loss followed by asking clients to draw a picture that represents how they remember the person, pet, or things they lost; and (d) directing clients to draw anything they would like about their own experience with loss (this will prompt clients to draw feelings/thoughts that the story evoked in them). These activities are followed by allowing group members time to share what they did.

Puppets. Melanie Klein (1929) was the first therapist to document the therapeutic power of puppets when working with children and teens. The author stated that puppets provide psychological safety by allowing for emotions, thoughts, and struggles to be projected. The use of puppets to help children deal with bereavement and separation has been documented (Butler, Guterman, & Rudes, 2009) and recommended to allow grieving children to express feelings about their lost in the here and now (Edgar-Bailey & Kress, 2010). Due to the level of abstract thinking required, the puppet activity proposed below, slightly modified from Bratton and Ray (1999), can be used in a grief and loss group with preadolescents instead of younger children.

The school counselor should first ask each group member to choose a puppet and introduce the puppets to the group. After the introduction, ask group members to create a story about death/loss that has a beginning, middle, and an end. After allowing a few minutes to create the story, ask group members to play-out their story with the puppets. For processing, Bratton and Ray (1999) recommended that the therapist first address each puppet directly by reflecting on the puppet's feelings and actions during the play and by encouraging the puppets to reconstruct a better end to the story and/or provide better coping mechanisms. Finally, the school counselor can encourage members to talk about their puppet by asking questions such as "What part of your puppet is like you?" "How is the way your puppet dealt with the loss similar/different from how you are dealing with your own loss?" "Do you see yourself doing the same things your puppet was doing when feeling sad/angry?"

Clay. Sholt and Gavron (2006) described the therapeutic use of clay by stating "clay-work makes possible an entire non-verbal language or communication for the creator, through which his or her mental realm, emotional life, and primary object relations can be expressed" (p. 67). The authors also explained that clay allows for the product to be modified, providing clients power to change their perceptions at any moment. Oaklander (1988) describes clay as a medium that is flexible, malleable, messy, and due to its origin brings the user to be in touch with earth and water. In cases where clay is not available, school counselors can use Model Magic or Play-Doh; however, these media may not have the same therapeutic power as clay because as media, these do not offer the same qualities described by Oklander.

The following ideas are modified from Oklander (1988) regarding how clay can be used when dealing with grief and loss. School counselors can ask clients to make figures that represent their feelings about their grief. Emphasizing that these figures do not have to resemble anything in particular and can be "out of space" figures is important because it allows clients not to feel self-conscious about what they are doing. Another possibility is to ask group members to create an object that reminds them of the person/things they lost. This object can be used as a way to commemorate the loss. Following these activities, members can introduce their creation to the group.

Sample Outline of 3-5 Group Sessions in a School Environment

Samide and Stockton (2010) recommended that counselors develop a framework guided by weekly themes and goals to organize group sessions. Finn (2003) proposed using the stages of one of the grieving models to plan the sessions throughout treatment. Following the author's recommendation, we outline five sessions using Fox's (1988) grieving model, previously explained in the introduction. Each individual goes through the process in different ways and at different times, thus school counselors should use clinical judgment in deciding when to modify treatment for each client. The following sample sessions outline a group conducted for preadolescents ages 11 and 12 whose families have divorced within the last 12 months.

Session 1. The goals for the first session are to (a) allow group members to introduce themselves, (b) establish group rules, and (c) explain that the group will center on issues of grief and loss. While explaining the purpose of the group, the school counselor can explain the concept of divorce and emphasize how each individual's situation is similar and different at the same time. As part of the introduction, the school counselor can talk about the importance of feeling safe in the group and instruct group members to create rules for the group.

One activity for creating group rules is to have a large piece of paper in the middle of the group and ask members to create a name for the group and a group "logo." Once they describe their name and logo, the counselor can ask them to develop the rules they want for the group, so everyone feels safe. The school counselor can write these on a piece of paper. It is important to add rules about confidentiality if group members do not bring them up. It is recommended to limit the time of this activity to the first 20 minutes. School counselors are encouraged to keep the name, logo and rules of the group and place them on the wall prior to starting every session.

This can be followed by an activity for members to introduce themselves. For this activity, the school counselor can use sand-trays and tell group members

> You will be introducing yourself to other members, but instead of talking about who you are, you can use the miniatures and the sand-tray to represent who you are. Take a moment to think about what you want others in the group to know about you; then choose some miniatures that represent those things and arrange them in the sand-tray in front of you. You will have about ten minutes to do this.

Once group members finish their sand-trays, the counselor allows members to have a turn to describe their sand-trays. The school counselor can invite other members to ask questions or make comments.

Session 2. According to Fox (1988), the first stage of the grieving process is comprehending the loss. Thus, the goal of this session is to promote children's understanding of divorce. The school counselor can use the puppet activity previously described and instruct group members to choose a puppet that represents them. After each member has selected a puppet, the members are directed to jointly create a play about divorce.

During processing time, the counselor can ask each puppet to share feelings and thoughts regarding the play. Because children will project upon the puppets their inner-self (Edgar-Bailey & Kress, 2010), the dialogue between the counselor and puppet is an opportunity to learn and reflect on each group member's understanding and experience of dealing with divorce. School counselors can encourage puppets to share ideas about how to deal with feelings in a positive way. Finally, the school counselor talks to each member about his or her experience using the puppets, with questions such as "What did you like/dislike about your puppet? "What did you like/dislike about the story?" Group members are given the last 10 to 15 minutes to engage in self-directed time.

Session 3. Fox's second stage is focused on accepting the loss by grieving (Fox, 1988). The school counselor starts by reading a story book about divorce. We recommend reading *I Don't Want to Talk about It* (Ransom & Finney, 2000), which tells the story of a girl trying to deal with her feelings regarding her parents' divorce. The book ends with the character coping positively with the new situation in her life and adapting to the changes the divorce brought. Although we are recommending this book, the reader is encouraged to consider individual members' culture, characteristics and circumstances when choosing a book. Pehrsson, Allen, Folger, McMillen, and Lowe (2007) offer an extensive list of books that can be used to discuss divorce with preadolescents (e.g., *Dinosaur's Divorce*). After reading the story, members can be directed to use the materials available to draw their own feelings about the story. Once they have finished drawing, they can share what they created. The school counselor can link members' feelings and experiences as they talk about their drawings. The last 15 minutes are used for nondirective time to foster empowerment in group members and allow them the opportunity to bring up issues they may want to process.

Session 4. Fox's (1988) next stage is commemorating the loss. The idea of commemorating the loss means that children will have an opportunity to express feelings that have not been expressed as a way to adapt to the loss and accept the reality of the situation. For this task, group members can be given the choice of creating a memory box in which to place memories (stories or pictures) about the way their family used to be or they can use clay to create an object that represents their predivorce family. Group members can choose what they want to share with the group. They can either take the memory box or clay objects home or leave them behind. During this activity, school counselors can process how it is difficult at times to let go of the memories we have and adapt to changes that happen when we go through a divorce.

Session 5. The next task in Fox's (1988) grieving model is "going on." The goal of this task is to allow children adapt to the changes that the loss created in their lives. For children experiencing divorce, adapting to the new lifestyle (e.g., going back between two homes, having limited contact with one of the caregivers, moving to a new place) can be difficult. Learning to deal with transitions that can bring up various feelings is important. For this task, sand-trays can be used by asking each member to divide the sand-tray in the middle to represent on one side what life used to be like before the divorce and on the other half what life is like after the divorce. Once they finish, each group member can talk about their sand-trays. It is important for school counselors to reflect on the strengths and positive coping skills that each group member is sharing regarding how they are adjusting to their new lifestyle.

Session 6: Providing grieving children the opportunity to process feelings regarding ending counseling is vital. Thus, the last session should focus on: (1) allowing group members process their feelings about termination, and (2) facilitating interpersonal learning as well as transference of skills. For this session, group members can use craft materials to create a story book about the group experience. Members can be asked to include at the end of the story two or three things they can do outside of the group when they feel bad about their parents' divorce. Once group members have finished, they can take turns sharing their stories. The school counselor can focus on reflecting similarities among members' story books. Similarly, it is important to emphasize the ideas they had about things they could do outside of group when feeling bad about their parents' divorce. The school counselor should remind group members they can come back to counseling if needed. Allowing group members the opportunity to engage in self-directed play can be helpful during this last session. This time can provide members the opportunity to process feelings they were not able to process through the activity.

CASE STUDY WITH APPLICATION OF TREATMENT RECOMMENDATIONS

Roberto is an 8 year-old Latino male referred to the school counselor by his teacher, Ms. Smith. After meeting with Roberto's' mother, the school counselor learned that Roberto's parents brought him to the United States when he was 6 years old. Prior to coming to the United States, Roberto lived with his grandparents for 2 years in El Salvador. Roberto has not seen his grandparents since he arrived in the U.S., but talks to them over the phone at least twice a month. Roberto's mother said that her husband was deported back to his country about 3 months ago. Ms. Smith stated that since Roberto's father was deported, Roberto started having behavioral problems in the classroom, becoming more aggressive and engaging in fights with other boys while also becoming more withdrawn from peers. Ms. Smith stated that Roberto is not participating in class as much as he used to do before and appears to be angry and sad. Roberto's mother said that since her husband left, she has observed how Roberto appears to be more dependent on her (e.g., asking her to do things for him that he used to do by himself) and he also seems to be getting upset more easily and frequently.

Treatment Recommendations. The changes in Roberto's behavior caused concern for both his teacher and his mother. Roberto has experienced a great deal of change in his young life, first the loss of the presence of his grandparents and, most recently, his father. Roberto's situation is not atypical of how an 8-year-old may react to loss. In general, children of this age will act out rather than talk about what is bothering them. Roberto met once a week for 30 minutes sessions with the school counselor for 4 weeks before placing him in group play therapy. In Roberto's case, the following recommendations were implemented:

Session 1. Roberto used the sand-tray in the playroom to represent his world. His sand-tray had a lot of divisions such as rivers and fences separating the miniatures one from another. As Roberto explained his sand-tray, he expressed how the people were not able to see each other because of the rivers and mountains (represented by the fences). This allowed the school counselor to reflect Roberto's feelings of loneliness, sadness, confusion, and anger.

Session 2. The school counselor read *My Daddy's Going Away* by McGregor (2009), a story that focuses on a child's feelings about his father going away. After reading the story, the school counselor told Roberto that he could draw a picture of his feelings about not having his grandparents and his father at home. Roberto drew a picture of an angel at the top of the page, in the middle, with tears coming down and touching the three human figures he drew at the bottom of the page. When asked about the drawing, Roberto did not want to talk about it. Thus, the school counselor gave him the option to engage in self-directed play. During the last ten minutes of the session, Roberto played with the building blocks, making buildings. The school counselor only tracked Roberto's behaviors and reflected back his feelings. It is important to notice that this could have been Roberto's way of gaining some sense of control by engaging in activities he could master and that allowed him to feel in power. The importance of not forcing children to verbalize or do activities they do not want to engage in cannot be overstated.

Session 3. The session started with the school counselor talking about feelings we have when we cannot be close to people we love. The school counselor used puppets to retell the story *My Daddy's Going Away,* but focused specifically on the coping skills the character in the story used. The school counselor invited Roberto to pick a puppet to tell the character of the story what other coping skills he can use when feeling sad. Roberto came up with ideas such as talk to the teacher, talk to the school counselor, and play with your toys. Roberto was given self-directed time, and he used the sand-tray to bury animal figures and placed different toys (e.g., the sword, the sand scoop, and building blocks) to symbolize crosses. Roberto turned to the school counselor and asked if they (the animals) could come back. The school counselor said she was not sure, and Roberto decided that some animals may come back and took some out of the sand-tray. This play could have symbolized Roberto's attempt to comprehend the losses in his life.

Session 4. The school counselor reminded Roberto this was their last weekly session, but that he would continue coming for group play therapy. Roberto was given the option to engage in self-directive play. Roberto decided to use puppets to create a story about a group of animals who were lost in the middle of the ocean without food and water. He then introduced a puppet who was an angel who came down to help the animals. He had one puppet who did not believe the angel could help, and another puppet that was convinced the angel could help. The story ended with the angel helping the animals get to land where food and water was waiting for them. Then, he said that if needing help, children can call 1-800-play therapy room and ended the story. It is noteworthy to mention that Roberto's mother was Catholic and always talked to Roberto about how the angels were protecting them and how praying would help them. In addition to representing his understanding of religion, Roberto also seemed to have represented in this play a positive way of overcoming his feelings.

The school that Roberto attended had a large population of immigrants. Thus, the school counselors at the school often offered group play therapy for immigrant children who were dealing with feelings regarding moving away from home and/or being away from a caregiver. Because Roberto was starting to withdraw from peers, after individual play therapy, he participated in five group sessions. Participating in this group allowed Roberto to find peer support, experience universality (Yalom, 1995) by realizing other children had similar problems/feelings, develop coping skills, and practice socialization skills. The social skills that Roberto gained throughout group, such as expressing his feelings and engaging in enjoyable interactions with other group members, were important given his presenting problem included being socially withdrawn and displaying anger outbursts.

Roberto's mother was given referrals for social services in the community that could help her financially as well as emotionally by providing her with peer support. Additionally, Roberto's mother was given a referral to have Roberto enrolled on a soccer team that a community center offered for free and to have Roberto paired with a mentor through the Big Brother program. This helped Roberto engage in age-appropriate activities outside of school and provided a positive outlet for his feelings regarding his loss. In addition, the school counselor guided Roberto's mother on how to talk about the situation with Roberto to ensure there was an open communication between the two of them. Similarly, the school counselor consulted with Roberto's teacher. During brief consultations, the school counselor helped Roberto's teacher to understand issues of grief and loss, which allowed the teacher to empathize with Roberto and have more patience with him. The teacher was taught how to respond empathically to Roberto's feelings, which made their relationship better.

Through these interventions, Roberto was able to manage his emotions in a positive way. The teacher and the mother reported noticing Roberto making changes, being more sociable and having less anger outbursts. Roberto's case highlights the benefits of individual and group play therapy while reminding readers of the importance of also collaborating with caregivers and teachers. When conducting interventions for bereaved children in schools, it is recommended to work with the child, the teacher, and the caregivers as a way to intervene holistically (Heath et al., 2008). This can be done by addressing grief and loss throughout the delivery system proposed in the American School Counseling Association's *National Model* (ASCA, 2005).

ADDRESSING GRIEF THROUGH A COMPREHENSIVE SCHOOL COUNSELING PROGRAM

Because children experience many types of losses (Fiorini & Mullen, 2006), finding the exact number of school age children who will be exposed to grief and loss is difficult. However, statistics indicate that over 1 million children each year are affected by divorce (U.S. Census Bureau, 2005) and one child out of every 20 will experience the death of a parent by the time they graduate from high school (Caring Foundation, 2012). These statistics indicate the need for school counselors to be ready to address grief through different venues. Thus, we recommend incorporating issues related to grief and loss in guidance lessons. These lessons can focus on providing children with coping skills as well as information that can assist them in understanding feelings associated with grief. Additionally, responsive services can be used to provide individual and group play therapy and to offer teachers and parents helpful information regarding how to best assist children experiencing grief and loss. For example, school counselors can provide workshops for teachers and parenting classes to teach caregivers about the effects of grieving on children and the best ways to help children work through the grief process. It is also important to locate referrals in the community that can assist students and families with the process of grieving when necessary.

CONCLUSION

Children and adolescents experience many types of losses (Fiorini & Mullen, 2006; Goldman, 2004) that can potentially negatively affect their socioemotional well being (Goldman, 2006). The grieving process can be worsened for children by the fact that most adults erroneously think that children are not affected by the loss or ignore the child's experience of grief for fear of bringing-up in children the pain of the loss (Crenshaw, 2002). Additionally, because children express their grief through actions and activities instead of expressing it through verbalization (Crenshaw, 2002; Landreth, 2002), traditional talk therapy is not developmentally appropriate. In response, school counselors need to be prepared to deliver developmentally appropriate play therapy to children and teens dealing with grief and loss.

This chapter provided an overview of how children view and experience grief and loss. In addition, the chapter offered readers examples of play therapy media and treatments that can be used to help children and preadolescents process grief. While intervening at the individual level through offering one-on-one or group play therapy is important, school counselors should also address grief and loss through classroom guidance. In addition, consulting with teachers and parents on how to help children process feelings associated with grieving is important.

REFERENCES

Achenbach, T. M., & Rescorla, L. A. (2001). *Manual for the ASEBA school age forms and profiles.* Burlington, VT: University of Vermon, Research center for Children, Youth, & Families.

Allen, B., Oseni, A., & Allen, K. (2011, Aug. 15). The evidenced-based treatment chronic posttraumatic stress disorder and traumatic grief in an adolescent: A case study. *Psychological Trauma: Theory, Research, Practice, and Policy.* Advance online publication. doi:10.1037/a0024930

American School Counselor Association. (2005). *The ASCA national model: A framework for school counseling programs.* Alexandria, VA: Author.

Baggerly, J., & Abugideiri, S. E. (2010). Grief counseling for Muslim preschool and elementary school children. *Journal of Multicultural Counseling and Development, 38,* 112-124. doi:10.1002/j.2161-1912.2010.tb00119.x

Boik, B. L., & Goodwin, E. A. (2000). *Sandplay therapy.* New York, NY: W. W. Norton.

Bratton, S. C., Ceballos, P. L., & Ferebee, K. W. (2009). Integration of Structured Expressive Activities within a Humanistic Group Play Therapy Format for Preadolescents. *The Journal for Specialists in Group Work, 34*(3), 251-275.

Bratton, S. C., & Ferebee, K. W. (1999). The use of structured expressive art activities ingroup activity therapy with preadolescents. In D. S. Sweeney & L. E. Homeyer (Eds.), *Group play therapy: How to do it, how it works, whom it's best for* (pp. 192–214). San Francisco, CA: Jossey-Bass.

Bratton, S. C., & Ray, D. (1999). Group puppetry. In D. S. Sweeney & L. E. Homeyer (Eds.), *The handbook of group play therapy: How to do it, how it works, whom it's best for* (pp. 267-277). San Francisco, CA: Jossey-Bass.

Bratton, S. C., & Ray, D. (2002). Humanistic play therapy. In D. Cain & J. Seeman (Eds.), *Humanistic psychotherapies* (pp. 369-402). Washington, DC: American Psychological Association.

Bratton, S., Ray, D., & Rhine, T., & Jones, L. (2005). The efficacy of play therapy with children: A meta-analytic review of treatment outcomes. *Professional Psychology: Research and Practice, 36*(4), 376-390. doi:10.1037/0735-7028.36.4.376

Butler, S., Guterman, J. T., & Rudes, J. (2009). Using puppets with children in narrative therapy to externalize the problem. *Journal of Mental Health Counseling, 31*(3), 225-233. doi:10.1080/03124070600985970

Caring Foundation. (2012). Children's grief awareness day fact sheet. Retrieved from http://www.highmarkcaringplace.com/cp2/cgad/factsheet.shtml

Carey, L. (1991). Family sandplay therapy. *The Arts in Psychotherapy, 18,* 231-239. doi:0.1016/0197-4556(91)90117-S.

Chesley, G. L., Gillet, D. A., & Wagner, W. G. (2008). Verbal and nonverbal metaphor with children in counseling. *Journal of Counseling and Development ,86*(4), 399-411. doi:10.1002/j.1556-6678.2008.tb00528

Cohen, J. A., & Mannarino, A. P. (2011). Supporting children with traumatic grief: What educators need to know. *School Psychology International, 32*(2), 117-131. doi:10.1177/0143034311400827

Crenshaw, D. (2002). Disenfranchised grief of children. In K. Doka (Ed.), *Disenfranchised grief: New concepts and research findings* (pp. 293-306). Champaign, IL: Research Press.

Doka, K. J. (Ed.). (1989). *Disenfranchised grief: Recognizing hidden sorrow.* New York, NY: Lexington Books.

Draper, K., Ritter, K. B., &Willingham, E. U. (2003). Sand tray group counseling with adolescents. *Journal for Specialists in Group Work, 28*(3), 244-260. doi:10.1177/0193392203252030

Edgar-Bailey, M., & Kress, V. E. (2010). Resolving child and adolescent traumatic grief: creative techniques and interventions. *Journal of Creativity in Mental Health, 5*(2), 158-176. doi:10.1080/15401383.2010

Evie, A. (1988). *Expressive group therapy for teen survivors of sexual abuse* (Report No. CG 020836). Chicago, IL: Annual Convention of the American Association for Counseling and Development. Retrieved from ERIC database. (ED 295096)

Finn, C. A. (2003). Helping students cope with loss: incorporating art into group counseling. *Journal for Specialists in Group Work, 28*(2), 155-165. doi:10.1080/714860157

Fiorini, J. J., & Mullen, J. A. (2006). *Counseling children and adolescents through grief and loss.* Champaign, IL: Research Press.

Flahive, M. W., & Ray, D. (2007). Effect of group sandtray therapy with preadolescents. *Journal for Specialists in Group Work, 32*(4), 362-82. doi:10.1080/01933920701476706

Fox, S. (1988). *Good grief: Helping groups of children when a friend dies.* Boston, MA: New England Association for the Education of Young Children.

Ginott, H. G. (1994). *Group psychotherapy with children.* Northvale, NJ: Jason Aronson.

Goldberg, F. R., & Harriet, L. (1998). Left and left out: Teaching children to grieve through a rehabilitation curriculum. *Professional School Counseling, 2*(2), 123-127. doi:10.9624/091400702

Goldman, L. (2004). Counseling with children in contemporary society. *Journal of Mental Health Counseling, 26,* 168-187. doi:10.4028/6112840805

Goldman, L. (2006). Best practice grief work with students in schools. In C. Franklin, M. B. Harris, & P. Allen-Meares (Eds.), *The school services sourcebook: A guide for school based professionals* (pp. 567-575). New York, NY: Oxford Press.

Green, E. J., & Connolli, M. E. (2009). Jungian family sandplay with bereaved children: Implications for play therapists. *International Journal of Play Therapy, 18*(2), 84-98. doi:10.1037/a0014435

Greenberg, K. R. (2003). *Group counseling in K-12 schools: A handbook for school counselors.* Boston, MA: Allyn & Bacon.

Hagood, M. (2000). *The use of art in counseling children and adult survivors of sexual abuse.* Philadelphia, PA: Jessica Kingsley.

Heath, M., Leavy, D., Hansen, K., Ryan, K., Lawrence, L., & Sonntag, A. (2008). Coping with grief: Guidelines and resources for assisting children. *Intervention in School & Clinic, 43*(5), 259-269. doi:10.1177/1053451208314493

Huss, S. N., & Ritchie, M. (1999). Effectiveness of a group for parentally bereaved children. *Journal for Specialists in Group Work, 24,* 186-196. doi:10.1080/01933929908411429

Jimerson, S. R., & Miller, D. N. (2008). Treating the illness: The school's response to health-related student death and children's grief. *Journal of Applied School Psychology, 24*(2), 285-302. doi:10.1080/15377900802093306

Kalff, D. (1980). *Sandplay* (2nd ed.). Santa Monica, CA: Sigo Press.

Kestly, T. (2005). Adolescents sand tray therapy. In L. Gallo-Lopez & C. Schaefer (Eds.), *Play therapy with adolescents* (2nd ed., pp. 18-29). Lanham, MD: Rowman & Littlefield.

Klein, M. (1929). Personification in the play of children. *The International Journal of Psychoanalysis, 10,* 193-204.

Kübler-Ross, E. (1997) *On death and dying*. New York, NY: Scribner.

Kulic, K. R., Dagley, J. C., & Horne, A. M. (2001). Prevention groups with children and adolescents. *Journal for Specialists in Group Work, 26*(3), 211-218.

Landreth, G. (2002). *Play therapy: The art of the relationship* (2nd ed.). New York, NY: Brunner-Routledge.

Leavy, D. G. (2005). Facilitating communication about death between mothers and adolescent sons using fictional children's literature (Unpublished master's thesis). Provo, UT: Brigham Young University.

Malchiodi, C. A. (2002). *The soul's palette: Drawing on art's transformative powers for healing and well-being*. Boston, MA: Shambhala.

McGregor, C. (2009). *My daddy's going away*. London, England: BPR.

McNally, S. P. (2001). *Sandplay: A source book for play therapists*. Bloomington, IN: Writers Club Press.

Oaklander, V. (1988). *Windows to our children*. Highland, NY: Gestalt Journal Press.

Pehrsson, D. E., Allen, V. B., Folger, W. A., McMillen, P. S., & Lowe, I. (2007). Bibliotherapy with preadolescents experiencing divorce. *The Counseling Journal: Counseling Journal for Couples and Families, 4*, 409-414.

Piaget, J. (1977). *The development of thought: Equilibrium of cognitive structures*. New York, NY: Viking Press.

Ransom, F. J., & Finney, K. F. (2000). *I don't want to talk about it*. Washington, DC: Magination Press.

Robson, M. (2008). The driver whose heart was full of sand: Leigh's story-a play therapy case study of a bereaved child. *British Journal of Guidance & Counselling, 36*(1), 71-80.

Salloum, A., & Overstreet, S. (2008) Evaluation of individual and group grief and trauma interventions for children post-disaster. *Journal of Clinical Child and Adolescent Psychology, 37*(3), 495-507.

Samide, L. L., & Stockton, R. (2010). Letting go of grief. Bereavement groups for children in the school setting. *Journal for Specialists in Group Work, 27*(2), 192-204.

Shen, Y., & Armstrong, S. A. (2008). Impact of group sandtray therapy on the self-esteem of young adolescent girls. *The Journal of Specialists in Group Work, 33*(2), 118-137.

Sholt, M., & Gavron, T (2006). Therapeutic qualities of clay-work in art therapy and psychotherapy: A review. *Art Therapy: Journal of the American Art Therapy Association, 23*(2), 66-72

Stroebe, M., & Schut, H. (1999). The dual process model of coping with bereavement: Rationale and description. *Death Studies, 23*, 197-224.

Tonkins, S. A. M., & Lambert, M. J. (1996). A treatment outcome study of bereavement groups for children. *Child and Adolescent Social Work Journal, 13*, 3-21.

Trozzi, M. (1999). *Talking with children about loss*. New York, NY: Putnam.

U. S. Census Bureau. (2005). Detailed tables—number, timing, and duration of marriage. Retrieved from http://www.census.gov/population/socdemo/marri-div/2004detailed_tables.html

Waas, H. (2003). Death education for children. In I. Corless, B. B. Germino, & M. A. Pittman (Eds.), *Dying, death, and bereavement* (pp. 25-41). New York, NY: Springer.

Webb, N. B. (2011). Play therapy for bereaved children: Adapting strategies to community, school, and home settings. *School Psychology International, 32*(2), 132-143. doi:10.1177/0143034311400832

Wolfelt, A. D. (2001). *Healing your grieving heart: 100 practical ideas*. Fort Collins, CO: Companion Press.

Worden, J. W. (1991). *Grief counseling and grief therapy: A handbook for the mental health practitioners.* New York, NY: Springer.

Yalom, I. D. (1995). *The theory and practice of group psychotherapy.* New York, NY: Basic Books.

CHAPTER 3

USING PLAY TECHNIQUES FOR FAMILY SUBSTANCE ABUSE CONCERNS

Jonathan H. Ohrt, Jenifer N. Ware, and Dodie Limberg

Family substance abuse is a serious concern that is experienced by millions of children each year. When one or more family members abuse a substance, it can create an unsettling environment where children are exposed to conflict, poor communication, or neglect of their physical and emotional needs. Unfortunately, family substance abuse can have serious, negative consequences for children's academic, social, and emotional development. However, in accordance with the American School Counselor Association's (ASCA, 2012) *National Model*, professional school counselors (PSCs) work to remove barriers to all students' academic and personal/social and emotional development. Through the delivery of responsive services, PSCs provide short-term counseling to assist students with personal concerns or relationship difficulties. Additionally, through a prevention-based school guidance curriculum, PSCs can help children to learn specific skills to cope with future challenges and maintain healthy psychosocial development (ASCA, 2012). Play therapy is a developmentally appropriate modality for individual and small group counseling with children. Therefore, in this chapter we discuss the psychosocial effects of

Integrating Play Techniques in Comprehensive School Counseling Programs, pp. 43–65

family substance abuse and describe practical play therapy techniques PSCs can use with their students.

Vignette 1

Lizzie is a 9-year old female in the fourth grade. Recently, she has appeared to be very withdrawn at school. She rarely plays with her friends during recess and does not participate in class activities as often as she did previously. Her grades have dropped significantly from the previous quarter. Lizzie's teacher sometimes finds her crying at her desk during independent reading time. Lizzie does not receive much support at home and she rarely sees her father. He often stays out late at a bar after work and spends much of the weekend drinking at home while watching sports. When Lizzie tries to talk to him he doesn't pay much attention to her. He tells Lizzie that he is too busy to help her with her homework or to spend time playing with her. He often seems distant from the rest of the family members. Things at home are very hectic because Lizzie's mom is also very busy taking care of her younger brother and sister. Lizzie tries to stay out of the way and spends a lot of time in her room alone. Lizzie's teacher is very concerned about her and refers her to the school counselor.

Vignette 2

David is an 8-year old male student in third grade. His teacher has noticed a steady decline in the quality of his work in class. David often appears distracted during different reading and activity times in class. He is having difficulty concentrating and also distracts his peers by talking to them at inappropriate times. David's teacher suspects that he is having some difficulty at home; however, when she has parent conferences, David's mom assures her that there are no serious problems in the household. In reality, David's home life is very chaotic. His mother often passes out early in the evening after taking an excessive dose of prescription pills. David is left to fend for himself and his younger brother when it comes to making dinner and getting ready for bed. These extra responsibilities make it difficult for David to complete his homework. Unfortunately, it is hard for David to keep friends because his friends' parents suspect that there is a conflict in David's house. They often discourage their own children from being friends with David. David's teacher eventually gets the feeling that something "just isn't right" and decided to refer him to the school counselor.

LITERATURE REVIEW

Substance abuse is a pervasive problem that affects many families throughout the United States (U.S.). Children who grow up in environments where they are exposed to adult substance abuse often experience long-term consequences. The American Psychiatric Association (American Psychiatric Association [APA], 2000) defines substance abuse as a maladaptive pattern of substance use within a 12-month period that causes significant impairment or distress and affects one's (a) ability to fulfill his or her major life obligations, (b) physical safety, (c) social or interpersonal functioning, or (d) results in substance-related legal problems. Substance abuse is a prevalent concern in the U.S. with an estimated 5% of the population meeting the diagnostic criteria for alcohol abuse, 1.2% for cannabis abuse or dependence, and 0.2% for cocaine abuse or dependence in a given year (APA, 2000). According to the *National Household Survey on Drug Use and Health* (Office of Applied Studies, Substance Abuse, and Mental Health Statistics, 2010), approximately 22.1 million Americans over the age of 12 were abusing or dependent on alcohol or other illicit drugs. These statistics are indicative of an alarming rise in the number of children growing up in substance-abusing families. Specific to alcohol abuse, in a recent national longitudinal study, Grant (2000) found that 1 in 4, or approximately 19 million children under the age of 18 were exposed to alcohol abuse or dependence. Such estimates may be conservative due to the fact that many families tend to keep the "family secret" by hiding knowledge of the addiction from those outside of the family system (Edwards, 2003).

When one or more family members engage in substance abuse or dependence, it can create an unstable environment, particularly for young children. Further exacerbating the situation is the fact that a high percentage of those abusing substances also meet the criteria for another psychiatric disorder (dual diagnosis). Specifically, it is estimated that approximately 50% of people who abuse substances are diagnosed with an additional mental illness. Unfortunately, individuals with dual diagnoses are also at a greater risk for suicide attempts and completion (Brooner, King, Kidorf, Schmidt, & Bigelow, 1997; Halikas, Crosby, Pearson, Nugent, & Carlson, 1994). Such dynamics make it difficult for an abusing individual to participate in good parenting. Researchers have found that alcoholic parents are less satisfied in their role as a parent (Watkins, O'Farrell, Suvak, Murphy, & Taft, 2009), are less likely to exhibit positive affect toward their child (Fitzgerald, Zucker, & Yang, 1995), and are more likely to engage in frequent, punitive behavior (Schuler & Nair, 2001). Additionally, individuals abusing substances may engage in behaviors that disrupt the family system. They may deny using, socialize with other users, and exclude friends and family members who do not use. These isolating behaviors also limit the children's access to appropriate role models. Ultimately, relationships within the family become strained and members often display higher levels of conflict and negativity, poor communication, deficient problem-solving skills, and may lack consistency (Fals-Stewart, Kelley, Cooke, & Golden, 2003).

Despite the turbulent and chaotic environment often associated with substance abuse, families, like other systems, seek to maintain homeostasis or equilibrium. In other words, family members adapt to the new dynamic introduced by the substance abuser in order to maintain balance within the family system; thus, the family establishes patterns of communication and interaction that serve to protect the family secret (substance abuse) and maintain the status quo. Unfortunately, this often leads to developmental delays within the family (Lambie & Rokutani, 2002) and causes children to develop unhealthy compensatory behaviors to maintain homeostasis when substance abuse is present. Kinney (2003) outlined three strategies that family members use to adapt to the new dynamic: (a) take care of oneself and avoid the member abusing substances, (b) become a caregiver and support and control the dysfunction system, or (c) accept the dysfunctional system and work to maintain the appearance that nothing is wrong (i.e., "family secret").

Children in families where substance abuse is occurring may also adapt by developing roles. For example, Wegscheider-Cruse (1981) outlined specific roles that children of alcoholics (COAs) may develop as a coping mechanism. The following are five potential roles that PSCs may observe among COAs in the school setting. The first role is *Chief Enabler.* The family member in this role denies family dysfunction and protects the substance abuser from consequences of his or her behavior. This role is most often occupied by the spouse of the abuser and may not be displayed often in children. However, this role may be identifiable during parent conferences or in interactions where the school counselor sees the family together (e.g., open house, parent conferences). The second role is that of the *Family Hero*. This member attempts to cover up the dysfunction and work hard to make the family appear healthy. A student who is in the role of *Family Hero* may be a high achiever, hard worker, and may seem very well adjusted. Additionally, students in this role may isolate themselves and avoid social situations in order to avoid drawing attention to the family and the substance abuse problem. The third role is the *Family Scapegoat*. This member diverts attention away from the substance abuser by acting out and taking blame for dysfunction. This may be seen as the child who gets blamed for everything, is often in trouble, and this dynamic may be identified during interactions among the family (e.g., parent teacher conference or child study team where the parent(s) is present). The fourth role is the *Lost Child* who attempts to escape the dysfunction by hiding and avoiding dependence on caregivers. This child may be very quiet and withdrawn, not asking for help, support, or accepting attention. Finally, the *Family Mascot* exhibits characteristics of a "class clown" who diverts attention away from the painful situation through humor, foolishness, wit, or charm. Although this model may be helpful for PSCs in conceptualizing students, it's important to note that the roles are generalizations and not necessarily indicative of all family substance abuse situations. Further, they should not be used to label individuals and families because those not experiencing substance abuse may exhibit such roles as well (Alford, 1998). Rather, the roles are included here to help identify coping strategies that may be used by various family members when there is a substance abuse issue in the family system.

Psychosocial Consequences

In addition to developing maladaptive coping behaviors, children living in families with substance abuse issues are also at an increased risk for long-term negative consequences related to their psychological, academic, and social development. First, COAs are at a much greater risk for developing alcohol abuse or dependence problems themselves. In particular, researchers have found that COAs are 4 times more likely to develop abuse or dependence problems than their non-COA peers (Brook et al., 2003). The environment for children who live with a substance-abusing parent is often uncertain and chaotic and may lack structure and consistency (Lawson & Lawson, 2005). Unfortunately, they typically have little control over their situation and are unable to escape it, sometimes resulting in maladaptive coping strategies, emotional distress, or behavioral problems. Children may also develop a sense of helplessness to change their situation, resulting in a more external locus of control (Mun, Fitzgerald, Puttler, Zucker, & Von Eye, 2000). Despite COAs lack of control over their situation, they might develop a sense of guilt or shame if they take responsibility for their parent's substance abuse. They may believe that if they were better behaved or were a better student, then their parent's alcohol abuse would stop. Thus, these children may develop a sense of worthlessness or low self-esteem (Fields, 2004; Kinney, 2003)

Another problematic symptom for children who grow up in families with alcohol or drug-abusing parents is that they are more likely to display internalizing and externalizing behaviors compared to their peers with non substance-abusing parents (Christensen & Bilenberg, 2000). For example, COAs often experience fear of conflict or losing control and have difficulty expressing their emotions (Rubin, 2001). Further, they also experience increased rates of anxiety and depression (Kessler et al., 1994). Because some forms of abuse are more prevalent in substance-abusing families, children may experience posttraumatic stress disorder resulting in various symptoms such as anxiety, depression, nightmares, crying, and bedwetting (Kinney, 2003). Children of alcoholics also exhibit higher level of conduct disorders and impulsivity (Fitzgerald et al., 1995).

Family substance abuse can also have significant negative effects on children's academic progress. The stressful and chaotic home environment may make it difficult for children to concentrate, complete homework, and receive parental academic support and encouragement (Arman, 2000; Fields, 2004; Kinney, 2003). Consequently, COAs suffer from lower academic achievement (Poon, Ellis, Fitzgerald, & Zucker, 2000) including lower verbal, writing, and mathematics scores. Additionally, COAs suffer from lower cognitive performance (Fitzgerald et al., 1995) and poorer neurological functioning (Poon et al., 2000). Finally, COAs are more likely to be diagnosed with a learning disability, be truant from school, retained, and eventually drop out of school.

Children from families experiencing substance abuse also struggle with relationships and social skills. Children are often confused or hurt by their relationships with the substance abuser, leading to difficulty with attachment and trust (Rubin, 2001). Additionally, children may lack appropriate communication skills to develop intimate relationships or friendships with peers and may isolate themselves (Fields, 2004; Kinney, 2003). Sadly, many of these consequences persist into adulthood, resulting in maladaptive relationship patterns with peers, romantic partners, and their own children later in life (causing problematic communication and interpersonal dynamics that are intergenerational). Therefore, it is imperative for children experiencing family substance abuse to receive early interventions to support their long-term progress and development.

EVIDENCE-BASED TREATMENTS

Unfortunately, there is limited research specific to counseling services for children experiencing family substance abuse and most do not receive counseling services (Doweiko, 2002). Rather, most recent research is related to interventions for adult children of alcoholics. The current focus in addictions treatment consists of including other family members in addition to treating the abuser. Although PSCs do not provide long-term psychotherapy or family counseling, they are responsible for collaborating with parents and can support students' academic and personal/social development within the school environment (ASCA, 2012). Lambie and Sias (2005) recommended the following activities for PSCs to assist COAs in their development: (a) increase PSC's knowledge of substance abuse and COAs, (b) educate other educators about COAs, (c) be accessible and an effective listener, (d) facilitate classroom guidance relating to substance abuse and COAs, (e) offer counseling groups to COAs, and (f) accept and acknowledge professional competencies and limitations. Arman (2000) developed a group model for PSCs to utilize with COAs that emphasized group components that have been effective in improving peer relations and a sense of belonging (Price & Emshoff, 1997) and instilling resiliency (Rak & Patterson, 1996); which are all potential concerns for children experiencing family substance abuse.

Although play therapy has not been specifically studied with family substance abuse concerns, it does have demonstrated effectiveness with a variety of presenting concerns experienced by these children. In a meta-analytic review of play therapy effectiveness, Bratton, Ray, Rhine, and Jones (2005) found that play therapy was effective in treating children with either externalizing behaviors or internalizing behaviors or both. Additionally, the authors reported that play therapy was effective in treating children with social adjustment, behavior concerns, or family functioning/relationships problems. More recently, Blanco and Ray (2011) found that play therapy was effective in improving children's academic achievement. Thus, play therapy appears to be a promising approach when working with children experiencing family substance abuse.

Proposed Treatment Approaches and Techniques

Play is essential for healthy physical, intellectual, and social-emotional development. According to Elkind (2007), play is an innate drive that fuels human thought and behavior throughout the lifecycle. Learning occurs as children use play to explore themselves and the world around them. Play and activity are a child's natural language. It is a way for children to communicate and explore their experiences, their reactions to those experiences, and their wants and needs (Landreth, Baggerly, & Tyndall-Lind, 1999).

Because play is a natural part of a child's life, it is important to include it in the counseling process for children. Play therapy provides a similar experience for children as talk therapy does for adults, giving children the opportunity for self-expression in a way that is natural and familiar. When feelings are inaccessible to a child at a verbal level, one should not expect a child to come up to an adult's verbal abilities to express thoughts and feelings. Rather, play therapy is about the adult meeting the child at the child's developmental level and communicating in ways that are comprehensible for that child. Landreth (2012) described play therapy as a

> dynamic interpersonal relationship between a child (or person of any age) and a therapist trained in play therapy procedures who provides selected play materials and facilitates the development of a safe relationship for a child (or person of any age) to fully express and explore self (feelings, thoughts, experiences, and behaviors) through play, the child's natural medium of communication, for optimal growth and development. (p. 16)

Theoretical Underpinnings of Play Approach

There are many different theoretical approaches to play therapy, each having a unique perspective on conceptualizing children and their needs. The most popular forms of play therapy are child-centered, cognitive-behavioral, and Adlerian approaches (Ray, 2011). Counselors are encouraged to engage in self-reflection to gain a deeper sense of awareness and understanding of their beliefs about human nature, effects of the environment, and personality development and change. Counselors can then develop an increased understanding about a theoretical orientation that fits best for them and can serve as a guide as they make decisions about implementing play therapy.

Adlerian play therapy combines the principles of play therapy with the concept of Alfred Adler's Individual Psychology. From an Adlerian perspective, people are purposeful, creative, and motivated by a need to belong (Ansbacher, & Ansbacher, 1956; Watts & Carlson, 1999). Maladjustment is a form of discouragement felt when one is unable to effectively cope with perceived problems in their life. In Adlerian play therapy, the role of the counselor is to understand the client's assets, lifestyle, goals, and behaviors, looking for opportunities to encourage them (Kottman, 2009).

Adlerian play therapists build an egalitarian relationship with the child based on mutual trust and respect. Because the relationship is collaborative in nature, the child and therapist share responsibility and power in the sessions. The therapist takes an active role in sessions, both by her own initiative as well as the child's request. Adlerian play therapy has four phases of therapy: (1) building a relationship, (2) exploring the child's lifestyle, (3) helping the child gain insight, and (4) reorienting and re-educating the child (Kottman, 2003). The role of the play therapist changes depending on the phase of counseling. After the first phase of building a relationship, Adlerian therapists become more directive in the second phase, going from partner to active explorer to educator. The third phase is more of a partnership again, as the therapist communicates important information. Again, the role switches in the fourth phase, with the therapist becoming an active teacher and encourager.

Adlerian play therapy is a useful intervention for school counselors in providing helpful strategies for children, teachers, and parents to change negative feelings and behaviors (Kottman & Johnson, 1983). Parent and teacher consultations are an important component of Adlerian play therapy and school counselors have the opportunity to engage in both. Being in the schools, school counselors have a unique opportunity to work with teachers, providing education and support that can positively affect the functioning of a classroom. School counselors can also provide a teacher with specific recommendations that can support a child's positive changes in play therapy. In addition to working with teachers, school counselors can also engage in parent consultations. Many school counselors are busy and may not have time to meet in-person with parents on a weekly basis, but they can set up times to talk over the phone periodically. School counselors can teach specific parenting strategies and educate parents on insights gained about their child.

Specific Play Techniques With Description

Family drawing. When a child experiences trouble at home, it can be helpful to create family drawings in play therapy. This gives the play therapist information about the child's perception of the family atmosphere and can also be used to help the child gain insight. One approach is a kinetic family drawing (Burns & Kaufman, 1972; Knoff & Prout, 1985). In this technique, the play therapist instructs the child to draw a picture of everyone in her family with everyone doing something. After the child has completed her drawing, the play therapist asks questions about the drawing and the family members, such as what they are doing, how they feel, and characteristics of the individual family members. This gives the therapist increased understanding about the child's perception of characteristics of and interactions between family members.

Creating cartoon helpers. Creating cartoon helpers (Kottman, 2003) is an expressive arts activity that can incorporate a variety of different art supplies and materials. A play therapist prompts a child to create a cartoon helper for the purpose of helping the child cope with a difficult situation. When using this technique, the child has the opportunity to gain insight as the play therapist makes suggestions about alternate ways of viewing self, others, and the world. It can also be used to help a child discover problem-solving strategies, develop coping skills, and discover positive self-attributes. This technique can be used in a variety of ways. For example, a child can draw a picture of a problematic situation or feeling and then create a cartoon, drawing and describing how it helps them with their problem. The child can also draw a picture of when the problem is resolved to help them gain insight about stressors and problem-solving strategies. The play therapist engages in dialogue with the child, processing through feelings about the situation; alternative thoughts, feelings, and behaviors; and/or strengths and resources that can help the child. When the session ends, the child can take the cartoon helper with them to serve as a reminder of helpful coping strategies to use throughout the week.

Symbolic representations. Children can use symbolic representations for people and situations in their lives, helping them gain insight and make changes in their perceptions, thoughts, feelings, and behaviors. There are many ways to use this technique, so the play therapist can be creative and make adjustments based on the child's interests and needs. One example is prompting the child to choose an animal for each member of the family, following with questions about the ways in which the animal is like the family member. Another suggestion is using puppets and prompting the child to create a puppet show with the family members. These types of activities can provide insight about the feelings and interactions among family members. It can also be taken a step further and serve as a means to explore problem-solving strategies and coping mechanisms, as it is sometimes easier for children to talk about external objects.

Feelings drawing. Children, depending on their level of development, can have trouble recognizing and verbalizing their feelings. In times like this, it can be helpful to use artwork as a means of self-expression and gaining insight. There are a variety of ways that feelings can be incorporated into artwork, one of which involves the child using different colors to represent their feelings. A play therapist can use a page already created, such as the one in *When A Family is in Trouble: Children Can Cope with Grief from Drug and Alcohol Addiction* by Marge Heegaard (1993). Alternatively, the therapist can create an outline of the child's body by tracing the child as they lay down on a large piece of paper or prompt the child to draw their own outline on any size of paper. Once the outline is created, the child can choose a color for each feeling that they want to use. It is recommended that the therapist have a feelings chart close by for the child to use if they need to do so. Instructions can be given to the child to color their feelings inside the body. Once the child has completed the activity, the school counselor processes it with them, discussing which colors they decided to use, where they put the color, and how much of the color they used. This activity can be used to gain information about the child's emotions or increase the child's self-awareness about feelings. Additionally, the activity can be taken a step further to start a conversation about what is happening when a child feels a particular feeling and how it might be changed (see Table 3.1).

Table 3.1. Sample Outline of Five Play Therapy Sessions in a School Environment

Session Number	*Content of Session*
Prior to First Session	Meet with parent/caregiver(s) and teacher(s) to collect information about the child's developmental history, family and social relationships, and concerns. This is also a time to build rapport with those involved in the child's life, as their involvement is important to making and maintaining positive changes in the child's life.
1	Introduce child to playroom by saying "This is our playroom and, in here, you can do many of the things you want to do."
	Continue building collaborative relationship between counselor and client.
	Prompt client to create a kinetic family drawing to gain awareness of client's perceptions of family atmosphere.
2	Prompt client to do a symbolic representation activity, choosing an animal that is like her and creating a home in the sand.
3	Prompt client to create a cartoon helper.
4	Create drawing about feelings.
5	Follow-up with client.
	Terminate.

CASE STUDY

As an elementary school counselor, Mrs. Davis received a referral for counseling with Lizzie, a student who appeared sad and increasingly withdrawn from her peers. Through parent and teacher consultations, Mrs. Davis gathered information about Lizzie and discovered that her dad had recently left home to receive treatment for alcoholism.

As the school counselor, Mrs. Davis already had a relationship with Lizzie from interactions in her classroom and other school programs. She was aware that Lizzie had become more withdrawn and, therefore, wanted to be particularly mindful of creating a safe environment in the playroom while also utilizing the five play therapy sessions she had with her. As it became evident that Lizzie felt comfortable in the playroom and the counselor-client relationship was established, Mrs. Davis felt comfortable moving forward into the next play therapy phase (Adlerian phase two, exploring the child's lifestyle). Mrs. Davis already had information from Lizzie's parents and teacher, but wanted to learn more about her perception of self and her environment. She also wanted to facilitate Lizzie's development of self-awareness and insight as she learned to cope with her difficult situation at home.

For the first session, Mrs. Davis brought Lizzie to the playroom and introduced it by saying, "This is our playroom and, in here, you can do many of the things you want to do" To build the therapeutic relationship and help Lizzie feel safe and connected, Mrs. Davis used a variety of techniques, such as tracking behavior, reflecting feeling, encouragement, restating content, and actively interacting with Lizzie. For a thorough discussion of specific skills, see Landreth (2012) or Kottman (2003). Consistent with Moustakas' (1955) finding of some children in a first session, Lizzie was quiet during the first portion of the session, seeming unsure of what to do. As the session progressed, she started exploring the playroom and engaging with Mrs. Davis. Mrs. Davis prompted Lizzie to create a kinetic family drawing to gain an understanding of her perception of her home environment. Lizzie drew her mother and brother playing with the dog and herself playing a video game in her room. She drew her dad on the opposite side of the page and explained that he was away getting help with a doctor. Lizzie described feeling sad that her dad was gone and unsure if he would come back.

During the second session, following the guidelines suggested by Homeyer and Sweeney (2011), Mrs. Davis prompted Lizzie to choose an animal for each member of her family and then create their home in the sandbox. Lizzie chose a dinosaur to be her dad, a big giraffe for her mom, a small giraffe for her brother, and a baby panda bear for herself. She put them in the sandbox with the two giraffes together, the dinosaur on one side and the panda bear on the opposite side. Mrs. Davis processed Lizzie's creation with her and Lizzie identified that the two giraffes were always together and leave everyone else out. Mrs. Davis pointed out that the panda was alone, wondering if there were times that Lizzie felt alone. Lizzie identified feeling left out by her mother and brother and sad about her dad leaving, unsure when he would come back or if he would come back at all.

Mrs. Davis knew that Lizzie's parents were planning for her dad to return home after he completed his treatment program. Mrs. Davis wanted to help Lizzie continue gaining insight about her feelings regarding her dad being gone and develop coping skills to get through this difficult time. Mrs. Davis prompted Lizzie to create cartoon helpers as a way to generate helpful problem-solving strategies and alternatives of looking at self, others, and the world (Kottman, 2003). First, she asked Lizzie to draw a picture of home while dad was away getting help. Lizzie drew herself feeling sad and lonely. Mrs. Davis then prompted Lizzie to draw a cartoon helper that would help her with her feelings until her dad got back. Lizzie drew an angel-looking creature, Belle, who had magical powers and explained that Belle flew back and forth between her and her dad, delivering messages to and from each other. Lizzie explained that Belle always told her that her dad loved her, missed her, and was coming home soon. Next, Mrs. Davis prompted Lizzie to draw a picture of the time when she feels happier at home. She drew a picture of her and her family, including her dad, playing a game together and explained that she wanted her dad to come home so they could all be a family again. Lizzie decided to create Belle out of craft sticks and take her home as a reminder that her dad loves her and that she would be ok until he came back home.

During Lizzie's fourth session, Lizzie and Mrs. Davis worked together on a feelings drawing. Mrs. Davis prompted Lizzie to lay on a large piece of butcher paper and traced the outline of her body. Next, they created a list of feelings together and Lizzie chose a different color for each feeling. Mrs. Davis then prompted Lizzie to color her outline with all of the feelings that she feels. Lizzie used several different colors representing happy, sad, angry, nervous, and guilty. Mrs. Davis asked Lizzie about her drawing and times that she felt the various feelings represented in her picture. Lizzie identified multiple feelings related to her dad being gone and her parents fighting during the past few months before he left, emphasizing her sad feelings. Mrs. Davis reflected Lizzie's feelings and then prompted her to draw or write new thoughts on her picture that might help her feel less sad. Lizzie generated hopeful thoughts about her dad coming home. Lizzie might find it helpful to engage with other children at recess instead of sitting alone.

Lizzie came into her last session and described feeling happier when she played with her friends and decided to no longer spend time alone at recess. Mrs. Davis encouraged Lizzie for her effort to engage with friends and try to think more positively. As the session ended, Mrs. Davis reminded Lizzie that she was available in the school counselor's office if Lizzie needed to talk in the future. After Lizzie's last play therapy session, follow-up consisted of Mrs. Davis providing insight to Lizzie's parents and teachers as well as helpful tools to use in their specific environments, such as feeling reflection and encouragement.

Children who experience family substance abuse are at a higher risk for negative consequences related to their academic, emotional, and social development. PSCs possess unique therapeutic counseling skills to assist these students within the context of a comprehensive school counseling program. Play therapy techniques are effective and developmentally appropriate interventions for PSCs to use as part of the responses services component of the delivery system. These interventions can help to ensure that these students continue healthy growth and development and experience academic, career, and personal/social success.

PREVENTION CURRICULUM

A framework for developing a preventative guidance curriculum is established in the delivery system of the ASCA *National Model* (2012). Professional school counselors have an ethical obligation to provide education and prevention of academic, career, and personal and social concerns for all students (ASCA, 2010). School counselors should exemplify the competency to develop a comprehensive, developmental guidance curriculum that aligns with the *ASCA National Model* (2012) and addresses the relationship of academic performance to personal/social needs and family life (ASCA, 2007). The *ASCA National Standards* regarding personal/social development of students provide direction for school counselors to develop an effective curriculum that increases student competence in three standards: (1) respect for self and others, (2) making decisions and goal setting, and (3) acquiring personal safety skills. These standards promote student development of healthy coping skills and address the concern of emotional and physical dangers of substance use and abuse.

According to the U.S. Department of Health and Human Services (2010), ten percent of youth between the ages of 12 to 17 were classified as needing treatment for substance abuse. In addition, Grant (2000) estimated that approximately 1 in 4 students in the United States, before the age of 18 is exposed to a family member who abuses substances. Therefore, the school is an ideal setting to implement a substance abuse prevention and awareness program, including issues regarding family substance abuse.

Proposed Curriculum Development Approaches and Theory Foundations

Developmentally, it is important to recognize the cognitive difference of children and adults. Children between the ages of 2-11 are developing the language skills and logical thinking (Piaget, 1962). Play therapy techniques provide students a way to communicate in their natural language, which is play (Landreth, 2012). Play techniques support the implementation of the *ASCA National Standards* (2004) which can assist children in developing coping skills (Ray, Armstrong, & Balkin, 2005). Promoting healthy coping skills within a prevention guidance curriculum may inhibit the effects of family substance abuse or future abuse of substances. Students who have poor parent-child relationships and who are involved in risk taking behaviors are at risk of future substance abuse (Lambie & Rokutani, 2002). Therefore, it is important to conduct guidance lessons that focus on: (a) family roles, (b) healthy decision making, and (c) coping skills. In the following section, we present sample guidance lesson plans that can be facilitated by PSCs.

SAMPLE LESSON PLANS

Family Roles

Title: Which Role Do I Play in My Family?

Standard: Students will acquire the knowledge, attitudes, and interpersonal skills to help them understand and respect self and others. (ASCA Standard A; Personal/Social Domain)

Competency:

1. Identify and recognize changing family roles (ASCA:PS:A1.12)
2. Recognize, accept, respect and appreciate individual differences (ASCA: PS: A2.3)
3. Use effective communication skills (ASCA: PS:A2.6)

Learning Objectives: After participating in the discussion, completing the activity, and processing with the group, students will be able to: (a) identify family roles, (b) recognize that all families are different and (c) use effective communication skills with family members.

Materials: Dry erase board, sand trays, and miniatures

Play Therapy Learning Activity: Sand Tray

Introduction: The school counselor will discuss the different roles within a family and how these roles can change. The school counselor will solicit responses from students about what roles students play in their own family. Depending on the age and developmental level of the children, specific roles within a family can be discussed (i.e., family hero, placater, scapegoat, lost child, and mascot). Next, the school counselor will ask the students to brainstorm in pairs what is means to be a family member. The counselor will then solicit responses from the pairs about what it means to be a family member. The counselor will write the responses on a dry erase board.

Activity:

1. The students will create a visual representation of what their family looks like (sand tray).
2. The students will share their creation in small groups.
3. The counselor will facilitate large group sharing.

 Conclusion: The counselor will facilitate discussion about what the students learned about themselves, specifically their role in the family, as a result of the activity.

Connection to Family Substance Abuse: The student's disclosure during this activity may allow the school counselor to identify possible substance abuse issues within a family or specific roles associated with substance abuse.

Assessment/Evaluation:

1. The students will complete a family role awareness form before and after the lesson.
2. Students will identify what it means to them to be a family member.

Follow-up: In a subsequent guidance lesson on respect towards self and others, the counselor will check-in with the students about how they have applied the knowledge they learned during this lesson. The counselor will address immediate concerns of students through responsive services.

MAKING HEALTHY DECISIONS

Title: How Do I Decide?

Standard: Students will make decisions, set goals and take necessary action to achieve goals. (ASCA Standard B; Personal/Social Domain)

Competency:

1. Use a decision-making and problem-solving model (ASCA: PS:B1.1)

2. Understand consequences of decisions and choices (ASCA: PS:B1.2)
3. Demonstrate when, where and how to seek help for solving problems and making decisions (ASCA: PS: B1.5)

Learning Objectives: After participating in the discussion, completing the activity, and processing with the group, students will be able to: (a) apply a decision-making model, (b) identify consequences of decisions and (c) demonstrate how to seek out resources to help with making decisions.

Materials: The school counselor will create scenarios that are developmentally appropriate and provide the students with a dilemma or decision to make (i.e., their friend at lunch stole a candy bar or on the bus students were making fun of their friend). Dry erase board, note cards

Play Therapy Learning Activity: Role Play

Introduction: The school counselor will brainstorm with students about what decisions they have to make and who influences their decisions. Next, the school counselor will explain role plays (psychodrama) and divide the students into groups to act out the scenarios.

Activity:

1. The students will create a role play from one of the scenarios the teacher created (or scenarios can be created from the brainstorm activity).
2. The school counselors will help students identify the decisions within each scenario and solicit responses about what positive and negative things they noticed about the role plays.
3. The counselor will explain the decision-making model and write the steps on the dry erase board
4. The school counselor will ask the students to implement the decision-making model into the role plays.

Conclusion: The counselor will facilitate discussion about what impact the decision making-model had on the outcomes of the decisions. Next, the counselor will help the students brainstorm resources available to them to help them make decisions. The counselor will ask each student to identify one new thing they will do the next time they have to make a difficult decision.

Connection to Family Substance Abuse: This will provide a preventative structure for students when they make decisions regarding future substance use. This lesson will also provide students an awareness of resources outside of their family they may help them cope with decisions/problems within their family regarding a family member's substance abuse.

Assessment/Evaluation:

1. The students will identify ways they make decisions before the activity.
2. The students will list the steps of the decision-making model on a note card for them to take with them.

Follow-up: In a subsequent guidance lesson on decision making, the counselor will check-in with the students about how they have used the decision-making model they learned during this lesson. The counselor will connect the decision-making model to coping with peer pressure.

HEALTHY COPING SKILLS

Title: Healthy Coping Skills

Standard: Students Will Understand Safety and Survival Skills (Asca Standard C; Personal/Social Domain)

Competency:

1. Learn techniques for managing stress and conflict (ASCA: PS:B1.2).
2. Learn coping skills to for managing life events (ASCA: PS: C1:11).

Learning Objectives: After participating in the discussion, completing the activity, and processing with the group, students will be able to: (a) identify techniques for managing stress and conflict and (b) demonstrate the use of healthy coping skills.

Materials: Dry erase board, puppets, book

Play Therapy Learning Activity: Puppets & Bibliotherapy

Introduction: The school counselor will ask each student to pick a puppet and to introduce themselves (as the puppet). The counselor will use a puppet to facilitate a discussion about what stress and conflict are, and feelings someone has when experiencing stress and/or conflict (i.e., sadness, anger, frustration). The counselor will ask the students (puppets) what they do when they have these feelings.

Activity:

1. The counselor will read a book (as the puppet).
2. The counselor will ask the students (puppets) about a time when they were like the character in the book.

   Conclusion: The counselor will facilitate a discussion about healthy ways to cope with these feelings.

Connection to Family Substance Abuse: This will provide a preventative structure for students, who may have a family member who is a substance abuser, to find healthy coping skills to deal with feelings surrounding interactions with the family member. The counselor should encourage that speaking with an adult (i.e., counselor) is a healthy coping skill; this may influence students to seek support from the school counselor regarding a family member's substance abuse.

Assessment/Evaluation:

1. Students will identify their current coping skills before the activity.
2. Students will identify one new coping skill they learned during the lesson.

Follow-up: In a subsequent guidance lesson, the counselor will check-in with the students about how they have applied their new coping skills. The counselor will address immediate concerns of students through responsive services.

CONCLUSION

Professional school counselors address their students' personal and social needs and work to remove barriers to their learning. Inevitably, all students will face some challenges related to their social and emotional health. Unfortunately, a high percentage of students will face challenges related to family substance abuse. Within the school guidance curriculum, PSCs can implement preventative developmental guidance to instill healthy coping mechanisms, communication, and problem-solving skills that may assist students in navigating future challenges. By integrating play techniques into developmental guidance, PSCs meet students at their developmental level and help them to better understand the concepts and skills that will help to ensure their healthy personal, social, and academic growth and development.

REFERENCES

Alford, K. M. (1998). Family roles, alcoholism, and family dysfunction. *Journal of Mental Health Counseling, 20,* 250-261.

Ansbacher, H. L., & Ansbacher, R. R. (Eds.). (1956). *The individual psychology of Alfred Adler: A systematic presentation of his writing.* New York, NY: Basic Books.

American Psychiatric Association (APA). (2000). *Diagnostic and statistical manual of mental disorders* (4th ed., Text Rev.). Washington, DC: Author.

American School Counselor Association. (2004). *ASCA National Standards for students*. Alexandria, VA: Author.

American School Counselor Association. (2012). *The ASCA National Model: A Framework for School Counseling Programs* (3rd ed.). Alexandria, VA: Author.

American School Counselor Association. (2007). *School counselor competencies*. Alexandria, VA: Author.

Arman, H. P. (2000). A small group model for working with elementary school children of alcoholics. *Professional School Counseling, 3,* 290-294.

Blanco, P., & Ray, D. (2011). Play therapy in elementary schools: A best practice for improving academic achievement. *Journal of Counseling and Development, 89,* 235-243. doi:10.1002/j.1556-6678.2011.tb00083.x

Bratton, S. C., Ray, D., Rhine, T., & Jones, L. (2005). The efficacy of play therapy with children: A meta-analytic review of treatment outcomes. *Professional Psychology: Research and Practice, 36,* 376-390. doi:10.1037/0735-7028.36.4.376

Brook, D. W., Brook, J. S., Rubenstone, E., Zhang, C., Singer, M., & Duke, M. R. (2003). Alcohol use in adolescents whose fathers abuse drugs. *Journal of Addictive Disease, 2,* 11-43. doi:10.1300/J069v22n01_02

Brooner, R. K., King, V. L., Kidorf, M., Schmidt, C. W., & Bigelow, G. E. (1997). Psychiatric and substance use comorbidity among treatment-seeking opioid users. *Archives of General Psychiatry, 54,* 71-80. doi:10.1001/archpsyc.1997.01830130077015

Burns, R., & Kaufman, S. (1972). *Action, styles, and symbols in kinetic family drawings.* New York, NY: Brunner/Mazel.

Christensen, H. B., & Bilenberg, N. (2000). Behavioural and emotional problems in children ofalcoholic mothers and fathers. *European Journal of Child and Adolescent Psychiatry, 9,* 219–226.

Doweiko, H. E. (2002). *Concepts of chemical dependency* (5th ed.). Pacific Grove, CA: Brooks/Cole Thomson Learning.

Edwards, J. T. (2003). *Working with Families: Guidelines and Techniques* (6th ed.). Durham, NC: Foundational Place Publishing.

Elkind, D. (2007). *The power of play: Learning what comes naturally.* Philadelphia, PA: Perseus.

Fals-Stewart, W., Kelley, M. L., Cooke, C. G., & Golden, J. C. (2003). Predictors of the psychosocial adjustment of children living in households of parents in which fathers abuse drugs: The effects of postnatal parental exposure. *Addictive Behavior, 28,* 1013-1031. doi:10.1016/S0306-4603(02)00235-6

Fields, R. (2004). *Drugs in perspective: A personalized look at substance use and abuse* (5th ed.). New York, NY: McGraw-Hill.

Fitzgerald, H. E., Zucker, R. A., & Yang, H. (1995). Developmental systems theory and alcoholism: Analyzing patterns of variation in high-risk families. *Psychology of Addictive Behaviors, 9,* 8-22. doi:10.1037/0893-164X.9.1.8

Grant, B. F. (2000). Estimates of US children exposed to alcohol abuse and dependence in the family. *American Journal of Public Health, 90,* 112-115.

Halikas, J. A., Crosby, R. D., Pearson, V. L., Nugent, S. M., & Carlson, G. A. (1994). Psychiatric comorbidity in treatment-seeking cocaine users. *American Journal on Addiction, 3,* 25-35.

Heegaard, M. E. (1993). *When a family is in trouble: Children can cope with grief from drug and alcohol addiction.* Minneapolis, MN: Woodland Press.

Homeyer, L., & Sweeney, D. (2011). *Sandtray therapy: A practical manual* (2nd ed.). New York, NY: Routledge.

Kessler, R. C., McGonagle, K. A., Zhao, S., Nelson, C. B., Hughes, M., Eshleman, S., Wittchen, H. U., & Kendler, K. S. (1994). Lifetime and 12-month prevalence of DSM-III-R psychiatric disorders in the United States: Results from the National Comorbitity Study. *Archives of General Psychiatry, 51,* 8-19. doi:10.1001/archpsyc.1994.03950010008002

Kinney, J. (2003). *Loosening the grip: A handbook of alcohol information.* New York, NY: McGraw-Hill.

Knoff, H., & Prout, H. (1985). *Kinetic drawing system for family and school: A handbook.* Los Angeles, CA: Western Psychological Services.

Kottman, T. (2003). *Partners in play: An Adlerian approach to play therapy* (2nd ed.). Alexandria, VA: American Counseling Association.\

Kottman, T. (2009). Adlerian play therapy. In K. J. O'Connor & L. D. Braverman (Eds.), *Play therapy theory and practice: Comparing theories and techniques* (2nd ed., pp. 237-282). Hoboken, NJ: John Wiley & Sons.

Kottman, T., & Johnson, V. (1983). Adlerian play therapy: A tool for school counselors. *Elementary School Guidance and Counseling, 28,* 42-51.

Lambie, G. W., & Rokutani, L. J. (2002). A systems approach to substance abuse identification and intervention for school counselors. *Professional School Counseling, 5*, 353-359.

Lambie, G. W., & Sias, S. M. (2005). Children of alcoholics: Implications for professional school counseling. *Professional School Counseling*, 266-273.

Landreth, G.L. (2012). *Play therapy: The art of the relationship* (3rd ed.). New York, NY: Routledge.

Landreth, G., Baggerly, J., & Tyndall-Lind, A. (1999). Beyond adapting adult counseling skills for use with children: The paradigm shift to child-centered play therapy. *The Journal of Individual Psychology, 55*, 272-587.

Lawson, A. W., & Lawson, G. W. (2005). Families and drugs. In R. H. Coombs (Ed.), *Addiction counseling review: Preparing for comprehensive, certification, and licensing examinations* (pp. 175-199). Mahwah, NJ: Lawrence Erlabaum Associates.

Moustakas, C. (1955). Emotional adjustment and the play therapy process. *Journal of Genetic Psychology, 86*, 79-99.

Mun, E.-Y., Fitzgerald, H. E., Puttler, I. I., Zucker, R. A., & Von Eye. A. (2000). Temperamental characteristics as predictors of externalizing and internalizing behavior problems in the contexts of high and low parental psychopathology. *Infant Mental Health Journal, 22*, 393-415.

Office of Applied Studies, Substance Abuse and Mental Health Statistics. (2010). Results from the 2010 National Survey on Drug use and Health: National Findings. Retrieved from http://www.samhsa.gov/data/NSDUH/2k10ResultsTables/Web/HTML/Sect5peTabs1to56.htm#ab5.1B

Piaget, J. (1962). *Play, dreams, and imitation in childhood*. New York, NY: Routledge.

Poon, E., Ellis, D. A., Fitzgerald, H. A., & Zucker, R. A. (2000). Intellectual, cognitive and academic performance among sons of alcoholics during the early elementary school years: Differences related to subtypes of familial alcoholism. *Alcoholism: Clinical and Experimental Research, 24*, 1020-1027. doi:10.1111/j.1530-0277.2000.tb04645.x

Price, A. W., & Emshoff, J. G. (1997). Breaking the cycle of addiction: Prevention and intervention with children of alcoholics. *Alcohol Health and Research World, 21*, 241-246.

Rak, C. F., & Patterson, L. E. (1996). Promoting resiliency in at-risk children. *Journal of Counseling and Development, 74*, 368-373. doi:10.1002/j.1556-6676.1996.tb01881.x

Ray, D. C. (2011). *Advanced play therapy: Essential conditions, knowledge, and skills for child practice*. New York, NY: Routledge.

Ray D. C., Armstrong, S. A., & Balkin, R.S. (2005). Play therapy practices among elementary school counselors. *Professional School Counseling, 8*, 360-365.

Rubin, D. H. (2001). *Treating adult children of alcoholics: A behavioral approach*. New York, NY: Academic Press.

Schuler, M. E., & Nair, P. (2001). Witnessing violence among inner-city children of substance abusing and non-substance abusing women. *Archives of Pediatrics & Adolescent Medicine, 155*, 342-346.

U.S. Department of Health and Human Services. (2010). *Report of the Results from the 2010 National Survey on Drug Use and Health: Summary of National Findings*. Washington, DC: Author.

Watkins, L. E., O'Farrell, T. J., Suvak, M. K., Murphy, C. M., & Taft, C. T. (2009). Parenting satisfaction among fathers with alcoholism. *Addictive Behaviors, 34*, 610-612. doi:10.1016/j.addbeh.2009.01.006

Watts, R., & Carlson, J. (Eds.). (1999). *Interventions and strategies in counseling and psychotherapy*. Philadelphia, PA: Accelerated Development.

Wegscheider-Cruse, S. (1981). *Another chance: Hope and help for the alcoholic family*. Palo Alto, CA: Science & Behavior Books.

CHAPTER 4

FINDING THEIR VOICE

Empowering Students With Selective Mutism

Angela I. Sheely-Moore

School counselors are challenged on a daily basis to enhance the academic, socioemotional, and career development of students from various cultural backgrounds. In our work with culturally diverse students, Murphy and Dillon (2011) reported how some cultural identities are "invisible" (p. 35) to the naked eye. One childhood mental disorder that might not be readily apparent to adults is selective mutism. The following two vignettes detail common presentations of selective mutism in the classroom setting that might go undetected by school staff.

Vignette 1

The third quarter of the school year has begun for Marie and yet she has not spoken directly to her first-grade teacher, Ms. Fields. Marie is well-liked by her classmates and remains at grade-level regarding her academic ability. Yet, Marie only speaks to two students within the entire school. Today, the students are working on arithmetic problems using small wooden blocks to assist in finding solutions. While other students are collaborating to complete the math worksheet, Ms. Fields observes

Integrating Play Techniques in Comprehensive School Counseling Programs, pp. 67–80

Marie sitting quietly in the back table of the classroom working on the assignment with no assistance from her peers. Marie looks to her right and taps the shoulder of her friend, Marisol. Marie cups her right hand alongside Marisol's ear to whisper something to her. Marisol immediately drops the counting blocks within her hands and approaches Ms. Field's desk to inform her that Marie needs to go to restroom.

Vignette 2

During a recent parent-conference meeting, Sally's parents described their first-generation Mexican American daughter as a "chatterbox" at home. The family self-identifies as bilingual and Sally is fluent in both Spanish and English with the tendency to speak "nonstop" at home according to her parents. However, when Sally enters her kindergarten classroom, she does not speak to any adults or children in the school. Instead, Sally uses hand gestures and head movements to communicate with her peers and teachers. Sally's teacher, Mr. Munoz, has attempted to engage verbally with Sally with no successful outcomes. In response to Mr. Munoz's attempts, Sally would immediately shift her eyes towards the carpet, while fidgeting with her hands in discomfort.

The phenomenon of children having the capacity to talk, but not talking within specific social contexts and with certain individuals was initially termed *aphasia voluntaria* in the late 1800s by Kussmaul, a German physician (McHolm, Cunningham, & Vanier, 2005; Remschmdt, Poller, Herpertz-Dahlmann, Henninghausen, & Gutenbrunner, 2001). In the 1930s the terminology shifted to emphasize the child's *choice* to refrain from speaking in certain settings—hence, Tramer's use of the term *elective mutism* (McHolm et al., 2005; Remschmdt et al., 2001). Earlier assumptions of children's oppositional behavior of refusing to speak were deemphasized with the term selective mutism (SM), which was first coined in the *Diagnostic and Statistical Manual of Mental Disorders* (DSM-IV; American Psychiatric Association [APA], 1994). The current diagnostic criteria for SM include: (1) consistent failure to speak in certain environments, such as school; (2) impediment towards academic achievement or social communication; and (3) duration occurring at least one month after the start of school (APA, 2000). According to the *DSM-IV Text Revision* (APA, 2000), ruling out other disorders (e.g., phonological disorder, stuttering, pervasive developmental disorder) is also necessary to facilitate an accurate diagnosis of SM.

PREVALENCE OF SELECTIVE MUTISM

Several authors reported the prevalence of children with SM as a rarity, ranging from 0.03%-1% of referred cases (Carbone et al., 2010;

Remschmdt et al., 2001) or a ratio of 0.8 per 1,000 individuals (Kumpulainen, Räsänen, Raaska, & Somppi, 1998). Such reported rates correspond to the DSM-IV-TR estimation of 1% of individuals referred to mental health services for SM (APA, 2000). However, other authors (Busse & Downey, 2011; Cline & Baldwin, 2004; Cunningham, McHolm, Boyle, & Patel, 2004) questioned the accuracy of the reported incidence and prevalence of SM in previous research due to criteria selection for SM, geographic and institutional setting (e.g., school, community clinic) of conducted studies, age of children, and immigrant status. For example, Elizur and Perednik (2003) reported a higher incidence rate of SM (2.2%) with immigrant preschoolers living in Jerusalem. Higher rates of SM are also being reported in studies conducted within the school setting. Kumpulainen et al. (1998) reported a 2% prevalence rate of SM in their survey of 2,010 second-graders. Such results indicate the possibility of SM being underreported in the general population, due to potential misdiagnoses of children with SM and the dominant use of verbalization within the school setting (Cohan, Chavira, & Stein, 2006). Regarding gender differences, research has indicated a higher incidence of SM in females compared to their male counterparts (Black & Uhde, 1995; Cunningham et al., 2004; Dummit et al., 1997; Elizur & Perednik, 2003; Kumpulainen et al., 1998).

With the manifestation of SM typically occurring outside of the home environment, the onset of referral for SM occurs when children enter the school setting, usually between 6 to 10-years of age (Kumpulainen et al., 1998). In fact, based on previous research studies, McHolm et al. (2005) reported children with SM are "most likely to speak at home … and least likely to speak at school" (p. 9). Several researchers (e.g., Busse & Downey, 2011; Stone, Kratochwill, Sladezcek, & Serlin, 2002; Wright, Miller, Cook, & Littmann, 1985) stressed the need for early intervention as a critical component to effective treatment of SM for elementary school-aged children. In fact, Stone et al. (2002) reported age of onset and duration of SM as two strong predictor variables for the effective treatment of SM. Key personnel in highly verbalized settings, such as schools, could serve to ameliorate short- and long-term socioemotional and behavioral consequences for children diagnosed with SM.

ACADEMIC CONSEQUENCES FOR CHILDREN WITH SELECTIVE MUTISM

Despite the reported onset of SM typically occurring within the first years of school (Kumpulainen et al., 1998), there are very few controlled studies that examine the academic, socioemotional, and behavioral characteristics of children with SM. Based on the limited conducted number of studies conducted, the impact of SM on children's academic achievement seems to be unaffected. Some authors (Busse & Downey, 2011; Cunningham et al., 2004; Kumpulinen et al., 1998; McHolm et al., 2005) suggested similar math and reading abilities of children with SM when compared to their counterparts who are not selectively mute. For instance, in a study of 52 children with SM, Cunningham et al. (2004) reported a lack of group differences on overall academic performance when compared to the control group. The authors also found no significant between-group differences in parents' reporting of academic activities conducted in the home (e.g., child reading to the parent, using the computer; Cunningham, et al., 2004). Kumpulainen et al.'s (1998) study indicated almost half of the second grade students meeting the diagnostic criteria for SM performed at an average level at school. Teacher ratings also indicated a higher frequency of children refusing to speak to the teacher were performing at or above grade level when compared to those who were performing below average (Kumpulainen et al., 1998).

SOCIOEMOTIONAL AND BEHAVIORAL IMPACT OF SELECTIVE MUTISM

In a review of existing literature, the socioemotional and behavioral consequences for children with SM are not as benign when compared to academic achievement. For example, based on teacher and parent reports, Black and Uhde (1995) indicated elevated levels of anxiety for children with SM. Cunningham et al.'s (2004) work supported previous studies indicating heightened anxiety levels for children with SM (Black & Uhde, 1995; Bergman, Piacentini, & McCracken, 2002; Dummit et al., 1997), in addition to other socioemotional and behavioral challenges when compared to a control group: propensity of obsessive tendencies and higher somatic complaints. Furthermore, Cunningham et al. (2004) indicated parent reports of children with SM indicate less social assertion, social responsibility, and social control. On the other hand, teachers within the same study reported children with SM as being less socially assertive, but not statistically different to the control group in the areas of social cooperation and social control (Cunningham et al., 2004). In addition to the previous studies (Black & Uhde, 1995; Bergman, Piacentini, & McCracken, 2002; Cunningham et al., 2004; Dummit et al., 1997) indicating socioemotional and behavioral challenges for children with SM, Vecchio and Kearney (2005) reported higher levels of reported internalizing behavioral problems when compared to the control group.

With a dearth of studies examining the socioemotional and behavior impact of SM into adulthood, Remschmidt et al.'s (2001) 12-year follow up study of individuals with SM indicate remarkable findings. Remschmidt et al. reflected upon the lack of earlier follow-up studies that included a control group. In fact, the authors only identified three prior studies that included a control group (Remschmidt et al., 2001). In addition to the limited controlled studies, many past follow-up studies included small samples sizes and were conducted as early as the 1960s (Remschmidt et al., 2001). Remschmidt et al.'s follow-up study revealed nearly half of the participants with a history of SM described themselves as less independent, less self-confident, less motivated toward academic pursuits, and overall less healthy and physically mature than the control group (p. 291). Furthermore, the authors reported less than half of the participants reporting complete remission of SM at follow-up, which correlates to less than favorable trajectory outcomes including communication and psychopathological issues (Remschmidt et al., 2001).

REVIEW OF EVIDENCE-BASED TREATMENT APPROACHES FOR SELECTIVE MUTISM

As indicated earlier, research conducted with large sample sizes or individual case studies with strong experimental control are quite limited within the literature on SM (Busse & Downey, 2011; Cline & Baldwin, 2004; Cohan et al., 2006; Cunningham et al., 2004; Stone et al., 2002). The rarity of the occurrence of SM within the general population could also serve as another challenge to conducting research (APA, 2000; Carbone et al., 2010; Kumpulainen et al., 1998; Remschmdt et al., 2001). Despite this setback, Stone et al. (2002) conducted the "first systematic analysis of the effectiveness of treatments for selective mutism using quantitative and qualitative data" (p. 184). In their comprehensive analysis of 114 studies consisting of experimental, quasi-experimental, and nonexperimental designs, Stone et al. indicated support for the use of behavioral approaches in the effective treatment of SM. Specifically, the use of behavioral treatment approaches were reported to be more effective than no treatment (Stone et al., 2002). Comparisons between distinct behavioral treatment modalities (e.g., cognitive behavioral therapy, social learning theory) were not analyzed due to insufficient data; hence Stone et al. were limited to examining the effectiveness of behavioral treatments when compared to no treatment. The most common technique employed within the behavioral framework was positive/social reinforcement, followed by shaping and contingency management (Stone et al., 2002).

Based upon a systematic review of refereed journal articles dating from 1990 to 2005, Cohan et al. (2006) reported the utilization of play therapy in the treatment of SM in a few studies within a multimodal approach.

However, Cohan et al. (2006) indicated the lack of descriptive methods which makes it unclear as to the specific type and duration of the various treatments provided within a multimodal approach. A psychodynamic play therapy approach is also utilized for children with SM, but the effectiveness of this approach remains unclear due to the lack of robust single case research designs (Cline & Baldwin, 2004; Cohan et al., 2006). Given the consensus in the literature of the reported effectiveness of behavioral approaches when working with individuals with SM (Cline & Baldwin; Cohan et al., 2006; Stone et al., 2002), it behooves professional school counselors to integrate such strategies within a developmentally responsive approach when working with children—play therapy.

THEORETICAL UNDERPINNINGS OF PLAY THERAPY

The core of play therapy involves the use of developmentally appropriate toys and play-based materials to facilitate a broad range of verbal and nonverbal expression within children. Although toys serve a tremendous role in the works of play therapists, the therapeutic relationship is an essential precursor to change. For children diagnosed with SM, the ability for school counselors to accept the child "as is"—that is, when the child is verbal *and* nonverbal—is critical in the facilitation of a therapeutic alliance grounded in safety, trust, and acceptance. The need for school counselors to communicate the core counseling conditions of empathy, unconditional positive regard, and genuineness is paramount to facilitate client growth and development (Landreth, 2012). In fact, Nims (2011) indicated the therapeutic relationship to be an essential component prior to the implementation of a solution-focused play therapy (SFPT) treatment approach.

TENETS OF SOLUTION-FOCUSED PLAY THERAPY

With an emphasis on the present and identifying solutions to problems, the solution focused (SF) approach runs counter to other traditional theories that explore problems (Fall, Holden, & Marquis, 2010). Using "solution talk" (Sklare, 2005, p. 11) as a critical mode of addressing problems, another assumption of SFPT is the belief of students experiencing problem-free moments, which can serve as momentum toward solutions. For instance, students with SM are not completely mute all the time; rather, there are exceptions when students with SM *will* engage in verbal communication with others. Identifying circumstances under which the child with SM is problem-free can serve as a catalyst to increase the frequency of verbalizations in different contexts. Given the assumption of problem-free moments, according to this theoretical approach, it is evident that the ability to resolve one's problems lies within the individual (Sklare, 2005). In alignment with one of the Rogerian tenets, the SFPT approach also postulates the inherent capacity of individuals to grow in a positive, constructive manner (Fall et al., 2010). In conjunction with the innate capacity to solve one's problems, the final assumption of SFPT is the notion of trusting the student to identify the treatment goal using positive statements (Sklare, 2005).

Nims (2011) stressed the need for student-directed goals for potential change: "the first and most important step in the SFPT process is establishing clear and concrete goals that fit the individual need of the child or adolescent.... The important thing is that the child wants this goal to happen" (p. 299). Nims's statement could not be emphasized enough when working with students with SM. With possible external pressures from parents, teachers, and peers to "just talk," the potential success of a SFPT approach is based on the school counselor's ability to empower students by developing their own goals for treatment. The following SFPT techniques are based on the two vignettes presented at the start of this chapter and on the assumption of Sally's and Marie's desire to increase the frequency of verbalizations in new settings.

Solution-Focused Based Play Therapy Techniques

Goal setting and the miracle question. As indicated earlier, goal setting serves as the critical starting point within the SFPT approach (Nims, 2011). Given the behavioral manifestation of children with SM, play therapy serves as a respectful and responsive approach to meet individuals at their developmental level. Hence, rather than forcing students with SM to verbalize their goal, school counselors can provide expressive art materials to provide students with a nonverbal approach to identify potential goals. For example, school counselors can provide the following prompt for students with SM, such as Marie and Sally: "Draw me a picture of what school would look like if you were talking to your teachers and other students in the classroom." This approach is also referred to in SFPT as the miracle question. With this technique, the school counselor would use toys and play-based materials to describe specific changes if the problem was magically resolved overnight (Nims, 2011). Sklare (2005) provided a common prompt when using the miracle question technique:

> Suppose when you go to sleep tonight, a miracle occurs, and because you are sleeping, you don't know it happens. The miracle solves the problem

> that brought you here. When you wake up in the morning ... what will you notice you will be doing differently? (p. 28)

Again, depending upon the severity of the condition, the school counselor will have to be creative to ensure accurate understanding of the goals when the student does not verbalize the outcome of the "miracle" occurrence. Hence, once the student has completed the drawing using various arts and crafts materials, the school counselor will have to reflect their observations based upon the finished product and check-in with the student to confirm the accuracy of their observations. Providing nonverbal means for students to communicate is critical during this process. For example, supplying a variety of hand puppets would grant students with SM the opportunity to respond to questions about the completed drawing using hand movements for "yes" or "no." Using red (no or stop) and green (go or yes) construction paper in the shape of a circle and taped to a wooden stick is another medium for students to assist the school counselor in clarifying the student's goals.

Exceptions. Using the technique of exceptions consists of highlighting occurrences when the problem is not being displayed. The use of various toy materials, especially toy miniatures, which characterize the school setting and other contexts (e.g., supermarket, shopping mall, park) will allow students with SM to visualize instances when they are speaking to others. For example, having an array of toy miniatures, the school counselor could use the technique of exceptions by providing the following prompt: "Using the toys, describe for me a time in school when you have talked to someone." Depending upon the severity of the condition, a more appropriate prompt for students might focus on approximations of actual verbalizations such as mouthing words or whispering. While the student arranges the miniatures, the school counselor remains engaged in this process by utilizing basic play therapy skills of tracking, reflecting feeling, and encouragement (Landreth, 2012).

Scaling. This common SFPT technique provides the opportunity for students to rate their progress of reaching their goal on a scale from 0 to 10 (Sklare, 2005). In the case of working with students diagnosed with SM, the score of 0 would indicate situations when they do not talk when there is an expectation to talk (e.g., classroom setting). On the other end of the continuum, a score of 10 would represent the resolution of the presenting problem. For younger children, Sklare (2005) provided a visual scale within his textbook depicting corresponding facial expressions to represent each number on the continuum (e.g., pronounced sad face representing the number 0 to a prominent very happy face for a score of 10). Using Sklare's graphical depiction of scaling or creating one's own would serve as another effective means to allow students with SM to communicate their experience in a less threatening mode of communication. Students with SM can simply point to the number and corresponding face that represents where they currently rate themselves in relationship to their overall goal. To assist student's movement to reach their goal, school counselors can have students create a silent movie using puppets and cue cards with written dialogue to describe how they will move one number closer to their goal (Sklare, 2005). For example, school counselors can present the following task for the student: "Today, you're going to be the director of your very own silent movie. Using the materials available to you, create a short movie of what will look different if you moved from a 6 to a 7."

A SCHOOL-BASED COMPREHENSIVE APPROACH TO TREATMENT

Given the multitude of roles and responsibilities of the contemporary school counselor in serving various stakeholders (e.g., students, teachers, parents/caregivers, support staff), the need for a collaborative approach in addressing the needs of students with SM is essential. The national student-to-school-counselor ratio averaging 459-1 for the 2009-2010 school year (American School Counseling Association [ASCA], n.d.) provides a tremendous challenge for school counselors to develop individual, long-term counseling services. With the duration of treatment for individuals with SM ranging from 5 sessions to a span of 3.5 years (Cohan et al., 2006), it would be critical for school counselors to work in tandem with the parents and caregivers of children with SM to explore community resources to locate a primary mental health care provider for their child.

School counselors must utilize a systemic approach and work with key stakeholders to implement strategies and programs to support the academic, socioemotional, and career development of students with SM. The American School Counselor Association's *National Model* (ASCA, 2012) can serve as a framework for school counselors to organize and implement a comprehensive program of services for students with SM. Specifically, school counselors can plan several activities to address the needs of students with SM and also those students who present characteristics of SM: (1) increasing awareness of SM through workshops for school staff, parents, and caregivers; (2) providing individual counseling services using SFPT; and (3) involving teachers and parents in the implementation of behavioral strategies to increase verbalization in the classroom and at home, respectively. The following discussion will exemplify the aforementioned strategies with Marie, the first-grade student with presenting characteristics of SM, described at the start of this chapter.

Increase awareness. With the onset of referral for SM occurring at the age when children enter the school setting (Kumpulainen et al., 1998), it seems important to inform teachers, support staff, and parents of the common characteristics of SM. Busse and Downey (2011) recommended strategies such as composing a letter to parents at the start of the school year or having school mental health professionals lead in-service workshops to describe SM and other anxiety related problems, in addition to clarifying SM from other communication issues such as social anxiety or English language learners. Additional strategies to disseminate general information about SM can be accomplished through brochures and web-based media, such as the school counseling website. Providing local and national resources on this issue would also serve to empower parents and teachers to learn more about the signs and symptoms, in addition to available treatment approaches.

In the case of Marie, preventative services would have begun during her first year at school. In addition to receiving the student handbook and other critical paperwork at the start of the school year, Marie's parents would have received a welcoming letter from the school counselor introducing the various services offered through the school counseling program. Within this letter, the school counselor introduced the possibility of socioemotional and academic difficulties students might experience in their transition to beginning school. The school counseling website link is included to provide additional information on various student challenges, including characteristics of SM and other anxiety-related issues. To facilitate the goal of capturing the widest audience possible, Marie's school counselor also has various brochures available in her office highlighting several common issues facing young children. You would also find posted on the school counselor's bulletin board upcoming workshops for teachers and parents regarding common childhood disorders—including SM as one of the featured topics.

Provide individual counseling services. It is commonplace for teachers and parents to request assistance from the school counselor when students exhibit socioemotional or behavioral problems in the classroom setting. It is not uncommon for school counselors to work with children who exhibit more externalizing behaviors as they are typically more disruptive to the learning environment. Informing teachers and parents of characteristics of internalizing problems, such as SM, would perhaps lead to earlier treatment (Busse & Downey, 2011). In establishing a strong therapeutic rapport with students referred for SM characteristics would facilitate the use of the aforementioned SFPT techniques discussed earlier in the chapter. Depending upon the severity of the presenting symptoms, school counselors should include consultations with the parent to share their clinical impressions of the student and possible referrals to receive treatment at a local community mental health clinic, if warranted.

For Marie's case, the school counselor would have collaborated with Ms. Fields to schedule meeting times to conduct play-based counseling session. These meeting times are varied throughout the week and limited to 25 minutes per session to ensure that Marie does not miss critical academic content. Specific examples of implementing the techniques of goal setting, use of the miracle question, finding exceptions to the problem, and scaling were discussed earlier in the chapter.

Incorporate behavior techniques within the classroom and home environment. Extending counseling techniques that compliment a SFPT approach would seem appropriate, especially in light of various researchers (e.g., Busse & Downey, 2011; Cline & Baldwin, 2004; Stone et al., 2002) who identified behavioral approaches as the most effective treatment approach to SM. The SFPT approach provides a safe and less-threatening approach in establishing therapeutic rapport and identifying specific student-directed goals. Using the SFPT approach grants students with SM the opportunity to communicate their thoughts, emotions, and behaviors in nonverbal means. To build upon this foundation of non-verbal communication via play, school counselors can also consider infusing behavioral techniques in the classroom and at home which would also serve to reach the client's stated goal. Contingency management, stimulus fading, and systematic desensitization are three behavioral techniques that would complement the works conducted during individual counseling sessions.

Contingency management. Also referred as token economies within the behavioral perspective, contingency management involves the use of positive reinforcement by rewarding appropriate behaviors with tokens that can be exchanged for rewards or privileges (Fall et al., 2010). In working with Marie, the school counselor can create a reward system based upon a designated amount of times during the week when the teacher or other school staff observes Marie whispering to another person that she did not whisper to in the past. Notice that Marie's contingency management program is not based on speaking in a typical tone of voice, as this goal might be too challenging for her at this time. Hence, when a teacher or other support staff member in the school noticed Marie whispering to another student who she has not whispered to before, Marie will earn a microphone sticker that will be affixed to her weekly calendar. At the end of the first week of the implementation of this technique, if Marie earns one microphone sticker, Marie can exchange the reward for an extra 10 minutes of recess time. Using contingency management, the school counselor can also adjust the frequency of the appropriate response and the amount of tokens earned to receive a reward or privilege.

Stimulus fading. Busse and Downey (2011) described this technique as reducing the exposure to a stimulus while incorporating a new stimulus into the environment. For example, in collaboration with Marie's parents, Mr. and Ms. Thompson, the school counselor has requested Marie to have a special play time at home with Lisa, a peer she feels comfortable in talking to, at least three times a week. The parents have been instructed to introduce another peer whom Marie does not feel comfortable talking to, at small increments, while simultaneously fading out Lisa from this special play time. The overarching goal of stimulus fading is for Marie to feel as comfortable talking with the new peer as she does with Lisa. Providing Marie toys and toy materials will facilitate the opportunity to begin communication with the new stimulus—the peer—in a format that is less threatening.

Systematic desensitization. Sharing common characteristics of scaling, contingency management, and stimulus fading, systematic desensitization involves a hierarchical structure of behavioral substeps, simultaneously paired with relaxation techniques, which ultimately lead to the targeted goal (Cohan et al., 2006). In order to reach Marie's targeted goal of speaking in a conversational, nonwhisper, voice to Ms. Fields by the end of the year, the school counselor will collaborate with Marie, Ms. Fields, and Marie's parents to identify and rank situations from the least anxiety-eliciting situation to the most anxiety-eliciting situation. Next, Marie will learn basic relaxation techniques such as breathing and imagery. Starting with the least anxiety-eliciting situation, Marie will utilize learned relaxation techniques to work on maintaining a calm state while simultaneously being exposed to the anxiety-eliciting situation. It is the goal for Marie to remain relaxed while slowly progressing through each of the hierarchical steps until she reaches her most anxiety-eliciting situation—talking to her homeroom teacher, Ms. Fields.

SUMMARY

Despite the reported rarity of individuals affected with SM, professional school counselors are charged to meet the academic, socioemotional, and career development of all students. The need for early intervention is critical for children with SM in order to avoid short- and long-term behavioral and socioemotional challenges (e.g., Busse & Downey, 2011; Stone et al., 2002; Wright et al., 1985). School counselors can serve as leaders in serving to help identify and assist in the treatment of students with SM, in addition to students exhibiting characteristics of SM. In collaboration with key stakeholders in the school and the parents of children with SM, these children will no longer have to remain in silence by finding their voice.

REFERENCES

American Psychiatric Association. (2000). *Diagnostic and statistical manual of mental-disorders: DSM-IV-TR* (4th ed.). Washington DC: Author.

American Psychiatric Association. (1994). *Diagnostic and statistical manual of mental-disorders: DSM-IV* (4th ed.). Washington DC: Author.

American School Counselor Association. (n.d.). New ratio released. Retrieved from http://www.schoolcounselor.org/

American School Counselor Association. (2012). *ASCA National Model: A framework for school counseling programs* (3rd ed.). Alexandria: VA: Author.

Bergman, L. R., Piacentini, J., & McCracken, J. T. (2002). Prevalence and description of selective mutism in a school-based sample. *Journal of the American Academy of Child and Adolescent Psychiatry, 41*, 938-946.

Black, B., & Uhde, T. (1995). Psychiatric characteristics of children with selective mutism: A pilot study. *Journal of the American Academic of Adolescent Psychiatry, 34*(7), 847-856.

Busse, R. T., & Downey, J. (2011). Selective mutism: A three-tiered approach to prevention and intervention. *Contemporary School Psychology, 15*, 53-63.

Carbone, D., Schmidt, L. A., Cunningham, C. C., McHolm, A. E.., Edison, S. E., St. Pierre, J., & Boyle, M. H. (2010). Behavioral and socio-emotional functioning in children with selective mutism: A comparison with anxious and typically developing children across multiple informants. *Journal of Abnormal Child Psychology, 38*, 1057-1067. doi:10.1007/s10802-010-9425-y

Cline, T. C., & Baldwin, S. (2004). *Selective mutism in children* (2nd ed.). London, England: Whurr.

Cohan, S. L., Chavira, D. A., & Stein, M. B. (2006). Practitioner review: Psychosocial interventions for children with selective mutism: a critical evaluation of the literature from 1990-2005. *Journal of Child Psychology and Psychiatry, 47*(11), 1085-1097. doi:10.1111/j.1469-7610.2006.01662.x

Cunningham, C. E., McHolm, A., Boyle, M. H., & Patel, S. (2004). Behavioral and emotional adjustment, family functioning, academic performance, and social relationships inchildren with selective mutism. *Journal of Child Psychology and Psychiatry, 45*(8), 1363-1372. doi:10.111/j.1469-7610.2004.00327.x

Dummitt, E. S., Klein, R. G., Tancer, N. K., Asche, B., Martin, J., & Fairbanks, J. A. (1997). Systematic assessment of 50 children with selective mutism. *Journal of the American Academy of Child Adolescent Psychiatry, 36*, 653-660.

Elizur, Y., & Perednik, R. (2003). Prevalence and description of selective mutism in immigrant and native families: A controlled study. *Journal of the American Academy of Child Adolescent Psychiatry, 42*(12) 1451-1459.

Fall, K. A., Holden, J. M., & Marquis, A. (2010). *Theoretical models of counseling and psychotherapy* (2nd ed.). New York, NY: Routledge.

Kumpulainen, K., Räsänen, E., Raaska, H., & Somppi, V. (1998). Selective mutism among second-graders in elementary school. *European Child & Adolescent Psychiatry,* 7(24-29),24-29.

Landreth, G. L. (2012). *Play therapy: The art of the relationship* (3rd ed.). New York, NY: Routledge.

McHolm, A. E., Cunningham, C. E., & Vanier, M. K. (2005). *Helping your child with selective mutism: Practical steps to overcome a fear of speaking*. Oakland, CA: New Harbinger.

Murphy, B. C., & Dillon, C. (2011). *Interviewing in action in a multicultural world* (4th ed.). Pacific Grove, CA: Brooks-Cole.

Nims, D. R. (2011). Solution-focused play therapy. In C. E. Schaefer (Ed.), *Foundations of play therapy* (pp. 297-309). Hoboken, NJ: John Wiley & Sons.

Remschmidt, H., Poller, M., Herpertz-Dahlmann, B., Henninghausen, K., & Gutenbrunner, C. (2001). A follow-up study of 45 patients with elective mutism. *European Archives of Psychiatry and Clinical Neuroscience, 251*(6), 284-296.

Sklare, G. B. (2005). *Brief counseling that works: A solution-focused approach for school counselors and administrators*. Thousand Oaks, CA: Corwin Press.

Stone, B. P., Kratochwill, T. R., Sladezcek, I., & Serlin, R. C. (2002). Treatment of selective mutism: A best-evidence synthesis. *School Psychology Quarterly, 17*(2), 168-190.

Vecchio, J. L., & Kearney, C. A. (2005). Selective mutism in children: Comparison to youths with and without anxiety disorders. *Journal of Psychopathology and Behavioral Assessment, 27*, 31-37.

Wright, H. H., Miller, M. D., Cook, M.A., & Littman, J. R. (1985). Early identification and intervention with children who refuse to speak. *Journal of the American Academy of Child and Adolescent Psychiatry, 24*, 739-746.

CHAPTER 5

ADLERIAN PLAY THERAPY IN A SCHOOL SETTING FOR CHILDREN WHOSE CAREGIVERS ARE MENTALLY ILL

Barbara B. Hebert

Professional school counselors (PSCs) are specifically trained to provide responsive services to students within the school environment. These responsive services include individual counseling, group counseling, consultation, peer facilitation, and referrals (American School Counselor Association [ASCA], 2012). While school counselors do not provide therapy, they do play an integral role in facilitating the academic, social, and emotional well-being of students. PSCs have the opportunity to provide much needed support to students who have a family member struggling with a mental illness, some examples of which are depression, bipolar disorder, schizophrenia, substance abuse or even a personality disorder.

For the scope of this chapter, the term "children" refers to both children and adolescents within the school setting. PSCs generally perceive individuals from a wellness perspective rather than a medical perspective. That being the case, the term "mental illness" may cause discomfort. However, the term "mental illness" is used throughout the chapter for the

Integrating Play Techniques in Comprehensive School Counseling Programs, pp. 81–103

sake of simplicity and is not intended to be derogatory in any manner. This term refers to those individuals who have been diagnosed with psychiatric symptoms that are chronic and potentially disabling (Reupert & Maybery, 2010).

Vignette 1

Eight year old Mary came to school every day. She was very compliant with all of the school rules and regulations and was never disruptive. Mary made every effort to please her teacher while in class. However, Mary frequently forgot to bring her homework back to school and her homework folder was rarely signed by her parents. Mary never attended field trips. Her school uniforms were sporadically dirty and wrinkled, but her personal hygiene seemed typical. Mary ate both breakfast and lunch at school; however, after she ate, she played quietly by herself on the playground, not interacting with the other children. One day, the teacher on duty noticed that Mary was catching small bugs and quietly stepping on them with her shoe. Later that same day, the school counselor received a call from Mary's grandmother, Mrs. Johnson. Mrs. Johnson reported that Mary's mother had been hospitalized for a suicide attempt and that Mary was the one who found her mother hanging in the closet and called 911. Mrs. Johnson also reported that Mary's mother had been diagnosed with bipolar disorder and that Mary was staying with the grandmother for the next few weeks.

Vignette 2

Joseph was a 10-year old boy in the fifth grade. He had an older sister, Joy, who was 12 years old and was also in the fifth grade. Joseph's younger sister, Cindy, was 7 years old and was in the second grade. Joseph's father, Mr. Morrison, contacted the school counselor because he was concerned about Joseph. Even though Joseph was in gifted classes and was making good grades, he was being disruptive at home. He was lying about having completed his homework when he had not actually done so. Joseph had also been hitting and kicking both of his sisters. Yesterday, Joseph's teacher contacted Mr. Morrison at work and reported that Joseph had tried to stab another boy in his class with a pencil. The teacher said she had not reported the incident because she didn't want Joseph to get in trouble, but she thought the Morrison's should know. Mr. Morrison reported that when he confronted Joseph about his behavior at school, Joseph ran away from home and was gone for several hours before the police found him. When the school counselor asked about the situation at home, Mr. Morrison reported that he works two jobs to support the family. He also said that after years of misdiagnoses, his wife was diagnosed with general anxiety disorder, major depressive disorder, and borderline personality disorder and has been periodically hospitalized for suicidal ideation. Mr. Morrison also reported that at times his wife heavily uses alcohol. Mr. Morrison apologized for sharing all of his family's "dirty laundry," but said he does not know what else to do. He was worried about Joseph but was at a loss as to how to help him. He was considering divorcing but was concerned about leaving the children with their mother.

LITERATURE REVIEW

Caregivers With Mental Illness

Individuals with mental illness may have symptoms that are wide ranging and that impact functioning in a variety of areas, including relationships and social interactions, energy level, degree of patience, education, financial skills, and employment (Nicholson, 2007; Reupert & Maybery, 2010a). Mental illness can affect parenting skills as well as the relationship between the parent and children (Bibou-Nakou, 2003). Children, like adults, must be viewed holistically; thus, the events and occurrences at home impact functioning in the school setting. Therefore, if a family member, especially a parent, struggles with mental illness, students may also struggle academically, socially and/or emotionally. According to Nicholson (2007), "if parents do better, children do better" (p. 32). For parents who struggle with mental illness, even the smallest problems, obstacles, or situations can quickly become massive and easily spiral out of the parent's control (Nicholson, 2007). These difficulties can be as seemingly innocuous as forgetting to pack the children's school lunch or neglecting to wash the children's clothes or as complicated as long-term hospitalization or becoming homeless. It is when these struggles occur and the children are impacted that professional school counselors can play a significant role through responsive services in the school setting.

Statistics

According to Nicholson et al., (2004) "the majority of adults with mental illness, or co-occuring psychiatric and substance use disorders are parents" (p. 1). Another study by Maybery, Reupert, Patrick, Goodyear, & Crase (2009) indicates that at least one parent in 21-23% of all families has or has a history of mental illness. Additionally, Nicholson et al. analyzed data from the National Co-Morbidity Survey and found that of the individuals living with a serious and persistent mental health illness over 67% of women were mothers and over 75% of men were fathers; furthermore, they analyzed the National Comprehensive Mental Health Services for Children and Families Program and found that in the family members of these children 66% had a history of substance abuse, 45% had a history of mental illness, and 19% had a parent with a history of psychiatric hospitalization. These results are not limited to the United States alone. For example, Walsh (2009) states that in England and Wales, over 2 million children are living with a caregiver who has a mental health problem; moreover, Reupert and Maybery (2007a) report that in Australia over 20% of children live in situations where one parent is either currently experiencing or has had a history of mental illness. Similarly, Mordoch (2010) reports estimates that in Canada 50% of individuals with mental illness are parents. Extrapolating the smallest of these statistics onto a school population of 500 students, it may be assumed that approximately 100 children are living in situations in which at least one of the caregivers has a mental illness; conversely, extrapolating the largest of these statistics onto a school population of 500 students, it may be assumed that approximately 335 to 375 of the students may be living with a caregiver who has a mental illness. What risk, then, does the mental illness of a parent or caregiver place on children?

IMPACT ON CHILDREN

While the impact of a parent or caregiver affects children differently, research indicates that children have increased risks of both psychiatric and behavioral problems (Beardslee, Versage, & Gladstone, 1998; Costea, 2011; Foster, 2010; Fraser & Pakenham, 2008; Goodyear, Cuff, Maybery, & Reupert, 2009; Meadows, McLanahan, & Brooks-Gunn. 2007; Mordoch, 2010; Morson, Best, de Bondt, Jessop, & Meddick, 2009; Mowbray, Bybee, Oyserman, Allen-Mears, 2006; Olliver-Kneafsey, Thornton, & Williamson, 2008; Singleton, 2007; Walsh, 2009). While there are certainly biological factors that may increase the risk of mental health issues for children, there are also environmental factors, including parental behaviors and family functioning (Costea, 2011). According to Bibou-Nakou (2003), citing several studies from 1985 through 2002, it is the psychosocial disturbances within the family setting rather than the mental illness itself that provide the most risk for children. Johnson and Flake (2007) also report that psychosocial disturbances can exacerbate the risks for children with mentally ill parents. For example, individuals with mental illness may experience greater negative emotions such as hostility, irritability, and sadness which may then impact the parent-child relationship (Bibou-Nakou, 2003). Furthermore, individuals with mental illness may experience chaotic interpersonal relationships, not just with the children, but also with other significant individuals For instance in the second vignette at the opening of this chapter, the father is considering divorce. Marital discord is certainly indicative of a chaotic interpersonal relationship. Other examples of these chaotic interpersonal relationships include social isolation, such as limited contact with extended family members, or financial hardship in which the family becomes homeless. This chaos may culminate in lower family cohesion, poverty, and less education, all of which impact children (Costea, 2011). Research indicates that children who have a mentally ill parent are impacted behaviorally, socially, and academically (Bibou-Nakou, 2003; Costea, 2011; Farahati, Marcotte, Wilcox-Gok, 2003; Fraser & Pakenham, 2008; Johnson & Flake, 2007; Mowbray, Oyserman, & Ross 2004; Reupert & Maybery, 2007a). The professional school counselor can provide responsive services to children when they are impacted behaviorally, socially, and/or academically.

In preparation for providing responsive services, it is essential to understand the specific ways in which children may be impacted. Research that focuses on the developmental and academic areas can provide understanding for the professional school counselor. Additionally, qualitative research documents that both the children's perspective and the parent's perspective are valuable in facilitating understanding of the impact on children.

Impact From the Children's Perspective

One way to understand the impact of a mentally ill caregiver on children is through a review of the literature that has investigated the situation from the children's perspective. Mowbray, Bybee, Oyserman, MacFarlane, and Bowersox (2006) studied adult children raised with a mentally ill mother and found that these children experienced academic issues, psychological problems, and social problems including social avoidance, lower self-esteem, and poor social adjustment. In 2007(b) Reupert and Maybery reviewed the literature and found that children who have a caregiver with a mental illness frequently perceive their environments as chaotic and unstable, perceive a lack of connectivity with the parent who is mentally ill, have increased caregiving responsibilities, have maladaptive coping strategies, and have misconceptions about mental illness. More recent studies support the work of Reupert and Maybery. For instance, Foster (2010) conducted a qualitative study and found four prevalent themes. These themes include (1) children's perceptions of feeling uncertain, (2) having difficulty connecting with the parent, (3) assuming a caregiver role, and (4) wanting to be in control. Mordoch (2010) found that children struggle because mental illness is not openly discussed and therefore they have limited information which is based primarily on their own observations supplemented with periodic comments made by family members, teachers, or counselors. Furthermore, Gladstone, Boydell, Seeman, and McKeever (2011) also indicated that children's understanding of mental illness is limited and that children want to be recognized as an important component in their parents' well-being.

Impact From the Caregiver's Perspective

When reviewed from the parental perspective, research indicates that many parents worry about the impact of their mental illness on their children (Costea, 2011). According to Costea, mentally ill parents may have unrealistic expectations regarding the development and behavior of the children. Ackerson (2003) qualitatively researched the experience of parents with mental illness and found the following themes: (a) pride in being a parent, (b) difficulties with diagnosis and treatment, (c) perceptions of stigma and discrimination due to the mental health diagnosis, (d) chaotic interpersonal relationships including struggles in relationships with children, (e) difficulties of single parenthood, (f) custody issues, and (g) struggles with social support. On the other hand, a number of studies found that although parental mental illness is perceived as a risk factor for children, many mentally ill caregivers are able to parent effectively and many children of mentally ill caregivers thrive (Ackerson, 2003; Mowbray et al., 1995; Mowbray et al., 2004; Olliver-Kneafsey et al., 2008; Walsh, 2009). It is important to remember, then, that caregiver mental illness does not always signify that the children will be at risk.

Social and Behavioral Impact

Beyond the perspectives of the children and the parent, it is important to understand the developmental influence a mentally ill parent may have on children which then impacts them socially or behaviorally. Depending on the type and severity of the mental illness of the parent, the attachment bond between the parent and children may be an issue of concern (Morson et al., 2009; Reupert & Maybery, 2007b; Schwartz & Davis, 2006; Singleton, 2007). If the parent's mental illness disrupts the bonding process, the relationship becomes inconsistent and/or neglectful as opposed to responsive nurturing; the children may experience difficulty with both cognitive and emotional development (Reupert & Maybery, 2007b). In some instances when children are severely maltreated or neglected, they may be diagnosed with reactive attachment disorder (Schwarz & Davis, 2006). Schwarz and Davis (2006) continue by stating that when the bonding process is disrupted to this degree, children may exhibit an inability to regulate emotions, develop insecure attachment relationships with primary caregivers, and have difficulty adapting to the school environment. Even if the attachment bond is not of concern, some mentally ill parents may struggle with the ability to be responsive to children and may struggle with emotions such as hostility, sadness, and irritability (Costea, 2011).

Both the struggle with responsiveness and the struggle with emotions, according to Costea (2011), may be related to developmental delays in language, attention, and social competence as well as disrupted attachment in infants and toddlers. Costea points out, however, that the stronger predictor of disrupted attachment is the quality of the relationship rather than the parent's mental illness. Children initially learn social interactions through the parent-child relationship (Singleton, 2007). Through the security of home and the parent-child relationship, children learn to establish and maintain relationships, deal with life's stressors, and regulate their emotions (Johnson & Flake, 2007). Additionally, children must negotiate the normal developmental tasks of childhood; however, if the children also take on the role of caregiver, either for the parent or for the household, then the children's own developmental needs may be adversely impacted (Morson et al., 2009). For instance, some of the developmental tasks of adolescents include the development of a sense of self, decreased dependence on the family, and the establishment of mature interpersonal relationships; however, when raised by a mentally ill caregiver, the adolescent may not successfully achieve these tasks (Johnson & Flake, 2007).

Furthermore, according to Mowbray et al. (2004), parental depression is significantly related to adolescent problems, in particular, with peer interactions and reduced social competency. Children of mentally ill parents may also struggle with feelings of isolation, guilt, loss, shame, and fear (Costea, 2011; Olliver-Kneafsey et al., 2008; Singleton, 2007). Some parents with mental illness may struggle with boundary setting and maintaining limits, their children may experience difficulty with security, confidence, and anxiety (Olliver-Kneafsey et al., 2008). Furthermore, Olliver-Kneafsey et al. (2008) point out that depressive parents have a more difficult time providing spontaneous praise and enthusiasm to children thus, potentially impacting the children's self-esteem and sense of self-worth. Studies indicate that children with mentally ill parents may internalize their struggles thus increasing the possibility of anxiety, depression, and stress (Hofnagels, Meesters, & Simenon, 2007, Johnson & Flake, 2007; Meadows et al., 2007; Mordoch, 2010; Reupert & Maybery, 2007b). Children with a mentally ill caregiver may externalize their feelings, thus exhibiting behavioral issues (Bibou-Nakou, 2003; Costea, 2011; Fraser & Pakenham, 2008; Johnson & Flake, 2007; Meadows et al., 2007; Mordoch, 2010; Mowbray et al., 2004; Mowbray et al., 2006; Olliver-Kneafsey et al, 2008). Behavioral issues may be far-ranging. For example, these behaviors may be maladaptive coping strategies that have been developed in order to cope with a mentally ill caregiver (Johnson & Flake, 2007; Reupert & Maybery, 2007b), or they may include behaviors that are oppositional, noncompliant, and/or aggressive in nature (Mowbray, et al, 2004).

Academic Impact

Finally, children with a mentally ill caregiver may also experience academic difficulties (Bibou-Nakou, 2003; Fraser & Pakenham, 2008; Olliver-Kneafsey et al., 2008). Mowbray et al. (2004) cite research studies that found a significant relationship between parental depression and adolescent problems in school as well as lower grade point averages for students. Johnson and Flake (2007) report that school-age children of depressed mothers are more likely to experience impaired academic performance and adolescent children of depressed mothers are more likely to have decreased school attendance and academic problems. The issue of decreased school attendance is substantiated by Olliver-Kneafsey et al. (2008) who state that academic issues may include truancy. Farahati et al. (2003) analyzed the National Comorbidity Study and found that parental mental illness can have a strong impact on children's schooling and can also increase the likelihood of dropping out of high school.

EVIDENCED BASED APPROACHES

Clearly, children of mentally ill caregivers may be profoundly impacted socially, behaviorally, and academically. What then are the evidenced-based approaches that mitigate the impact of mentally ill parents on children and adolescents? According to Nicholson (2009), there is a "dearth of evidence regarding interventions for children and families living with parental mental illness" (para. 2). However, in a review of the literature that does exist, there are a few evidenced-based approaches for working with children of mentally ill caregivers (Fraser & Pakenham, 2008; Goodyear et al., 2009; Morson et al., 2009; Nicholson, 2009; van Doesum & Hosman, 2009). Discussions regarding these evidenced-based approaches indicate the value of group work, psychoeducational sessions that provide information about mental illness, and individual counseling focusing on emotional expression and developing adaptive and proactive coping strategies. All of these evidenced-based approaches are strengths-based and focused on the development of resiliency. While many of these approaches extend beyond the generally accepted realm of the professional school counselor, there are several components that fit easily into the school environment. School is an important factor in the growth and development of children and as such can play an integral role in facilitating the healthy development and functioning of children whose caregivers struggle with mental illness (Bibou-Nakou, 2003; Olliver-Kneafsey et al., 2008; Reupert & Maybery, 2007b). Therefore, professional school counselors can play an integral role in facilitating this healthy development and functioning, especially in the social, behavioral, and academic realms.

THEORETICAL PERSPECTIVE

Given the number of children in schools who are likely to have caregivers struggling with mental illness, it makes a great deal of sense to implement some type of responsive service that provides support for the students. In order to implement responsive services, it also makes sense to choose a theory from which to work. Theories provide direction and allow us to organize our perspectives "about human experience, life, the universe, and our clients" (Murdock, 2004, p. 4). Theory provides a schemata so that the information we glean from our clients can be organized in such a way so that we can not only understand our client's struggles more clearly, but we can also be more efficient and directed in our work with that client (Murdock, 2004). Each counselor learns to work from his/her own theoretical perspective.

Individual Psychology or Adlerian Theory

One theoretical orientation that is effective for children who have caregivers with mental illness is individual psychology or the Adlerian theoretical approach to counseling children. While a thorough discussion regarding Adlerian theory is beyond the scope of this chapter, a general understanding of individual psychology is useful. Individual psychology or Adlerian theory, developed by Alfred Adler (1931) views human beings from an optimistic perspective, perceiving that individuals are inherently social beings with a subjective perspective on the world and who have the ability to change, to be creative and to be responsible (Kelly & Lee, 2007; Kottman & Johnson, 1993; Morrison, 2009; Murdock, 2004). Furthermore, according to Murdock (2004), Adlerian theory promotes the idea that life is a goal-oriented journey and that each individual is motivated to strive for superiority and for a sense of community or belonging. Kelly and Lee (2007) identify the underlying assumptions of Adler's theory of personality that behavior is both purposeful and goal directed. Adler believed that the individual's *style of life* is set by about four to five years of age (Thompson, Rudolph, Henderson, 2004). This lifestyle is derived from conclusions made by children through observation of the environment (Henderson & Thompson, 2011).

Because children may perceive themselves as inadequate or unimportant, they incorporate these perceptions into their lifestyle (Kottman & Johnson, 1993). As children mature, this lifestyle, or life pattern, becomes more solidified (Kelly & Lee, 2007). According to Carlson, Watts, and Maniacci (2006), lifestyle is the way an individual perceives life and the manner in which the individual can achieve significance and belonging. The individual seeks out experiences that augment this subjectively derived lifestyle (Kottman & Johnson, 1993). Therefore, lifestyle determines the children's (and ultimately the adult's) behavior (Henderson & Thompson, 2011). According to Adlerian theory, "healthy people … have well-developed social interest and therefore contribute to society as they go about solving the tasks of life" (Murdock, 2004, p. 82). On the other hand according to Kottman and Johnson (1993), the foundation of maladjusted behavior rests upon either the individual's lifestyle that was created in part by mistaken beliefs or the individual's lack of connection with others.

In terms of maladjusted behavior, it is helpful to understand the work of Rudolph Dreikers, a student and colleague of Adler's. Dreikers (1947) believed that the basis for most childhood maladjusted behavior incorporates one or more of the following mistaken goals: (1) attention seeking, (2) power, (3) revenge, and (4) assumed disability, also referred to as inadequacy or withdrawal (Kelly & Lee, 2007). According to Kelly and Lee (2007), Dreikers also believed that children generally direct these misbehaviors toward the significant individuals in their lives, such as parents and teachers. For example, according to this perspective, children who are attention-seeking believe "that he or she is insignificant and unimportant unless at the center of adult attention" (p. 138). Children exhibit behaviors, either in a socially positive manner (achieving success, being reliable, behaving conscientiously, etc.) or in a maladaptive manner (being a "show-off," causing mischief, being irresponsible about school work or chores at home) (Henderson & Thompson, 2011; Kelly & Lee, 2007; Murdock, 2004; Thompson et al., 2004). Children whose goal is power engage in power struggles and feel both significant and self-important when they win those struggles (Kelly & Lee, 2007). Similarly, children whose goal is revenge perceive themselves as both significant and self-important when they have "gotten even" with others (Henderson & Thompson, 2011). Finally, Henderson and Thompson (2011) indicate that some children simply feel inferior and incapable of handling life's issues; therefore, they adopt the mistaken goal of inadequacy or withdrawal with the goal of hiding their inferiority through "giving up." Other children, according to Kelly and Lee (2007), who fail to achieve a sense of significance through one or more of the other mistaken goals, may ultimately move toward the goal of assumed disability or inadequacy. "At this point, the child ceases to be an active behavior problem … [acting out behavior] is replaced with a level of inactivity and passivity that reflects an attitude of 'giving up'" (p. 139). Regardless of how children arrive at the mistaken goal of assumed disability or inadequacy, the behaviors exhibited by these children are "passively destructive" (Henderson & Thompson, 2011, p. 359) and are designed to get others (parents, teachers, etc.) to give up on them as well so that children do not have to continue facing failure, humiliation, and defeat (Kelly & Lee, 2007). This behavior may manifest in children not completing homework or refusing to even attempt any academic work (i.e., putting their head down, not picking up their pencil, staring off into space instead of working). Unfortunately, these types of behaviors are often misinterpreted in schools by teachers and counselors as children lacking academic motivation.

Play Therapy

Using Adlerian theory as the springboard, it is most useful to add the modality of play therapy. Play therapy has been shown to be an effective intervention for children because play is their natural mode of communication (Landreth, 2002). Landreth (2001) states "Play is to children what verbalization is to adults" (p. 10). According to Landreth (2002), "Play is the child's symbolic language of self-expression and can reveal (a) what the child has experienced; (b) reactions to what was experienced; (c) feelings about what was experienced; (d) what the child wishes, wants, or needs; and (e) the child's perception of self" (p. 18). Watts and Garza (2008) state that play is an essential component in children's development, specifically in the development of cognitive, motor, language, and social skills. Along these same lines, Schaefer (1993) states that play is not only important in the normal developmental process of children, but that it can also assuage maladjusted behavior. In addition to the power of play, the play therapist and the play therapy environment are also vital aspects of the process. For example, the play therapist creates a therapeutic atmosphere that is both child-centered and in which the children can make decisions and choices for themselves (Landreth, 2002). Within the therapeutic process of play therapy, children are fully accepted and respected as unique and sensitive beings who are both resilient and capable; thus, it is a strengths-based perspective that provides understanding and acceptance in a nonjudgmental manner. According to Landreth (2002) the "creative potential" that already exists within children is released through this process (p. 109).

Adlerian Play Therapy

When the modality of play therapy is infused into the theoretical perspective of individual psychology, Adlerian play therapy arises. Kottman applies the principles of play therapy to the foundation of Adler's Individual Psychology (Morrison, 2009). Adlerian theory provides a realistic explanation for understanding children and their behavior. Adlerian play therapy promotes pragmatic techniques for working with children, teachers, and parents. Thus, the practical and sensible nature of Adlerian play therapy makes it valuable for professional school counselors (Kottman & Johnson, 1993). If children are older than 4 to 5 years of age, the assumption is made that they have already constructed life patterns that most likely include mistaken goals and a lack of connection.

Kottman (2003) indicates that children who are referred for counseling are most likely to have drawn negative conclusions about themselves and their environment and are thus engaging in behaviors that are not only self-defeating but that are also indicative of discouragement. According to Snow, Buckley, and Williams (1999), the egalitarian nature of Adlerian play therapy is intrinsically encouraging to children. The counselor further encourages children by facilitating an understanding of the behavior patterns as well as an understanding of the capacity to change those patterns (Cash & Snow, 2001). Thus, Adlerian play therapy focuses on encouragement to reduce discouragement and hence improve self-efficacy. Kottman applied the "Crucial Cs" to Adlerian play therapy (Morrison, 2009). These Crucial Cs address Kottman and Johnson's (1993) statement that maladjusted behavior is based not only on the mistaken goals that make up an individual's lifestyle, but also that maladjusted behavior is based on a lack of connection with others. The Crucial Cs include feeling *connected* to others, feeling *capable*, perceiving self as valuable or as someone who *counts,* and gaining the *courage* to explore and face new challenges (Kottman, 1999, as cited in Henderson & Thompson, 2011, p. 375). Furthermore, Kottman (1999) states that the Crucial C's can be utilized as a framework for the counselor to both assess and intervene, dependent upon the children's status and strength in each area. Thus, Adlerian play therapists build an egalitarian relationship with children, working to understand the children's lifestyles (including mistaken goals and the children's status in terms of the Crucial Cs), facilitate the children's insight into that lifestyle so that they can accomplish life's tasks in a healthy, well-adjusted manner, and facilitate the conversion of that insight into action (Kottman, 2001). Through this work, children regain a sense of superiority as well as a sense of connection with others.

Phases of Adlerian Play Therapy

According to Adlerian play therapy, the therapeutic process advances through four phases that include the creation of an egalitarian relationship, understanding children's lifestyles, facilitating children's understanding of that lifestyle, and empowering and reeducating children so that changes can be made (DeOrnellas, Kottman, & Millican, 1997; Kottman, 1999; Kottman & Johnson, 1993; Morrison, 2009; Snow et al., 1999; Watts & Garza, 2008). The first phase, the development of an egalitarian relationship with children, provides the foundation for the therapeutic relationship and is accomplished through the basic play therapy techniques of tracking, restatement of content, reflection of feeling, returning responsibility to children (i.e., not doing things for children that they can do for themselves, such as tying shoes or pouring cereal) and limit setting (Kottman, 1999; Kottman & Johnson, 1993). The use of encouragement also facilitates the building of an egalitarian relationship and is embedded in the play therapy process through the counselor's respect for children's abilities and strengths (Kottman & Johnson, 1993). Once an egalitarian relationship has been established, the counselor then works to understand the children's lifestyle. Both the toys and the play provide insight regarding the atmosphere of the children's family, the children's perspective of the family constellation, the goals of the children's behavior, and the early recollections of the children (Kottman, 1999). Also at this stage of the process, information is gathered through interviewing the children's caregivers and teachers (Snow et al., 1999). Consultation, according to Kottman and Johnson (1993) plays an integral role in Adlerian play therapy. The counselor gains an understanding of the family dynamics from the information gathered and thus forms tentative hypotheses about the family and about the children (Kottman, 1999). It is from these hypotheses that the counselor creates goals and strategies for intervention (Kottman, 1999). In the third phase of Adlerian play therapy, the play therapist facilitates the children's understanding of their lifestyle, goals of behavior, and maladaptive beliefs through the sharing of hypotheses with the children, the caregivers, and the teacher as appropriate (Kottman, 1999; Watts & Garza, 2008). Techniques that can be used to share these hypotheses with the children include tentative guesses, expressive arts, mutual storytelling, use of metaphors in play, role playing, and bibliotherapy (Snow et al., 1999). The fourth and final phase of Adlerian play therapy involves the empowerment and education of the children through the conversion of the newly acquired insight into action. It is in this phase that the children implement alternative behaviors that address the inherent desire for superiority and connectedness (Snow et al., 1999; Watts & Garza, 2008). Techniques that facilitate the implementation of these new behaviors include the use of metaphors in play, problem-solving strategies, and expressive arts (Kottman & Johnson, 1993). Woven throughout these four phases of Adlerian play therapy is the awareness of and assessment for the Crucial Cs. According to Kottman (1999), as the counselor works with the children throughout the phases of Adlerian play therapy, the children's strengths in each "C" can be incorporated into the process and areas of difficulty can be remediated through the process.

Techniques in Adlerian Play Therapy

Techniques that Kottman and Warlick (1989) suggest might be useful in Phase 2 (understanding the children's lifestyle) involve gathering information about early recollections from the children. Depending upon the age of the children, the counselor might simply ask the children to talk about different memories that he or she has. If the children are not of a developmental age to easily verbally recount these memories, the counselor might either ask the children to use the dolls and dollhouse or puppets to "play out" some memories or ask the children to draw pictures of memories. Along these same lines, it seems that the use of a sandtray would also be an efficacious method for illustrating memories of a time when the children were younger.

In Phase 3 of Adlerian play therapy, the counselor may use a gentle form of disclosure through metaphoric play (Kottman & Warlick, 1993). For instance, when the children are playing with dolls in the dollhouse and a mother doll becomes irritated with a little girl doll, the counselor may say something such as "I'm wondering if the way that mommy doll talks to the little girl doll is like the way your mommy sometimes talks to you?" Another example of this gentle disclosure could occur when the children are playing in the sand and use very small action figures to "kill monsters" that are much bigger. At this point, the counselor might say

"Those [figures] are very powerful to kill such big monsters. I'm wondering if you feel powerful when you pick on the other kids at recess?" A third example of this type of disclosure could possibly occur when the children use all of the soldiers, jungle animals, and dinosaurs to surround one lone figure and state that the one lone individual is going to be "eaten up." At this point, the counselor might say "That seems scary. I'm wondering if that's what it feels like to you when you get in trouble."

Watts and Garza (2008) use drawings to facilitate the "as if" technique in Phase 4 of Adlerian play therapy. Using art to implement the "as if" technique, Watts and Garza asked children to draw a picture based upon questions such as "If you were acting the way you want to be acting, how would you behave differently?" or "If someone saw you several months from now and you had changed your behavior to be the way you want it, what would that person see?" Watts and Garza stated that the counselor may have to assist children by asking questions that facilitate the drawing such as "who would be near you?", "what is happening around you?", "what are you thinking?", and "what shows that you are behaving differently?" In addition to this first drawing, children may also be asked to create additional drawings that facilitate understanding of how to move in the direction of the goal. For instance, the counselor may ask children to draw a picture that shows they are headed in the direction of their goal. The counselor may support that drawing by asking questions such as "How would someone know you were moving in that direction?" "Who do you think will notice this change?" or "What do you think that person will notice first?" The second component of this technique as outlined by Watts and Garza includes the construction of a list of "as if" behaviors. The children and the counselor collaboratively create the list and then rank items according to difficulty. After the list has been created and ranked, the third component involves the children choosing one or two of the least difficult behaviors to implement. Once those behaviors are implemented, the process continues through the implementation of all items on the list as children move from insight into action. Throughout this process, as in all aspects of the counseling relationship, the counselor conveys encouragement by avoiding evaluative language and by focusing on children's self-efficacy (Watts & Garza, 2008).

CONCLUSION

In conclusion, professional school counselors have the opportunity to provide much-needed support for children whose caregivers struggle with mental illness. These children are frequently at-risk for social, emotional, and behavioral issues; therefore, professional school counselors can implement the responsive service of individual counseling. Adlerian play therapy provides a pragmatic framework from which children can be understood and through which appropriate interventions can be implemented. These interventions, applied through the four phases of Adlerian play therapy, help children move from behavior that indicates a sense of disconnectedness and mistaken goals of behavior that are maladaptive to feelings of connection with behaviors that are well-adjusted and socially productive.

SAMPLE OUTLINE FOR SESSIONS IN A SCHOOL SETTING

(Please note that each phase may take significantly longer than indicated.)

Session 1: Phase 1

(a) Establish an egalitarian relationship: nondirective play therapy with the counselor tracking, reflecting, restating, returning responsibility to children, setting limits (as necessary).
(b) Use of encouragement throughout interactions.
(c) Counselor observes children's play to assess the lifestyle.

Session 2: Phase 1

(a) Continue to establish an egalitarian relationship: nondirective play therapy with the counselor tracking, reflecting, restating, returning responsibility to children, setting limits.
(b) Use of encouragement throughout interactions.
(c) Continue observation of children's play to assess the lifestyle.

Session 3: Phase 2

(a) Continue establishing an egalitarian relationship.
(b) Continue encouragement throughout interactions.
(c) Continue observation of children's play to assess the lifestyle.
(d) Talk with the parents (if possible) and pertinent teachers to gather information that might implement the formation of tentative hypotheses regarding the children's lifestyle.

(e) Ask children to draw a picture of the first thing they can remember about their family.
(f) Ask children to draw a picture of the most important thing that ever happened to them when they were little.
(g) Ask children to draw a picture of anything they remember about when they were little.
(h) Have the children describe each picture.

Session 4: Phase 2

(a) Continue establishing an egalitarian relationship.
(b) Continue observation of children's play to assess the lifestyle.
(c) Talk with children about any other memories they might have; ask children to show those memories through puppets, dollhouse or sandtray.
(d) Ask children to draw a picture of their family as it is now.

Session 5: Phase 3

(a) Continue establishing an egalitarian relationship.
(b) Continue observation of children's play to assess the lifestyle.
(c) As the children play, use the toys as metaphoric tools to gently and tentatively disclose information to children about their lifestyle.

Session 6: Phase 4

(a) Continue establishing an egalitarian relationship.
(b) Continue observation of children's play to assess the lifestyle.
(c) Use "as if" technique with drawing to facilitate the children's movement from insight into action.

CASE STUDY WITH TREATMENT RECOMMENDATIONS

Sally is a 7-year old second grader. This is her first year at your school. She was registered at your school by her maternal grandmother who indicated that Sally's mom wasn't feeling well and could not come for registration. Sally's teacher, Ms. Gardner, has come to you stating that Sally periodically comes to school in dirty, wrinkled uniforms and seemingly has not had a bath for several days. Ms. Gardner also reports that Sally rarely completes her homework and only occasionally attempts to do her classwork. Ms. Gardner tells you that Sally does not have any friends, even though she has now been in school for 3 months, and that Sally frequently ignores the other children when they invite her to play. Ms. Gardner informs you that yesterday two of the children in her class had an extremely loud argument. One of the boys began to shout loudly at a girl in the classroom and called her "Stupid" and "Crazy." Initially, Sally appeared to be "frozen" in her desk when the yelling began. However, when the little girl became upset and started to cry, Sally ran over to the boy and shoved him down, then she went to the girl and began to comfort her. When Ms. Gardner tried to talk with Sally about her actions, Sally refused to make eye contact with Ms. Gardner and refused to do any classwork for the remainder of the day.

Recommendations

Phase 1: Creation of an Egalitarian Relationship

Begin an egalitarian counseling relationship with Sally, using basic play therapy techniques such as tracking, restating content, reflecting feeling, returning responsibility to the children, and setting limits.

Phase 2: Understanding Children's Lifestyle

Gather information about Sally from her family (if possible) and from teachers who may come into contact with her. Using this information, begin to draw tentative hypotheses about Sally's lifestyle. For example, from the information gathered from teachers you may conclude that Sally appears to have the mistaken goal of inadequacy or withdrawal because she does not even make attempts to do schoolwork. Additionally, Sally does not appear to have any sense of connection with either the teacher or the other children. From information gathered from Sally's grandmother, you learn that Sally's mom was diagnosed with Major Depressive Disorder when Sally was 4 years old. You also learn that Sally has two younger siblings, ages 3 and 4, and that Sally's father left the family shortly after the youngest child was born. Sally's mother has been hospitalized several times in the last 8 years due to psychosis. During these episodes of psychosis, Sally's mother hears voices that tell her aliens are trying to steal her children. When these psychotic episodes occur, Sally's mother hides the children in a closet. Sally's grandmother tries to monitor the situation, but during the last psychotic episode, the children were hidden in the closet for almost 10 hours before the grandmother realized what was happening. When Sally was taken from the closet, she simply went to her room and sat on the bed. From this information, it may be surmised that Sally may have limited connection with her mother and no connection with her father. It may also be assumed that due to the chaotic situation at home, Sally may have had the mistaken goal of power at some point; however, now it appears that her mistaken goal may have devolved into inadequacy and withdrawal.

In addition to the information gathered from Sally's grandmother and from teachers, information may be gathered about Sally from her play in the playroom. This information is manifested in patterns of play that represent concerns or themes. For instance, each week when Sally returns for counseling she consistently plays with a dollhouse. As Sally plays with the dollhouse, you notice that she populates it with a mother, a little girl, and two babies. Sally consistently puts the mother doll in the bed or on the sofa and has the little girl doll taking care of the two babies. Every once in a while, Sally pretends that the mother yells at the little girl doll for not cleaning up, calling her "stupid." When the mother doll yells, Sally pretends that the little girl doll cries. This theme continues as Sally plays with the puppets and with the barnyard animals over the next few weeks. The "mother" does little or nothing while the "child" takes care of the younger "children," periodically gets yelled at, and then cries. Occasionally, Sally has the little girl and the babies hide in different locations around the playroom. By about the fourth week, Sally incorporates a grandmother figure into her play. Sally has the grandmother and mother argue frequently. When the grandmother and mother argue, the grandmother calls the mother "Crazy." By about the sixth week, the grandmother doll makes the mother leave the dollhouse and the little girl cries again. When asked why the little girl is crying, Sally responds that she is crying because her mother had to leave and that her mother had to leave because the little girl didn't hide well enough.

During this phase, you may also ask Sally to draw a picture of when she was "little." Sally says she can't draw it, but a few minutes later she begins to play in the sandtray. Sally puts a telephone into the sand. Then, she puts all of the emergency vehicles into the sandtray and has the emergency workers rescue a female adult. When you ask Sally about what is happening, she says that one day her mommy made her hide in the closet for a long time, so she used the phone and called her grandmother. Sally tells you that her grandmother came to the house and that she had a big argument with mommy. Then, mommy had to go to the hospital for a long time because she (Sally) called grandmother instead of hiding like a good girl.

At the next session, you ask Sally if she has remembered anything else from when she was "little." Sally says "yes" and goes immediately to the sandtray. She creates a scene in the tray that she calls a "party" with several little girls playing together and one little girl sitting by herself. Sally identifies the lone child as herself and says she is watching other girls at the party.

Tentative hypotheses from Sally's play indicate the likelihood that Sally has no connection at home or with friends, feels responsible for her mother's hospitalization, and is feeling inadequate. These hypotheses reinforce the information gathered from Sally's grandmother and teachers.

Phase 3: Facilitating Children's Understanding of Their Lifestyle

As Sally continues to play out her themes, gently and tentatively share hypotheses with her. For instance, when Sally pretends that the little girl is crying because her mother calls her "Stupid," you might say "I'm wondering if sometimes your mom yells at you and calls you 'Stupid.' I'm wondering if you believe you're 'stupid?'" Sally quickly nods her head and begins to play with different toys. Later, when Sally has several dolls playing together, you may say "I'm wondering if sometimes you watch the other children play but feel separated from them" or "I'm wondering if you feel different than the other children sometimes." Continuing these gently and tentatively phrased hypotheses about Sally's metaphoric play, you continue to facilitate Sally's insight into her own lifestyle pattern.

Phase 4: Empowering and Reeducating Children

Once Sally has begun to gain insight into her lifestyle pattern, you may choose to use the "as if" drawing technique (Watts & Garza, 2008). For example, you might ask Sally to draw a picture of what she would like for her day at school to look like. Sally draws two pictures. The first picture illustrates Sally surrounded by other children, smiling, and playing happily. The second picture shows Sally sitting at her desk with a paper in front of her that has a big, red, A+ on it. You and Sally talk about the pictures individually, encouraging Sally to problem-solve behaviors that can help her get to these places. With Sally, construct a list of behaviors that she could try that will help her move toward achieving these goals. Sally lists behaviors such as talk to the girl sitting next to her, asking the other kids if she can play jump rope with them at lunch, smiling at the other kids in her class, doing her math worksheets, practicing her spelling words, etc. When encouraged to choose two behaviors from her list, Sally chooses to smile at the other kids in her class and to practice her spelling words. At the next session, Sally happily tells you that she made a "B" on her spelling test and that the girl sitting next to her in class talked to her. Continue working with Sally on the list, choosing one or two behaviors each week for her to implement. Each week, encourage Sally in this process as she moves toward feeling both connected and superior.

REFERENCES

Ackerson, B. J. (2003). Coping with the dual demands of severe mental illness and parenting: The parents' perspective. *Families in Society, 84*(1), 109-118. Retrieved from http://ezproxy.selu.edu/login?url=http://search.proquest.com/docview/230166674?accountid=13772

Adler, A. (1931). *What life should mean to you.* New York, NY: Grosset & Dunlap.

American School Counselor Association. (2012). *The ASCA National Model: A framework for school counseling programs* (2nd ed.) Alexandria, VA: Author.

Beardslee, W. R., Versage, E. M., & Gladstone, T. R. G. (1998). Children of affectively ill parents: A review of the past 10 years. *Journal of the American Academy of Child and Adolescent Psychiatry, 37,* 1134-1141.

Bibou-Nakou, I. (2003). Helping teachers to help children living with a mentally ill parent. *School Psychology International 24*(3), 5-23.

Carlson, J., Watts, R., & Maniacci, M. (2006). *Adlerian therapy: Theory and practice.* Washington, DC: American Psychological Association.

Cash, R. O., & Snow, M. S. (2001). Adlerian treatment of sexually abused children. *The Journal of Individual Psychology, 57*(1), 102-115.

Costea, G. D. (2011). Considering the children of parents with mental illness: Impact on behavioral and social functioning. *The Brown University Child and Adolescent Behavior Letter 27*(4). doi:10.1002/cbl20137

DeOrnellas, K., Kottman, T., & Millican, V. (1997). Drawing a family: Family art assessment in Adlerian therapy. *The Journal of Individual Psychology, 53*(4), 451-460.

Dreikurs, R. (1947). The four goals of the maladjusted child. *Nervous Child, 6,* 321-328.

Farahati, F., Marcotte, D. E., Wilcox-Gok, V. (2003). The effects of parents' psychiatric disorders on children's high school dropout. *Economics of Education Review, 22*(2), 167-178.

Foster, K. (2010). "You'd think this roller coaster was never going to stop": Experiences of adult children of parents with serious mental illness. *Journal of Clinical Nursing, 19*(21/22), 3143-3151. doi:10.1111/j.1365-2702.2010.03293.x

Fraser, E., & Pakenham, K. I. (2008). Evaluation of a resilience-based intervention for children of parents with mental illness. *Australian & New Zealand Journal of Psychiatry, 42*(12), 1041-1050. doi:10.1080/00048670802512065

Gladstone, B. M., Boydell, K. M., Seeman, M. V., & McKeever, P. D., (2011). Children's experiences of parental mental illness: A literature review. *Early Intervention Psychiatry 5*(4), 271-289.

Goodyear, M., Cuff, R., Maybery, D., & Reupert, A. (2009). CHAMPS: A peer support program for children of parents with a mental illness. *Australian e-Journal for the Advancement of Mental Health, 8*(3), 296-304.

Henderson, D. A., & Thompson, C. L. (2011). *Counseling children* (8th ed., pp. 343-383), Belmont, CA: Brooks/Cole.

Hofnagels, C., Meesters, C., & Simenon, J. (2007). Social support as predictor of psychopathology in the adolescent offspring of psychiatric patients. *Journal of Children and Family Studies, 16,* 91-101.

Johnson, P. L., & Flake, E. M. (2007). Maternal depression and child outcomes. *Pediatric Annals, 36*(4), 196-202. Retrieved from http://ezproxy.selu.edu/login?url=http://search.proquest.com/docview/217555191?accountid=13772.

Kelly, F. D., & Lee, D. (2007). Adlerian approaches to counseling with children and adolescents. In H. T. Prout & D. T. Brown (Eds.), *Counseling and psychotherapy with children and adolescents: Theory and practice for school and clinical settings* (4th ed., pp. 131-179). Hoboken, NJ: Wiley.

Kottman, T. (1999). Integrating the Crucial Cs into Adlerian play therapy. *The Journal of Individual Psychology, 55*(3), 288-297.

Kottman, T. (2001). Adlerian play therapy. *International Journal of Play Therapy, 10*, 1-12.

Kottman, T. (2003). *Partners in play: An Adlerian approach to play therapy* (2nd ed.). Alexandria, VA: American Counseling Association.

Kottman, T., & Johnson, V. (1993). Adlerian play therapy. A tool for school counselors. *Elementary School and Guidance Counseling, 28*(1), 42-51.

Kottman, T., & Warlick, J. (1989). Adlerian play therapy: Practical considerations. *The Journal of Individual Psychology 45*(4), 433-446.

Landreth, G. L. (2001). Facilitative dimensions of play in the play therapy process. In G. L. Landreth (Ed.), *Innovations in play therapy: Issues, process and special populations* (pp. 3-22). Philadelphia, PA: Brunner-Routledge.

Landreth, G.L. (2002). *Play therapy: The art of the relationship* (pp. 9-26). New York, NY: Brunner-Routledge.

Maybery, D., Reupert, A., Patrick, K., Goodyear, M., & Crase, L. (2009). Prevalence of children whose parents have a mental illness. *Psychiatric Bulletin, 33*, 22-26.

Meadows, S. O., McLanahan, S. S., & Brooks-Gunn, J. (2007). Parental depression and anxiety and early childhood behavior problems across family types. *Journal of Marriage and Family, 69*(5), 1162-1177. Retrieved from http://ezproxy.selu.edu/login?url=http://search.proquest.com/docview/219767201?accountid=13772

Mordoch, E. (2010). How children understand parental mental illness: "You don't get life insurance. What's life insurance?" *Journal of the Canadian Academy of Child and Adolescent Psychiatry, 19*(1), 19-24.

Morrison, M. O. (2009). Adlerian play therapy with a traumatized boy. *The Journal of Individual Psychology, 65*(1), 57-68.

Morson, S., Best, D., de Bondt, N., Jessop, M., & Meddick, T. (2009). The Koping Program: A decade's commitment to enhancing service capacity for children of parents with a mental illness. *Advances in Mental Health, 8*(3), 286-295.

Mowbray, C. T., Oyserman, D., & Ross, S. (1995). Parenting and the significance of children for women with a serious mental illness. *The Journal of Mental Health Administration, 22*(2). 189-201.

Mowbray, C. T., Bybee, D., Oyserman, D., & Allen-Mears, P. (2004). Diversity of outcomes among adolescent children of mothers with mental illness. *Journal of Emotional and Behavioral Disorders, 12*(4). 206-221.

Mowbray, C. T., Bybee, D., Oyserman, D., MacFarlane, P., & Bowersox, N. (2006). Psychosocial outcomes for adult children of parents with severe mental illnesses: Demographic and clinical history predictors. *Health & Social Work, 31*(2), 99-108. Retrieved from http://ezproxy.selu.edu/login?url=http://search.proquest.com/docview/210570015?accountid=13772

Murdock, N. L. (2004). *Theories of counseling and psychotherapy: A case approach* (pp. 67-107). Upper Saddle River, NJ: Pearson Education.

Nicholson, J. (2007). Helping parents with mental illness. *Behavioral Healthcare, 27*(5), 32-33. Retrieved from http://ezproxy.selu.edu/login?url=http://search.proquest.com/docview/227948811?accountid=13772

Nicholson, J. (2009). Building the evidence base for families living with parental mental illness. *Australian e-Journal for the Advancement of Mental Health, 8*(3), 222-226.

Nicholson, J., Albert, K., Bairos, M., Banks, S., Biebel, K., Clayfield, J., ... & Williams, V. (2004). Families living with mental illness. *Psychiatry Issue Briefs, 1*(2). Retrieved from http://escholarship.umassmed.edu/pib/vol1/iss2/1

Olliver-Kneafsey, K., Thornton, E., & Williamson, W. (2008). The impact of parental bipolar affective disorder on adolescent behavior: Positive messages to young people, parents, teachers and other professionals working with children whose parents suffer from mental health problems. *Pastoral Care in Education, 26*(3), 181-185. doi:10.1080/02643940802246567

Reupert A., & Maybery, D. (2007a). Strategies and issues in supporting children whose parents have a mental illness within the school system. *School Psychology International 28*(2), 195-205.

Reupert, A., & Maybery, D. (2007b). Families affected by parental mental illness: A multiperspective account of issues and interventions. *American Journal of Orthopsychiatry,* 77(3) 362-369. doi:10.1037/0002-9432.77.3.362

Reupert A., & Maybery, D. (2010). Families affected by parental mental illness: Australian programs, strategies and issues. The (missing) role of schools. *International Journal for School-Based Family Counseling, II* (August 2010).

Schaefer, C. E. (1993). What is play and why is it therapeutic? In C. E. Schaefer (Ed.), *The therapeutic powers of play* (pp. 1-15). New York, NY: Aronson.

Schwartz, E., & Davis, A. S. (2006). Reactive attachment disorder: Implications for school readiness and school functioning. *Psychology in the Schools, 43*(4), 471-479. doi:10.1002/pits.20161

Singleton, L. (2007). Parental mental illness: The effects on children and their needs. *British Journal of Nursing, 16(*14), 847-850.

Snow, M. S, Buckley, M. R., & Williams, S. C., (1999). Case study using Adlerian play therapy. *The Journal of Individual Psychology 55*(3), 328-341.

Thompson, C. L., Rudolph, L. B., Henderson, D. (2004). *Counseling children*, (6th ed., pp. 294-329). Belmont, CA: Brooks/Cole.

Van Doesum, K. T. M., & Hosman, C. M. H. (2009). Prevention of emotional problems and psychiatric risks in children of parents with a mental illness in the Netherlands: Interventions. *Austrialian E-Journal for the Advancement of Mental Health, 8*(3), 264-276.

Walsh, J. (2009). Children's understanding of mental ill health: Implications for risk and resilience in relationships. *Child and Family Social Work, 14*, 115-122.

Watts, R.E., & Garza, Y. (2008). Using children's drawings to facilitate the Acting "As If" technique. *The Journal of Individual Psychology, 64*(1), 113-118.

CHAPTER 6

USING PLAY THERAPY TECHNIQUES IN COUNSELING CHILDREN WITH DEPLOYED PARENTS

Jennifer R. Curry

In this time of war, and in memory of our fallen heroes, we must be mindful to do everything in our power to keep our troops safe as they keep us safe. We must do better to take care of their families, who sacrifice in ways too many to count.

—Senator John Kerry

Military families face many unique challenges including frequently moving and parent separation (Barker & Berry, 2009; Chartrand, Frank, White, & Shope, 2008; Laser & Stephens, 2011). One particular difficulty is the stress experienced by family members when someone is deployed; this especially rings true when the deployment is for combat. For children, having a parent deployed for military service is a significant life event as they cope with the normal concerns of childhood in addition to the stress of time lost with their parent, fear of injury and death, changes

Integrating Play Techniques in Comprehensive School Counseling Programs, pp. 105–123

in the family dynamics and much more (Chawla & Solinas-Saunders, 2011; Cozza, Chun, & Polo, 2005; Lincoln, Swift, & Shorteno-Fraser, 2008). Further complicating the difficulties of parental deployment, there is growing disapproval and a noted decrease in popular support for current U.S. military occupation and war; this sentiment can lead to declines in the "hero status" of deployed personnel. Specifically, antiwar sentiment may be internalized for children and military families as rejection or lack of community support, further injuring children with deployed parents (Tunac de Pedro et al., 2011). This chapter is dedicated to the children of military families and highlights a play therapy technique, filial therapy, which can be used in schools to address issues that arise during parent military deployment. Following are two vignettes demonstrating the stress faced by military children, a literature review of the effects of parental deployment on children, and a three session outline for parent workshops that can be conducted by school counselors.

Vignette 1

Kylie is a fourth grade student at Wilcox Elementary. Her father, a staff sergeant, was recently deployed and will be gone for at least 1 year. Kylie is normally vivacious, hard-working, responsible, academically successful and socially engaged during class. Her teacher, Mr. Simon, reported to the school counselor that Kylie seems very withdrawn, is not eating during lunch, and is no longer playing with other children during recess. Mr. Simon noted that Kylie no longer volunteers to answer questions in class, preferring instead to sit quietly and doodle. Mr. Simon also tells the school counselor that he knows Kylie's mother is also scheduled to be deployed and that Kylie's grandmother will be coming to stay with her and her three little brothers.

Vignette 2

Sampson is a second grade student who has recently transferred to Shenandoah Elementary school. Sampson and his little sister (a 4-year old in pre-K) were enrolled in Shenandoah by their mother. Sampson's family has come to live in the Shenandoah area with Sampson's grandmother because Sampson's father was deployed. Since coming to Shenandoah, Sampson displays aggressive and impulsive behaviors. He interrupts class frequently, is bossy with other students, bullies others, and has been in two fights on the playground and one fight on the school bus. Sampson's teacher, Mrs. Shelby, referred Sampson for anger management to the school counselor. Miss Chandler, the counselor, called Sampson's mother. Sampson's mother was grateful that Sampson could receive counseling services at school and she mentioned to the school counselor that Sampson has not been the same since his father left for Iraq. She also told the counselor that Sampson has difficulty adjusting and that the family has moved 4 times in the last 5 years. Sampson's mother cried during her conversation with the counselor and disclosed that she is dealing with her own depression and anxiety and that she has no idea how to help her children cope with their father's deployment.

MILITARY FAMILIES

Although there is little empirical research exploring the effects of military deployment on children (Sheppard, Malatras, & Israel, 2010), it is important to review what is known. Currently, about 1% of the U.S. population serves in the military (Miles, 2011); further, there are 23.4 million veterans in the United States and an additional 2.2 active service personnel including volunteer service members (Esposito-Smythers et al., 2011; Substance Abuse and Mental Health Services Administration [SAMHSA], n.d.). According to Chartrand et al. (2008), since the beginning of the war in Iraq (post September 11, 2001), over 2 million children have been affected by parent deployment. Moreover, military deployments have been longer in duration due to staging and lengthy training sessions for preparing soldiers (Chawla & Solinas-Saunders, 2011).

Military families have unique stress and concerns compared to other family constellations. Specific concerns related to parent deployment that affect children's healthy growth and development include: (1) challenges to the mental health of nondeployed and deployed family members including trauma, (2) risk of parent physical injury and death, and (3) changes in family dynamics. How these stressors affect children is largely dependent on personal characteristics (i.e., resilience), resources (family economic stability, extended family and support network) and caregiver reactions to stress (e.g., parental depression).

Mental Health and Trauma Concerns

During deployment, there are many layers of family functioning that can affect children's ability to cope. The mental health of the deployed family member is one concern, but the mental health of remaining family members may be equally, if not more, critical. For example, when a father is deployed, the mental health of the mother has a significant impact on children in the home (Chartrand et al., 2008; Lincoln et al., 2008); indeed, maternal well-being is a noted predictor of children's adjustment (Andres & Moelker, 2010; Davis, 2010). According to Esposito-Smythers and colleagues (2011), the nondeployed spouse may experience compromised emotional health with higher rates of depressive episodes, anxiety, loneliness, insomnia, and acute stress reaction. This decrease in emotional well-being can matriculate into poor parenting practices and deteriorate the child-caretaker relationship. Furthermore, things do not necessarily become stable once the deployed parent has returned home; there are many complexities of the deployment process.

Specifically, the American Psychological Association (APA, 2007) denotes four phases of deployment: predeployment (from notification to departure), deployment, reunion (time of preparation for return of deployed person), and postdeployment or reunification. Although it seems logical that there would be significant family stress in the predeployment and deployment phases, there is an incredible amount of stress in the postdeployment phase once families are reunited. The reasons for post deployment, reintegration stress include: conflicts associated with roles and boundaries in the home (i.e., which parent will get up to care for children in the night); household management conflict (e.g., loss of independence for the non-deployed spouse); resurrection of old, unresolved problems; the reactions of children to the retuning parent (i.e., response to discipline, taking sides when parents argue), worry over future deployments and much more. Thus, there are special challenges to the mental health of family members in each phase of deployment. Additionally, the mental well-being of all family members can be largely affected by concerns over the mental health of the deployed parent.

The results of one study indicated that during combat deployment, the majority of individuals seeking mental health services are seen primarily for anxiety disorders followed by adjustment and mood disorders (primarily depression) (Schmitz et al., 2012). It may be particularly stressing for the nondeployed spouse and children to realize that their deployed loved one is suffering mental health stress. During postdeployment and reintegration phases, military service personnel remain at higher risk than civilians for depression, anxiety, posttraumatic stress disorder (PTSD), and substance abuse (APA, 2011). According to SAMHSA (n.d.), one in five veterans deployed to Iraq or Afghanistan has posttraumatic stress disorder. For veterans with PTSD, there is an increased risk of legal problems, use of alcohol and other substances, psychiatric symptoms, and poor general health. According to the *Medical Surveillance Monthly Report* (2012), published by the Armed Forces, between the years of 2000-2011 there were a reported 936, 283 military service members diagnosed with *at least one* mental disorder. Additionally, combat stress was shown to increase irritability, reckless and high risk behaviors, and difficulty controlling anger (SAMHSA, n.d.). Of even greater concern, many service personnel may not get mental health service postdeployment due to the perception that receiving such services and admitting there is a problem would have a negative impact on their career (i.e., loss of promotion) (APA, 2011; Kim, Thomas, Wilk, Castro, & Hoge, 2010). Thus, mental health concerns exist in all deployment phases and school counselors should not assume that children will resume happy, healthy lives once a deployed parent has returned home.

Risk of Physical Injury and Death

The possibility of physical injury and death are ever present during a military deployment and add to the daily anxiety and stress experienced by primary caregivers and children. More concerning, according to Cozza et al. 2005), it is not uncommon for the family to receive news of a soldier's injuries that is characterized by incomplete or inaccurate information. When an injury does occur, anxiety is further increased for children who may be left with family members or friends as the non-deployed parent joins the injured parent at a military hospital away from home. Moreover, when children aren't left with family members and are taken to a treatment facility, they are exposed to the daily pain and suffering of the injured parent or may even be confronted with the reality that a parent is permanently disfigured, a potentially shocking experience for children (Cozza et al., 2005). Most importantly, as noted by Cozza et al.(2005) parents may be unsure of how much information about an injury to share with children and this can lead to sharing too much or too little information. Once the injured parent is returned home, the family must adjust to the necessary modifications that are physically necessitated by the injury. For example, a parent with an amputated limb might need help maneuvering around the house or may need a wheelchair in the home. In these circumstances, the family must adjust to learning how much help to offer or give to the injured parent and redistribution of family responsibilities will also need to be explored. Moreover, financial burdens of a disability as well as making the physical structure of the home accommodating (i.e., adding a wheelchair ramp) to the injured individual are also added stressors.

Statistical prevalence of injuries to combat troops includes a wide range of physical injuries. For example, according to the *Medical Surveillance Monthly Report* (2012), published by the Armed Forces Health Surveillance Center, from 2000-2011 there were a reported 6,144 incidents of amputation with the majority being minor amputations (i.e., fingers) and an approximate 3,000 being major amputations e.g., leg). Suicide rates for active duty members from 1998-2011 were also concerning with a total of 2,290 suicides in that period, and suicide rates were higher for service members who had been divorced or separated rather than those who had never married. Though there is a dearth of empirical evidence on the effects of deployed military parents' death on their children (Cozza et al., 2005), it may be assumed that this type of tragedy is a major trauma with long lasting effects on children.

Changes to Family Dynamics

Stress in military families during a deployment may impact how parents relate to their children. For example, Chartrand et al. (2008) noted that "military families who experience repeated or prolonged deployments were at risk for child maltreatment" (p. 1010); it is possible that increased risk of abuse occurs when the nondeployed spouse feels overwhelmed and lacks the coping skills to manage the daily demands of life with the emotional distress of deployment. Even when abuse isn't occurring, the stress of deployment is challenging for the remaining parent (generally the wife) who must become more assertive and independent in order to expand role responsibilities such as single parenting, dealing with financial concerns, and coping with the overwhelming lack of certainty about a spouse's safety (Baptist et al., 2011). The lack of stability in the family structure often leads to a redistribution of responsibilities and adolescents may have to pick up some extra roles such as babysitting, helping younger children with homework, cooking and added household chores. This can cause anger, resentment, and strain in the relationship between the non-deployed parent and their children (Mmari, Roche, Sudhinaraset, & Blum, 2009).

Even as the system stabilizes during deployment, small challenges to stability, even something benign and positive, such as a telephone call from the deployed parent, can cause confusion in the family structure. For example, if a mother has stepped into the role of disciplinarian and household authority during a father's deployment, then the child may be confused if the father calls and says, "*I'm expecting you to be a good boy. You need to do your homework, clean your room, and take care of your mom.*" This kind of communication may inadvertently suggest to the child that the father is still the authority that should be followed and that the mother is not truly capable of being the head of the household.

Further complications to family life stability may arise when the deployed parent returns home. Recent research on marital discord and intimate partner violence indicates a high propensity for service personnel returning from combat to be more violent to their spouses and to have more severe violent incidents than civilian families (Klostermann, Mignone, Kelley, Musson, & Bohall, 2012). Moreover, returning combat service personnel are more likely than civilians to experience unstable marital relationships (Klostermann et al., 2012). Thus, even when the deployed parent returns home, children may be exposed to increased conflict and violence in the home, further adding to systemic stress.

Although violence is not present in every home with a parent returning from deployment, there are still changes to family constellation, redefining roles and responsibilities, and adjustments to family members' expectations of each other. Some expected changes include organization, activities, and childrearing practices: caretaking responsibilities (i.e., which parent will make sure kids get their bath and dinner), discipline structures, and family recreation (Lincoln et al., 2008; Mmari et al., 2009). This source of stress, changing roles and responsibilities can be significant and prolonged particularly in families with poor structure stability during nondeployment (Mmari et al., 2009).

IMPACT OF DEPLOYMENT ON CHILDREN: BEHAVIORAL, MENTAL HEALTH, AND EMOTIONAL AFFECTS

As aforementioned, in spite of concern for how deployment may affect children's social and emotional well-being, there is limited research investigating children's behavior related to parental deployment (Sheppard et al., 2008). Although there are patterns of evidence that indicate the effects on children during parent military deployment (especially for combat), readers should be cautioned that individual differences will factor into how stress manifests. Individual factors that may shape children's behaviors include resiliency, internal locus of control, coping mechanisms, temperament, external supports, and so forth. In spite of these individual differences, research indicates that in general, girls demonstrate more internalizing behaviors (crying, sadness) and boys display more externalizing behaviors (i.e., disciplinary problems) (Chartrand et al., 2008).

For children, the stress of military deployment can lead to depression, behavior problems, clinginess, demands for attention, emotional difficulties, and anxiety (Barker & Berry, 2009; Chandra et al., 2010; Esposito-Smythers et al., 2011; Lester et al., 2010). For children in extreme distress, parental deployment can lead to regression to an earlier stage (i.e., a 5 year old wetting the bed), sleep disturbances and night terrors, and frequent crying (Lincoln et al., 2008). Adolescents with deployed parents had higher measured heart rates and perceived stress levels (Chartrand et al., 2010) and children in general have more discipline problems and demands for attention during combat deployment (Barker & Berry, 2009; Lester et al., 2010). Moreover, Lester et al. (2010) concluded that cumulative deployments (more than 1) may have a significant, long term effect on children. This effect may be due in part to the parent being gone for major events in the child's life (beginning kindergarten, graduating from high school) or missing major developmental milestones (i.e., seeing the child walk for the first time). Similarly, Chandra et al. (2010) also found evidence indicating that the number of months a parent is deployed correlates with increases in behavioral difficulties, an indication, according to the researchers, that maintaining family mental health gets harder over time.

Of concern for the school environment, children with a deployed parent display more academic difficulties than their peers without deployed parents and greater levels of emotional disregulation (e.g., less emotional stability and greater displays of anger and sadness) (Lester et al., 2010) or difficulty expressing emotions (Mmari et al., 2009). Specifically, Lyle (2006) found small but negative relationships between academic achievement and parent deployment, but he cautioned that multiple and prolonged deployments may have a cumulative effect on children's academic outcomes.

In spite of the difficulties associated with deployment, many children are very resilient and adjust rather quickly. In a study of Dutch children whose parents were deployed, 38% of mothers noted that their children's sense of loss declined a few weeks after their father was deployed (Andres & Moelker, 2010). Indeed, all children will not need counseling. Most children will experience sadness in the initial weeks of deployment followed by a stabilization of affect and behavior. School counselors should assess which children are in need of responsive services (individual or small group counseling) based on emotional, behavioral and academic responses to deployment. Once assessed, myriad services could be provided to address needs: individual counseling, small group counseling, classroom presentations, faculty in-services, parent workshops, and so forth. Further, a range of theoretical approaches and techniques could be used to address parental deployment including expressive arts therapy (Kim, Kirchhoff, & Whitsett, 2011), packaged counseling curricula, manualized treatment and programs for small or large groups (i.e., Families Over Coming Under Stress [FOCUS]) (Lester et al., 2012), bibliotherapy, and play therapy. In this chapter we explore a play therapy intervention that includes the nondeployed parent: filial therapy.

FILIAL PLAY THERAPY

In a qualitative study using focus group protocol, Mmari et al. (2009) found that school personnel (including school counselors) felt unprepared to deal with children's concerns during deployment. This is largely because school counselor training is focused on core counseling knowledge and skills (e.g., individual and group counseling, theory, development) rather than cultural specifics or needs of particular populations and practical applications to meet those needs (i.e., military families). Therefore, many school counselors may feel unsure of how to help children during parent deployment.

As previously noted, the well-being of a spouse during another spouse's deployment (e.g., the mother's well-being in the absence of the father), critically affects the mental well-being of children in the family; this fact underscores the importance of helping the remaining spouse or caregiver cope with deployment separation (Andres & Moelker, 2010). Further, Barker and Berry (2009) found that parent support (specifically warmth and family cohesion) mitigated some of the effects of deployment in young children. Therefore, school counselors should consider interventions that involve the remaining caregiver, spouse or partner, such as filial therapy.

One of the most influential and seminal authors of filial therapy, Rise Van Fleet, notes that there are several principles underlying the use of a filial approach: (1) play is a critical component in children's development; (2) parents have the greatest impact on their children's lives and can learn how to play therapeutically with their children; (3) most problems that children face are based on difficulties in the environment and adjustment to environmental challenges so education and skill development can alleviate most of these problems (Van Fleet, 2005). Filial therapy is a means of using psychoeducation to train parents to conduct nondirective play experiences with their child (Sori, 2006). Specifically, in filial therapy the parent is taught by the counselor how to use child centered skills (positive responses, validation) through play experiences with their child. Filial therapy is used to strengthen the parent-child bond, create parental understanding and acceptance of the child, empower parents to communicate effectively with their children, and assist parents in discovering some of the joys of parenting—even during difficult life circumstances (Ray, 2006). According to Van Fleet (2005), the following are some therapeutic goals for parents engaging in filial therapy (p. 4):

1. To increase parents' understanding of child development in general.
2. To increase parents' understanding of their own children in particular.

3. To help parents recognize the importance of play and emotion in their children's lives as well as in their own.
4. To decrease parents' feelings of frustration with their children.
5. To aid parents in the development of a variety of skills that is likely to yield better child-rearing outcomes.
6. To increase parents' confidence in their ability to parent.
7. To help parents open the doors of communication with their children and then keep them open.
8. To enable parents to work together better as a team.
9. To increase parent's feelings of warmth and trust toward their children.
10. To provide a nonthreatening atmosphere in which parents may deal with their own issues as they relate to their children.

All of these therapeutic goals have significance for families with children during a combat deployment. As part of a comprehensive school counseling program (American School Counselor Association, 2012), parent workshops are used to promote the emotional, social, and academic growth of children. In the next section we explore how one school counselor implemented a three part workshop series on filial interventions for caregivers of children with a deployed parent.

PARENT WORKSHOPS: FILIAL THERAPY TRAINING

Gabby Nelson was a school counselor at an elementary school located three miles from a military base. The troops at the base were notified in spring that they would be deployed for combat to Iraq in fall of the same year. Miss Nelson had about 6 months to prepare for her anticipated interventions to meet students' needs during the deployment. Nearly half of the students in her school (270 out of about 600) were from military families and the majority of those were expecting to have at least one parent deployed. Miss Nelson set up a three part workshop series to help the remaining caregivers (nondeployed parents, grandparents, other family members) assist children when their parents were deployed through filial therapy.

Logistics

To encourage parents to attend the workshops, Miss Nelson knew she needed to provide childcare, food, materials, and other incentives to make the workshops fun. However, she had a minimal budget for the necessary resources and spent a couple of months establishing community and stakeholder partnerships in order to procure the help needed. Miss Nelson began by contacting a church whose property adjoined the school's property to ask for support. The church was very willing to help and provided volunteers to run a nursery, playground, gym activities, and study hall for children while their caregivers attended the workshops. All volunteers were screened through a background check at the school. Additionally, the church provided dinner for children and the caregivers attending the training.

A local veteran's affairs post donated a gift bag for each family attending which included the book *Over There* by Dorinda Silver Williams, a activity book called *My Parent is in the Military* (published by Military Community Awareness), a set of crayons, a stationary tablet and envelopes (for writing to deployed parents), and U.S. flag stickers. Additionally, the Parent Teacher Association (PTA) at the school contacted local businesses and were able to get door prizes for each of the three workshops including massages at a local spa, restaurant gift cards, gift baskets from a local baker, gift cards for local retailers, and so forth. The point of the door prizes was to provide extra incentives and rewards for the parents who came. Therefore, every person attending received free childcare, dinner, and some materials to take home for working with their child(ren).

Finally, parents were asked to register ahead of time to ensure that there were enough materials and food available for everyone. The school PTA donated a folder for each parent and paid for copies of all training materials (copy of power points for each workshop, homework sheets, flyer with wellness information, and a sheet with examples of filial techniques). Workshops were held over a 6 week period (one meeting every two weeks) and lasted from 5:30 P.M.-8:00 P.M. (including child drop off and pick up time) on Thursday nights. All of the workshops were designed to help non-deployed parents and caregivers work with children between the ages of 4-10 through filial therapy techniques during deployment. All of the workshops followed the training process described by Van Fleet (2005) and included demonstrations, training, and mock play sessions.

Parent Workshop Session 1

The first workshop was designed to help caregivers understand the developmental needs of children. Only adults attended the meeting. Children were at the neighboring church playing games, eating dinner, or doing homework. This allowed parents to focus on the content of the session. Before the program began the school counselor highlighted some of the reasons that self-care is particularly important for the non-deployed parent. The counselor indicated that in the packet of materials given out was a flyer that listed reduced fee services for counseling, nutrition, and other services for caregivers having difficulty managing their own stress, depression, and anxiety.

Once the presentation began, a power point was shown that addressed the cognitive development and emotional needs of children. Parents were cautioned about continued exposure to media, especially when death or injuries of soldiers are being reported as this may cause long-term negative psychological concerns, such as prolonged anxiety, in children (Cozza et al., 2005). Parents were encouraged to keep children in a structured routine (setting bed times, limiting time on social media like video games, and structuring family activities).

Next, filial therapy was introduced. The school counselor, Miss Nelson, discussed what filial therapy is, describing it as nondirective, positive play techniques that parents can use with their children. Miss Nelson explained that nondirective means that the child chooses what to play and how the toys are used within the filial session. Before demonstrating filial therapy, Miss Nelson described several techniques the parents would be using (tracking, reflections of feeling, setting limits, and undivided attention). Miss Nelson gave a description and several examples of each technique. For example, when describing reflections of feeling, Miss Nelson stated that "*reflections of feelings are statements that show that you understand the feelings being expressed by your child.*" Examples of reflections of feeling included: "*You feel sad right now*" and "*You are excited about playing with your doll.*" Parents were also instructed to not direct play but to have limits for safety (i. e., no throwing toys at someone else, crayons can only be used on paper and not walls or furniture). (For more information about teaching parents these techniques please see Sori, 2006; Chawla & Solinas-Saunders, 2011).

Next, parents watched a video excerpt on filial therapy (Van Fleet, 2008) that demonstrated these techniques (this video can be ordered through the APA or through Van Fleet's website: http://play-therapy.com). Afterward, parents were given time to practice with one other adult. Finally, parents were asked to set aside 15 minutes each day for the next 2 weeks as filial time with each of their children (for children between the ages of 4-10 only). During this time, parents were instructed to give undivided attention including turning off cell phones, not checking e-mail, and so on. Parents were given a worksheet to track the days, times and locations of filial therapy and a rating sheet to rate the skills they used during each filial session. Parents were also given a feeling faces wall chart (Please see Appendix A), so that they could help children identify their feelings. The last activity was a drawing for door prizes and this concluded the first workshop.

Parent Workshop 2

The second workshop began the same way (children dropped off at church and meals provided by the church members). The parent meeting began with parents getting in groups of 4-5 and discussing the filial sessions they had experienced in the last 2 weeks. Parents were asked to share their successes and their frustrations and to list their successes and frustrations on pieces of butcher paper which were then placed around the room. Some examples of successes listed by parents included feeling closer to their child, feeling proud that they truly listened to their child, sensing that their child was feeling less stressed, and fewer behavior problems. Frustrations included having difficulty ending the session, being unsure of how many limits to impose, and feeling awkward tracking. After hanging the lists on the wall, Miss Nelson started the power point. The power point went through common problems in filial therapy including limit-setting, nondirection, and getting the child to end the session without crying or begging for more time. Parents were given more information on each of these skills.

Then, Miss Nelson walked around the room and addressed some of the frustrations for the week that had not already been covered in the power point. For example, one parent stated that she had difficulty with empathic listening, especially coming up with reflections of feeling. She said, "*I just kept repeating 'You feel mad.'*" Miss Nelson had the group make a list of other feeling words and talked about the importance of helping children expand their feeling vocabulary. Miss Nelson reminded parents that they could use the feeling faces wall chart to let assist the child in identifying his or her feelings. The parent with this frustration agreed to take her feelings list with her to the next filial session and to use it to come up with additional feeling words when she feels stuck. She also committed to have her child point out her feelings on the feeling faces wall chart.

After brainstorming ways to deal with their frustrations, Miss Nelson asked if any parents would like to role play a filial session in order to get feedback. One parent volunteered right away and said she would love to get feedback. Miss Nelson asked another parent to play the child and gave the "child" a basket of toys. The role play lasted for 5 minutes. Miss Nelson let the parent conducting the filial session state what she thought were her strengths during the session and what she was most frustrated with. Then Miss Nelson asked for positive feedback only from the other parents. Afterward, Miss Nelson asked the group to help the volunteer fix her frustrations with the session through suggestions and helpful feedback. Miss Nelson had time to do this same activity with two more volunteers before ending the second parent workshop.

At the conclusion of the second workshop, parents were asked to conduct daily 20 minute filial activities in their home over the next 2 weeks and to continue logging their times/progress. This time, Miss Nelson added a homework assignment. Each parent had to take their child(ren) to a park, playground, or an activity center with games (such as an indoor play center) and use filial techniques in a public setting. The workshop ended with a drawing for door prizes.

Parent Workshop 3

The third parent workshop began with parents dropping off their children at the church and having dinner. At the beginning of the training session, parents got in groups of four and five and shared their successes and frustrations for the week. The group spent about 20 minutes trouble shooting. Then Miss Nelson conducted a 20 minute question and answer session. Last, the parents joined the children at the church in the gym and each parent and their child(ren) were given a structured filial activity. Families were asked to create a picture of their perfect day together using crayons or markers and butcher paper. Parents were asked to use their filial skills during the session. Afterward, parents were encouraged to contact the counselor if they have difficulties with filial therapy in the future. At the end of the workshop a drawing was done for door prizes.

OTHER INTERVENTIONS

Beyond prevention and intervention strategies for parents, school counselors may need to also provide responsive services for children during deployment. One such service is small group counseling. School counselors considering small group counseling for students with deployment concerns may wish to consider using a curriculum, expressive arts techniques, and a play therapy approach. Individual counseling may also be warranted and should be given on an as needed basis. For material suggestions please see Appendix A.

CONCLUSION

Military families face many unique challenges including the stress of combat deployment. Research indicates that during deployment the family unit destabilizes as the stress of mental health concerns, physical injury or death, financial problems, family dynamics, and relocation are experienced by family members. Yet, many school counselors are unprepared to respond to military families in crisis due to lack of preparation and training for such events. One major consideration for school counselors is that the nondeployed parent's mental health and well-being are highly influential in how a child copes with deployment; therefore, it is best practice to include the nondeployed parent in counseling. One approach for doing this is through filial therapy. In this chapter, filial therapy for military families was demonstrated through a three part parent workshop conducted by a school counselor. However, school counselors should also be prepared to deliver individual and small group counseling to children with deployed parents when necessary. Finally, it is notable that most children will adjust to having a deployed parent and may not need services at all; for those children not in need of service, the school counselor and staff can provide a safe, supportive environment where the sacrifices of the military are acknowledged and honored.

APPENDIX A. MATERIAL RESOURCES FOR WORKING WITH CHILDREN OF DEPLOYED PARENTS

Same Sky Sharing from the Children's Institute, small group counseling curriculum, Retrieved from www.childrensinstitute.net/programs/same-sky-sharing

Military Children: A Primer for School Personnel (activities begin on page 37), downloadable pdf. Retrieved from http://support.militaryfamily.org/site/DocServer?docID=642

Helping Children Cope When a Loved One is on Military Deployment, PDF with helpful tips for school personnel. Retrieved from http://wisconsinmilitary.org/wp-content/uploads/2009/12/KidsCopeDeployment.pdf

Military Community Awareness, purchase books and more. Retrieved from http://www.4mca.com/c-87-militarykids.aspx

Military Kids Connect, Resources for educators. Retrieved from https://www.militarykidsconnect.org/educators

NC National Guard Family Programs 2012 Educator Guide: No Military Child Left Behind, retrieved from http://www.ncpublicschools.org/docs/militarysupport/resources/ncfpresourceguide.pdf

Daddy, Will You Miss Me? by Wendy McCormick. Illus. by Jennifer Eachus. 1999. Grades K–2.

Daddy, You're My Hero! by Michelle Ferguson-Cohen. 2002. Grades K-1.

The Magic Box: When Parents Can't Be There To Tuck You In, by Seymour Epstein and Marty Sederman. Illus. by Karen Stormer Brooks. 2003. Grades K-2.

Mommy, You're My Hero! by Michelle Ferguson-Cohen.2002. Grades K-2.

My Daddy Is a Soldier, by Kirk Hilbrecht and Sharron Hilbrecht. 2002. Grades K-1.

Soldier Mom, by Alice Mead.1999. Grade 3.

Uncle Sam's Kids: When Duty Calls, by Angela Sportelli-Rehak. 2002. Grades K–3.

When Dad's at Sea, by Mindy Pelton. Illus. by Robert Gantt Steele. 2004. Grades K-3.

While You Were Away, by Eileen Spinelli. Illus. by Renee Graef. 2004. Pre-K-2.
A Year Without Dad, by Jodi Brunson. Illus. by Cramer. 2003. Grades K-3.
A Yellow Ribbon for Daddy, by Anissa Mersiowsky. Illus.by Rey Contreras. 2005. Grades K-3.

APPENDIX B. FEELING FACES WALL CHART

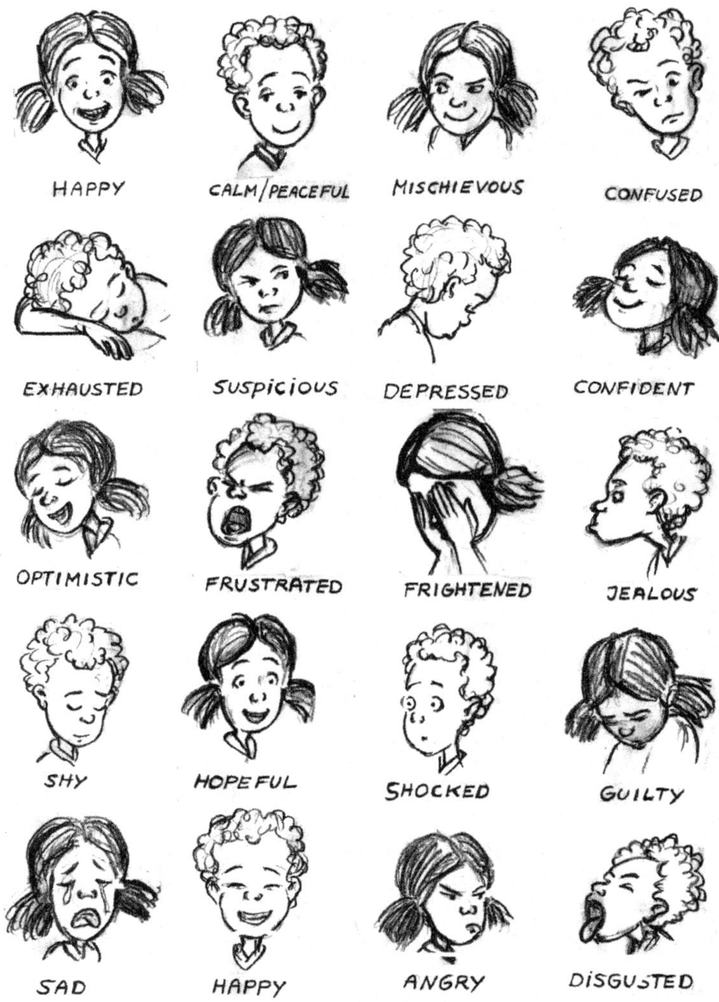

REFERENCES

American Psychological Association. (2007) Presidential Task Force on Military Deployment Services for Youth, Families, and Service Members. The psychological needs of U.S. military service members and their families: A preliminary report. Retrieved from http://www.ptsd.ne.gov/publications/military-deployment-task-force-report.pdf

American Psychiatric Association. (2011). Military. Retrieved from http://www.healthyminds.org/More-Info-For/Military.aspx

American School Counselor Association. (2012). *ASCA National Model: A Framework for School Counseling Programs* (3rd ed.). Alexandria, VA: Author.

Andres, M. D., & Moelker, R. (2010). There and back again: How parental experiences affect children's adjustments in the course of military deployments. *Armed Forces & Society*, 1-30. doi:10.1177/0095327X10390461

Armed Forces Health Surveillance Center. (2012). *Medical Surveillance Monthly Report, 19*(6). Silver Springs, MD: Author.

Baptist, J. A., Amanor-Boadu, Y., Garret, K., Goff, B. S. N., Collum, J., Gamble, ... & Wick, S. (2011). Military marriages: The aftermath of Iraqi Freedom (OIF) and Operation Enduring Freedom (OEF) deployments. *Contemporary Family Therapy, 33,* 199-214. doi:10.1007/s10591-011-9162-6

Barker, L. H., & Berry, K. D. (2009). Developmental issues impacting military familes with young children during single and multiple deployments. *Military Medicine, 174,* 1033-1040.

Chandra, A., Lara-Cinisomo, S., Jaycox, L. H., Tanielian, T., Burns, R. M., Ruder, T., & Han, B. (2010). Children on the homefront: The experience of children from military families. *Pediatrics, 125,* 16-25. doi:10.1542/peds.2009-1180

Chartrand, M. M., Frank, D. A., White, L. F., & Shope, T. R. (2008). Effect of parents' wartime deployment on the behavior of young children in military families. *Archives of Pediatric and Adolescent Medicine, 162,* 1009-1014. doi:10.1001/archpedi.162.11.1009

Chawla, N., & Solinas-Saunders, M. (2011). Supporting military parent and child adjustment to deployments and separations with filial therapy. *The American Journal of Family Therapy, 39,* 179-192. doi:10.1080/01926187.2010.531647

Cozza, S. J., Chun, R. S., & Polo, J. A. (2005). Military families and children during operation Iraqi Freedom. *Psychiatric Quarterly, 76*(4), 371-378. doi:10.1007/s11126-005-4973-y

Davis, B. E. (2010). Parental wartime deployment and the use of mental health services among young military children. *PEDIATRICS, 126*(6), 1215-1216.

Esposito-Smythers, C., Wolff, J., Lemmon, K. M., Bodzy, M., Swenson, R. R., & Spirito, A. (2011). Military youth and the deployment cycle: Emotional health consequences and recommendations for intervention. *Journal of Family Psychology, 25*(4), 497-507. doi:10.1037/a0024534

Kim, J. B., Kirchhoff, M., & Whitsett, S. (2011). Expressive arts group therapy with middle-school aged children from military families. *The Arts in Psychotherapy, 38,* 356-362. doi:10.1016/j.aip.2011.08.003

Kim, P. Y., Thomas, J. L., Wilk, J. E., Castro, C. A., & Hoge, C. W. (2010). Stigma, barriers to care, and use of mental health services among active duty and national guard soldiers after combat. *Psychiatric Services, 61*(6), 582-588. doi:10.1176/appi.ps.61.6.582

Klostermann, K., Mignone, T., Kelley, M. L., Musson, S., & Bohall, G. (2012). Intimate partner violence in the military: Treatment considerations. *Aggression and Violent Behavior, 17*, 53-58. doi:10.1016/j.avb.2011.09.004

Laser, J. A., & Stephens, P. M. (2011). Working with military families through deployment and beyond. *Clinical Social Work Journal, 39*, 28-38. doi:10.1007/s10615-010-0310-5

Lester, P., Saltzman, W. R., Woodward, K, Glover, D., Leskin, G., Bursch,B., Pynoos, R., & Beardslee, W. (2012). Evaluation of a family-centered prevention intervention for military children and families facing wartime deployments. *American Journal of Public Health, 102*, S48-S54. doi:10.2105/AJPH.2010.300088

Lester, P., Peterson, K., Reeves, J., Knauss, L., Glover, D., Mogil, C., ... & Beardslee, W. (2010). The long war and parental combat deployment: Effects on military children and spouses. *Journal of the American Academy of Child & Adolescent Psychiatry, 49*(4), 310-320. doi:10.1016/j.jaac.2010.01.003

Lincoln, A., Swift, E., & Shorteno-Fraser, M. (2008). Psychological adjustment and treatment of children and families with parents deployed in military combat. *Journal of Clinical Psychology, 64*(8), 984-992. doi:10.1002/jclp.20520

Lyle, D. S. (2006). Using military deployments and job assignments to estimate the effect of parental absences and household relocations on children's academic achievement. *Journal of Labor Economics, 24*(2), 319-350. doi:10.1086/499975

Miles, D. (November 28, 2011). Survey shows growing gap between civilians, military. *American Forces Press Service*. Retrieved from http://www.defense.gov/news/newsarticle.aspx?id=66253

Military Community Awareness. (n.d.). *I'm a proud military child.* Woodbury, NY: Author.

Mmari, K., Roche, K. M., Sudhinaraset, M., & Blum, R. (2009). When a parent goes off to war: Exploring the issues faced by adolescents and their families. *Youth & Society, 40*(4), 455-575. doi:10.1177/0044118X08327873

Ray, D. C. (2006). Supervision in play and filial therapy. In T. Kerby Neill (Ed.) *Helping others help children: Clinical supervision of child psychotherapy* (pp.89-108). Washington, DC: American Psychological Association.

Schmitz, K. J., Schmied, E. A., Webb-Murphy, J. A., Hammer, P. S., Larson, G. E., Conway, ... & Johnson, D. C. (2012). Psychiatric diagnoses and treatment of U. S. military personnel while deployed to Iraq. *Military Medicine, 177*(4), 380-389.

Sheppard, S. C., Malatras, J. W., & Israel, A. C. (2010). the impact of deployment on U. S. military families. *American Psychologist, 65*(6), 599-609. doi:10.1037/a0020332

Sori, C. F. (2006). Filial therapy: An interview with Rise VanFleet. In C. F. Sori (Ed). *Engaging children in family therapy: Creative approaches to integrating theory and research in clinical practice.* (pp. 91-116). New York, NY: Routledge.

Substance Abuse and Mental Health Services Administration. (n.d). Co-occurring disorders in veterans and military service members. Retrieved from http://www.samhsa.gov/co-occurring/topics/military/index.aspx

Tunac De Pedro, K. M., Astor, R. A., Benbenishty, R., Estrada, J., Smith, G. R. D., & Esqueda, M. C. (2011). The children of military service members: Challenges, supports, and future educational research. *Review of Educational Research, 81*(4), 566-618. doi:10.3102/0034654311423537

Van Fleet, R. (2005). *Filial therapy: Strengthening parent-child relationships through play* (2nd ed.). Sarasota, FL: Professional Resource Press.

Williams, D. S. (2006). *Over there.* Washington, DC: Zero to Three.

CHAPTER 7

INTEGRATING PLAY TECHNIQUES WITH STUDENTS EXPERIENCING ACADEMIC CHALLENGES

Jonathan H. Ohrt, Dodie Limberg, and Jenifer N. Ware

Academic achievement refers to students' skill development and overall understanding of information (Ebel & Frisbie, 1986). Academic problems can manifest in many different ways for students within the school setting. Students may have difficulty concentrating in class, engaging in class discussions, grasping concepts related to subject matter, or attending school regularly. Some signs of academic struggles include poor grades, low levels of class participation, incomplete assignments, refusing to attempt class work or not focusing on academic tasks, and low scores on standardized tests. Unfortunately, poor academic achievement in early grades can have a lasting impact on students' psychosocial development and educational progress. Professional school counselors are in a unique position to address students' academic and personal/social development through developmental guidance and responsive services within the delivery system of the American School Counselor Association *National Model* (ASCA, 2012). In this chapter, we discuss the effects of poor academic achievement and present practical play therapy techniques that school counselors can use to assist students in their development.

Integrating Play Techniques in Comprehensive School Counseling Programs, pp. 125–148

Vignette 1

Tyler is an 8 year old male in third grade who is struggling in school. He wakes up every morning dreading school and begs his parents to let him stay home. In class, Tyler is withdrawn and rarely interacts with the other children. His teacher, Mrs. Robinson, reports that he does not pay attention to instructions and is usually off task. When students are instructed to work on assignments in class, Tyler will often sit and stare, rarely accomplishing anything. When approached, Tyler usually states that the work is too hard and he does not want to do it. At home, Tyler's parents report that homework is a daily struggle. Tyler avoids doing his homework and will sometimes lie, saying that he has none. When his parents become insistent about him working on schoolwork, he often cries and says that the he cannot do it. Despite his parents' efforts to help him, Tyler is resistant to receiving their help. After three months of this behavior, Tyler's parents and teacher see a continual decline in Tyler's grades and report that he appears increasingly sad and withdrawn. Mrs. Robinson decides to refer Tyler to the school counselor due to her concerns about his emotions, self-esteem, and academic performance.

Vignette 2

Ashley is seven years old and in second grade. Two months into the school year, her teacher noticed that she was falling behind in her schoolwork and had several incomplete assignments. After the school received standardized test scores, it was determined that Ashley was below competency in reading and she was placed in a program where she received additional help learning to read. Ashley felt embarrassed when she was pulled out of class to attend the reading program. Her classmates were beginning to tease her about her incompetency in reading. Ashley's parents reported that she came home crying every day and refused to talk to them about school. At school, Ashley started breaking the classroom rules, refusing to do her work and interrupting others. She became aggressive towards other children, both in class and at recess, and did not respond to consequences. After several instances of hitting and pushing others, Ashley was referred to the school counselor for behavior concerns.

LITERATURE REVIEW

The No Child Left Behind Act (NCLB, 2002) resulted in increased focus on student achievement and accountability for schools. Consequently, states are now required to develop standards, accountability systems, and standardized tests to assess student performance. Although NCLB was implemented to reduce educational inequities, it also resulted in increased pressure on schools and teachers to demonstrate accountability for student outcomes and increased the practice of high stakes testing (Hursh, 2005). These pressures on schools and teachers may also affect students at an early age. For instance, students are often exposed to standardize testing for the first time in third grade (Felton & Akos, 2011).

Although some of the policies in NCLB may be controversial, a focus on academic performance is important because students often encounter difficulties related to their academic achievement. Many children struggle in academic areas such as reading, writing, science, and mathematics (Fletcher & Vaughn, 2009). For example, on the National Assessment of Educational Progress in 2009, approximately 67% of fourth-grade students failed to score at proficiency on the reading scale, 61% failed to score at proficiency on the mathematics scale, and 66% failed to score at proficiency on the science scale (Aud et al., 2011). Additional indicators of academic struggles include poor grades, low teacher ratings of performance, and low scores on state or national standardized tests. Unfortunately, early academic struggles appear to have a compounding effect. Students who struggle in reading and math in first grade tend to fall even further behind in third grade (Kainz & Vernon-Feagans, 2007).

Increased attention to student outcomes at a young age is critical because, in general, academic difficulties (e.g., grades, test scores, academic track) in early elementary grades are linked to later school dropout (Alexander, Entwisle, & Horsey, 1997). Currently, approximately 7,000 students drop out of school each day and it is estimated that the cost to the nation of dropouts in 2010 is $337 billion (Alliance for Excellent Education, 2010). The financial consequences are far reaching for the U.S. economy: decreased purchasing power, lower tax revenue, and lower productivity. Additionally, the need for students to persist in their education is highlighted by the fact that by 2018, the U.S. will need 22 million new college degree earners. The projection for 2018 is that approximately 66% of all jobs will require some college education or postbaccalaureate degree (Carnevale, Smith, & Strohl, 2010).

Risk Factors

There are many reasons why children struggle academically and various factors can influence children's risk for academic problems and failure. Individual characteristics, mental health concerns, and environmental and family factors often influence academic performance. Multiple individual factors have been linked to poor academic achievement. For instance, students' intrinsic academic motivation is often predictive of their achievement. Students who are less curious and display low persistence typically perform worse than their peers who are more curious, persistent, and enjoy the learning environment and challenging tasks (Gottfried, Gottfried, Cook, & Morris, 2005). Additionally, students who have higher intrinsic academic motivation tend to have less academic anxiety and more positive perceptions of their academic competency (Marcoulides, Gottfried, Gottfried, & Oliver, 2008).

Students' beliefs about themselves and their competence are also predictive of academic achievement. Self-concept is an individual's perception of competence in a variety of areas including academics, physical appearance, social skills, family, and athletics (Quilliams & Beran, 2009). Academic self-concept refers to students' beliefs about their ability to be successful academically and is linked to other outcomes such as persistence and academic achievement. Students who are at risk for poor academic achievement often report a low self-concept.

Additional individual factors that can influence students' academic performance are certain mental health diagnoses. Prevalent diagnoses that negatively impact academics are those associated with learning difficulties. Specifically, an estimated 4% to 6% of all public school students are diagnosed with an identified learning disability (LD) (Learning Disabilities Association of America [LDA], n.d.). Learning disabilities are defined by the LDA (n.d.) as a "neurologically-based processing problem. These processing problems can interfere with basic skills such as reading, writing, or math calculating" (p. 1). Unfortunately, children diagnosed with LDs are at greater risk for poor academic development.

Children who struggle with inattention, hyperactivity, or impulsivity are also at increased risk for poor academic performance. Multiple studies have demonstrated that children diagnosed with attention deficit hyperactivity disorder (ADHD) perform poorer academically than their peers who do not have this diagnosis. In a review of the literature, Frazier, Youngstrom, Glutting, and Watkins (2007) reported that the largest differences between children diagnosed with ADHD and those who are not are in reading and mathematics achievement. Other studies indicate that elementary school children with ADHD also score lower on standardized tests and exhibit lower social functioning than their peers (McConaughy, Volpe, Antshel, Gordon, & Eiraldi, 2011)

Other children may struggle with disruptive behaviors and may be diagnosed with conduct disorder (CD) or oppositional defiant disorder (ODD). Children diagnosed with ODD often throw temper tantrums, argue with or defy adults, or purposely annoy people. Additional characteristics include: being angry or vindictive, blaming others for misbehavior, and easily annoyed (American Psychiatric Association [APA], 2000). Conduct disorder order is considered more severe and is characterized by aggression towards other, theft, or destruction of property (APA, 2000). Not surprisingly, these disruptive behaviors can severely interfere with children's ability to behave at school and succeed academically. Children with these diagnoses often suffer from long-term consequences such as substance abuse, arrests, learning disorders, and dropping out of school (Bernstein, 2012).

Finally, children who struggle with various attachment concerns may also experience academic problems. For example, between 4% and 5% of all children and young adolescents are diagnosed with separation anxiety disorder (SAD) (Masi, Mucci, & Millepiedi, 2001). Children who are diagnosed with SAD experience excessive distress when they separate from primary attachment figures (i.e., parent or guardian). They are typically afraid to be separated from their caretakers or to be alone, and consequently they often refuse to attend school or ask to leave with minor illnesses (Masi et al., 2001). When children diagnosed with SAD miss educational time, it can greatly disrupt their academic development.

Beyond individual characteristics, there is considerable research suggesting that family factors strongly influence students' academic achievement. In particular, parental involvement may influence student achievement. Students whose parents are more involved in their education (e.g., attend parent conferences, assist with homework) and encourage a positive learning environment at home, tend to perform better academically. For example, when students have a space to do homework (e.g. a clean desk, or a dining room table) and necessary resources (i.e., materials such as markers, crayons, internet access), as well as adult support, they are more likely to be successful in completing homework assignments and long term projects. Conversely, students who do not have access to necessary materials (i.e., no paper, no pencil), live in a single-parent home, in poverty, or whose parents have a low-level of education are at an increased risk for poor academic achievement (National Institute of Child Health and Human Development [NICHD] Early Child Care Research Network, 2005).

Psychosocial Consequences

Students who experience academic difficulties are at greater risk for negative psychosocial outcomes. Additionally, poor school performance can have serious implications for students' long-term educational progress and development. Students who do not meet minimum academic requirements or state standards may be retained; meaning they will have to repeat the same grade including content and materials from the previous year. The grade retention rate for students in kindergarten (K) through Grade 8 remained consistently between 9 and 11% between the years 1996 and 2007. In 2007, the retention rate for K-8 students was approximately 10% (Planty et al., 2009). National data tends to demonstrate unfavorable academic progress for those who are retained. For example, in 2004, among students age 16-19 who had dropped out of school, 21.4% had been retained at least once; whereas only 3.8% of those who graduated high school had been retained (U.S. Department of Education, National Center for Education Statistics [NCES], 2006). Further, in their review of 17 studies, Jimerson, Anderson, and Whipple (2002) reported a significant link between grade retention and school dropout in every study.

The consequences of poor academic success reach far beyond the school environment. Academic difficulties are also associated with negative mental health concerns. For example, poor academic performance is associated with depressive symptoms and other internalized distress among children (Schwartz, Gorman, Nakamoto, & Toblin, 2005). Additionally, academic problems are highly associated with externalizing behaviors such as bad conduct and social problems. Woods (1995) summarized the consequences for students who eventually dropout, including increases in high-risk behavior such as: alcohol and drug abuse, early pregnancy, delinquency, crime, violence, and suicide. Further, approximately 75% of prison inmates in the U.S. are school dropouts (Harlow, 2003).

EVIDENCE BASED TREATMENT APPROACHES

Recently, many school districts throughout the U.S. have adopted a response to intervention (RTI) model to assist students who struggle academically. The RTI model consists of providing interventions to students at increasing levels of intensity based on students' responses to interventions and progress. Although RTI models vary in terms of implementation, the early interventions are typically provided by teachers, learning specialists, and special educators, and range from differentiated instruction in the large classroom to intensive, small group interventions. As the intervention plan moves to greater intensity, students may receive more one-on-one assistance (Rock & Leff, 2011).

Positive behavior support (PBS) is also a recently established policy that seeks to address student discipline, social/emotional development, and academic achievement (Rock & Leff, 2011). The PBS system is implemented at three levels. The first level is structured to include all students in the school through positive teaching and reinforcement of school expectations. The second level is structured for students who may be encountering minor problems and are at risk for more serious concerns.

Students needing the second level participate in interventions such as counseling groups, peer tutoring, or after school programs. Students needing the third level are those who exhibit serious academic, social/ emotional, or behavior concerns and therefore may receive more intense one-on-one interventions including specific behavioral management plans and contracts. The use of school-wide positive behavior support, in conjunction with other preventive interventions has demonstrated positive changes in school engagement and academic achievement (Sprague & Walker, 2004). For more information on PBS programming, please see Osher, Dwyer, and Jackson (2004) and Sprague and Golly (2004).

Other interventions target specific academic areas for students. For example, READ 180 is a literacy program that targets students in upper elementary through high school who are struggling with reading or who score poorly on state reading assessments. The program includes strategies such as teacher instruction, independent reading, and computer-based reading lessons and address phonemic and phonological awareness, vocabulary, spelling, fluency, reading comprehension and writing. Multiple studies have demonstrated reading improvement for students who participate in the READ 180 program (Scholastic, Inc., 2011).

Although specific academic interventions are certainly important, the significant psychosocial consequences of poor academic performance indicate that students also need mental health services to support their development. For example, play therapy is a developmentally appropriate modality for working with children (Landreth, 2012) and is effective when working with a variety of presenting concerns such as externalizing behaviors, attention deficit/hyperactivity disorder, teacher-child relationships, and aggression (Bratton, 2010). Specifically, there is recent evidence that play therapy is effective in helping students improve their academic achievement (Blanco & Ray, 2011; Quayle, 1991; Shechtman, Gilat, Fos, & Flasher, 1996). Blanco and Ray (2011) found that children who participated in play therapy improved their achievement levels significantly when compared to a control group that did not receive treatment. Thus, in the following sections we describe practical play therapy techniques that school counselors can use when working with students who are experiencing academic difficulties.

PROPOSED TREATMENT APPROACHES AND TECHNIQUES

Play is essential for healthy physical, intellectual, and social-emotional development. It propels healthy brain development and helps us learn and adapt to the world around us (Brown, 2009). Through play, children can learn about themselves and the world in a way that nurtures their need for imagination and fantasy. Piaget (1962) identified that children do not develop abstract reasoning until approximately age 11. Play, therefore, allows children to use concrete objects to represent individual experiences within their environment. It gives them manageable ways to discover their inner world, allowing increased feelings of security and control.

As described by Landreth (2012),

> play therapy is defined as a dynamic interpersonal relationship between a child (or person of any age) and a therapist trained in play therapy procedures who provides selected play materials and facilitates the development of a safe relationship for a child (or person of any age) to fully express and explore self (feelings, thoughts, experiences, and behaviors) through play, the child's natural medium of communication, for optimal growth and development. (p. 11)

Children are active beings and play therapy allows this need to be met. Play therapy to children is what talk therapy is to adults. Play therapy gives children the opportunity to express his inner world. Feelings are often inaccessible to children at a verbal level; therefore it would be too much pressure to expect them to come up to an adult's verbal abilities to express thoughts and feelings. Instead, play therapy is about the adult meeting children at their developmental level and communicating in ways that are comfortable for them.

Theoretical Underpinnings of Play Approach

There are multiple approaches to counseling children when utilizing play therapy. Each approach has unique ways of explaining the goal of the client-counselor relationship, conceptualizing one's world, and interacting with caregivers in the child's environment. As counselors utilize play therapy, it is gravely important that each counselor spend time self-reflecting to better understand themselves and their beliefs in order to understand which approach will be most effective based on self-assessment. According to Ray (2011), the most widely used theoretical orientations of play therapy are child-centered, cognitive-behavioral, and Adlerian approaches. For the purpose of this chapter, the focus will be on Adlerian play therapy.

Adlerian play therapy is based on Alfred Adler's individual psychology (Adler, 1954), combining it's concepts with the basic principles of play therapy. From this theoretical perspective, people are purposeful, creative, and motivated by a need to belong (Ansbacher & Ansbacher, 1956; Watts & Carlson, 1999). Maladjustment is a form of discouragement that one feels when unable to find ways to cope with self-perceived problems in one's life. It is the counselor's role to look for ways to encourage the client by exploring the client's assets, lifestyles, goals, and behaviors, finding what makes them special and unique (Kottman, 2009).

Adlerian play therapy has four phases: (a) building an egalitarian relationship, (b) exploring the child's lifestyle, (c) helping the child gain insight, and (d) reorienting and reeducating the child (Kottman, 2011). The therapeutic relationship is an equal partnership based on trust and respect where the counselor and client share responsibility and power. The therapist takes an active role in sessions, both by her own initiative and the child's request. Building this relationship is a continual process throughout the entire length of play therapy. As the relationship is established, the Adlerian play therapist focuses on understanding the child by observing the child in the playroom, understanding how the child's play represents one's lifestyle, and then communicating this understanding to the child (Kottman, 2003).

Adlerian play therapy is a practical tool for school counselors, providing concrete strategies for children, teachers, and parents to alter negative behaviors and feelings (Kottman & Johnson, 1983). Parent and teacher consultation are an essential part of Adlerian play therapy. School counselors have a unique position in the child's life, being able to work with teachers to increase their understanding of the child in the classroom context. School counselors can also make recommendations to teachers to help support the behavioral changes the child makes in play therapy. Although school counselors' time is limited, which would indicate a lack of time to meet with parents in person on a weekly basis, phone calls can be made every other week or as needed. School counselors can use this time to provide insights to parents and consult with them regarding appropriate parenting strategies for their child and to provide parent training. These conversations are also a great way to follow up on the parents' perceptions of the child's progress throughout the intervention process.

Specific Play Techniques

Encouragement. Encouragement is an essential technique in Adlerian play therapy that is used throughout all four phases. It is a way for the counselor to communicate acceptance of the child and faith in his or her ability. Adlerian play therapists avoid doing anything for a child that he or she can do for him or herself. If the therapist believes that the child cannot do something, the therapist can then offer for them to do it together. Encouragement is especially important during the last phase of counseling as the child formulates new goals and ideas for gaining significance in his or her life (Kottman & Warlick, 1989). The focus should be on the child's attitude and efforts instead of a final product. This concept is important for a child with academic struggles who finds schoolwork challenging and does not believe that her or she can make improvements. To show encouragement, Kottman (2003) recommended that counselors do the following: (a) convey unconditional acceptance; (b) show faith in the child's abilities; (c) give recognition for effort; (d) focus on strengths and assets; (e) emphasize the deed and the joy of doing, not the doer; (f) give credit for the good part of what was done and ignore the parts that do not come up to standards; (g) show involvement in the child's interests; (h) let the child know that sometimes you make mistakes, modeling the courage to be imperfect; (i) help the child realize that mistakes do not have to be negative and can be learned from; and (j) make sure the child discovers a positive way to gain significance. Examples of encouragement responses include: "you figured out how to do it," "you worked hard to bring up your grade and you are proud of yourself," "you are working to get that picture just the way you want it," and "you seem upset about spilling the sand; sometimes accidents happen in here."

School artwork. Art techniques can be used in Adlerian play therapy to help the counselor gain an understanding of the child's view of self, others, and the world. Various materials can be used, such as markers, sidewalk chalk, colored pencils, paint, sculpting clay, Play-Doh, collage materials, or anything else that may facilitate self-expression. One specific example is the kinetic school drawing (KSD; Knoff & Prout, 1985), where the counselor prompts the client to draw a school picture with everyone is doing something, including herself, her teacher, and a friend or two. Specific instructions can be added or altered if trying to understand something specific about the child (e.g., his special education classroom). After the child completes the drawing, the counselor then asks questions about the drawing to understand the child's perception of herself and the world around him. Later in the therapeutic process, the counselor can ask the child to create a drawing of her ideal school environment, asking questions about this picture as well. The counselor can use both of these pictures to facilitate a conversation about goals or problem-solving strategies.

Mutual storytelling. Developed by Richard Gardner, mutual storytelling is a metaphoric counseling technique that is well-suited for Adlerian play therapy (Kottman, 2003). The counselor asks the client to choose several figures, puppets, or dolls; pretend they can talk; and tell a story using them as characters. As the child tells the story, the play therapist listens for metaphors that represent the child's lifestyle, such as perceptions of herself, ways of problem-solving, and relationships with others. Later in the session, or in a subsequent session, the play therapist retells the story, using the same characters with a different middle and end to the story. The new version of the story demonstrates an alternative problem-solving strategy and view of self and others. The school counselor can prompt a child to use puppets to tell the story of a day in the classroom or a particular event, such as working on an assignment in a group. The school counselor would then listen for metaphors and proceed as explained above.

Body drawing. Sometimes children may struggle with recognizing their thoughts and feelings about themselves and in play therapy, the therapist can facilitate children's self-awareness. This can be done a number of ways. One option is having the child lay on a large piece of butcher paper and the therapist drawing an outline of her body. Alternatively, the child can draw an outline of herself on any size of paper. The play therapist can then prompt the child to identify words to describe herself; coloring the picture and writing inside their outline. For example, if a child identifies herself as a fast runner, she might draw a pair of running shoes on the picture or write the words "fast runner" inside the feet. If the child struggles to identify positive characteristics, the therapist can ask the child what she thinks parents, friends, or teachers might think and then process her thoughts about it. The therapist can also offer suggestions about what she has seen in the playroom and in their relationship, such as noticing that the child is focused, likes to laugh, figures out ways to solve a problem, or cares about others. This drawing can be completed in one session and taken home as a reminder of the child's positive assets. It can also be a continual creation that is worked on and referred to throughout multiple sessions as the child gains new levels of self-awareness and self-confidence (see Table 7.1).

Case Study

As an elementary school counselor, Mrs. McIntyre received a counseling referral for a second grade student named Ashley due to increasing behavior concerns and recent academic difficulty. Before starting counseling with Ashley, Mrs. McIntyre scheduled parent and teacher consultations to gain information about Ashley and her environment, both at home and school. She also used the opportunity to build partnerships with them so that they could all work together to help Ashley.

As the school counselor, Mrs. McIntyre was actively involved with many children in the school. She knew Ashley prior to the start of counseling and believed they already had an established foundation for a positive counseling relationship. Knowing that the number of counseling sessions was limited, she gathered information from Ashley's parents and teachers prior to the first session. Due to the brief nature of

Table 7.1. Sample Outline of Five Play Therapy Sessions in a School Environment

Session Number	*Content of Session*
Prior to First Session	Meet with parent/caregiver(s) and teacher(s) to collect information about the child's developmental history, family and social relationships, and concerns. This is also a time to build rapport with those involved in the child's life, as their involvement is important to making and maintaining positive changes in the child's life
1	Introduce child to playroom by saying "This is our playroom and, in here, you can do many of the things you want to do"
	Continue building collaborative relationship between counselor and client
	Prompt client to do a kinetic school drawing to elicit child's perceptions and feelings about school and self
2	Start mutual storytelling—child tells story
3	Continue mutual storytelling—counselor retells story
4	Role-play familiar situation that has occurred in the classroom, using puppets and/or client and counselor to act out situation
5	Follow-up with client about role-play situation
	Terminate

counseling in the school environment and gathering information ahead of time, Mrs. McIntyre determined that a play therapy approach would be the most effective form of counseling for Ashley and that the focus of counseling would be on the third and fourth phases of Adlerian play therapy.

For the first session, Mrs. McIntyre took Ashley out of class to a playroom that was set up with a variety of toys allowing for a range of emotional expressions. She introduced the playroom by saying, "This is our playroom and, in here, you can do many of the things you want to do." Mrs. McIntyre used multiple techniques to build the relationship, including encouragement, tracking behavior, restating content, metacommunicating (i.e., making interpretations about interaction patterns), reflecting feelings, and actively interacting with Ashley. Ashley engaged in a lot of exploratory play during the first session, engaging Mrs. McIntyre in some of her activities. During her play, Ashley made a few statements about not liking school and having no friends. Mrs. McIntyre was interested in learning about Ashley's perception of the school environment and her interactions with others, so she prompted Ashley to create a KSD (Knoff & Prout, 1985). She instructed Ashley to draw a school picture with everyone doing something, including herself, her teacher, and a friend or two.

When she completed the picture, Mrs. McIntyre asked questions and processed the picture with Ashley. Ashley identified feeling stupid and embarrassed when she had to leave class to receive special help for her reading. She recalled other students looking at her as she left and thought that they must think she is stupid.

During the third phase of Adlerian play therapy, *gaining insight*, Mrs. McIntyre's goal was to help Ashley gain clarity about her perceptions, attitudes, behaviors, thoughts, and feelings. Once Ashley had a deeper understanding of herself, she could then make choices about behavioral changes that she might want to make. Mrs. McIntyre used a metaphoric counseling technique called mutual storytelling (Kottman, 2003) to help Ashley gain insight into her feelings and behavior in the classroom, and to generate healthy, alternative responses. Mrs. McIntyre asked Ashley to choose dolls, animal figures, or puppets to create a story that involved a problem to solve or an adventure to experience. Ashley told a story about a bird that fell out of a tree and hurt its wing, afraid to fly again because it was painful. She eventually gave up trying after the other birds around her did not help and, instead, spent their time flying high above her.

In the next session, Mrs. McIntyre reminded Ashley of her story and told her that she was going to retell the story, using the same characters with a different middle and end to the story. This demonstrated an alternative way to solve the problem and view self and others. Mrs. McIntyre told the story with the same beginning where the bird fell out of the tree, hurt its wing, and felt afraid to fly again. She changed the story to annotate the bird's positive thoughts of not giving up when it was hard and continually trying again. She added that two of the other birds were willing to help this bird and cheered for her when she was finally able to fly again. Mrs. McIntyre processed the story with Ashley, asking for her thoughts and feelings about the story. Ashley identified the bird as brave and lucky to have friends around that helped her. Mrs. McIntyre then prompted Ashley to identify people around her that might be willing to help her or cheer for her. Ashley identified her teacher and one friend in her class, feeling encouraged and recognizing that she was not completely alone.

During the fourth session, Mrs. McIntyre wanted to help Ashley generate alternative thoughts, feelings, and behaviors for problematic situations at school. She showed Ashley her drawing from the first session which was kept in a file with her case notes. Ashley remembered the drawing and identified that she continued leaving her class to work on her reading skills. Mrs. McIntyre reflected Ashley's embarrassment and sadness about leaving and then prompted her to brainstorm ideas for what to do when she gets pulled out of class or teased by her classmates. Together, Ashley and Mrs. McIntyre came up with several ideas and then Ashley chose one to try in a role-play. Ashley role-played ignoring others' negative behaviors and being attentive to those who were supportive. She practiced walking with confidence and thinking positive thoughts. Ashley planned to practice these behaviors before the next session.

During Ashley's last counseling session, Mrs. McIntyre followed-up with her about the situation they previously role-played. Ashley stated that it was sometimes difficult to think positive but was getting easier with practice. Ashley's confidence increased as she felt better prepared for how to handle the difficult transition. Mrs. McIntyre affirmed Ashley for her efforts in gaining insights, generating new ideas, and practicing them in the classroom. As this was the last session, Mrs. McIntyre reminded Ashley that she was available in the school counselor's office if Ashley needed to talk in the future.

After Ashley's last play therapy session, Mrs. McIntyre followed-up with Ashley's parents and teacher to consult with them about helpful tools to use, such as encouragement and reflection of feelings. Mrs. McIntyre provided resources for Ashley's parents and gave suggestions for ways to help Ashley at home, such as giving her breaks while doing her homework and encouraging her efforts. She also gave suggestions to Ashley's teacher, such as creating a signal between the two of them as a way for Ashley to communicate that she does not understand and that she feels discouraged.

Children experiencing academic difficulties are at serious risk for long-term psychosocial consequences. Fortunately, PSCs work to eliminate barriers to all students' success and development. As a responsive service within the delivery system of the ASCA (2012) *National Model* short-term play therapy is a developmentally appropriate modality to address students' academic and personal needs. Therefore, PSCs can utilize play therapy techniques during individual counseling to ensure that students continue healthy academic, personal, and social growth and development.

PREVENTION CURRICULUM

Student academic development is a main focus within the school environment, and school counselors need to recognize the implications of students' academic needs in delivery of their comprehensive, developmental school counseling program (ASCA, 2012). School counselors have both an ethical and professional responsibility to provide students with equitable access to academic resources through a program that is consistent with the *ASCA National Model* (ASCA, 2010). The academic development of students refers to their skill development and overall understanding of information (Ebel & Frisbie, 1986). Student's academic development can be addressed through the implementation of a comprehensive guidance curriculum that includes preventative developmental guidance.

The delivery system of the *ASCA National Model* (2012) provides a framework for school counselors to implement a guidance curriculum that provides preventive measures for academic challenges. The guidance curriculum consists of lessons that are tailored to the developmental needs of each grade level. According to Gysbers and Henderson (2012) 100% of children have developmental needs. The ASCA *National Model* recommends that 35% to 45% of an elementary school counselor's time should be focused on implementing a curriculum to address these needs. Additionally, "The school counseling core curriculum consists of a planned, written instructional program that is comprehensive in scope, preventive in nature and developmental in design" (ASCA, 2012, p. 85).

Proposed Curriculum Development Approaches and Theory Foundations

The topics within a guidance curriculum to address the academic needs of elementary students should be focused on developing their skills, behaviors, and self-efficacy to create a foundation for their future learning. Play therapy techniques integrated within the guidance curriculum can promote student developmental growth (Ray, Armstrong, & Balkin, 2005). Piaget's (1962) developmental theory suggests that it is challenging for students to think abstractly; therefore, the curriculum should provide students the opportunity to cognitively and concretely understand the information within the guidance lesson. Play therapy provides students with a way to connect concrete concepts to abstract thought while mastering behaviors needed for change (Ray, Armstrong, & Balkin, 2005). Blanco and Ray (2011) found in a pilot study that child-centered play therapy improved elementary student's academic achievement. Play therapy techniques that enhance academic topics prepare students for more productive learning in the classroom (Landreth, 2012). Suggested topics may include: (a) individual and cooperative learning, (b) learning styles, and (c) balance and time- management. These topics are suggested because they are emphasized in the *ASCA National Model Standards* (2004).

SAMPLE LESSON PLANS

Individual and Cooperative Learning

Title: With or Without

Standard: Students will acquire the attitudes, knowledge and skills that contribute to effective learning in school and across the life span. (ASCA Standard A; Academic Development Domain)

Competency:

1. Students will take responsibility for their actions (ASCA: A:A3.1.)
2. Students will demonstrate the ability to work independently, as well as the ability to work cooperatively with other students (ASCA: A:A3.7)

Learning Objectives: After participating in the activity and the discussion students will be able to: (a) take responsibility for their actions within the classroom, and (b) understand how to work independently and cooperatively within in the classroom.

Materials: Dry erase board, a simple word-search (created by counselor), Poster board (one for each group), markers/crayons, Hula-hoop

Play Therapy Learning Activity: Cooperative Play

Introduction: The school counselor will explain to the students that they will be doing three different types of activities: (1) an individual activity, (2) a small group activity, and (3) a large group activity

Activity:

1. The students will complete a word-search. The counselor will discuss what it was like for students to work on their own and record their ideas on the dry erase board.
2. The students will create a group drawing in a small group (3-4) of students. The counselor will discuss what it was like for students to work in a small group and record their ideas on the dry erase board.

3. All students will participate in the hula-hoop game: All participants join hands and form a circle. Two participants drop hands and put their arms through the hula hoops. They then join hands again. The hula hoops are then dangling from their arms. The objective of the game is to send the hula hoops completely around the circle and return them to the starting point without releasing hands. This means that each person has to go through the hula hoops as they make their way around the circle. The counselor will discuss what it was like for students to work in a large group and record their ideas on the dry erase board.

   Conclusion: The counselor will use the information on the dry erase board to facilitate a discussion about the comparison (positives/negatives) of working in each of these settings. The counselor will ask students to identify their responsibility in each activity and what they learned about themselves. The counselor will facilitate discussion about how these activities connect to their schoolwork and overall learning.

Assessment/Evaluation:

1. The students will identify if they prefer to work independently or with a group before the lesson.
2. The students will identify a benefit of working independently and cooperatively.
3. The students will identify something they were responsible for in one of the activities.

Follow-up: In a subsequent guidance lesson, the school counselor will check-in with students about their preference of working independently or in a group and how it has helped their learning.

LEARNING STYLES

Title: Secret Handshake

Standard: Students will complete school with the academic preparation essential to choose from wide range of substantial post-secondary options, including college. (ASCA Standard B; Academic Development Domain)

Competency:

1. Use knowledge of learning styles to positively influence school performance (ASCA: A:B1.6)
2. Become a self-directed and independent learning (ASCA: A:B1.7)

Learning Objectives: After participating in the discussion and completing the activities students will be able to: (a) identify 3 different learning styles (visual, auditory, kinesthetic) and (b) apply their learning style to their independent learning.

Materials: Dry-erase board, create three different secret hand shake, a picture of one of the secret handshakes

Learning Activity:

Introduction: The school counselor will ask students to brainstorm how they think they learn. The students they will learn a secret handshake in three different ways.

Activity:

1. Show students a picture of one of the secret handshakes, ask students to try the secret handshake. For those who got the secret handshake right, put their name on the dry erase board in one color.
2. Tell students how to do a different secret handshake, ask students to try the secret handshake. For those who got the secret handshake right, put their name on the dry erase board in a different color.
3. Demonstrate how to do a different handshake (without any words), ask students to try the secret handshake. For those who got the secret handshake right, put their name on the dry erase board in a different color.

Conclusion: The counselor will facilitate discussion about what was the easiest or hardest way to learn a secret handshake. The counselor will define and describe the three different learning styles used to teach them the secrete handshake. The counselor will discuss how these learning styles are connected with school performance. The students will identify ways they can use this knowledge to improve their learning.

Assessment/Evaluation:

1. The students will brainstorm how they think they learn.
2. The students will describe their preferred learning style.
3. The students will identify one way to apply their preferred learning style to their schoolwork.

Follow-up: In a subsequent guidance lesson, the counselor will implement different learning styles. The school counselor will check-in with students about their awareness of their learning style and how it has improved their learning.

DEVELOPING BALANCE AND TIME-MANAGEMENT

Title: My Week, My Day, My Life

Standard: Students will understand the relationship of academics to the world of work and to life at home and in the community (ASCA Standard C; Academic Development Domain) and Students will acquire the attitudes, knowledge and skills that contribute to effective learning in school and across the life span (ASCA Standard B; Academic Development Domain).

Competency:

1. Students will demonstrate the ability to balance school, studies, extracurricular activities, leisure time and family life (ASCA: A:C1.1.)
2. Students will apply time-management and task management skills (ASCA: A:A2.1.)

Learning Objectives: After participating in discussion, completing the activity, and processing with the group, students will be able to: (a) identify different ways they spend their time, and (b) describe ways to create a balance in their life.

Materials: Paper, Markers/Crayons

Play Therapy Learning Activity: Drawing

Introduction: The school counselor will ask student to stand-up and balance on one foot. The counselor will facilitate a discussion about what balance means.

Activity:

1. The students will draw a picture of their week.
2. The students will draw a picture of the day.
3. The students will draw a picture of their life.
4. The students will share their creation in small groups.

Conclusion: The counselor will facilitate discussion about what is similar and different about the three pictures and what aspects of the student's life are represented (i.e., school, extracurricular activities, free time, and family). The counselor will discuss ways to for students to create balance between these aspects of their lives.

Assessment/Evaluation:

1. The students will complete a brief assessment of how they spend their time before the activity.
2. The students will identify one way their life is off balance and something they can do to create more balance.

Follow-up: In a subsequent guidance lesson, the students will complete the same brief assessment of how they spend their time and compare it to the previous assessment to identify ways they have created balance in their lives.

CONCLUSION

Academic development is one of the three domains that PSCs address within a comprehensive school counseling program. Additionally, student academic competencies and indicators are outlined in the ASCA *National Standards* (2004) for students. As part of the school guidance curriculum, PSCs implement preventive developmental guidance to help students learn skills to cope with future challenges. Play techniques provide PSCs with a helpful way to meet students at their developmental level during guidance lessons. By delivering proactive guidance services, PSCs help equip students with the necessary skills to navigate future academic challenges and avoid delays in their academic development and progress.

REFERENCES

Adler, A. (1954). *Understanding human nature*. New York, NY: Fawcett Premier.

Alexander, K. L., Entwisle, D. R., & Horsey, C. S. (1997). From first grade forward: Early foundations of high school dropout. *Sociology of Education, 70*, 87-107. doi:10.2307/2673158

Alliance for Excellent Education. (2010). *High school dropouts*. Retrieved from http://www.all4ed.org/files/HighSchoolDropouts.pdf

American Psychiatric Association. (2000). *Diagnostic and statistical manual of mental disorders* (4th ed., Text rev.). Washington, DC: Author.

American School Counselor Association. (2004). *ASCA National Standards for students*. Alexandria, VA: Author.

American School Counselor Association. (2012). *The ASCA National Model: A Framework for School Counseling Programs* (3rd ed.). Alexandria, VA: Author.

American School Counselor Association. (2010). *The ASCA ethical standards*. Alexandria, VA: Author.

Ansbacher, H. L., & Ansbacher, R. R. (Eds.). (1956). *The individual psychology of Alfred Adler: A systematic presentation of his writing*. New York, NY: Basic Books.

Aud, S., Hussar, W., Kena, G., Bianco, K., Frohlich, L., Kemp, J., & Tahan, K. (2011). *The condition of education 2011* (NCES 2011-033). U.S. Department of Education, National Center for Education Statistics. Washington, DC: U.S. Government Printing Office.

Bernstein, B. E. (2012). *Conduct disorder.* Retrieved from http://emedicine.medscape.com/article/918213-overview#a1

Blanco, P. J. and Ray, D. C. (2011). Play therapy in elementary schools: A best practice for improving academic achievement. *Journal of Counseling & Development, 89,* 235-243. doi:10.1002/j.1556-6678.2011.tb00083.x

Bratton, S. C. (2010). Meeting the early mental health needs of children through school-based play-therapy: A review of outcome research. In A. A. Drews & E. Schaefer (Eds.), *School-based play therapy* (2nd ed., pp. 17-58). Hoboken, NJ: Wiley.

Brown, S. (2009). *Play: How it shapes the brain, opens the imagination, and invigorates the soul.* New York, NY: Penguin Group.

Carnevale, A. P., Smith, N., & Strohl, J. (2010). *Help wanted: Projections of jobs and education requirements through 2018.* Georgetown University, Center on Education and the Workforce.

Ebel, R. L., & Frisbie, D. A. (1986). *Essentials of educational measurement* (4th ed.). Englewood Cliffs, NJ: Prentice-Hall.

Felton, K. A., & Akos, P. (2011). The ups and downs of third grade. *Educational Leadership, 68*, 28-31.

Fletcher, J. M., & Vaughn. S. (2009). Response to intervention: Preventing and remediating academic difficulties. *Child Development Perspectives, 3*, 30-37. doi:10.1111/j.1750-8606.2008.00072.x

Frazier, T. W., Youngstrom, E. A., Glutting, J. J., & Watkins, M. W. (2007). ADHD and achievement: Meta-analysis of the child, adolescent, and adult literatures and a concomitant study with college students. *Journal of Learning Disabilities, 40*, 49-65. doi:10.1177/00222194070400010401

Gottfried, A. W., Gottfried, A. E., Cook, C. R., & Morris, P. E. (2005). Educational characteristics of adolescents with gifted academic intrinsic motivation: A longitudinal investigation from school entry through early adulthood. *Gifted Child Quarterly, 49*, 172-185. doi:10.1177/001698620504900206

Gysbers, N. C., & Henderson, P. (2012*). Developing & Managing Your School Guidance & Counseling Program*. Alexandria, VA: American Counseling Association.

Harlow, C. W. (2003). *Education and Correctional Populations,* NCJ 195670, Bureau of Justice Statistics, U.S. Department of Justice.

Hursh, D. (2005). The growth of high-stakes testing in the USA: Accountability, markets and the decline in educational quality. *British Educational Research Journal, 31*, 605-622. doi:10.1080/01411920500240767

Jimerson, S. R., Anderson, G. E., & Whipple, A. D. (2002). Winning the battle and losing the war: Examining the relation between grade retention and dropping out of high school. *Psychology in the Schools, 39*, 441-457. doi:10.1002/pits.10046

Kainz, K., & Vernon-Feagans, L. (2007). The ecology of early reading development for children in poverty. *Elementary School Journal, 107*, 407-427. doi:10.1086/518621

Knoff, H., & Prout, H. (1985). *Kinetic drawing system for family and school: A handbook.* Los Angeles, CA: Western Psychological Services.

Kottman, T. (2003). *Partners in play: An Adlerian approach to play therapy* (2nd ed.). Alexandria, VA: American Counseling Association.

Kottman, T. (2009). Adlerian play therapy. In K. J. O'Connor, & L. D. Braverman (Eds.), *Play therapy theory and practice: Comparing theories and techniques* (2nd ed., pp. 237-282). Hoboken, NJ: John Wiley & Sons.

Kottman, T. (2011). *Play therapy: Basics and beyond* (2nd ed.). Alexandria, VA: American Counseling Association.

Kottman, T., & Johnson, V. (1983). Adlerian play therapy: A tool for school counselors. *Elementary School Guidance and Counseling, 28,* 42-51.

Kottman, T. T., & Warlick, J. (1989). Adlerian play therapy: Practical considerations. *Individual Psychology: The Journal of Adlerian Theory, Research & Practice, 45*(4), 433.

Landreth, G. L. (2012). *Play therapy: The art of the relationship* (3rd ed.). New York, NY: Routledge.

Learning Disabilities Association of America. (n.d.). *Types of learning disabilities.* Retrieved from http://www.ldaamerica.org/aboutld/teachers/understanding/types.asp

Learning Disabilities Association of American. (n.d.). *Learning disabilities: Signs, symptoms and strategies*. Retrieved from http://www.ldaamerica.org/aboutld/parents/ld_basics/ld.asp

Marcoulides, G. A., Gottfried, A. E., Gottfried, A. W., & Oliver, P. H. (2008). A latent transition analysis of academic intrinsic motivation from childhood through adolescence. *Educational Research and Evaluation, 14*, 411-427. doi:10.1080/13803610802337665

Masi, G., Mucci, M., & Millepiedi, S. (2001). Separation anxiety disorder in children and adolescents: Epidemiology, diagnosis, and management. *CNS Drugs, 15*, 94-104. doi:10.2165/00023210-200115020-00002

McConaughy, S. H., Volpe, R. J., Antshel, K. M., Gordon, M., & Eiraldi, R. B. (2011). Academic and social impairments of elementary school children with attention deficit hyperactivity disorder. *School Psychology Review, 40*, 200-225.

National Institute of Child Health and Human Development Early Child Care Research Network. (2005). Duration and developmental timing of poverty and children's cognitive and social development from birth through third grade. *Child Development, 76*, 795-810.

Osher, D., Dwyer, K., & Jackson, S. (2004). *Safe, supportive and successful schools: Step by step.* Longmont, CO: Sopris West Educational Services.

Piaget, J. (1962). *Play, dreams, and imitation in childhood.* New York, NY: Routledge.

Planty, M., Hussar, W., Snyder, T., Kena, G., KewalRamani, A., Kemp, J., Bianco, K., & Dinkes, R. (2009). *The Condition of Education 2009* (NCES 2009-081). National Center for Education Statistics, Institute of Education Sciences, U.S. Department of Education, Washington, DC.

Quayle, R. L. (1991). The Primary Mental Health Project as a school-based approach for prevention of adjustment problems: An evaluation. *Dissertation Abstracts International: Section A. Humanities and Social Sciences, 52*, 1268.

Quilliams, L., & Beran, T. (2009). Children at risk for academic failure: A model of individual and family factors. *Exceptionality Education International, 19*, 63-76.

Ray, D. C. (2011). *Advanced play therapy: Essential conditions, knowledge, and skills for child practice.* New York, NY: Routledge.

Ray D. C., Armstrong, S.A., & Balkin, R.S. (2005). Play therapy practices among elementary school counselors. *Professional School Counseling, 8*, 360-365.

Rock, E., & Leff, E. H. (2011). The Professional School Counselor and Students with Disabilities. In B. T. Erford (Ed.), *Transforming the school counseling profession* (3rd ed., pp. 314-341). Upper Saddle River, NJ: Pearson Education.

Shechtman, Z., Gilat, I., Fos, L., & Flasher, A. (1996). Brief group therapy with low-achieving elementary school children. *Journal of Counseling Psychology, 43*, 376-382. doi:10.1037/0022-0167.43.4.376

Scholastic, Inc. (2011). *Compendium of READ 180 Research*. Retrieved from http://read180.scholastic.com/reading-interventions-program/research

Schwartz, D., Gorman, A. H., Nakamoto, J., & Tobin, R. L. (2005). Victimization in the peer group and children's academic functioning. *Journal of Educational Psychology, 97*, 425-435. doi:10.1037/0022-0167.43.4.376

Sprague, J. R., & Golly, A. (2004). *Best behavior: Building positive behavior supports inschools*. Longmont, CO: Sopris West Educational Services.

Sprague, J. R., & Walker, H. M. (2004). *Safe and healthy schools: Practical prevention-strategies*. New York, NY: Guilford Press.

No Child Left Behind (NCLB) Act of 2001, Pub. L. No. 107-110, § 115, Stat. 1425 (2002).

U.S. Department of Education, National Center for Education Statistics. (2006). *The Condition of Education 2006*, NCES 2006-071, Washington, DC: U.S. Government Printing Office.

Watts, R., & Carlson, J. (Eds.). (1999). *Interventions and strategies in counseling and psychotherapy.* Philadelphia, PA: Accelerated Development.

Woods, E., G. (1995). *Reducing the Dropout Rate*. School Improvement Research Series. Office of Educational Research and Improvement (OERI), U.S. Department of Education.

CHAPTER 8

PLAYING IN PERIL

Integrating Play Therapy With Responsive Services Following a Natural Disaster

Jennifer N. Baggerly and Eric J. Green

Vignette 1

Juanita, a 5-year-old third generation Mexican American girl, whimpers as she is reluctantly led down the hallway to her kindergarten class room. The stench of smoke still permeates her hair and clothing from the wildfires that consumed her family's modest home days ago. She is late to school because she is staying with relatives in a different school district. Usually outgoing, Juanita now clutches her blanket and refuses to move past the classroom doorway. Some of her friends go to her in an unsuccessful attempt to coax her in while other children tease her for being a "scaredy cat". She begins to cry because her cat was killed by the fire. In exasperation, the teacher calls the school counselor for help.

Integrating Play Techniques in Comprehensive School Counseling Programs, pp. 149–165

Vignette 2

Michael, an 8-year-old African American boy, slams into several children in the lunch line as he yells "tornado" and laughs loudly in an exaggerated fashion. His family, as well as numerous others, was displaced to a temporary shelter after a F4 tornado leveled their neighborhood. Although Michael has been a model student prior to the disaster, he now begins to fight with other boys who were angered by his behavior. "I was just playing," he yells after two other boys shove him back. They say, "Go play with your grandfather!" Michael raises his fist and curses in revenge. As a teacher escorts him to the principals' office, he tearfully states his grandfather was killed during the tornado.

With 385 disasters worldwide in 2010 and an increase of natural disasters within the last decade (Guha-Sapir, Vos, Below, & Ponserre, 2010), school counselors may encounter children such as these in their careers. Fortunately, the American School Counselor Association's (ASCA) *National Model* (2012) provides a framework so school counselors can implement disaster preparedness and intervention services into their comprehensive, developmental guidance program. This chapter will guide school counselors in fulfilling their mission of creating a safe environment for children by implementing the following: (a) a school guidance curriculum that prepares children to cope with natural disasters, (b) individualized student planning to identify children adversely impacted by natural disasters, (c) responsive services of small group counseling and individual counseling for impacted children, as well as consultation for their teachers and parents, and (d) systems support by developing collaborative relationships with disaster relief organizations.

NATURAL DISASTERS AND STUDENT PERFORMANCE

Natural Disasters

Natural disasters are destructive events caused by nature that meet the following seven criteria: (a) destruction of property, injury, or loss of life, (b) identifiable beginning and end, (c) sudden and time-limited, (d) adversely affects a large group of people, (e) public event that impacts more than one family, (f) out of realm of ordinary experience, and (g) psychologically traumatic enough to induce stress in almost anyone (Rosenfeld, Caye, Ayalon, & Lahad, 2005). Distinctions in this definition are important to note. The breadth of impact is a key criterion in the definition of disaster. Even though a single house fire is disastrous for a family, it is not considered a natural disaster by federal definitions. Therefore certain entities such as the Federal Emergency Management Agency (FEMA) and nongovernment organizations (NGOs) (i.e., American Red Cross, Save the Children, Children's Disaster Services, etc.) will not be deployed. A destructive event is only considered a disaster when local capacity and external resources have been overwhelmed. Likewise, the definition of disaster implies the event causes psychological trauma that would overwhelm almost anyone. Just as first responders rush to meet physical needs of overwhelmed survivors, so must school counselors rush to meet psychological needs of overwhelmed child survivors.

Natural disasters are categorized into five subgroups (Guha-Sapir et al., 2010): geophysical, meteorological, hydrological, climatological, and biological. Specifically, geophysical events originate from solid earth and include earthquake, volcano, landslides, and dry mass movement. Meteorological events are caused by short-lived atmospheric processes such as storms, tornados, and hurricanes. Hydrological events are caused by deviations in normal water cycles or overflow of water from wind such as floods and title waves. Climatological events come from long-lived processes resulting in extreme temperature, drought, or wildfire. Lastly, biological events are caused by exposure to germs, toxic substances, or animals including viral infectious disease epidemics and insect infestation.

Prevalence

Prevalence of natural disasters varies each year. According to World Health Organization Centre for Research on the Epidemiology of Disaster, in 2010 "a total of 385 natural disasters killed more than 297,000 people worldwide, affected over 217 million others and caused $123.9 billion of economic damages" (Guha-Sapir et al., 2010, p. 1). In a representative sample survey of 2,030 U.S. children ages 2 to 17, Becker-Blease, Turner, and Finkelhor (2010) found that approximately 14% reported a lifetime exposure to a disaster and 4.1% in the past year.

Hydrological and meteorological disasters are the most prevalent in the United States. In 2008, floods impacted over 11 million people in the United States. In 2005, a total of 1,833 people in the U.S. were killed after Hurricane Katrina. Moreover, "Many experts believe that climate change has caused an increase in weather systems resulting in unprecedented rain and flooding this past decade and that this will continue in the future" (Guha-Sapir et al., 2010, p. 24). Unfortunately, this prevalence indicates that hundreds of thousands of U.S. children will be impacted by natural disasters in the years to come.

Social, Academic, and Behavior Functioning

Natural disasters can contribute to short-term and long-term disruptions in children's psychosocial, academic, and behavior functioning. Black (2001) summarized the short and long term impact of natural disasters as follows:

> Children who live through a disaster usually have two life-changing experiences. First, they endure the trauma itself, which might forever alter their sense of security and their ability to cope with life's problems. Second, they face ongoing disorder and dishevelment in their day-to-day lives. (p. 54)

After a disaster, children ages 6 to 11 may exhibit typical reactions such as anxiety about family members' safety, fear that another disaster will occur, clinging or dependent behavior, bed-wetting, social withdrawal, increased fighting, hyperactivity, inattentiveness, irrational fears, irritability, sleep disruption, stomachaches, and refusal to attend school (Brymer et al., 2006; La Greca, 2008). For adolescents (ages 12 to 18), common reactions include flashbacks and nightmares, emotional numbing, avoidance of reminders, substance abuse, depression, headaches and stomachaches, risk-taking behaviors, lack of concentration, apathy about school performance, and rebellion at home or school (Brymer et al., 2006; La Greca, 2008). After disasters, both elementary and secondary school children who are displaced may have decreased school performance including lower standardized test scores, tardiness, absenteeism, fights, verbal abuse of teachers, bullying, cutting class, and theft (Briere, 2006; Pane, McCaffrey, Kalra, & Zhou, 2008).

Although these reactions to disasters typically resolve within 30 days, some children may experience severe and ongoing symptoms such as depression, anxiety, and posttraumatic stress disorder (PTSD) for months and years if left untreated (Kronenberg et al., 2010). For example, moderate to very severe symptoms were reported by 55% of school aged children 3 months after Hurricane Andrew and 34% at 10 months postdisaster (La Greca, Silverman, Vernberg, & Prinstein, 1996). Similarly, 1 year after Hurricane Katrina, 61% of elementary school children living in high impact areas screened positive for elevated PTSD symptoms (Jaycox et al., 2010). Approximately 2 years after Hurricane Katrina, 31% of parents surveyed reported their children had clinically-diagnosed depression, anxiety, or behavior disorders and 18% reported notable decreases in academic achievement (Abramson, Stehling-Ariza, Garfield, & Redlener, 2008).

To determine which children are more likely to have severe symptoms after disasters, school counselors need to find the answers to the following several questions (Rosenfeld, Caye, Ayalon, & Lahad, 2005).

1. *What were the characteristics of the disaster?* Longer duration and higher intensity results in more severe symptoms (La Greca, 2008).
2. *What was the child's exposure to the disaster?* Closer exposure and particularly perceived life threat results in more severe symptoms (La Greca, Silverman, Lai, & Jaccard, 2010).
3. *What are the characteristics of the student including age, gender, and prior victimization?* Females and younger children tend to have more severe symptoms as do children with prior abuse or victimization (Becker-Blease et al., 2010).
4. *What is the student's interpersonal, cultural, and social context?* Children with stronger interpersonal support from caring family members and peer support tend to have less severe symptoms (La Greca et al., 2010). Children from groups with less economic and sociopolitical power such as ethnic minorities and other marginalized populations tend to have more severe symptoms. Differing cultures and religions attribute different meaning and respond differently to a disaster. For example, some Mexican American Catholics may view a disaster as a consequence for a sin while some European American Protestants may view the disaster as a random act of nature.
5. *What is the wider, social, political, and economic context including disaster planning and relief efforts?* Children who perceive and receive more support and resources from community members, government agencies, NGOs, tend to have less severe symptoms. In contrast, children who perceive the government is against them may have more severe symptoms (Abramson et al., 2008).

In addition to using these questions to identify children at-risk, school counselors can screen children by using assessments such as the *Child's Reaction to Traumatic Events Scale-Revised* (Jones, Fletcher, & Ribbe, 2002) or the *Disaster Experiences Questionnaire* (Scheeringa, 2005).

EVIDENCE-BASED APPROACHES FOR TREATMENT

Evidence-based approaches for the prevention and treatment of severe symptoms in children after a disaster are selected based on the phase of disaster (La Greca & Silverman, 2009). The first phase of a disaster is pre-impact, at which time planning, training, and preparation is conducted before a disaster occurs. Evidence from La Greca and Silverman (2009) suggest the most appropriate intervention during this phase is cognitive behavioral psychoeducation to increase understanding of disasters and coping mechanisms in children and faculty members. The second phase is the impact phase, which occurs immediately after a disaster. La Greca and Silverman stated that the intervention with the most evidence is psychological first aid (PFA) (Brymer et al., 2006). "PFA is an evidence-informed modular approach to help children, adolescents, adults, and families ... designed to reduce the initial distress caused by traumatic events and to foster short- and long-term adaptive functioning and coping" (p. 5). This intervention is delivered one-on-one in about 15 to 20 minutes usually at a disaster relief center, medical facility, or near the site of the disaster after safety has been established.

The third phase of disaster recovery is short-term adaptation, which usually occurs days and weeks after a disaster. One approach with strong evidence that has been used with children in fourth grade and above is cognitive behavioral interventions after trauma in schools (CBITS) (Jaycox et. al., 2010). CBITS was designed to be delivered in 10 group sessions and one to three individual sessions in a school setting. After CBITS was provided to 57 fourth through eighth grade children with high trauma exposure during Hurricane Katrina and resulting clinical symptoms. These children showed clinically and statistically significant reduction in PSTD and depression (Jaycox et al., 2010).

The fourth phase of disaster recovery is long-term adaptation, which usually occurs months and years after disaster. La Greca and Silverman (2009) stated the intervention with the strongest evidence during this phase is trauma focused-cognitive behavioral therapy (TF-CBT; Cohen, Mannarino, & Deblinger, 2012). TF-CBT helps resolve trauma symptoms in children through strategies summarized in the acronym PRACTICE as follows: **P**sychoeducation and parenting skills, **R**elaxation, **A**ffect modulation, **C**ognitive coping and processing, **T**rauma narrative, **I**n vivo mastery of trauma reminders, **C**onjoint child-parent sessions, and **E**nhancing future safety and development. After TF-SBT was provided to 22 fourth through eighth grade children with high trauma exposure during Hurricane Katrina and resulting clinical symptoms, these children showed clinically and statistically significant reduction in PSTD and depression (Jaycox et. al., 2010). It is important for school counselors to note that in the Jaycox et. al. (2010) study, 98% of the children randomly assigned to the school based intervention actually participated while only 37% of the children randomly assigned to the community-based clinic participated. Thus, school counselors should make every effort to facilitate disaster interventions in the school setting.

PROPOSED TREATMENT APPROACHES AND TECHNIQUES

Theoretical Underpinning of Play Approach

Play therapy is commonly used by elementary school counselors because it is a developmentally appropriate approach that is an essential tool for counseling children (Ray, Armstrong, Warren, & Balkin, 2005). According to the Association for Play Therapy (APT, 2012), play therapy is the systematic use of a theoretical model to establish an interpersonal process wherein trained play therapists use the therapeutic powers of play to help clients prevent or resolve psychosocial difficulties and achieve optimal growth and development. Landreth (2012) stated that the premise of play therapy is to use the therapeutic, nonjudgmental, permissive relationship between counselor and child to promote healing in children ages 3 through 10 years old. Counselors utilize toys, art, sand, and other play media as the primary medium for communication with clients.

The evidence base for effective play therapy practice has grown in the new millennium (Baggerly, Ray, & Bratton, 2010). Bratton, Ray, Rhine, and Jones' (2005) meta-analysis of 93 play therapy research studies demonstrated an effect size of .80, indicating a large treatment effect. There is also evidence that play therapy is an effective intervention for school children's academic achievement and their disaster recovery. Blanco and Ray (2011) showed that child centered play therapy (CCPT) significantly improved elementary school children's academic achievement as measured by the *Young Children's Achievement Test* when compared to the control group. After a large earthquake struck Taiwan, Shen (2002) demonstrated that CCPT significantly decreased children's anxiety and suicidal risk when compared to the control group.

When providing play therapy to traumatized children, there are three commonly used theoretical approaches: (1) CCPT (Landreth, 2012), (2) cognitive behavioral play therapy (CBPT) (Knell & Dasari, 2009); and (3) trauma-focused integrative play therapy (TF- IPT) (Gil, 2011). The premise of CCPT is to facilitate a healing therapeutic relationship between counselor and child and allow the child to lead the session while the counselor provides therapeutic responses (Landreth, 2012). Through CCPT, children can express their emotions and thoughts about the disaster on their own timetable to gradually make meaning of their experience and achieve mastery over their emotions and behavior.

In contrast to the child-directed approach of CCPT, some school counselors use a more directive play therapy approach: CBPT (Knell & Dasari, 2009). CBPT has been shown to have a small to moderate treatment effect size when utilized with traumatized children (Drewes, 2009). Cognitive behavioral play therapy's premise is that cognitions shape behaviors and the reconceptualization of distorted or faulty thinking or attributions of traumatic events by children will change their maladaptive behaviors and relieve anxieties. Young children's egocentric thinking may cause them to believe that they are solely responsible for problematic or disastrous occurrences. By utilizing therapeutic toys such as puppets or relaxation exercises, the school counselor educates students to promote understanding of traumatic event and master coping behaviors.

In an effort to combine both the child-directed approach of CCPT and the directive approach of CBPT, Gil (2011) developed trauma-focused integrative play therapy (TF-IPT) to provide posttraumatic treatment for children. TF-IPT integrates tenets of CCPT (e.g., nonjudgmental therapeutic relationships) and CBT strategies into play and expressive arts therapies. By using TF-IPT, school counselors can provide the integrative work that respects the student's pacing, defensive mechanisms, and symbolic play as well as more directive interventions to assist the student's processing of trauma. Additionally, the TF-IPT model advocates for guardian/parental involvement in treatment as an effective adjunct to any type of traumatic treatment intervention.

Play Therapy Interventions

Although CBITS and TF-CBT have strong evidence for decreasing trauma symptoms after disasters, the study by Jaycox et al. (2010) was implemented with children fourth through eighth grade rather than younger children. Play is a developmentally appropriate approach for younger children (Landreth, 2012) and school counselors commonly implement play therapy (Ray et al., 2005). Play therapy has a growing evidence base in treating younger children (Baggerly et al., 2010; Green & Christensen, 2006). Therefore, we recommend school counselors integrate play, PFA, CBITS, and TF-CBT as well as play therapy (CCPT, CBPT, or TF-CBT) into different components of their comprehensive developmental school guidance program. According to the ASCA's *National Model* (2012), the delivery system of a comprehensive school guidance program entails school guidance curriculum, individual student planning, responsive services, and system support (ASCA, 2012). The following paragraphs describe methods for integrating play and play therapy into these components as part of a disaster response plan.

Guidance Curriculum

Once school is resumed after a disaster, school counselors are encouraged to implement several play therapy activities in classroom guidance lessons to achieve the goals of TF-CBT (Shelby & Felix, 2005). First, school counselors can normalize common postdisaster symptoms via puppet shows. For example, a wise puppet such as an owl can reassure a scared puppet such as a kitten that being scared, wetting the bed, and having stomach aches usually last only a short time. Second, school counselors can teach relaxation strategies by asking children to tighten their muscles like a soldier and relax like a ragdoll. Third, school counselors can facilitate affect modulation by teaching students soothing mantras such as, "Take deep breaths in through your nose and out through your mouth" and leading them in art activities that depict a safe, calm place. Finally, school counselors can encourage positive cognitive coping and processing by teaching students to "Change the CD" so scary thoughts are replaced by their favorite inspirational song.

Individual Student Planning

As discussed above, school counselors need to screen students to determine which ones are likely to have severe reactions to the disaster. Children at-risk are ones (a) closest to exposure to the disaster, (b) experienced destruction of property or life including pets, (c) have limited support systems, and (d) have prior trauma such as abuse or family loss. Children who are at-risk should be provided responsive services as described below.

Responsive Services of PSA

All school counselors are strongly encouraged to download the free PSA manual and participate in online training at www.nctsn.org so they will be ready to implement PSA at their school as needed. Strategies for integrating play into PSA have been demonstrated in a video by Baggerly (2006) and include using puppets to make contact with children, art activities and games to teach coping skills, as well as many other play based strategies described above.

Responsive Services of Small Group Play Therapy

Since research demonstrates that peer support is one of the biggest influences in long term disaster recovery (La Greca et al., 2010), small group play therapy is essential for children at risk for PTSD after a disaster. Small group play therapy is facilitated between counselors and perhaps two to four children where play-based activities are introduced for a common psychotherapeutic goal that meets the needs of all children involved. The following play therapy activities are recommended for implementation in three to five small group counseling sessions. These activities can be initiated either before or after 20 minutes of CCPT and after each student has participated in the guidance lessons described above.

The first group play therapy activity is "The Coping Box" (Baggerly, 2007; Green, 2007; Shelby & Felix, 2005). It is based upon the trauma-focused cognitive behavioral paradigm, which includes children utilizing art to discover new and effective coping strategies. First, the school counselor obtains an old shoe box for each child and prompts them to place construction paper around the box and use a lid to cover it. Next, children look through magazines and cut out symbols or images that represent parts of their identity or something they can do to feel better during distress. The children glue the pictures on the box. The school counselor and the children write 10 coping strategies on 10 precut squares of construction paper. The children place the paper in their box, another child draws out a strategy, and the school counselor guides them in a role play to practice the coping strategy.

After children have demonstrated the consistent ability to use coping mechanisms, the next group play therapy activity is bibliotherapy. The school counselor reads a children's story about trauma recovery such as *A Terrible Thing Happened* (Holmes, 2000) or *Brave Bart* (Shephard, 1998) in a soothing, calm voice. The purpose of bibliotherapy is to facilitate systematic desensitization by verbally and symbolically facing fears through interaction with the book's content, character, and images. The school counselor can ask children to use puppets or toys to demonstrate how the book character's responded to the disaster. Then they can discuss how the character's response was similar to, or different, from their own reactions.

A similar bibliotherapy activity is for school counselors to read, "Life Doesn't Frighten Me at All" by Maya Angelou (Green, Crenshaw, & Drewes, 2011). The school counselor asks the children to identify an image in the story that was prominent. Next, the school counselor asks the students to draw a line down the middle of the page and create a scene of something they fear on the left side of the paper. The school counselor observes in attentive silence. After the students are finished, the school counselor discusses the scene by discussing the symbols in the image: (a) "Did the story remind you of anything from your own life?" (b) "If you were in this image, how would you be feeling?" (c) "What story does this scene tell?" (d) "What occurred before/after this scene?" "If you could give this scene a title, what would it be?" Last, the school counselors ask the students to illustrate the concept of finally conquering their fear and anxiety so that it is manageable by illustrating it on the right side of the paper.

In the final group play therapy session, school counselors can re-emphasize coping strategies. Yet, rather than externalizing the coping mechanisms as in the Coping Box, students will be asked to internalize the coping mechanisms through "A Coping Heart" (Baggerly, 2007;

Green, 2009; Shelby & Felix, 2005). The purpose of this intervention is to increase children's awareness of internalized coping strategies that can enhance future safety and development. The school counselor provides students with a piece of red construction paper with a predrawn large heart on it outlined in a dark color. The school counselor instructs the children to draw a line down the middle of the heart and a line across the middle of the heart so that there are roughly four equal sections. The children then consider activities they typically engage in to make themselves feel better when they are afraid or distressed. The children draw one of their coping activities in each of the four sections on the heart. After they are finished drawing, two small holes on the top edge of the heart are made by a hole puncher. The school counselor cuts a piece of yarn long enough to go around a child's neck and ties the heart around each child's neck. The school counselor instructs each child to tell others in the group what their coping strategies are and possibly role play them for the group. Last, school counselors remind students that they have the ability to protect their heart and keep it safe from harm by practicing and implementing these adaptive ways of coping with traumatic anxiety.

Responsive Services of Individual Play Therapy

If students continue to exhibit severe symptoms after they have received classroom guidance lessons and small group play therapy, school counselors should consider providing individual play therapy. The school counselor can implement CCPT, CBPT, or TF IPT depending on the training of the school counselor. The purpose of individual play therapy after disasters is to provide a safe and protected space for the student to gradually play out their trauma narrative in a symbolic manner with the toys (Baggerly, 2006). In vivo mastery of trauma reminders can be achieved as children play with toys or materials that represent aspects of the disaster while school counselors provide soothing therapeutic responses such as reflecting feelings, facilitating understanding, or enlarging the meaning. After children appear to reach a sense of mastery in their individual play, school counselors can facilitate a restorative re-telling of the child's trauma narrative by asking the child to draw or use sand tray miniatures to show what happened before, during, and after the disaster. The school counselor can reinforce the child's resilience by highlighting his or her strengths, courage, sense of meaning, and bright future.

System Support

School counselors are caring and competent leaders who provide system support after a disaster. One way of providing system support is to implement the following tasks recommended by the National Child Traumatic Stress Network (2012):

1. Provide support, consultation, training, and technical assistance, as needed, to school staff
2. Provide mental health recovery information, referrals, and support to parents
3. Promote staff self-care and teach adults stress-reduction techniques
4. Maintain close contact and open communication with children, staff, and parents
5. When authorized by the principal, serve as a liaison with community-based agencies and monitor the work of community mental health professionals providing services to children on campus

School counselors can also provide parents and teachers helpful guides, available at www.nctsn.org and http://www.7-dippity.com/other/op_storm.html. In addition, school counselors can collaborate with local disaster relief agencies and provide resource lists for government agencies (e.g., FEMA) and NGOs (e.g., the American Red Cross and Save the Children).

CASE STUDY WITH APPLICATION OF TREATMENT RECOMMENDATIONS

Juanita and Michael, the children described in the beginning of this chapter, are case composites to protect the confidentiality of the children. Both children exhibited common reactions after a disaster, specifically uncharacteristic withdrawal and aggression. The school counselors first provided PFA with play activities infused to help stabilize the children. Juanita particularly enjoyed having a stuffed animal to hug as well as blowing soap bubbles to calm down. Michael enjoyed containing his picture of a tornado in a sealed envelope and doing muscle relaxation by stiffening muscles like a soldier and relaxing like a ragdoll.

The school counselor phoned the children's parents to inform them of their children's difficulty and provided emotional support. The school counselor sent home a parent's guide from NCTSN (National Child Traumatic Stress Network) as well as a donated department store gift card for the family. After a consultation with Juanita and Michael's teachers, the school counselor provided a guidance lesson in the children's classrooms. The puppet show that identified common disaster responses seemed to engender empathy in other children. Several of Juanita's classmates said they would invite her over to their homes to play with toys. Michael's classmates agreed to play dodge ball with him during recess.

Two weeks after the disaster, teachers and parents indicated that Juanita and Michael were having nightmares and avoiding things related to the disaster. The school counselor identified other children of similar ages who were exhibiting ongoing difficulty and scheduled three small group counseling sessions. In session one both groups made a coping box. In session two, the school counselor read *A Terrible Thing Happened* to Juanita's group and *Life Doesn't Frighten Me at All* to Michael's group followed by art activities. In session three, Juanita's group made a coping heart necklace while Michael's group made a coping shield to remind them of the skills they learned.

Sensing that both Juanita and Michael needed to process their trauma story individually, the school counselor scheduled three individual play therapy sessions for each child. Juanita played with the doll house during CCPT. She exhibited play themes of danger and loss as she repeatedly placed snakes on top of the doll house which would "eat' the farm animals. Eventually, she demonstrated mastery by having army men chase the snakes away and having an angel take the animals to farm heaven. At the end of each session, the school counselor prompted Juanita to use the sand tray miniatures to show what happened before, during, and after the fire. In the first session, Juanita did so quietly without much affect. In response to the school counselor's prompt in the second session, she verbalized her feelings of terror and as well as her thought that she should have saved her cat. The school counselor validated her with "You were really scared and sad just like most people would be. You wish you could have saved your cat. It was not your fault. You did the smartest thing by keeping yourself safe. Tell me about the happy memories of your cat that you will hold in your heart." By the third session, Juanita was able to verbalize the entire story with appropriate affect and a sense of resolution, indicating internalized mastery.

During Michael's individual CCPT sessions, he played with the blow up punching doll (i.e. "Bobo"). His play theme was aggression as exhibited by repeatedly punching and sitting on the Bobo. Gradually, he developed mastery by dressing up like a police man and handcuffing Bobo in the corner. At the end of the first session, the school counselor guided him in drawing a cartoon story of what happened before, during, and after the tornado. His heavy scribbling with red and black colors indicated his anxiety despite a flippant attitude. At the end of the second session, the school counselor prompted him to draw thought and feeling bubbles for each cartoon section. He reluctantly wrote, "I thought I was going to die" and "Mad and sad that grandpa did die." The school counselor reflected his courage with, "You were smart enough to know how dangerous it really was. You feel mad and sad that grandpa died. Your sadness shows what a caring boy you are." In the third session, Michael drew a picture of himself as a super hero with a shield coving a big heart. He said he was flying in the sky so his grandfather could see him from heaven. The school counselor validated his intent with, "You want your grandpa to know you are a brave, strong, and caring boy and most importantly you know that you are."

SUMMARY

Professional school counselors who utilize the ASCA *National Model* (2012) to generate and execute a comprehensive, developmental guidance program can address the potentially decimating psychological aftermath in traumatized students following a natural disaster. Specifically, competent school counselors are prepared to follow their school's crisis plan in conjunction with the faculty and staff personnel so that it is a seamless, coordinated effort that minimizes student chaos and systemic confusion. In the predisaster phase, school counselors deliver classroom guidance lessons to increase students' understanding of disasters and coping strategies. In the impact phase, school counselors integrate play therapy interventions into PSA. In the short-term adaptation phase, school counselors provide classroom guidance lessons to reenforce previously developed coping strategies, screen for at risk students, schedule small group play therapy sessions, provide parent and teacher behavioral consultations, and coordinate external disaster relief resources for families. In the long term adaptation phase, school counselors provide individual play therapy (Blanco & Ray, 2011) to help students master a restorative retelling of their trauma narrative, mostly symbolically and/or creatively, for trauma integration to occur.

To effectively implement this integrative responsive services paradigm, as part of the school counselors' comprehensive developmental guidance program after a natural disaster, all school counselors are encouraged to pursue professional development by completing the Psychological First Aid online training, attending advanced disaster recovery and play therapy training, and developing resource lists of local disaster relief agencies. The most essential feature for school counselors to remember during and immediately following a natural disaster is to remain calm, reassure students that they are safe, and begin working in collaboration with staff, parents, and the community to coordinate efforts so that every student is ensured an equal chance at recovery. Resilience in elementary school-aged students following a natural disaster begins simply with a warm, caring school counselor who provides the psychological safe space for students to freely play out their fears at their own pace. Ultimately, through the safety and strength inherent in compassionate and caring school counselor-student relationships, children begin to feel OK about themselves and re-imagine a life of enjoyment again.

RESOURCES

After the Storm: A guide to help children. Retrieved from www.7-dippity.com/other/op_storm.html

Association for Play Therapy. Retrieved from www.a4pt.org

Child Trauma Academy. Retrieved from http://www.childtrauma.org

Disaster Mental Health & Crisis Stabilization for Children Video. Retrieved from http://www.emicrotraining.com/product_info.php?products_id=214

FEMA for Kids. Retrieved from http://www.fema.gov/kids/

National Center on Children and Disasters. Retrieved from http://www.childrenanddisasters.acf.hhs.gov/resources.html

National Child Traumatic Stress Network. Retrieved from http://www.nctsn.org

Psychological First Aid: Field Operations Guide. Retrieved from http://www.nctsnet.org/nccts/nav.do?pid=typ_terr_resources_pfa

Self Esteem Shop. Retrieved from http://www.selfesteemshop.com/

Trauma Focused Cognitive Behavioral Therapy. Retrieved from http://tfcbt.musc.edu/

REFERENCES

Abramson, D., Stehling-Ariza, T., Garfield, R., & Redlener, I. (2008). Prevalence and predictors of mental health distress post-Katrina: Findings from the Gulf Coast Child and Family Health Study. *Disaster Medicine and Public Health Preparedness*, *2*(2), 77-86.

American School Counselor Association. (2012). *The ASCA national model: A framework for school counseling programs* (3rd ed.). Alexandria, VA: Author.

Association for Play Therapy. (2012). *Play therapy clinical definition*. Retrieved from http://www.a4pt.org/ps.index.cfm?ID=2289

Baggerly, J. N. (2006). *Disaster mental health and crisis stabilization for children*. (Video). Framingham, MA: Microtraining Associates.

Baggerly, J. (2006). Preparing play therapists for disaster response: Principles and procedures. *International Journal of Play Therapy*, *15*(2), 59-81.

Baggerly, J. (2007). International interventions and challenges following the crisis of natural disasters. In N. B. Webb (Ed.), *Play therapy with children in crisis* (3rd ed., pp. 345-367). New York, NY: Guilford.

Baggerly, J., Ray, D., & Bratton, S. (Eds.). (2010). *Child-centered play therapy research: The evidence base for effective practice*. Hoboken, NJ: John Wiley.

Becker-Blease, K. A., Turner, H. A., & Finkelhor, D. (2010), Disasters, victimization, and children's mental health. *Child Development, 81,* 1040-1052. doi:10.1111/j.1467-8624.2010.01453.x

Black, S. (2001). Disaster's aftermath: Rebuilding schools is one thing—rebuilding children's lives is quite another. *American School Board Journal, 188*(4), 52-54, 56.

Blanco, P. J., & Ray, D. C. (2011). Play therapy in elementary schools: A best practice for improving academic achievement. *Journal Of Counseling & Development, 89*(2), 235-243. doi:10.1002/j.1556-6678.2011.tb00083.x

Bratton, S., Ray, D., Rhine, T., & Jones, L. (2005). The efficacy of play therapy with children: A meta-analytic review of the outcome research. *Professional Psychology: Research and Practice, 36*(4), 376-390.

Briere, J. (1996). *Trauma symptom checklist for children*. Odessa, FL: Psychological Assessment Resources.

Brymer, M., Jacobs, A., Layne, C., Pynoos, R., Ruzek, J., Steinberg, A., Vernberg, E., & Watson, P. (National Child Traumatic Stress Network and National Center for PTSD) (2006 July). *Psychological first aid: Field Operations Guide* (2nd Ed.). Retrieved from www.nctsn.org

Cohen, J. A., Mannarino, A. P., & Deblinger, E. (2012). *Trauma-focused CBT for children and adolescents: Treatment applications*. New York, NY: Guilford.

Drewes, A. (Ed.). (2009). *Blending play therapy with cognitive behavioral therapy: Evidence-based and other effective treatments and techniques.* Hoboken, NJ: John Wiley.

Gil, E. (2011). *Helping abused and traumatized children: Integrating directive and nondirective approaches*. New York, NY: Guilford.

Green, E. J. (2007). The crisis of family separation following traumatic mass destruction: Jungian analytical play therapy in the aftermath of hurricane Katrina. In N. B. Webb (Ed.), *Play therapy with children in crisis: Individual, Group, and Family Treatment* (3rd ed., pp. 368-388). New York, NY: The Guilford Press.

Green, E. J. (2009). Teaching self-empowerment skills gives children a voice. *ASCA School Counselor, 13*(3), 11-17.

Green, E. J., & Christensen, T. (2006). Children's perceptions of play therapy in school settings. *International Journal of Play Therapy, 15*(1), 65-85.

Green, E., Crenshaw, D., & Drewes, A. (2011, October 13). *Depth approaches to foster resilience in children following trauma.* A half-day workshop presented at the annual association for Play Therapy International Conference, Sacramento, CA.

Guha-Sapir, D., Vos, F., Below, R., & Ponserre, S. (2010). *Annual Disaster Statistical Review 2010: The Numbers and Trends. Brussels: CRED.* Retrieved from http://cred.be/sites/default/files/ADSR_2010.pdf

Holmes, M. (2000). *A terrible thing happened—A story for children who witnessed violence or trauma*. Washington, DC: Magination Press.

Jaycox, L. H., Cohen, J. A., Mannarino, A. P., Walker, D. W., Langley, A. K., Gegenheimer, K. L., ... & Schonlau, M. (2010). Children's mental health care following Hurricane Katrina: A field trial of trauma-focused psychotherapies. *Journal Of Traumatic Stress, 23*(2), 223-231.

Jones, R. T., Fletcher, K., & Ribbe D. R. (2002). Child's Reaction to Traumatic Events Scale-Revised (CRTES-R): A self-report traumatic stress measure.

Knell, S., & Dasari, M. (2009). CBPT: Implementing and integrating CBT into clinical practice. In A. Drewes (Ed.), *Blending play therapy with cognitive behav-*

ioral therapy: Evidence-based and other effective treatments and techniques (pp. 321-352). Hoboken, NJ: John Wiley.

Kronenberg, M. E., Hansel, T., Brennan, A. M., Osofsky, H. J., Osofsky, J. D., & Lawrason, B. (2010). Children of Katrina: Lessons Learned about Postdisaster Symptoms and Recovery Patterns. *Child Development, 81*(4), 1241-1259.

La Greca, A. (2008). Interventions for posttraumatic stress in children and adolescents following natural disasters and acts of terrorism. In R. C. Steele, T. D. Elkin, & M. C. Roberts (Eds.), *Handbook of evidence-based therapies for children and adolescents: Bridging science and practice* (pp. 121-141). New York, NY: Springer Science.

La Greca, A. M., & Silverman, W. K. (2009). Treatment and prevention of posttraumatic stress reactions in children and adolescents exposed to disasters and terrorism: What is the evidence? *Child Development Perspectives, 3*(1), 4-10. doi:10.1111/j.1750-8606.2008.00069.x

La Greca, A. M., Silverman, W. K., Lai, B., & Jaccard, J. (2010). Hurricane-related exposure experiences and stressors, other life events, and social support: Concurrent and prospective impact on children's persistent posttraumatic stress symptoms. *Journal Of Consulting And Clinical Psychology*, doi:10.1037/a0020775

La Greca, A. M., Silverman, W. K., Vernberg, E. M., & Prinstein, M. (1996). Symptoms of posttraumatic stress after Hurricane Andrew: A prospective study. *Journal of Consulting and Clinical Psychology, 64*, 712-723.

Landreth, G. (2012). *Play therapy: the art of the relationship* (3rd ed.). London, England: Routledge.

National Child and Traumatic Stress Network. (2012). Retrieved from http://www.nctsn.org/trauma-types/natural-disasters/tornadoes#tabset-tab-5

Pane, J., McCaffrey, D. F., Kalra, N., & Zhou, A. (2008). Effects of student displacement in Louisiana during the first academic year after the hurricanes of 2005. *Journal of Education for Children Placed at Risk, 13*(2), 168-211. Retrieved from http://www.rand.org/pubs/reprints/2008/RAND_RP1379.pdf

Ray, D. C., Armstrong, S. A., Warren, E., & Balkin, R. S. (2005). Play therapy practices among elementary school counselors. *Professional School Counseling, 8*(4), 360-365.

Rosenfeld, L. B., Caye, J. S., Ayalon, O., & Lahad, M. (2005). *When their world falls apart: Helping families and children manage the effects of disasters*. Washington, DC: NASW Press.

Scheeringa, M. S. (2005). *Disaster experiences questionnaire* (Unpublished manuscript). Tulane University, New Orleans, LA.

Shelby, J. S., & Felix, E. D. (2005). Posttraumatic play therapy: The need for an integrated model of directive and nondirective approaches. In L. A. Reddy, T. M. Files-Hall, & C. E. Schaefer (Eds.), *Empirical based play interventions for children* (pp. 79-104). Washington, DC: American Psychological Association.

Shen, Y. (2002). Short-term group play therapy with Chinese earthquake victims: Effects on anxiety, depression, and adjustment. *International Journal of Play Therapy, 11*(1), 43-63.

Shephard, C. (1998). *Brave Bart—A story for traumatized and grieving children*. Clinton Township, MI: Trauma and Loss in Children.

CHAPTER 9

CHILDREN WITH AN INCARCERATED PARENT

Child-Centered Play Therapy

M. Ann Shillingford, S. Trice-Black, and M. Whitfield-Williams

There can be no keener revelation of a society's soul than the way in which it treats its children.

—Nelson Mandela

Parental incarceration is a significant problem in today's society (The Sentencing Project, 2009). Children of incarcerated parents are often left with a single parent who has to struggle to make ends meet, or with relatives such as grandparents who themselves may be grappling with considerable personal challenges (i.e., financial concerns, health issues). Children with an incarcerated parent may experience an overwhelming amount of academic, social, and behavioral struggles and may be left with feelings of alienation and abandonment possibly resulting in long-term negative outcomes.

Integrating Play Techniques in Comprehensive School Counseling Programs, pp. 167–184

Vignette 1

George is a well-dressed 7-year-old who is walking down the hallway to his classroom. Mary, a kindergartener happily skipping down the same hallway accidentally bumps into George. He immediately grabs Mary by the arm and shoves her against the wall. George proceeds to scream at Mary that he never wants her to touch him again. The teacher separates the children and tries to calm George down. He is brought to the school counselor who tries to engage George in conversation or at best calm him down. During their conversation, the counselor discovers that George's father was recently incarcerated.

Vignette 2

Diamond is a 6-year-old who resides with her grandmother. Her mother, who raised her thus far, has been incarcerated for the past 8 months. Diamond's grandmother is also taking care of her ailing grandfather and four younger cousins. Today Diamond comes to school crying and when asked, expresses that she misses her mom. Her teacher shares that she cries often in class and will sometimes refuse to complete assignments. Diamond rarely completes homework and appears to be withdrawn and disengaged. The school counselor tries to decide the most appropriate approach for Diamond's situation.

DEFINITION OF THE ISSUE

Evidence suggests that children are greatly affected psychologically, socially, and financially when a parent is incarcerated (Ming, 2011). This disruption of the family unit serves as a critical barrier to the development of children (Rukuni, 2006). These children are often traumatized by sudden separation when their parent is abruptly taken away (Simmons, 2000). When parents are in and out of prison, the results are disturbances in a child's life. These disruptions can cause confusion and emotional damage if not handled properly.

According to the U.S. Department of Health and Human Services (2002), children may experience: withdrawal, anxiety, depression, and poor peer relations due to the absence of a parent and/or the disruptions caused by parental incarceration. In addition, these children contend with feelings like anxiety, shame, sadness, grief, social isolation and guilt (Phillips & Gates, 2011). Children of incarcerated parents may also begin to engage in high risk delinquent behaviors such as robbery, arson, and physical altercations (Aaron & Dallaire, 2010).

Moreover, children with incarcerated parents face dramatic emotional imbalance as a result of lack of communication with their parents and they may have no one else to whom they can turn. Children may experience feelings of helplessness and a sense of loss of control, decreased hope and lower emotional stability (Young & Smith, 2000). These feelings are aggravated as some parents and caregivers are too ashamed to explain the cause of separation or may refuse to answer questions posed by children. Mazza (2002) explains that many children feel confused and abandoned and may have no idea what happened to their parents (i.e., they may know their parents are gone but don't know *where* they are). Although some children's concerns are manifested through confusion, anger, or resentment towards their parents, others blame the criminal justice system and officers that took their parents away. Further complicating the feelings children of incarcerated parents may be experiencing, school personnel, including school counselors, may feel unsure of how to discuss the situation with the child and therefore may not mention the circumstances to the child; this complexity may add to the child's feelings of isolation, shame, and confusion.

PREVALENCE INCLUDING STATISTICS

There are over 10 million minor children in the United States who have experienced parental incarceration, including at least 2.3 million children with a currently incarcerated parent (Center for Children of Incarcerated Parents, 2011). Children of state and federal prisoners represented about 2.3% of all U.S. children in 2007, including 6.7% of all Black children, 2.4% of all Latino children and 0.9% of all White children (Glaze & Marushak, 2008). Today, there are approximately 810,000 incarcerated parents with more than 1.7 million children under the age of 18, one third of whom will turn 18 while their parent(s) is incarcerated (Glaze & Maruschak, 2008). Because incarcerated mothers are more likely than incarcerated fathers to live with their children prior to being incarcerated (Glaze & Maruschak, 2008; Smith, Krisman, Strozier, & Marley, 2004), increase in the number of children with an incarcerated parent largely reflects a doubling of the number of women in state or federal prison from 63,000 in 1990 to 116,000 in 2008 (West & Sabol, 2009). Additional statistics suggests that (a) approximately 6% of all children entered the foster care system due to parental incarceration in 2003 (Allard & Lu, 2006); (b) children with fathers who have been incarcerated are 25% more likely to experience economic hardship than children whose fathers have not been incarcerated (Bendheim-Thoman Center for Research on Child

Wellbeing, 2008); and (c) children of incarcerated parents are more likely to live with caregivers who abuse drugs and have mental health problems, and to experience sexual or physical abuse and neglect (Phillips, Burns, Wagner, Kramer & Robbins, 2002).

Unfortunately, children of inmates have a reduced opportunity to develop protective factors such as ability to communicate openly and connectedness. Stress resulting from a family member's incarceration reduces the ability of the family to promote optimal growth and development of its members. When a family experiences severe levels of stress, resources are often used to reduce stress, rather than promote positive outcomes.

IMPACT OF PARENTAL INCARCERATION ON CHILDREN'S SOCIAL, ACADEMIC AND BEHAVIORAL FUNCTIONING

Parental incarceration increases the risk that children will experience later behavioral and emotional problems, have troubles in school, and become involved in the juvenile and criminal justice system (e.g., Murray & Farrington, 2005). In addition to these challenges, many of these children are likely to live in single parent, impoverished households characterized by residential mobility, and their caregivers are likely to experience poor mental and physical health (Poehlmann, 2005). School counselors may be knowledgeable of familial instability including family violence, poverty, child abuse and/or neglect, parental mental illness, maternal history of sexual and physical abuse, high levels of neighborhood violence, and a host of other risk factors that, by themselves, could explain the elevated risk factors for children of incarcerated parents (Glaze & Maruschak, 2008; Parke & Clarke-Stewart, 2003).

However, longitudinal and quasi-experimental research studies have found that parental incarceration is not merely a proxy for preincarceration risk factors (e.g., family poverty, parental substance abuse, and child abuse/neglect) but has an independent effect on the emotional and behavioral development of children (Huebner & Gustafson, 2007; Murray & Farrington, 2005; Phillips et al., 2002). Children with an incarcerated parent are at an increased likelihood of exhibiting symptoms of depression, eating and sleep disorders, anxiety and hyperarousal (Lee, Genty, & Lavar, 2005; Parke & Clarke-Stewart, 2003), conduct disorder (Phillips et al., 2002), antisocial personality disorder (Murray & Farrington, 2005), and attention-deficit/hyperactivity disorder (Phillips et al., 2002). Thus, it is no surprise that children with an incarcerated parent are more likely to be expelled or suspended from school (i.e., for fighting and/or insubordination; see Hanlon et al., 2005), even after controlling for other risk factors such as child abuse or neglect, residential instability, parental substance abuse or mental illness, and poverty (Phillips et al., 2002).

Children sometimes cope with the stigma of having an incarcerated parent by withdrawing from pro-social groups and affiliating with non-conforming peers from whom they receive acceptance and support (Eddy & Reid, 2003). Affiliating with antisocial peer groups may partly explain why children with an incarcerated parent have an increased likelihood of engaging in delinquent and criminal behavior (Eddy & Reid, 2003) and are more likely to be arrested and/or incarcerated as juveniles (Murray & Farrington, 2005). Therefore, it is important that these students receive appropriate interventions to mitigate the potentially damaging effects caused by their parental incarceration. The American School Counselor Association (ASCA, 2000) reported in a position statement that school counselors should provide student assistance programs to better support students and their families who may be experiencing crisis or other traumatic incidents. The statement further explains that these programs should include identification of any problem behaviors that may be impacting the student and then continued with referral and follow-up services where needed. As such, school counselors are ideally placed to recognize effects of parental incarceration on their students social, academic and behavioral functioning.

REVIEW OF EVIDENCED BASED APPROACHES FOR TREATMENT

In spite of the challenges faced by children with an incarcerated parent, there is a paucity of evidence-based approaches noted in the literature. Approaches that have been introduced support the use of theoretical interventions. For example, Shillingford and Edwards (2008) noted positive results in a case study where Glasser's (1998) Reality therapy was utilized in individual sessions with a student who had been experiencing significantly negative behavioral difficulties in school and at home. Through individual meetings using a Reality therapy approach, this student was able to make more positive choices, thereby improving his academic and social functioning. Engstrom (2008) used a family intervention approach supported by Pearlin, Mullan, Semple, and Skaff's (1990) stress-process theory to support children whose mothers are incarcerated by including the grandmother caregivers in the counseling process. Engstrom underscored the importance of including the grandmothers as part of the intervention strategies as they may very well be the main source of support for the children of incarcerated parents. Engstrom found encouraging results by engaging grandmothers in this collaborative process.

In recognition of the growing number of children affected by parental incarceration and their heightened risk for adverse outcomes, several programs have been developed with a focus on youth and young children. These programs include mentoring and after-school programs. Examples of mentoring programs include the Seton Youth Shelters: Mentoring Children of Prisoners (MCP) Program in Virginia, which was founded in 2006. This program has demonstrated effectiveness for increasing children's interest in school, developing better relationships with their family, and improving communication skills in expressing their issues or problems. Family members report a positive change in the youth's attitude, increased interest in school, completion of homework, and greater interest in their well-being.

Another program, Project SEEK, conducted by the Michigan Department of Mental Health in Flint, Michigan intended to reduce the negative effects of parental incarceration. Starting in 1989, SEEK identified and recruited children through their imprisoned parents; provided services at a community site and in family homes; offered support groups for children; fostered communication between children and their incarcerated parents; provided caregivers with advocacy and referrals; and conducted an evaluation as part of all their activities. In 10 years of operation, Project SEEK increased caregiver ratings of children's cognitive skills, increased children's academic self-esteem, reduced the number of school changes per child, increased adolescents' locus of control, decreased adolescents' self-reported delinquent behavior and substance abuse, and decreased the rate at which incarcerated parents in participating families returned to prison (www.fcnetwork.org/reading/mott.html).

In addition to these mentoring approaches, a small number of agencies have offered after-school programs specifically for prisoners' children. These programs typically offer a combination of peer and academic support as well as social and recreational activities. Originally known as Aid to Imprisoned Mothers (AIM), then as Aid to Children of Imprisoned Mothers, the Forever Family program in Atlanta, Georgia began offering after-school services in 1997. This program was designed to help children cope with the psychological consequences of maternal incarceration, and includes academic support services, social-recreational activities, emergency assistance and referrals (Forever Family, 2012).

In light of the limited evidence-based interventions for children with incarcerated parents, the following section highlights the advantages of play therapy, which has long been supported in literature. Significant evidence for the benefits of using play therapy with children who experience varied psychological and behavioral concerns is presented. Due to the momentous research on the effects of play on children, the authors consider this approach to be a useful avenue for school counselors who are tasked with providing support for children living without a parent due to parental incarceration.

THEORETICAL UNDERPINNING OF CHILD-CENTERED PLAY THERAPY

Through child-centered play therapy (CCPT), professional school counselors can enter the world of elementary school students by using children's play and toys as a common language (Landreth, Ray, & Bratton, 2009). Children can express their feelings and thoughts through play, which is a developmentally natural form of communication for children. In comparison to adults, children are developmentally limited in cognitive verbalization as a primary means of communication and, therefore, play therapy presents an appropriate medium (Bokszczanin, 2007). Indeed, play therapy matches with Piaget's theory of cognitive development (Ray, 2005). Specifically, according to Piagetian theorists, play is the most developmentally appropriate means of communication for young children (ages 2-7) who are likely in the preoperational stage of cognitive development and may lack language skills in comparison to their internal awareness. Even as children mature into the concrete operations stage of cognitive development (ages 8-11) they are limited in abstract reasoning and can use play to bridge the gap between experiences, affect and cognition (Landreth, 2012). Through the vehicle of play, children are able to communicate feelings and thoughts that are often difficult to express verbally.

CCPT has its roots in person-centered therapy and was first developed by Virginia Axline, a former student of Carl Rogers. As with person-centered therapy, the nondirective approach to CCPT is based on the belief that everyone has the innate ability to strive towards self-actualization within a safe and nurturing environment. Axline (1947) outlined eight necessary principles for therapeutic relationships with children: (a) a warm, friendly relationship with the child; (b) acceptance of the child as he/she is; (c) an environment of safety in order to help the child freely express his/herself; (d) sensitivity, awareness, and reflection of the child's feelings; (e) respect for child's ability and responsibility to institute change; (f) trust in child as evidenced by allowing the child to lead; (g) awareness and respect for gradual process of CCPT; and, (h) the establishment of necessary limits.

Through child-centered play therapy, children are able to direct their own growth (Landreth, 2012). Children's feelings about themselves influence their development and their ability to produce change. Play allows children opportunities to experience control and self-confidence, and to process difficult experiences such as separation from an incarcerated parent (Kot & Tyndall-Lind, 2005; Schaefer & Carey, 1994).

The absence of an incarcerated parent threatens the safety and security of a child's environment. However, the safe, supportive, nurturing environment established when counselors use CCPT, allows children to communicate and process difficult, often intense emotions and thoughts, process their own needs and strive towards self-actualization. By projecting intense feelings and emotions towards toys, and experiencing control and mastery over situations in fantasy, children experience empowerment rather than helplessness (Robinson, 1999; Webb, 1999). As feelings of mastery become incorporated in a child's sense of self, self-concept and self-efficacy are enhanced. When provided with an appropriate, supportive environment, children can develop an awareness of their feelings, respect for these feelings, and expression and acceptance of these feelings, which in turn, allows children better control rather than being controlled by their feelings. Responsibility for one's self develops through mastery over one's feelings.

Trust, as an integral component of CCPT, allows the counselor to trust in the process and to trust that the child has the capacity to meet his or her own needs. It is often difficult for adults to trust that children can rely on their own innate abilities to problem solve. For example, in CCPT, children may struggle with a simple toy and ask for assistance. Although many adults may feel compelled to rush to assist children as a means of helping them, by allowing children to struggle, to rely on themselves, and to problem solve on their own, children develop a sense of mastery and belief in self. When working with children, it is often tempting for counselors to suggest activities or to direct the counseling session. By directing the child, the counselor thwarts the child's abilities to discover his or her own potential and inhibits the self-actualization process. This next section explains non-directive child centered play techniques followed by sample sessions applicable in the school setting.

SPECIFIC PLAY TECHNIQUES WITH DESCRIPTION

Specific play techniques for a CCPT approach include the establishment of an appropriate counseling environment, facilitative responses, and limit-setting. Within each of these techniques is the foundational belief that the child directs and leads counseling sessions. The application of these techniques allows children to discover their innate abilities and take responsibility for their own growth and progress.

Environment

A private, safe, welcoming environment is necessary for child-centered play therapy. Professional school counselors, who may not have access to a large, permanent playroom, can create their own play therapy bags or carts with selected toys. These mobile play therapy units can assist professional school counselors as they work with children in a variety of settings. Toys encourage children to communicate through play, thus, the selection of toys is an importance component of CCPT. Landreth (2012) stated that "toys should be selected rather than collected (p. 133)." Through the provision of a wide variety of toys, children may experience and demonstrate responsibility and decision-making in the counseling environment. Counselors should select real-life toys, acting-out aggressive release toys, and toys for creative expression and emotional release (Landreth, 2012). Examples of real-life toys include dolls, animals, puppets, kitchen kit, cars, and a phone, which can allow children to express lived-experiences. Acting-out aggressive release toys include soldiers, boxing gloves, stuffed wild animals, and a hammer. Aggression-release toys can provide avenues for children to express hostility and anger. Toys for creative expression and emotional release can include clay, crayons, and blocks, which can be mastered and manipulated easily as well as facilitate the development of a positive self-image (Landreth, 2012).

Facilitative Responses

Facilitative responses track children's behaviors, feelings, and thoughts in a nonjudgmental manner. Tracking may feel awkward as counselors begin their practice, yet tracking communicates to children that the counselor is present, aware, and accepting, which promotes security and the safety to explore difficult issues. For example, a child may begin painting to which the counselor may state, "You have decided to paint." With a smile on his/her face, the child may hold the completed picture up for the counselor to see. Many adults may be inclined to provide evaluative feedback, such as, "That's a beautiful picture," thus conveying a judgment (whether positive or negative) However, child-centered play therapy emphasizes the importance of nonevaluative statements, such as, "You are proud of your picture" in order to help children become aware of and rely on their own feelings, an integral part of the empowerment process.

Limit Setting

Limits are an essential component of child-centered play therapy (Landreth, 2012). Only necessary limits should be established in the therapeutic relationship. Some limits must be established such as not harming self or others. Even the simple fact that the counseling session must end is a limit that needs to be established and enforced; this is particularly crucial in a school environment where the structure of the environment is qualitatively different from clinical settings. Limits can be set in the form of choices, thereby honoring the child's natural ability to make positive behavioral choices. For example, the school counselor might say "you can play with all the toys in this play area however; they will need to remain in the play area and not outside of it." The child now has the choice of playing in the selected area (positive) or throwing toys outside of that area (negative). Landreth (2012) developed the A.C.T. method of limit setting in order to provide children with the opportunity to develop self-control and also to recognize that they have choices. The A.C.T method is three-fold and includes (a) *acknowledging the feeling* (e.g., reflecting the child's feelings with statements such as "I can see you're feeling angry…"); (b) *communicate the limit* (e.g., "you may throw the ball BUT the bat is not for throwing"); and (c) *target appropriate choices* (takes the child's attention away from the item of focus to an alternative choice "you can choose to throw the bean bags also if you like". By providing children with choices, CCPT counselors can still provide children with power and control over their own emotions and behaviors as well as promotes appropriate boundaries.

SAMPLE OUTLINE OF THREE TO FIVE SESSIONS IN A SCHOOL ENVIRONMENT

Objectives in child-centered play therapy are broad and focus on the person rather than the problem. An overriding objective is to provide a warm, caring, accepting environment where the child can discover and rely on internal strengths (Landreth, 2012). Guerney (2001) signified four stages in child-centered play therapy: the warm-up stage, the aggressive stage, the regressive stage, and the mastery stage. The four stages are ordered and gradual throughout the counseling process. Children's behaviors during these stages are as varied and unique as individual children themselves and thus should be compared to baseline behaviors. In the *warm-up stage*, the child experiences uncertainty about the counseling relationship and the establishment of trust. During the *aggressive stage*, children's aggressive behaviors, both internalized and externalized, reach a peak. During the *regressive stage* of CCPT, as children move away from aggressive behaviors, developmentally regressive behaviors often appear. Examples of behaviors during this stage could include acting like a baby or exhibiting helpless, dependent behaviors. Finally, in the *mastery stage*, children verbally express or use play to express their confidence in themselves. For example, children may competently play in age appropriate activities or may act out feelings of competence such as that of a superhero.

A sample of four sessions in the school setting, according to Guerney's four stages of CCPT, follows. However, it is important to note that children's progression through the stages is varied. Some children may move from one stage to the next in one session. Others may spend a few sessions leaving one stage and entering the next.

Stage 1/Warm-Up Stage

During the first session which falls within the warm-up stage, the counselor must introduce the child to him/herself and to the counseling environment, which should contain toys from each of the categories previously mentioned: scary, nurturing, expressive, fantasy, and aggressive toys. The most important part of the initial session is to begin building the relationship with the child, who may not be familiar with the professional school counselor other than through the guidance curriculum (classroom presentations). Sensitivity, gentleness, and acceptance are of paramount importance during this session as the counselor first makes contact with the child. Landreth (2012) suggests introducing the child to the counseling environment in a short phrase such as, "this is our playroom, and this is a place where you can play with the toys in a lot of the ways you would like to" (p. 183). This introduction encourages the child to begin leading and emphasizes the freedom that the child has to choose which, if any, toys to play with and to choose how, he/she would like to play with these toys. Limits are introduced from the initial session as the counselor explains to the child how long they will be meeting. Landreth (2002) recommends that the counselor sit in a chair rather than towering over the child authoritatively or sitting on the floor, which might communicate that the counselor expects to be a play participant. Although these counseling behaviors seem minimal, the verbal and nonverbal communication patterns employed convey to the child that the counselor accepts the child the way he/she is. This unconditional acceptance and affirming approach can be very powerful.

Stage 2/Aggressive Stage/Session 2

After a child becomes familiar and more comfortable with the counselor and the counseling environment, he/she moves into the aggressive stage. During this stage, children feel safe enough to begin to explore underlying issues, such as the feelings they experienced when their parent was incarcerated. As the child begins to explore through play, he/she is likely to test limits and to engage in behaviors of defiance. By continuing to provide unconditional positive regard and genuineness, along with setting limits when necessary, the professional school counselor can provide a nurturing space in which the child feels safe and accepted. Reflecting the child's feelings and tracking the child's behaviors as she/he explores through play consistently reinforces the counselor's acceptance of the child.

Stage 3/Regressive Stage/Session 3

Following the aggressive stage, children move into the regressive stage, which is marked by regression into earlier developmental behaviors. As mentioned previously, children may exhibit infant or toddler behaviors such as pretending to suck from a bottle, talking in a baby voice, or appearing helpless and asking for assistance. Although it is often difficult, as adults have a tendency to want to rescue or protect children, the counselor should restrain from assisting the child with activities, and instead allow him/her to struggle and to achieve mastery. Guerney (2001) notes that during this stage, children often vacillate between dependency and independence as a way of testing the safety of the environment and his/her abilities.

Stage 4/Mastery/Session 4

During the mastery stage, children exhibit fewer aggressive and regressive behaviors and, instead, begin to consistently exhibit behaviors of assurance and competence. In various ways, children communicate their sense of mastery to the counselor. For example, some children may simply engage in play that is age appropriate, thus signifying that he/she is comfortable and confident. Some children may act out their sense of mastery in fantasy, such as acting like a superhero. Other children may point out their accomplishments in building a tower or drawing a picture. Throughout the sessions, as the counselor provides nonevaluative reflections, the child can become aware of and rely on his or her own feelings and thoughts, thus developing mastery. Feelings that once were the master over the child, such as fear, anger, helplessness or shame regarding the circumstances of their incarcerated parent, are now accepted, controlled, and mastered.

It is important to remember that behavioral changes may be evolutionary; specifically, change occurs over time and may not be immediately observed. As each student goes through the four stages, the school counselor should communicate with parents/guardians, teachers, and other stakeholders how the child's actions are being influenced and what outcomes are expected. Parents and teachers may become increasingly frustrated as the child goes through each stage but particularly the aggressive and regressive stages, especially if the behaviors are being carried into the classroom or home environment. Clear and consistent communication will need to be conveyed as to what exactly is happening during these stages stakeholders should be provided with appropriate interventions for supporting the child when outside of the play environment.

CASE STUDY

The following case study is presented as an illustration of the application of CCPT, a nondirective approach for working with children with whose parent is incarcerated.

The Client and Presenting Problems

Samantha was a 7-year-old White female, who resided with her grandmother and four siblings. Her mother had been incarcerated for the past three years due to drug related charges. Samantha was referred to the school counselor by her teacher and grandmother who are both concerned about her disrespect for teachers and fighting with classmates.

The school counselor who had been employed at this school for several years was familiar with Samantha and had worked with her previously. Due to their familiarity with each other, Samantha appeared comfortable with the counselor and came into the meeting excited and in a rather talkative mood. The school counselor scheduled Samantha for 30-minute individual weekly meetings for 5 consecutive weeks. Her counseling schedule had been coordinated with her teacher and agreed upon by her grandmother, it was also agreed that any work missed would be made up later that day and at home.

Goals of Sessions

During the first session with Samantha (Warm-up stage), the goal was to introduce Samantha to the counseling environment. Although Samantha was familiar with the school counselor, it was still important to set a foundation of acceptance, freedom to express feelings, and necessary limit setting. During the first meeting, the professional school counselor sat in a chair and gestured around the room, stating, "this is a play area and you are welcome to play with all the toys." The counselor set limits which included explaining the times and dates of their meetings. The school counselor stated, "We will get together on Tuesdays mornings from 9:00 until 9:30 (points at a clock in the corner of the room). This is your time in the playroom." Samantha was initially hesitant to engage in play and expressed that "it is childish." Many adults may want to respond by reassuring the child that it is okay to play with toys. However, in child-centered play therapy, it is important to create an environment of acceptance of the child's feelings. Thus, the school counselor replied, "You think it is childish to play with the toys." Samantha responded, "I think playing with those is childish (points to some stuffed animals). Those are baby toys. I want to play with the dollhouse (points at the dollhouse, smiling and jumping up and down)." The counselor responded, "You don't want to play with the stuffed animals because you think they are childish. You are excited to play with the dollhouse." In the previous statement, the counselor communicated acceptance of Samantha's feelings and her desires, thus empowering her with the ability to make decisions.

During the subsequent sessions, moving from the Warm-Up to the Aggressive Stage, Samantha became more comfortable expressing her feelings and began to test limits. Difficult feelings such as frustration, anger, and sadness that she felt regarding the absence of her mother began to appear in play. For example, during the second meeting, Samantha was looking through the dollhouse for a doll she played with the previous week and could not find it. Samantha picked up one of the dollhouse toys and yelled, "Where's my doll?" The counselor responded, "You are frustrated because you can't find your doll." Samantha held the dollhouse toy in her hand and pulled, stating, "I am strong. I can throw this far." The counselor responded, "You are proud that you are strong and can throw a long way." Samantha pulled her arm back, as if to throw and seemingly aimed the toy at the counselor and stated, "I am stronger than you!" The counselor acknowledged her feelings and set necessary limits by responding, "You think that you are stronger than me and you want to throw the toy at me. You may not throw the toy at me, but you may throw the ball at those blocks (pointing at the building blocks)." By accepting Samantha's feelings and allowing her to express these feelings, while setting limits in a safe environment, the counselor conveyed acceptance of Samantha. More importantly Samantha became more aware of her own feelings, and began to feel more confident and empowered.

Following the Aggressive Stage and moving to the Regressive Stage, Samantha who was usually talkative and engaging selected a baby bottle and began to speak in a baby voice while feeding a small doll. The occurrence went as such:

Samantha: Drink baby, mama's gonna take good care of you.
Counselor: You are feeding the baby.
Samantha: Waaaaa—no more milk—waaaaa—milk all gone. (Samantha was crying).
Counselor: You are sad because there is no more milk for the baby.
Samantha: Samantha wants to sip her little bottle but there isn't any milk. Samantha is hungry.
Counselor: You are sad and hungry and want some more food but it's all gone.
Samantha: Can you get the baby something else? Find another bottle. I can't find one.
Counselor: You want to find something else to feed the baby. I think you can find something.
Samantha: (looking around the room, grabbed a spoon): This is the baby's spoon. She can eat big girl food now (begins putting the spoon in the baby's mouth).

In the previous exchange, the counselor encouraged Samantha to solve her own problems and achieve mastery, rather than attempting to fix the problem for her.

During the final stage, mastery, Samantha exhibited behaviors that reflected her sense of mastery over her feelings in comparison to her feelings of anger controlling her, which were expressed prior to counseling in fighting with other classmates and disrespect towards her teacher. Throughout her sessions with the school counselor, Samantha was able to express her feelings in an accepting and safe environment, which allowed Samantha to develop confidence in and acceptance of herself. In the final stage, Samantha communicated her sense of mastery through play. Samantha engaged in independent, age appropriate play. In playing with the dollhouse, Samantha decorated the rooms with the doll furniture in ways that she found pleasing and announced, "Look at my house. Doesn't it look good? I fixed it all by myself!" The school counselor reflected and reinforced her feelings of pride in stating, "You are proud that you fixed the house all by yourself!" Both teacher and grandmother reported positive changes in Samantha's behaviors in school and at home. The counselor recommended Samantha for one of her small counseling groups and continued to provide support to her.

SUMMARY

The need to support children surviving without a parent due to parental incarceration is imperative. These children are often struggling with numerous academic, social, and behavioral concerns as well as stigmatization from society due to their parent's incarceration. Because of the training that school counselors receive in their graduate programs, they are in an ideal position to provide necessary supports for these children. It is well understood, however, that due to the limited time and resources that may be available to these professionals, counseling services often need to be abbreviated. Play therapy provides that practical flexibility needed in the school setting to implement these services. This chapter provided school counselors with a CCPT approach to counseling and highlighted useful technique for successfully executing these services to students with an incarcerated parent.

REFERENCES

Aaron, L. & Dallaire, D. H. (2010). Parental incarceration and multiple risk experiences: Effects on family dynamics and children's delinquency. *Journal of Youth & adolescence, 39*(12), 1471-1484

Allard, P. E., & Lu, L. D. (2006). Rebuilding families, reclaiming lives. New York: Brennan Center for Justice. Retrieved from http://www.brennancenter.org/content/resource/rebuilding_families_reclaiming_lives/

American School Counselor Association. (2000). The professional school counselor and student assistance programs. Retrieved from http://schoolcounselor.org/content.asp?pl=325&sl=127&contentid=178

Axline, V. M (1947). *Play therapy.* Cambridge, MA: Houghton Mifflin.

Bendheim-Thoman Center for Research on Child Wellbeing. (2008). *Parental incarceration and child wellbeing in fragile families.* (Fragile Families Research Brief No. 42). Princeton, NJ: Princeton University. Retrieved from www.fragilefamilies.princeton.edu/briefs/ResearchBrief42.pdf

Bokszczanin, A. (2007). PTSD symptoms in children and adolescents 28 months after a flood: Age and gender differences. *Journal of Traumatic Stress, 20*, 347-351.

Center for Children of Incarcerated Parents. (2011). *Data sheet 3A: How many are there?* Retrieved from http://www.xilinx.com/support/documentation/data_sheets/ds529.pdf

Eddy, J. M., & Reid, J. B. (2003). The adolescent children of incarcerated parents: A Developmental perspective. In J. Travis, & M. Waul (Eds.), *Prisoners once removed: The impact of incarceration and reentry on children, families, and communities* (pp. 189-258). Washington, DC: The Urban Institute Press.

Engstrom, M. (2008). Involving caregiving grandmothers in family interventions when mother with substance abuse problems are incarcerated. *Family Issues, 47*(3), 357-371.

Foreverfamily. (2012). Surrounding children with the love of family. Retrieved from http://www.gadisciples.org/organizations/Women/ForeverFamily/foreverfamily.htm

Glasser, W. (1998). *Choice theory in the classroom.* New York, NY: HarperCollins.

Glaze, L. E., & Maruschak, L. M. (2008). Parents in prison and their minor children. Retrieved from http://bjs.ojp.usdoj.gov/index.cfm?ty=pbdetail&iid=823

Guerney, L. (2001). Child-centered play therapy. *International Journal of Play Therapy, 20*(2), 13-31.

Hanlon, T. E., Blatchley, R. J., Bennett-Sears, T., O'Grady, K. E., Rose, M., & Callaman, J. M. (2005). Vulnerability of children of incarcerated addict mothers: Implications for preventive intervention. *Children and Youth Services Review, 27,* 67-84.

Huebner, B., & Gustafson, R. (2007). The effect of maternal incarceration on adult offspring involvement in the criminal justice system. *Journal of Criminal Justice, 35*(3), 283-296.

Kot, S., & Tyndall-Lind, A. (2005). Intensive play therapy with child witnesses ofdomestic violence. In L. A. Reddy, T. M. Files-Hill, & C. E. Schaefer (Eds.), *Empirically based play interventions for children* (pp. 31-49). Washington, DC: American Psychological Association.

Landreth, G. L. (2012). *Play therapy: The art of the relationship*. New York, NY: Taylor & Francis.

Landreth, G. L., Ray, D. C., & Bratton, S. C. (2009). Play therapy in elementary schools. Psychology in the Schools, *46*(3), 281-289.

Lee, A., Genty, P. M., & Laver, M. (2005). *The impact of the adoption and safe families act on children of incarcerated parents*. Washington, DC: Child Welfare League of America.

Mandela, N. (n.d.). Children's quotes. Retrieved from http://www.brainyquote.com/quotes/keywords/children.html

Mazza, C. (2002). And then the world fell apart: The children of incarcerated fathers. *Families in Society: The Journal of Contemporary Human Services, 83*, 521-529

Ming, M. D. (2011). *The impact of family, community, and resilience on African-American young adults who had parents incarcerated during childhood.* (Unpublished dissertation). Andrews University, Michigan.

Murray, J., & Farrington, D. P. (2005). Parental imprisonment: Effects on boys' antisocial behaviour and delinquency through the lifecourse. *Journal of Child Psychology and Psychiatry, 46*, 1269-1278.

Parke, R., & Clarke-Stewart, K. A. (2003). The effects of parental incarceration on children: Perspectives, promises, and policies. In J. Travis (Ed.), *Prisoners once removed: The impact on incarceration and reentry on children, families, and communities* (pp. 189-282). Washington, DC: The Urban Institute Press:

Pearlin, L. I., Mullan, J. T., Semple, S. J., & Skaff, M. M. (1990). Caregiving stress and the stress process: An overview of concepts and their measures. *The Gerontologist, 30*, 583-594.

Phillips, S., & Gates, T. (2011). A conceptual framework for understanding the stigmatization of children of incarcerated parents. *Journal of Child & Family Studies, 20*(3), 286-294

Phillips, S. D., Burns, B. J, Wagner, H. R., Kramer, T. L., & Robbins, J. M. (2002). Parental incarceration among youth receiving mental health services. *Journal of Child and Family Studies, 11*, 385-399.

Poehlmann, J. (2005). Children's family environments and intellectual outcomes during maternal incarceration. *Journal of Marriage and Family, 67*, 1275-1285.

Ray, D. C. (2005). Play therapy practices among elementary school counselors. *Professional School Counseling, 8*, 360-365

Robinson, R. (1999). Unresolved conflicts in a divorced family: Case of Charlie, age 10. In N. B. Webb (Ed.), *Play therapy with children in crisis* (pp. 272-293). New York, NY: Guilford Press.

Rukuni, T. L. (2006). Human service professionals: Assessing the needs of children of incarcerated parents (Unpublished dissertation). Michigan State University, Michigan.

Schaefer, C. E., & Carey, L. (1994). Family play therapy. Northvale, NJ: Jason Aronson.

Shillingford, M. A., & Edwards, O. W. (2008). Application of choice theory with a student whose parent is incarcerated: A qualitative case study. *International Journal of Reality Therapy, 28,* 41-44

Simmons, C. W. (2000). Children of incarcerated parents. *California Bureau Note,* 7(2), 1-11

Smith A, Krisman K, Strozier, A. L., & Marley, M. A. (2004). Breaking through the bars: Exploring the experiences of addicted incarcerated parents whose children are cared for by relatives. *Families in Society, 85*(2), 187-195.

The Sentencing Project. (2009). Incarceration. Retrieved from http://www.sentencingproject.org/template/page.cfm?id=107

U.S. Department of Health & Human Services. (2002). From prison to home: The effects of incarceration and reentry on children, families, and communities. Retrieved from http://aspe.hhs.gov/hsp/prison2home02/parke&stewart.pdf

Young, D. S., & Smith, C. (2000). When moms are incarcerated: The needs ofchildren, mothers and caregivers. *Families in Society: The Journal of Contemporary Human Services, 81*(2), 130-147.

Webb, N. B. (1999). The child witness of parental violence: Case of Michael, age 4, and follow up at age 16. In N. B. Webb (Ed.), *Play therapy with children in crisis* (pp. 49-73). New York, NY: Guilford Press.

West, H., & Sabol, W. (2009). Prison Inmates at the midyear 2008-statistical tables. Bureau of Justice Statistics. Retrieved from http://www.bjs.gov/content/pub/pdf/jim08st.pdf

CHAPTER 10

DEMONSTRATING SCHOOL COUNSELOR EFFECTIVENESS IN COUNSELING USING PLAY THERAPY TECHNIQUES

Jolie Ziomek-Daigle and Kelly Cowart

The purpose of this chapter is to highlight the efficacy of play therapy used by school counselors. In this chapter we first discuss the evolution of the school counseling specialty over the last century. Next, a discourse on the transforming school counseling initiative (TSCI) (Education Trust, 1997) will follow and information will be provided as to how this movement took shape on the cusp of the era of accountability. Accountability and assessment measures of the No Child Left Behind Act (NCLB, 2002) will be presented as well as the American School Counselor Association's (ASCA) response with the introduction to the ASCA *National Model* (2012). In the next section we examine advocacy and social justice strategies used to increase student achievement. The practice of using play therapy in the schools to improve student achievement, behavior, and connectedness will be the following section. Finally, a case study is included so that the reader can integrate all of the content presented in this chapter.

Integrating Play Techniques in Comprehensive School Counseling Programs, pp. 185–207

A Brief History of the School Counseling Profession

At the turn of the 20th century, the roots of school counseling began through the work of Frank Parsons and the founding of the vocational guidance movement. Impending social issues at that time included child labor, immigration, and urbanization thus the vocational guidance movement was created to assist in transitions from school or home to the workforce (Herr & Erford, 2011). The next 2 decades brought related allied professionals to the vocational movement along with their respective knowledge gained from curriculum offerings and practices. Professionals in student personnel, psychology, social work, and psychiatry all began to contribute to the vocational guidance movement. Individuals working in the area of vocational guidance were now bringing discipline-specific strategies in administration, testing, behavior management, advocacy, systemic work, and diagnosis and treatment. Toward the middle of the 21st century, counseling theories began to emerge. Once such theory was the person-centered approach in which the client and counselor work more collaboratively to achieve goals rather than counselor directed interventions. Herr and Erford (2011) suggest that the arrival of collaborative counseling theories (i.e., developmental and systems), which were proactive and adaptive in nature, provided fertile soil for school counseling models to grow.

The next few decades brought further definition of the school counseling specialty as well as special recognition and support from the federal government. This change occurred post World War II. The launching of Sputnik in 1957 helped the government conclude that the country was behind in math and science advances. The concern resulted in the passing of the National Defense Education Act of 1958 so that high achieving students could be identified and attend college. Federal funds were now being spent on the preparation and employment of school counselors who, in turn, would identify talented students for college majors in engineering, mathematics, and science. Herr and Erford (2011) concluded that this was the era when legislation and professionalization defined the field of school counseling. This professionalization of the school counseling specialty included the birth of several national organizations such as the ASCA and state standards for school counselor certification.

Several acts passed during the following decades that increased responsibilities for school counselors. The Carl D. Perkins Act of 1984 and the Elementary School Counseling Demonstration Act of 1995, along with local and state mandates for school counselors to become involved in issues of child abuse, drug abuse, and career education, all took place during this time. Due to school counselors assuming more responsibilities across developmental domains, comprehensive program models began to emerge to ensure accountability and cohesion of program components (Gysbers & Henderson, 1994). Also, toward the end of this era, we saw the birth of the TSCI (Education Trust, 1997) and the passage of NCLB (2002). The following section will describe how the school counseling profession increased accountability measures in training and practice

Transforming School Counseling and Accountability

The mid-90s brought standards-based reform, accountability measures, and advanced technologies (House & Martin, 1998). Leaders in the field wanted school counselors engaged in critical conversations regarding student achievement and prepared to show evidence-based results; particularly in student outcomes. Discussions as to whether school counselors should address issues of equity and access, as well as assume roles as advocates and leaders, were occurring (Paisley & Hayes, 2003). This transformative shift in school counseling would leave behind a more clinical, mental health model focused on the individual needs of students and create a greater focus on comprehensive program development in the areas of academic, career, and college aspirations of all students. As a result of this discourse and a response to the educational climate, many training programs made a commitment to value all the contributions school counselors can offer and meet both the academic and mental health needs of youth. Presently, students are being trained under a model that develops counselors to become skilled practitioners and educational leaders in the schools (Paisley & McMahon, 2001; Ziomek-Daigle, McMahon, & Paisley, 2008).

Educational reform efforts during this time also stimulated organizations such as the ASCA to develop national standards for programs. Additionally, ASCA's standards development concentrated on student competence in three broad domains: personal/social, academic, and career. Later, ASCA published the *ASCA National Model: A Framework for School Counseling Programs* (ASCA, 2012) to assist counselors in developing standards-based programs in four primary areas: foundation, management system, delivery system, and accountability.

Given that this is the age of accountability and educational reform, school counselors should not be complacent by only developing programs based on comprehensive models but should also present results that show positive student outcomes. So, the question is reframed from "*What do counselors do*?" to "*How are students different because of what school counselors do?*" (ASCA, 2012, p. 17). As Brown and Trusty (2005) suggest, "If school counselors expect to be credited with raising student achievement, they must provide clear-cut evidence that this occurs because of their interventions" (p. 13). Demonstrating outcomes like increasing graduation rates, improving standardized test scores, and decreasing behavior referrals is important to mark yearly progress and is often included in school wide improvement goals. However, data must clearly establish that the results are linked to school counseling interventions. Mixed methods of data collection and analysis such as observations, document analysis, focus groups, and multiple assessments may offer school counselors additional support in terms of substantiating effectiveness. An example of a school counselor using multiple assessments and data points will be discussed in the case study section of this chapter.

ADVOCACY AND SOCIAL JUSTICE WORK IN SCHOOLS

Recent accountability measures and transformative practices have allowed school counselors to identify educational and attainment gaps of all students but particularly those who might be poor and underrepresented. The school counseling profession has progressed from appreciating diversity and promoting multiculturalism to using advocacy and social justice strategies in schools. The United States is more diverse than ever and it is estimated that minority groups will outnumber majority groups by 2020 (Wasow, 2005). Interestingly, ASCA's skills of collaboration, advocacy, and use of data support school counselors in discovering gaps and developing appropriate interventions for traditionally marginalized students. Guided by Brofenbrenner's (1979) theory of ecological systems, school counselors can work within contextual influences and collaborate multisystsemically at the microlevel (with teachers, principals, allied professionals, and parents), at the mesolevel (with community leaders, agency administrators, and school district supervisors), and at the macrolevel (within state or national entities that deal with counseling and student achievement matters). Students from marginalized groups could benefit from school counselors advocacy efforts that affect student outcomes. Examples include the efforts of a school counselor to sponsor a student-led organization for lesbian, gay, bisexual, transgender (LGBT) youth and families (micro), advocate to increase gifted and advanced placement testing for minority students (meso), and present research to lawmakers when potential bills may cut funding (macro).

Assessing the Effectiveness of Play Therapy in Schools

The evolution of the school counselor whose focus was on the individual adjustment of students to the current transformative practitioner has occurred. As aforementioned, training programs are graduating students who have skills to work with K-12 youth as mental health specialists and educational leaders. By responding to student needs in the personal/social domain, school counselor practices may have the potential to impact other aspects of student growth and development, for example academics. Counseling strategies that have been used in schools for decades, such as play therapy, can be linked to increasing student achievement (Blanco & Ray, 2011; Baggerly & Bratton, 2010).

School counselors are professional educators with expertise in mental health who deliver "comprehensive developmental school counseling programs that promote healthy development, and provide prevention and intervention services as needed" (ASCA, 2012, p. 3). Prevention services anticipate potential problem areas and proactively offer learning opportunities (Gysbers & Henderson, 1994). Further, school counselors have the skill set to recognize and intervene when students experience emotional distress, academic difficulties, social complications, behavior problems, or other prevailing concerns that may impact academic achievement (Ziomek-Daigle, McMahon, & Paisley, 2008). The school counselor is trained in issues of mental health and may be the first, if not only person to whom a student is referred (Paisley & Hubbard, 1994).

Identifying early interventions that are effective for children and can be delivered in a highly accessible setting such as schools is a critical need for the 21st century (Landreth, Ray, & Bratton, 2009). According to Kochhar-Bryant (2010) an increasing proportion of the general school population is at-risk of academic failure, school dropout, and suicide. In particular, one in five children between the ages of nine and 17 have diagnosable mental health or behavioral disorders (Kochhar-Bryant, 2010). Over 20% of school age children experience mental health concerns and nearly 80% of these students will not receive any mental health services (Blanco & Ray, 2011). Students of low socioeconomic status may lack social capital (i.e., social relations that have productive benefits) and are likely to only receive these services from a school counselor as they may not have access to resources in their own communities. Even when resources do exist in the community, families may encounter other barriers such as no transportation or parents who work during nonschool hours on nights and weekends and therefore can't take their child for counseling services.

Blanco and Ray (2011) state that younger children are susceptible to a lack of mental health attention and the subsequent effects on student outcomes. Academic achievement is a significant predictor of whether or not young people will have either stable or marginalized economic lives in our increasingly complex world (Lapan, 2004). As child development specialists in the schools, counselors are uniquely qualified to create educational environments that promote the optimal cognitive, emotional, social, and behavioral development of children (White & Flynt, 1999). Academic self-efficacy is enhanced when school counselors provide developmentally appropriate interventions aimed at improving attitudes toward learning and academic skills. Academic competence allows students to maximize the instruction offered by teachers (Landreth, 2002). Experts contend that play therapy with youth in grades prekindergarten through high school and with diverse populations is a research-based and developmentally appropriate method of facilitating student growth (Baggerly & Bratton, 2010; Ray, Bratton, Rhine, & Jones, 2001). Therefore, play therapy offers students the opportunities to develop in the academic as well as personal/social and career domains during 30-minute sessions, a typical intervention time in the schools (Blanco & Ray, 2011).

PLAY AS A COMPONENT OF A SCHOOL COUNSELING PROGRAM

Play has the power to facilitate normal child development as well as alleviate potentially delayed or disrupted behaviors (Reynolds & Stanley, 2001). Piaget (1962) identified play as being vital to the cognitive, social, and emotional development of children. It is the native language of children (Landreth, 2002) and the therapeutic modality of choice when working with children (Dougherty & Ray, 2007). School counselors can embrace play therapy as a viable method of addressing a variety of social, emotional, behavioral, and developmental issues and view that counseling through play is not an adjunct to the school counseling program but is ideally infused into large group guidance, small group interventions, and individual counseling (Landreth, Strother, & Barlow, 1985). School counselors who value play therapy are likely to also incorporate it into their work with teachers and parents (e.g., kinder training, filial therapy).

Comprehensively integrating play therapy into the school-wide counseling program requires conceptualizing the modality in a much broader form than playroom-based delivery (Ray, Muro, & Schumann, 2004); for example, play can be integrated in the classroom, the small group setting, and in one-on-one work with students School counselors deliver services to students through classroom guidance, small group counseling, and individual counseling. Careful planning is essential when a school counselor intends to infuse play therapy into the counseling program. When designing the guidance curriculum, several questions are helpful to consider: (a) What does this specific population of students need? (b) How will students be different as a result of the guidance curriculum? (c) Are play therapy lesson plans empirically? and (d) How will learning be assessed? (Dimmitt, 2009).

Play in Classroom Guidance

Classroom guidance is where prevention and developmental education primarily take place. It is an instructional program that is comprehensive in scope, preventative and proactive, and developmental in design (ASCA, 2012). Through well-crafted, engaging lessons counselors are able to provide every student with the knowledge, attitudes, and skills that prepare them for a successful academic career, healthy relationships, and a promising future.

The ASCA *National Model* (2012) recommends that elementary level counselors spend 45% of their time engaged in classroom guidance, while middle school and high school counselors dedicate 35 and 25% of their time respectively. With nearly half of their time committed to classroom guidance, this seems the most logical place for elementary counselors to begin implementing play and play therapy techniques. Class sizes can vary from fifteen to thirty or more students. Therefore, directive play therapy interventions such as games, art, music, drama, and bibliotherapy are best suited for this form of delivery. Many practitioners have authored articles and books filled with play therapy and play-based interventions that can be adapted or modified for classroom guidance (Ashby, Kottman, & Degraaf, 2008; Goodyear-Brown, 2002; Hall, Kaduson, & Schaefer, 2002; Kaduson & Schaefer, 2010; Lowenstein, 1999; Swank, 2008).

The standards and competencies of the ASCA *National Model (*2012) have been established to ensure that every student receives instruction in the domains of academic development, personal/social development, and career development. For example, a competency in the academic domain may read, "Students will articulate feelings of competence and confidence as learners" (ASCA, 2012, p. 114). The developmental crosswalking tool assists counselors in deciding if this competency will be taught K-2, 3-5, 6-8, and/or 9-12. In an elementary setting, for example, this particular competency might be delivered through classroom guidance kindergarten through second grade, remediated through small group counseling in third and fourth grade, and be identified as a strength during individual academic planning in fifth grade. As stated earlier, knowledge regarding the needs of specific populations drives the design of curricula at individual schools (Dimmitt, 2009). This knowledge is gained through needs assessment, review of critical data elements, and garnering the perspectives of multiple stakeholders (i.e., conversations with advisory council, interview with administrators). Once the competencies of each grade level have been identified, the curriculum crosswalking tool provides a written format for planning the scope, and sequence, of yearlong guidance curriculum plans. This is the time for counselors to plan for the systematic incorporation of play into the classroom through guidance lessons.

Play in Small Groups

Many children require additional supports in order to reach their full academic, social, and emotional potential. Small groups provide counselors a forum for offering individualized prevention and remediation instruction in a time-efficient manner. The types of groups that counselors implement are as varied as the student populations they serve. Traditional groups may be remedial in nature, crisis oriented, or preventative in design. Play therapy groups allow counselors to focus on individual and group issues concurrently (White & Flynt, 1999). Interactions in small groups often reflect how children interact with others in the classroom. Small group counseling is the most authentic medium for children to learn about others, the ways in which they interact with others, and their impact on others (Ziomek-Daigle, McMahon, Paisley, 2008).

Children can, but do not have to be grouped by similar concerns (White & Flynt, 1999). Scheduling is less of a challenge when groups are comprised of children with varying counseling needs. For example, a kindergarten play group may be comprised of three students from the same classroom. The group might consist of one student experiencing transition to school difficulties, another student exploring issues regarding retention in kindergarten, and a third student adjusting to a new sibling at home. Groups may also be structured around a similar issue with students of varying ages and relationships. Baggerly (2004) demonstrated that elementary-aged siblings whose family had recently become homeless benefitted from sibling group play therapy to process the dramatic change in life circumstances. Research indicates that group play counseling has been effective with children receiving speech therapy services at school (Danger & Landreth, 2005), raising the self-esteem of fourth, fifth, and sixth grade students (Post, 1999), increasing the moral reasoning of ninth grade students (Paone, Packman, Maddux, & Rothman, 2008), and reducing anxiety in children who have witnessed domestic violence (Tyndall-Lind, Landreth, & Giordano, 2001).

Play in Individual Counseling

Students who are experiencing crisis or intense levels of disruption in their lives may necessitate the use of individual play therapy. Some children are not candidates for group therapy due to aggressive behaviors, sexual acting out, or severe emotional issues and need one-on-one assistance (White & Flynt, 1999). While school counselors are not trained nor can they spend their day providing in-depth therapy, as previously mentioned, many children do not have access to healthcare or a mental health provider.

Students who are struggling in the classroom may benefit academically from individual play therapy. Blanco and Ray (2010) found that individual child-centered play therapy significantly improved the academic achievement for at-risk first grade students. Further, an increase in students' self-efficacy was seen after just six individual play therapy sessions (Fall, 1999). In a study conducted by Ray, Henson, Schottelkorb, Brown, and Muro (2008) individual play therapy occurring at least twice weekly was shown to reduce teacher's perceptions of relationship stress with children demonstrating behavioral and social issues. The play therapy literature is rich in efficacious interventions with individual children. A review and analysis of such studies may be beneficial to school counselors hoping to reproduce such effective outcomes through play.

COUNSELOR AS CONSULTANT IN TRAINING OTHER SCHOOL-BASED PROFESSIONALS

Current research indicates that the relationship between student and teacher impacts achievement, connectedness to school, and interactions with peers (Edwards, Varjas, White, & Stokes, 2009). Positive teacher-student relationships are characterized by support, understanding, and invigorating learning experiences (White, Flynt, & Draper, 1997). A quality relationship enhances students' social bonding, resilience, and brain development resulting in effective learning and functional peer relationships (Chaloner, 2001; Edwards et al., 2009). Children who dislike school or their teacher are at risk of developing such hostility that they withdraw from the educational process altogether (Kuykendall, 2004). These feelings manifest in multiple behaviors such as: refusal to enter the classroom, wandering around the classroom, noncompliance with directions, incomplete work, disengagement from group activities, continual arguing with and aggression toward peers, crying, refusal to be consoled, frequent visits to the school nurse, absenteeism, and poor academic growth exacerbate negative teacher-student relationships (Chaloner, 2001; Draper, White, O'Shaunghessy, Flynt, & Jones, 2001). School counselors may have the opportunity to develop positive relationships among teachers and students by using consultation or staff development to present the basic facilitative skills of play therapy.

An example of an intervention, known as kinder therapy, engages teachers as part of the therapeutic process and teaches the use of basic play therapy skills for the classroom (White, Flynt, & Draper, 1997). Kinder Therapy is an adaptation of filial therapy. The kinder training manual developed by White, Draper, Flynt, and Jones (2000) outlines teacher learning, facilitator supervision, and classroom coaching procedures. Additionally, it allows school counselors to maintain an emphasis on developmental and preventative interventions for greater numbers of students. Teachers who participated in kinder training reported improved classroom management skills and student behavior as well as enhanced teacher child relationships (Edwards et al., 2009).

ASSESSMENT OF PLAY THERAPY IN A SCHOOL COUNSELING PROGRAM

"Accountability and evaluation of the school counseling program are absolute necessities" (ASCA, 2012, p. 7). As Young and Kaffenberger (2009) emphasize:

> For school counseling programs to be considered a pivotal and valued resource to the learning environment requires school counselors to commit to formulating and executing services that link school counselors' work to the instructional mission and concretely demonstrate accountability for student academic success. (p. 59)

Fortunately, the ASCA *National Model* (2012) establishes clear steps for accomplishing this important task beginning with garnering support from administrators and stakeholders. Assessment of play therapy based interventions must be conducted and shared in order for school administrators and other stakeholders to clearly acknowledge the alignment of a play therapy infused curriculum with the academic mission of the school. By using play interventions that have shown positive outcomes, counselors are more likely to be able to communicate to administrators, teachers, parents how students are different because of a developmental, comprehensive counseling program (Reynolds & Stanley, 2001).

The ASCA *National Model* (2012) encourages the collection of process, perception, and results data to measure the evaluation of the effectiveness of interventions implemented as part of the counseling program. Dimmitt (2009) define the three types of data in the following way: (a) *process data* is evidence that the intervention took place. It is data that answers the questions of who received the services, when the client received the intervention, and duration of intervention; (b) *perception data* identifies what children learned as evidenced by a change in feelings or beliefs, mastery of new skills, or an increase in knowledge, and (c) *results data* is the application of process and perception data to prove that an intervention either has or has not positively impacted achievement or achievement-related behavior such as attendance, discipline, or work completion.

Perception data can be acquired through assessment. There are many ways to evaluate student learning such as multiple choice tests, rating scales or rubrics, role plays, skill demonstration, portfolios, journals, informal or formal observation of student behavior, or student self- assessment (Holcomb-McCoy, 2007). Surveys and scaled questions that use a Likert-type scale can be used to identify changes in beliefs, attitudes, or opinions. Packaged curricula typically include pre- and posttests to aid in identifying and measuring impact (Dimmitt, 2009; Holcomb-McCoy, 2007).

To demonstrate the effectiveness of a first grade classroom guidance lesson regarding the process of making mistakes in order to learn, a school counselor begins with a survey for the teacher (see Appendix A). The teacher is asked to list students whose grades are being impacted due to difficulty completing work because of a fear of making mistakes (i.e., perfectionism). Students are given a pre-test examining their beliefs about mistakes based on five scaled questions (see Appendix B). The pre-test provides information to the counselor regarding students whom the teacher has expressed concerns about, perceptions of students regarding the teacher's expectations of perfection, and reveals students who may have perfectionistic tendencies or anxieties that have gone unnoticed by the teacher.

A play-based lesson is then taught using bibliotherapy and drawing. The counselor reads *Ish* by Peter Reynolds. The counselor and children then discuss how beginning efforts when learning something new are close-*ish* but not perfect. A Mr. Potato Head is set up where every child can see it. Each child is given paper and crayons and then asked to draw a picture that looks Mr. Potato Head-*ish*. Students then discuss with partners the parts of their drawings they are proud of and the parts that are –*ish* and may improve with practice. The counselor leads a discussion of how it felt to know that the drawing was intended to be Mr. Potato Head-*ish* and not perfect. Students identify tasks at school that they are willing to be-*ish* and not perfect. The pictures, with names omitted to protect the confidentiality of the students, are then hung in the hallway in an "*Ish* Gallery." The counselor follows up two weeks when returning for the next guidance lesson. The students complete the scaled questions and the teacher reports on the grades and work attempts of the students previously identified on the survey (see Appendix C). The perception data is analyzed for any changes in student beliefs. The results data is determined by analyzing student grades and teacher reports regarding number of work attempts before and after the lesson. The amount of positive change indicates the degree of effectiveness of the lesson.

Any results data indicating an efficacious impact on change in student attitudes, behaviors, and grades can be shared with stakeholders, such as administrators and the advisory council, to illustrate exactly how counselor-led, play-based interventions positively influence student achievement. Expanding the discussion to include ways in which successful large group lessons are translated into small group and individual interventions enhances stakeholders' understanding of the varied ways school counselors use play to meet the academic, social, and career needs of students.

CASE STUDY

Macey is a White, energetic, bright, healthy 6-year-old. Macey lives with her mother who is employed part-time, and two older sisters. The children qualify for the free lunch program at school. One sister is in fourth grade and the other is in sixth grade. Macey is of average size for first grade, is athletically built, and enjoys playing with the boys in her class. Academically, she is mastering the knowledge and skills of first grade. Macey is referred to the school counselor after being sent to an administrator for continual verbal arguments and name calling with her peers.

Working from a holistic perspective, the school counselor consulted with the teacher and parent in order to fully understand the child's world. Operating from the belief that children and adults can use play-based media to express themselves, the school counselor placed a basket of fidget toys, a bowl of moon sand, and Silly Putty on the table used for consultations. The use of the toys by Mrs. Jenkins, the teacher, allowed her to engage in anxiety reducing behaviors while encouraging the discussion of her feelings regarding Macey. Mrs. Jenkins reported that Macey exhibits difficulty staying on task, completing work, and frequently disrupts instruction by bickering with other students. In the teacher's words, Macey is "bullying" other students on the playground. Mrs. Jenkins expressed that she has a difficult time liking Macey. She feels this may be due, in part, to the fact that she is exasperated with the number of times a day different students report to her that Macey is bothering them or calling them "fat," "annoying," or "rambunctious." Mrs. Jenkins is frustrated that Macey's mother has not responded to invitations for a parent conference and that Macey regularly does not have any completed homework. Feelings of resentment, anger, and hopelessness were expressed by the teacher.

The counselor reflected the teacher's feelings and frequently offered encouragement regarding the positive strategies implemented by Mrs.

Jenkins. The counselor offered to contact the mother for a conference and agreed to start seeing Macey individually in the play room. The school counselor asked the teacher to begin keeping data. Mrs. Jenkins would record daily the two significant behaviors creating concern: student reports regarding Macey's social interactions and the number of redirections Macey needed to complete her work. Weekly classroom assessments would be used as well for achievement data purposes.

The school counselor called Macey's mom, explained her role at the school, and stated that she had some ideas about how to improve things for Macey. The counselor appealed to mom as the expert on her child and explained that the school needed her expertise. Macey's mom agreed to come in 2 days later. Both the assistant principal and Mrs. Jenkins were in attendance for the meeting. During the course of the conference, Macey's mom articulated her own feelings of disconnectedness from her child. She reported that as a petite woman with two other petite daughters she often found herself commenting to Macey about her weight and allowing the other daughters to call Macey "fat." The two older sisters enjoy quiet activities and are soft spoken while Macey is "rambunctious" and frequently "annoying." Macey's mother reported that she frequently feels overwhelmed by Macey and can understand how other children might feel 'bullied' by Macey. The school counselor helped the mom reframe her vision of Macey using words such as "athletic," "exuberant," "lively," "assertive," and "outgoing."

Mrs. Jenkins left the conference with a new understanding of her student. Knowledge of her student's home life created a sense of urgency within the teacher to affirm and encourage Macey. Mrs. Jenkins and the counselor collaborated to create a plan allowing Macey to have 10 minutes of one-on-one play time with Mrs. Jenkins every day. The counselor discussed with the teacher how to improve her relationship with Macey by adopting the therapeutic attitude of Axline's (1969) eight basic principles for therapists who work with children:

1. The therapist is genuinely interested in the child and develops a warm, caring relationship;
2. The therapist experiences unqualified acceptance of the child and does not wish that the child were different in some way;
3. The therapist creates a feeling of safety and permissiveness in the relationship, so the child feels free to explore and express herself completely;
4. The therapist is always sensitive to the child's feelings and gently reflects those feelings in such a manner that the child develops self-understanding;

5. The therapist believes deeply in the child's capacity to act responsibly, unwaveringly respects the child's ability to solve personal problems, and allows the child to do so;
6. The therapist trusts the child's inner direction, allows the child to lead in all areas of the relationship, and resists any urge to direct the child's play or conversation;
7. The therapist appreciated the gradual nature of the therapeutic process and does not attempt to hurry the process;
8. The therapist establishes only those therapeutic limits necessary to anchor the session to reality and which help the child accept personal and appropriate relationship responsibility.

The counselor also provided instruction on the language of encouragement (Dinkmeyer, McKay, & Dinkmeyer, 1980; Kottman, 1993) and the basic tracking skills of play therapy (Landreth, 2002) to be used during the ten minutes of play time. Mrs. Jenkins also read *Responsibility in the Classroom* (Lew & Bettner, 1995) at the counselor's suggestion. Macey's mother was agreeable to learning strategies to enhance her relationship with Macey. Using a modified version of child-centered filial play therapy (Landreth & Bratton, 2006), Macey and her mother were able to share connections through play. Macey's mother began affirming strengths that she observed in Macey while enjoying time with her daughter. Macey also participated in small group play therapy with the school counselor. After 2 weeks of play therapy with the counselor, Mrs. Jenkins, and her mother, Macey's mother and teacher began noticing differences in Macey at home and at school. Macey became more cooperative with her sisters, more compliant with her mother's requests, and initiated friendly conversations with her peers. After 4 weeks of play therapy with her teacher and counselor, as well as filial play with her mother, Macey began reporting to her mother, teacher, and the assistant principal how much she enjoys school.

The achievement data from grades, achievement-related data from the time-on-task record (see Appendix D), parent perception survey, and the results from the peer interaction data (see Appendix E) at the end of eight weeks indicated that Macey was consistently finishing her work without redirection, few students were reporting incidents regarding Macey to Mrs. Jenkins, her math and reading grades had improved by one letter grade, and both Macey and her mother reported increased happiness at home. The school counselor created a data report for the administrators indicating the interventions used and pre- and postintervention achievement data. The principal later requested that the school counselor offer a staff development session to the faculty regarding the outcomes and the skills the teacher learned. The integration of play therapy into every facet of the intervention and the use of data to document its effectiveness confirms that the school counselor's work contributed substantially to the success of this student.

CONCLUSION

Integrating play therapy into a comprehensive program is a promising option for school counselors. It is helpful to remember that play therapy is not just about techniques, rather it is "a way of being with children based on a deep commitment to certain beliefs about children and their innate capacity for growth" (Landreth, Ray, & Bratton, 2009). A commitment to developmentally appropriate practice with students must be built on an evidence-based foundation. In this age of accountability, it is crucial for school counselors to show intent and impact in their work with students. The collection and analysis of process, perception, and results data are central practices of today's school counselors. As leaders in the school building, counselors must to advocate for children's rights to participate in programming conducted in their first language of play. Effectively assessing student learning and outcomes enables school counselors to articulate to all stakeholders that play and play-based interventions work in tandem with academic instruction to achieve the mission of schools in valuable, concrete ways.

APPENDIXES DISPLAYED STARTING ON NEXT PAGE

Appendix A

Perfectionistic or Risk Anxiety Referral Form

Teacher Name ________________

Please answer the following questions before the "Ish" guidance lesson. Thank you!

Name of Student	Academic Context of Behaviors	Types of behaviors displayed	Tally the # of times child exhibits behaviors during the academic context identified for 1 week	Number of assignments completed in academic context over 1 week
Example: *Ryder*	*Writer's Workshop (or any writing)*	*Starts and then erases over and over again, asks to go to the bathroom, can become irritable, doesn't complete work and hides it.*		

Appendix B

Pre- and Postassessment for *Ish* Lesson

What do you think about mistakes?

☺ = YES ☹ = I don't know ☹= NO

All of my work has to be completed perfectly.

☺ 😐 ☹

It is okay to try even if I might make a mistake.

☺ 😐 ☹

I am afraid to make a mistake on my work.

☺ 😐 ☹

My work can be close-ish.

☺ 😐 ☹

My teacher says it is okay to make mistakes.

☺ 😐 ☹

Appendix C

Perfectionistic or Risk Anxiety Follow-Up Form

Teacher Name ________________

Please record the following information

Name of Student	Academic Context of Behaviors	Types of attempted behaviors observed	Tally the # of times student attempts work in the identified context for 1 week	Number of assignments completed in context over 1 week
Example: *Ryder*	*Writer's Workshop (or any writing)*	*Starts and then erases and then starts again. Shows his work to another student to ask if it is "ish." Starts and seeks reassurance from teacher.*		

Appendix D

Time On-Task Record

Teacher Name ___________________ Student Name ________________________

Please place a tally mark in the box each time you redirect the student to get back on-task.

	Monday	**Tuesday**	**Wednesday**	**Thursday**	**Friday**
Week of: Total:					
Week of: Total:					
Week of: Total:					
Week of: Total:					

Appendix E

Peer Interaction Record

Teacher ______________________ Student ___________________________

Please tally the number of times ***other students*** *report ____________ engaging in any of the following behaviors:*

*name calling,

*instigating conflict,

*inappropriately touching others.

	Monday	Tuesday	Wednesday	Thursday	Friday	Totals
Week of:						
Week of:						
Week of:						
Week of:						

REFERENCES

American School Counselor Association. (2012). *The ASCA National Model: A Framework for School Counseling Programs, Third Edition.* Alexandria, VA: Author.

Ashby, J., Kottman, T., & Degraaf, D. (2008). *Active Interventions for Kids and Teens: Adding Adventure and Fun to Counseling.* Alexandria, VA: American Counseling Association.

Axline, V. (1969). *Play therapy.* New York, NY: Ballantine Books.

Baggerly, J. (2004). Applying the ASCA national model to elementary school students who are homeless: A case study. *Professional School Counseling, 8*(2), 116-123.

Baggerly, J., & Bratton, S. C. (2010). Building a firm foundation in play therapy research: Response to Phillips (2010). *International Journal of Play Therapy, 19*(1), 26-38.

Blanco, P. J., & Ray, D. C. (2011). Play therapy in elementary schools: A best practice for improving academic achievement. *Journal of Counseling & Development, 89,* 235-243.

Brofenbrenner, U. (1979). *Ecology of human development.* Cambridge, MA: Harvard Univeristy Press.

Brown, D., & Trusty, J. (2005). The ASCA National Model, accountability, and establishing causal links between school counselors' activities and student outcomes: A reply to Sink. *Professional School Counseling, 9*(1), 13-15.

Chaloner, W. B. (2001). Counselors coaching teachers to use play therapy in classrooms: The Play and Language to Succeed (PALS) early, school-based intervention for behaviorally at risk children. In A. Drewes, L. Carey, Y. C. Schaefer (Eds.), *School-based play therapy* (pp. 368-390). New York, NY: John Wiley.

Danger, S., & Landreth, G. (2005). Child-centered group play therapy with children with speech difficulties. *International Journal of Play Therapy, 14*(1), 81-102.

Dimmitt, C. (2009). Why evaluation matters: Determining effective school counseling practices. *Professional School Counseling, 12*(6), 395-399.

Dinkmeyer, D., McKay, G., & Dinkmeyer, D. (1980). *Systematic training for effective teaching.* Circle Pines, MN: American Guidance Services.

Dougherty, J., & Ray, D. (2007). Differential impact of play therapy on developmental levels of children. *International Journal of Play Therapy, 16*(1), 2-19. doi:10.1037/1555-6824.16.1.2

Draper, K., White, J., O'Shuaunghessy, T., Flynt, M., & Jones, N. (2001). Kinder training: Play based consultation to improve the school adjustment of discouraged kindergarten and first grade students. *International Journal of Play Therapy. 10*(1), 1-29.

Education Trust. (1997). *Transforming school counseling.* Retrieved from http://www.edtrust.org/main/school_counseling.asp

Edwards, N. A., Varjas, K. M., White, J. F., & Stokes, S. A. (2009). Teachers' perceptions of kinder training: Acceptability, integrity, and effectiveness. *International Journal of Play Therapy, 18(3),* 129-146. doi:10.1037/a0015170

Fall, M. (1999). A play therapy intervention and its relationship to self-efficacy and learning behaviors. *Professional School Counseling, 2*(3), 194-204.

Goodyear-Brown, P. (2002). *Digging for buried treasure: 52 Prop-based play therapy interventions for treating the problems of childhood*. Nashville, TN: Sundog.

Gysbers, N. C., & Henderson, P. (1994). *Developing and managing your school guidance program* (2nd ed.). Alexandria, VA: American Association for Counseling and Development.

Hall, T. M., Kaduson, H. G., & Schaefer, C. E. (2002). Fifteen effective play therapy techniques. *Professional Psychology: Research and Practice, 33*(6), 515-522. doi:10.1037//0735-7028.33.6.515

Herr, E. L., & Erford, B. T. (2011). Historical roots and future issues. In B. T. Erford (Ed.), *Transforming the school counseling profession* (3rd ed., pp. 19-43). Columbus, OH: Pearson Merrill Prentice Hall.

Holcolmb-McCoy, C. (2007). *School counseling to close the achievement gap*. Thousand Oaks, CA: Corwin Press.

House. R. M., & Martin, P. J. (1998). Advocating for better futures for all students: A new vision for school counselors. *Education, 779*, 284-291.

Kaduson, H. & Schaefer, C. (2010). *101 Favorite Play Therapy Techniques*. Lanham, MD: Jason Aronson.

Kochhar-Bryant, C. A. (2010). *Effective collaboration for educating the whole child*. Thousand Oaks, CA: Corwin.

Kottman, T. (1993). Adlerian play therapy: A tool for school counselors. *Elementary School Guidance & Counseling, 28*(1), 42-53.

Kuykendall, C. (2004). *From rage to hope: Strategies for reclaiming black and hispanic students*. Bloomington, IN: Solution Tree.

Landreth, G. (2002). *Play therapy: The art of the relationship* (2nd ed.) New York, NY: Brunner-Routledge.

Landreth, G., & Bratton, S. (2006). *Child parent relationship therapy* (CPRT): *A 10-session filial therapy model*. New York, NY: Brunner-Routledge.

Landreth, G., Ray, D. C., & Bratton, S. C., (2009). Play therapy in elementary schools. *Psychology in the Schools, 46*(3). doi:10.1002/pits.20374

Landreth, G., Strother, J., & Barlow, K., (1985). Child-centered play therapy: Nancy from baldness to curls. *School Counselor, 32*(5), 347-356.

Lapan, R. (2004). *Career development across the K-16 years: Building the present to satisfying and successful futures*. Alexandria, VA: American Counseling Association.

Lew, A., & Bettner, B. A. (1995). *Responsibility in the classroom: A teacher's guide to understanding and motivating students*. Newton, MA: Connexions Press.

Lowenstein, L. (1999). *Creative Interventions for Troubled Children & Youth*. Toronto, Canada: Champion Press.

No Child Left Behind (NCLB) Act of 2001, Pub. L. No. 107-110, § 115, Stat. 1425 (2002).

Paisley, P. O., & Hayes, R. L. (2003). School counseling in the academic domain: Transformations in preparation and practice. *Professional School Counseling, 6*, 198-205.

Paisley, P. O., & Hubbard, G. T. (1994). *Developmental school counseling programs: From theory to practice*. Alexandria, VA: American Counseling Association.

Paisley, P. O., & McMahon, H. G. (2001). School counseling for the 21st century: Challenges and opportunities. *Professional School Counseling, 5,* 106-115.

Paone, T. R., Packman, J. Maddux, C., & Rothman, T. (2008). A school-based group activity therapy intervention with at-risk high school students as it relates to their moral reasoning. *International Journal of Play Therapy, 17*(2), 122-137. doi:10.1037/a0012582

Piaget, J. (1962). *Play, dreams, and imitation in childhood.* New York, NY: Routledge.

Post, P. (1999). Impact of child-centered play therapy on the self-esteem, locus of control, and anxiety of at-risk 4th, 5th, and 6th grade students. *International Journal of Play Therapy, 8(2),* 1-18.

Ray, D. C., Bratton, S. C., Rhine, T., & Jones, L. (2001). The effectiveness of play therapy: Responding to the critics. *International Journal of Play Therapy, 10,* 85-108.

Ray, D. C., Henson, R. K., Schottelkorb, A. A., Brown, A. G., & Muro, J. (2008). Effect of short- and long-term play therapy services on teacher-child relationship stress. *Psychology in the Schools, 45(10),* 994-1009. doi:10.1002/pits.20347

Ray, D. C., Muro, J., & Schumann, B. (2004). Implementing play therapy in the schools: Lessons learned. *International Journal of Play Therapy, 13*(1), 79-100.

Reynolds, C., & Stanley, C. (2001). Innovative applications of play therapy in school settings. In A. A. Drewes, L. J. Carey, & C. E. Schafer (Eds.), *School-based play therapy.* New York, NY: John Wiley.

Swank, J. M. (2008). The use of games: A therapeutic tool with children and families. *International Journal of Play Therapy, 17(2),* 154-167. doi:10.1037/1555-6824.17.2.154

Tyndall-Lind, A., Landreth, G. L., & Giordano, M. A. (2001). Intensive group play therapy with child witnesses of domestic violence. *International Journal of Play Therapy, 10*(1), 53-83.

Young, A., & Kaffenberger, C. (2009). *Making data work*. Alexandria, VA: American School Counselor Association.

Wasow, B. (2005). *Majority minority.* Retrieved from http://www.tcf.org/list.asp?type=NC&pubid=1072

White, J., Draper, K., Flynt, M., & Jones, N. P. (2000). *Kinder training: Play-based teacher consultation to promote the adjustment and achievement of discouraged students.* Norcross, GA: Kid Choice.

White, J., & Flynt, M. (1999). Play groups in elementary school. In D. S. Sweeney & L. E. Homeyer (Eds.), *Group play therapy: How to do it, how it works, whom it's best for.* San Francisco, CA: Jossey Bass.

White, J., Flynt, M., & Draper, K. (1997) Kinder therapy: Teachers as therapeutic agents. *International Journal of Play Therapy, 6*(2), 33-49.

White, J., Flynt, M., & Draper, K. (1997). Kinder therapy: Teachers as therapeutic agents. *International Journal of Play Therapy, 2*(6), 33-49.

Ziomek-Daigle, J., McMahon, H. G., & Paisley, P. O. (2008) Adlerian-based interventions for professional school counselors serving as both counselors and educational leaders. *Journal of Individual Psychology, 64*(4), 450-467.

CHAPTER 11

INTEGRATING PLAYFUL ACTIVITIES AND GAMES WITHIN SCHOOL COUNSELING SMALL GROUPS

Jacqueline M. Swank

The integration of games and activities within school counseling small groups may creatively enhance a developmental school counseling program. This chapter focuses on ways to successfully utilize games and activities within small groups. The author discusses (a) areas to consider when integrating games and activities, (b) strategies for modifying and creating games, and (c) examples of games.

Vignette 1

Angelica, an elementary school counselor, was approached by a group of teachers about facilitating a small group with boys identified as struggling to stay on task and focus during class. In particular, the boys needed support to learn to interact appropriately with their peers during class activities, recess time, and during transition periods before and after

Integrating Play Techniques in Comprehensive School Counseling Programs, pp. 209–226

school. Angelica was familiar with the boys and knew that they had lots of energy. She was wondering what activities she could integrate within the small group to provide an opportunity for the boys to engage in some physical activity, while focusing on addressing the identified concerns.

Vignette 2

Terrance, a middle school counselor, was asked by the principal to facilitate a small group with students who were at-risk of dropping out of school. The students expressed limited interest in the group and Terrance wondered what types of activities he could integrate within the group to make it more appealing to the students and encourage their participation.

The two vignettes describe the challenges school counselors may experience in developing a small group curriculum that is appealing and appropriate for students. Additional challenges arise in devoting time to the multi-step process of facilitating small groups, including conducting needs assessments, planning, obtaining approval from school personnel and parents, recruiting and screening student participants, and scheduling. Without designating sufficient time for each of these steps, the school counselor may experience problems that hinder the success of the group (Stockton & Toth, 2007).

Beyond recruiting participants, the school counselor needs a curriculum that will motivate students to participate and learn from the group. Therefore, in planning a group curriculum, school counselors may consider integrating games and other activities. Children are naturally playful and enjoy engaging in activities and playing games with others (Greenberg, 2003). Additionally, games may support the concepts identified as areas of focus within counseling (e.g., social and problem-solving skills, creating a sense of cohesion and belonging, practicing new behaviors). Observing students' participation and interactions with others also provides the school counselor with useful assessment data (Reid, 2001). Thus, the inclusion of games and other activities within small group counseling may enhance students' interest, encourage participation, and support learning. However, school counselors may feel challenged in developing small group activities that are appropriate and appealing to their identified population. This chapter addresses these challenges by addressing the integration of playful activities and games within small group counseling in the elementary, middle, and high school setting.

Game play is described as having the following five basic characteristics: (a) oriented towards goals, (b) competitive, (c) invoking ego processes, (d) adhering to rules, and (e) fostering interpersonal interactions (Reid, 2001). Integrating activity and game play within counseling sessions may strengthen and expedite therapeutic change. In addition, game play provides an opportunity for emotional release and may assist with addressing issues that clients struggle to express or discuss with the counselor (Jordan, 2002). Game play also challenges the viewpoint that children must play to win by providing positive competition that reinforces children's strengths and talents (Livesay, 2008). Games promote relationships, communication, insight development, reality testing, rational thinking, and ego enhancement (Reid, 2001).

The integration of games in counseling was highlighted in the counseling literature in the 1950s, focusing on the use of checkers to reveal resistance to counseling (Loomis, 1957). Then, in the 1970s, two therapy games were developed (*The Talking, Feeling, Doing Game* [Creative Therapeutics] and the *Ungame* [Tailcor]), which focused on communication and social skills (Reid, 2001). Today, school counselors may use a myriad of therapy games that exist, in addition to using traditional games (e.g., *Candyland, Sorry, Trouble*) in counseling.

Group activity therapy (GAT) is a concept discussed by Bratton and Ferebee (1999) that encompasses both structured and unstructured play that is modeled from Landreth's (2002) child-centered play therapy approach. In facilitating GAT, the counselor provides children and adolescents with an opportunity to engage in self-expression without requiring them to verbally discuss everything. Thus, youth may feel more comfortable participating in group counseling using a GAT format, as opposed to using talk therapy (Paone, Packman, Maddux, & Rothman, 2008).

Researchers have explored the use of games and activity therapy in counseling. Botha and Dunn (2009) developed a board game to use as an assessment tool within Gestalt play therapy, which focuses on the therapeutic relationship, awareness, and the child's inner world (Carroll & Oaklander, 1997). In exploring the effectiveness of the game, Botha and Dunn reported that the game was useful for relationship building, sensory stimulation, and identification of problem-solving skills. Additionally, Paone and colleagues (2008) compared the effectiveness of GAT to talk therapy in enhancing moral reasoning among ninth graders (N = 61) and found that GAT was more effective than talk therapy. Packman and Bratton (2003) also examined the effectiveness of GAT among preadolescents with learning disabilities (N = 30) and found that individuals involved in GAT exhibited a reduction in behavior problems.

CATEGORIES OF GAMES

The integration of games within small group counseling may include board games, physical games, and video games. There are a variety of board games that school counselors may integrate within counseling, including popular board games designed for fun (e.g., *Candyland* and *Trouble*) and board games designed specifically for counseling (e.g., *The Talking, Feeling, Doing Game* and *Look Before You Leap*). Within the category of board games designed for fun, there are games focused on a popular culture figure or event (e.g., *Harry Potter*). These games may appeal to children and adolescents who enjoy the character(s) being portrayed in the game; however, the game might only be interesting for a period of time due to changes in pop culture (Livesay, 2008), and with limited budgets, school counselors need to choose games that may sustain children's interest over time. Using board games that are familiar to children and adolescents promotes confidence, empowerment, and open-mindedness (Nelson, 2005). Furthermore, board games may facilitate skill development in various areas, including problem-solving and decision-making, ethical behavior, emotional regulation regarding acceptance and disappointment, and impulse control (Livesay, 2008).

Physical games address fine and gross motor skills (Reid, 2001). This category of games may present challenges for the school counselor regarding spacing considerations. Additionally, the counselor may struggle with engaging students in processing because of the level of physical activity. Despite these challenges, physical games have been effective in helping children who are impulsive and hyperactive to obtain better self-control (Reid, 2001). Additionally, adventure based counseling (ABC) involves physical games and activities that promote problem-solving, teamwork, trust, and responsibility (Glass & Myers, 2001; Schoel & Maizell, 2002; Swank & Daire, 2010). Moreover, school counselors should be prepared to make accommodations as necessary for students with physical disabilities as equity in participation can promote a sense of belonging, acceptance, and cohesion. Thus, children and adolescents may benefit from the integration of physical games and activities despite the challenges.

School counselors may choose to integrate video games within counseling because they are growing in popularity among children and adolescents. Researchers are also beginning to explore the effects of integrating video games within counseling. Hull (2009) examined the use of video games focusing on sports (i.e., *NBA Street 2*), strategy and skill (i.e., *Lego Star Wars II*) and racing (i.e., *Need for Speed Hot Pursuit 2*) and reported their usefulness in working with children (boys ages 9-14) with emotional disturbances of sadness. Additionally, Ceranoglu (2010) reported that video games may assist school counselors with developing relationships with children, observing cognitive skills (i.e., motor, academic, tolerance for frustration), and discussing conflicts. Video game play also provides an opportunity for counselors to discuss with clients feelings that arise while playing the games. Furthermore, they may parallel life and strengthen problem-solving skills by presenting obstacles that the players must overcome in order to reach an identified goal (Enfield & Grosser, 2000). However, school counselors may experience challenges with integrating video games into counseling, including financial constraints to purchase game systems and games, and students using the games to avoid verbal communication with the counselor (Ceranoglu, 2010). School counselors, within a group setting, may also struggle with involving all group members in a session involving a video game due to the limited number of participants that can play a game simultaneously.

CONSIDERATIONS

When considering the integration of activities or games within small groups, there are several areas that school counselors will want to contemplate prior to facilitating the sessions. Some areas to ponder include: the developmental level of the students; the counselor's role; selection and preservation of materials; and rules, boundaries, and cheating. It is crucial to consider each of these areas prior to integrating games within the developmental school counseling program.

Development

There are three levels of cognitive development in play, as described by Piaget (1962): sensory motor and functional play during the sensorimotor stage of development (2 months to 2 years); dramatic, symbolic, and fantasy play during the preoperational stage (2 to 7 years); and games with rules during the concrete operational stage (7 to 11 years). In contrast, Vygotsky (1976) described game play as beginning in the preschool years. Preschool children may engage in simple games for skill testing and to challenging their past achievements, in addition to playing for fun (e.g., matching games). However, game play at this stage may involve frequently changing the rules while playing board games, cards, or guessing games (Jordan, 2002). During the school age years, children begin playing more complex, realistic games that have greater structure (Bellinson, 2002; Frost, Wortham, & Reifel, 2001; Reid, 2001). With greater structure, children follow the rules more rigidly in their play. Game play during this developmental stage may assist children in frustration tolerance and impulse control. Finally, during adolescence, game play assists youth with problem solving while continuing to provide opportunities for social interaction (Jordan, 2002).

The integration of games and activities within counseling influence play in all areas of development: cognitive, emotional, social, and identity construction (Reid, 2001). In the cognitive realm, play becomes more realistic as children grow and develop, which allows counselors to integrate games that address real life situations and promote problem-solving and decision-making skills. Within the emotional and social areas of development, children develop the capacity to express how they are feeling and relate to others. Additionally, children show a greater interest in interacting and socializing with their peers, which may also involve challenging their peers. Finally, games may assist children in gaining greater knowledge and an understanding of who they are and what they value (Reid, 2001). Thus, the integration of activities and games within counseling may support development in various areas; and therefore, be applicable for addressing the three domains of student development (academic, career, and personal/social development) emphasized within the ASCA *National Model* (2012).

Counselor's Role

In deciding to integrate games and activities into counseling, Streng (2002) emphasizes the importance of having trained counselors to facilitate them. The instructions and rules for the games and activities may appear simple and easy to follow; and therefore, acceptable for anyone to lead the group. However, it is crucial to remember that games and activities are used to facilitate processing feelings and experiences about a variety of counseling issues, and thus, it remains important to have trained counselors to facilitate the groups. Additionally, Bellinson (2002) and Reid (2001) discuss the importance of considering countertransference when integrating games within counseling. Counselors should reflect upon their own experiences and feelings about particular games before deciding to use them within counseling.

School counselors' level of involvement is also an area to consider in facilitating groups. Counselors may choose to remain in a facilitative role by focusing on observing group dynamics and facilitating discussions throughout group sessions. Alternatively, counselors may choose to take a more active role by participating in games or activities. This would likely occur during individual counseling because the game or activity may require two or more people; however, it is also a consideration during group counseling. If a counselor decides to actively play a game or be involved in an activity, it is important to be mindful of what is occurring within the group and to continue in the role of facilitator. As an active participant in the game, the counselor must also decide what personal information to share with the children or adolescents. Sharing personal information that is related to the topic and on the children's level can be helpful; however, sharing too much information or too personal information may create a negative environment where the group members feel uncomfortable and unsafe (Streng, 2002). Additionally, counselors should focus on feelings and discuss situations, without providing solutions (Bellinson, 2002). Thus, in deciding the level of participation, school counselors should consider the therapeutic needs of the students and what level of involvement will promote the success of the group.

Selection and Preservation of Materials

School counselors may select a variety of materials when integrating games and activities within counseling. In selecting materials it is crucial to consider the developmental level of students. For example, during a painting activity, young children may enjoy playing in the water when using watercolor paint; however, they may struggle with using paint and paint brushes to create pictures; this may be particularly true if they have had limited or no access to painting prior to the activity. Therefore, school counselors may prefer to use finger paint or tempera paint with young children. Additionally, school counselors consider what materials are appealing to students, which will vary by student. Counselors may ask students what they are good at or what they like to do, and then creatively integrate these areas within the games and activities used within the school counseling program. The integration of materials that are appealing to children promotes engagement and may reduce resistance (Swank, 2008). Furthermore, counselors should consider available space and allotted time. School counselors strive to facilitate an environment that promotes physical and emotional safety and security, while considering time required to facilitate and process games and activities. Hence, school counselors uses intentionality in selecting materials for the games and activities used within the school counseling program.

Modifying existing games and creating new games can be a time intensive process; therefore, it is also important to consider methods that may promote the longevity of the games. Laminating game materials is one strategy that helps promote game durability. Additionally, school counselors set rules and limits regarding the use of materials during game play. Furthermore, counselors may obtain storage containers (e.g., plastic storage bins, plastic bags) or create containers by recycling shoe boxes and other containers for game storage, which promotes sustainability, reduces the chance of losing game materials and pieces, and helps establish organization of games for future use.

Rules, Boundaries, and Cheating

Games and structured activities involve rules and directions. Within small group counseling, school counselors will want to facilitate a discussion about the rules prior to playing a game; however, there is flexibility in how the rules are established for a game. One approach involves reading the rules and instructions that are included with the game and ensuring that everyone understands and agrees to the rules. Alternatively, counselors may allow the group to create their own rules for a game, which emphasizes problem-solving skills and also provides counselors with opportunities to observe the behavior of the individual group members (Streng, 2002). Allowing group members to play on teams of two or three people, instead of playing individually also promotes teamwork and interpersonal skills (Streng, 2002). While rules are a component of games, Bellinson (2002) emphasizes the importance of focusing on the therapeutic value of the game, instead of focusing on controlling how children play the game to ensure that it is played in the proper manner. In addition to rules, counselors may need to set boundaries during game play to maintain physical and emotional safety, while also preventing materials from being destroyed. In setting boundaries, counselors should consider the purpose, necessity, intended outcome, and follow-up action if the boundaries are not followed by the students. Thus, counselors strive to maintain a balance between establishing rules and boundaries to promote the safety of the students, counselors, and materials while also allowing flexibility and encouraging self-expression.

Cheating may present during game play and counselors may choose to address it or allow it within sessions (Swank, 2008). However, within a group setting, the group members may choose to address cheating, even if the counselor does not draw attention to the issue. Reid (2001) suggests that counselors view cheating as a form of expression of feelings and coping skills, instead of viewing it as a problem. Therefore, the occurrence of cheating within game play provides an opportunity to identify feelings, behaviors, and coping skills, while also developing social skills.

APPROACH AND TECHNIQUES

A school counselor's approach to the integration of play, in the form of activities and games, should be grounded within a counseling theory and the context of play therapy. Then, when creating a small group curriculum, the counselor may integrate existing activities and games designed for therapy or utilize creativity to create/modify traditional games to address a variety of counseling issues. Therefore, the utilization of activities and games defined within a play therapy theoretical orientation may help school counselors facilitate small groups successfully.

Theoretical Premise

Game play has been explored within a variety of theories within the context of play therapy (i.e., child-centered, cognitive-behavioral, psychoanalytic, gestalt, Adlerian, and social learning). Child-centered play therapy (CCPT) is a nondirective approach to counseling, which Landreth and Sweeney (1997) reported does not support the integration of most board games because they are structured and directive. It is important to note that a structured, directive approach may better fit with the time constraints of school counselors in developing group play interventions. However, children may engage in game play during a CCPT counseling session by creating their own game to play using toys that are located within the play room, without being directed by the counselor.

A variety of theories support the integration of games within play therapy. Cognitive-behavioral play therapy (CBPT) focuses on the integration of cognitive and behavioral interventions within play and the counselor's role as an educator (Knell, 1997). In CBPT, counselors use games to address maladaptive behaviors and thoughts and promote healthy skill development (Swank, 2008). Within psychoanalytic theory, counselors are observers and focus on identifying motivations, conflicts, and defenses presented within game play (Lee, 1997). Gestalt play therapy also supports the integration of games within counseling to foster relationship building, awareness of emotions, and communication with the child's inner world when used as a projective technique (Carroll & Oaklander, 1997). Counselors may also use games to help children in various areas that are crucial tasks within Adlerian play therapy, such as increasing social interest, creating constructive goals, and developing new skills (Kottman, 2001). Therefore, counselors may use games to help clients connect with others and develop social skills. Social learning theory is a final area that supports the integration of game play (Reid, 2001; Serok & Blum, 1983). Within game play, children and adolescents have the opportunity and are encouraged to explore new behaviors within a social environment that is safe (Swank, 2008), which may assist them in developing confidence to try out the behaviors in their daily lives (Serok & Blum, 1983). Thus, school counselors should consider counseling theories grounded within play therapy to provide support for the integration of activities and games within small group counseling.

Play Techniques

School counselors may use existing activities and games or use creativity to develop new ones. Game modifications provide opportunities to meet the developmental needs of specific students or groups of students (Jordan, 2002; Swank, 2008). Additionally, in developing new games, counselors have opportunities to tailor the games to clients' ages, developmental levels, problem areas, and counseling settings. Using open-ended question cards in games may provide information about children or adolescents or assist with developing skills in the cognitive, affective, behavioral, and social domains (Jordan, 2002). Furthermore, game play is a fun, nonthreatening activity, which can be cost effective when counselors use creativity to create games (Jordan, 2002).

Swank (2008) described areas to consider when creating a game or modifying an existing game. The first step involves identifying the therapeutic purpose of the game. Additionally, Swank emphasizes the importance of integrating a component of fun within games, addressing a variety of learning styles and senses, considering whether it is applicable to diverse populations, and ensuring that it is developmentally appropriate for the intended population. In developing or modifying games, counselors may also integrate questions in a variety of formats, demonstrations, or dilemmas to discuss during the games (Swank, 2008). Then, when integrating the game or activity within play, Lowenstein (1999) emphasizes the importance of having a beginning, middle, and end, which allows a counselor to introduce the activity in the beginning, facilitate the activity, and then process the experience, while being mindful that the therapeutic value of the session focuses on the process, not the product. Thus, school counselors have various strategies to assist them with successfully integrating activities and games within small groups.

SAMPLE SESSIONS

The Talking Box

Theme: Communication

Age: Second grade and up (need ability to write or have individuals to help with this process)

Goals:

- Develop a safe environment for group
- Facilitate a discussion about a specific topic
- Encourage interpersonal interaction among group members

Materials:

- Paper or note cards
- Pencils or pens
- Box or container

Description:

The school counselor asks the group members to think about questions or situations related to the group topic that they have wanted to discuss, but have felt too embarrassed or uncomfortable to ask about during the group. The group members are told that they will have the opportunity to ask these questions anonymously during the group. Then, group members are instructed to write the questions or situations on slips of paper or note cards without adding their name. The questions are then put in a box and the counselor randomly selects them from the box, reads the question, and then facilitates a discussion with the group.

Considerations

The school counselor reads the questions, instead of having the group members take turns reading the questions to protect the anonymity of the process by preventing a group member from recognizing someone else's handwriting. Group members may want to have the box available during every session to add questions or situations that come up throughout the small group. The counselor may also add questions or situations to the box. Additionally, the school counselor may also modify the activity to use as an icebreaker during the first group by having group members write something about themselves on the paper and then giving group members an opportunity to guess which card belongs to each group member.

Guess the Feeling

Theme: Self-expression
Age: All ages

Goals:

- Promote expression of feelings
- Develop empathy for others

Materials:

- Paper
- Crayons, markers, colored pencils

Description:

The school counselor reads a story or presents a situation and asks the group members the feelings they might experience if they were the storybook character or the person in the situation. Then, group members are asked to draw a picture about a situation they have experienced that evoked strong feelings. The group members do not write the feeling word on their picture; however, they can portray the feeling in the picture. The group members then take turns guessing how others felt in the situations portrayed in the pictures. Group members can describe the situation in their picture, but not how they felt, until after group members have attempted to guess the feeling. After guessing the feelings portrayed in the pictures, the counselor facilitates a discussion about how people may feel different in various situations.

Considerations

Some individuals are self-conscious about their ability to draw; and therefore, they might be reluctant to participate in the activity. The school counselor may suggest drawing symbols to represent the situation or writing keywords that a group member could use to discuss the situation. However, the group members are encouraged to draw and the school counselor provides support during this process.

Choice and Consequences (Swank, 2008)

Theme: Problem solving
Age: Elementary level

Goals:

- Develop decision-making skills
- Foster interpersonal interactions

Materials:

- *Chutes and Ladders* board game
- Small objects/miniatures
- Index cards cut into squares the size of the board game sections
- Markers, crayons, pens, pencils
- Tape

Description:

The school counselor facilitates a discussion about decision-making skills, focusing on choices and consequences, using the situations portrayed on the board game. Then, the school counselor allows the group to play the game while continuing to discuss the choices presented on the board game. After playing the game, the school counselor invites the group members to discuss recent decisions that they've made and to illustrate the decisions on square index card pieces, with one square illustrating the situation and another square illustrating the choice made by the student. The students are encouraged to illustrate both positive and negative choices they made regarding various situations. After the students finish their squares, they are discussed in the group and then added to the board to replace the positive and negative choices displayed on the game. Finally, the students have the opportunity to play the game again using their situations and choices.

Considerations

This activity may take two sessions to complete and students may choose to use the game for multiple sessions illustrating additional situations and choices. Further, the school counselor may encourage students to take some blank squares home to play this modified game with their family, if they have the board game at home, or suggest creating the board out of cardboard. The counselor may offer a variety of small objects/miniatures for students to use in selecting a game piece. This addresses the problem of not having enough game pieces for each group member. Additionally, the school counselor may facilitate a discussion about the significance of the objects/miniatures (Swank, 2008).

What We Learned Tic Tac Toe

Theme: Review group topic
Age: All ages

Goals:

- Reinforce learning related to the topic addressed
- Evaluate group outcomes

Materials:

- Question cards
- Chalkboard, dry erase board, or large sheets of paper (flipchart)
- Chalk/markers

Description:

Group members are divided into two teams. The teams take turns answering questions about the information they have learned during the group sessions. If a team answers a question correctly, they place an "X" or "O" (the letter representing their group) in a section of the *Tic Tac Toe* board, in an attempt to get three letters in a row horizontally, vertically, or diagonally. The counselor may facilitate playing several rounds to answer all the questions.

Considerations

The school counselor may use other game formats to review the content addressed within the group sessions, such as Guess that Phrase (modified *Hangman* without using the concept of a hangman) or Charades (Swank, 2008).

CASE STUDY

Henry is an 8-year-old boy, who was referred to the school counselor by his teacher for having difficulty coping with his anger. Henry was in gifted classes and did well academically; however, the teacher referred him to the school counselor due to incidents of yelling at the teacher and peers when he became angry. The school counselor met Henry in her office and attempted to initiate a conversation with him; however, he sat quietly with his arms crossed and refused to talk with the counselor. Additionally, Henry stared at the floor, avoiding eye contact with the counselor during most of the session. The counselor invited Henry to participate in a small group that she was starting the following week. Henry looked up when the counselor began describing the group activities and stated that he wanted to participate.

The group focused on anger management and involved various games and activities. Henry showed a willingness to participate during the first group session. However, within the first 20 minutes of the group, Henry became angry about sharing materials with other group members and started yelling at a peer. The school counselor used this situation as a learning opportunity and modeled for Henry a healthy way to cope with his anger. Then, the counselor offered Henry the opportunity to practice the technique. Henry refused to practice the technique during the group session and remained disruptive during most of the group.

The counselor focused the next group session on learning strategies to cope with anger by having the students brainstorm strategies (e.g., asking permission to move away from the situation and then sitting in a quiet place, taking deep breaths, shifting the focus away from the situation) and then practice the techniques. Henry remained calm during this session and showed a willingness to practice moving away from the group to sit quietly until he calmed down. Group members continued to learn about the sources, triggers, and targets of anger and practiced anger management strategies each week during demonstrations integrated within several games (e.g., modified *Candyland* described in Swank, 2008) and activities used throughout the group sessions. Henry began showing progress in using the strategies when he became angry during group sessions.

He expressed that he liked having the option to move away from the group to calm down and then return when he was ready. The school counselor worked with the teacher to identify a place in the classroom where Henry and other students could go to calm down when needed throughout the day. The teacher reported that Henry started to use this strategy in class and also encouraged other students to use the "quiet time" spot when they became angry. Henry continued to have some disruptive anger incidents during class; however, they were reduced and Henry showed a greater ability to make healthy decisions. During the final group session, Henry discussed and demonstrated what he learned during the *What We Learned* game. The school counselor continued to offer Henry encouragement when seeing him in the hallway and occasionally Henry stopped by the counselor's office to play a game and practice his coping skills.

SUMMARY

Games and activities are often enjoyable, and therefore appealing to students of all ages. The integration of games and activities within counseling sessions provides an opportunity for school counselors to address issues that are interfering with students' academic, career, and personal/social development. When utilized in an intentional manner within small groups, games and activities may also foster interpersonal skills. Therefore, in designing the curriculum for a small group, school counselors are encouraged to be creative in developing new innovative activities and games, or modifying existing games to include in the therapeutic process. Thus, school counselors have the opportunity to enhance the small group counseling experience.

REFERENCES

American School Counselor Association. (2012). *The ASCA National Model: A framework for school counseling programs* (3rd ed.). Alexandria, VA: Author.

Bellinson, J. (2002). *Children's use of board games in psychotherapy.* Northvale, NJ: Jason Aronson.

Botha, E., & Dunn, M. (2009). A board game as Gestalt assessment tool for the child in middle childhood years. *South African Journal of Psychology, 39*(2), 253-262. Retrieved from http://www.journals.co.za/ej/ejour_sapsyc.html

Bratton, S. C., & Ferebee, K. W. (1999). The use of structured expressive art activities in group activity therapy with preadolescents. In D. S. Sweeney & L. E. Homeyer (Eds.), *The handbook of group play therapy: How to do it, how it works, whom it's best for* (pp. 192–214). San Francisco, CA: Jossey-Bass.

Carroll, F., & Oaklander, V. (1997). Gestalt play therapy. In K. O'Connor & L.M. Braverman (Eds.), *Play therapy theory and practice: A comparative presentation* (pp. 184–203). New York, NY: Wiley.

Ceranoglu, T. A. (2010). Video games in psychotherapy. *Review of General Psychology, 14*(2), 141-146. doi:10.1037/a0019439

Enfield, G., & Grosser, M. (2000). Picking up coins: The use of video games in the treatment of adolescent social problems. In L. C. Rubin (Ed.), *Popular culture in counseling, psychotherapy, and play-based interventions* (pp. 181-195). New York, NY: Springer.

Frost, J. L., Wortham, S. C., & Reifel, S. (2001). *Play and child development.* Upper Saddle River, NJ: Merrill Prentice Hall.

Glass, J. S., & Myers, J. E. (2001). Combining the old and the new to help adolescents: Individual psychology and adventure based counseling. *Journal of Mental Health Counseling, 23*(2), 104-114.

Greenberg, K. R. (2003). *Group counseling in K-12 schools: A handbook for school counselors.* Boston, MA: Pearson Education.

Hull, K. B. (2009). *Computer/video games as a play therapy tool in reducing emotional disturbances in children.* (Doctoral dissertation, Liberty University). Retrieved from http://digitalcommons.liberty.edu/cgi/viewcontent.cgi?article=1282&context=doctoral

Jordan, K. B. (2002). Create-a-Game. In R. E. Watts (Series Ed.), *Techniques in marriage and family counseling* (Vol. 2, pp. 105-108). Alexandria, VA: American Counseling Association.

Kottman, T. (2001). Adlerian play therapy. *International Journal of Play Therapy, 10*(2), 1-12. doi:10.1037/h0089476

Knell, S. M. (1997). Cognitive-behavioral play therapy. In K. O'Connor & L. M. Braverman (Eds.), *Play therapy theory and practice: A comparative presentation* (pp. 79-99). New York, NY: Wiley.

Landreth, G. L. (2002). *Play therapy: The art of the relationship* (2nd ed.). New York, NY: Brunner-Routledge.

Landreth, G. L., & Sweeney, D. S. (1997). Child centered play therapy. In K. O'Connor & L. M. Braverman (Eds.), *Play therapy theory and practice: A comparative presentation* (pp. 17-45). New York, NY: Wiley.

Lee, A. C. (1997). Psychoanalytic play therapy. In K. O'Connor & L. M. Braverman (Eds.), *Play therapy theory and practice: A comparative presentation* (pp. 46-78). New York, NY: Wiley.

Livesay, H. (2008). Passing go in the Game of Life: Board games in therapeutic play. In L. C. Rubin (Ed.), *Popular culture in counseling, psychotherapy, and play-based interventions* (pp. 197-224). New York, NY: Springer.

Loomis, E. A. (1957). The use of checkers in handling certain resistances in child therapy and child analysis. *Journal of the American Psychoanalytic Association, 5*(1), 130-135. doi:10.1177/000306515700500107

Lowenstein, L. (1999). *Creative interventions for troubled children and youth.* Ontario, Canada: Hignell.

Nelson, T. M. (2005). Therapy making use of *Games of Rapport*, *Games of Courtesy*, and *Good Habits*. In L. Gallo-Lopez & C. E. Schaefer (Eds.), *Play therapy with adolescents* (pp. 210-221). Lanham, MD: Jason Aronson.

Paone, T. R., Packman, J., Maddux, C., & Rothman, T. (2008). A school-based group activity therapy intervention with at-risk high school students as it relates to their moral reasoning. *International Journal of Play Therapy 17*(2), 122-137. doi:10.1037/a0012582

Packman, J., & Bratton, S. C. (2003). A school-based group play/activity therapy intervention with learning disabled preadolescents exhibiting behavior problems. *International Journal of Play Therapy, 12*(2), 7-29. doi:10.1037/h0088876

Piaget, J. (1962). *Play, dreams, and imitation in childhood.* New York, NY: Vintage.

Reid, S. E. (2001). The psychology of play and games. In C. E. Schaefer & S. E. Reid (Eds.), *Game play: Therapeutic use of childhood games* (2nd ed., pp. 1-36). New York, NY: Wiley.

Schoel, J., & Maizell, R. S. (2002). *Exploring islands of healing: New perspectives on adventure based counseling.* Beverly, MA: Project Adventure.

Serok, S., & Blum, A. (1983). Therapeutic uses of games. *Residential Group Care &Treatment, 1*(3), 3-14. doi:10.1300/J297v01n03_02

Stockton, R., & Toth, P. (2007). Small group counseling in school settings. In J. Wittmer & M. A. Clark (Eds.), *Managing your school counseling program: K-12 developmental strategies* (3rd ed., pp. 120-132). Minneapolis, MN: Educational Media Corporation.

Streng, I. C. (2002). Groupwork with children and adolescents using lifegames. *Groupwork, 13*(2), 49-71.

Swank, J. M. (2008). The use of games: A therapeutic tool with children and families. *International Journal of Play Therapy, 17*(2), 154-167. doi:10.1037/1555-6824.17.2.154

Swank, J. M., & Daire, A. P. (2010). Multiple family adventure based therapy groups: An innovative integration of two approaches. *The Family Journal, 18*(3), 241-247. doi:10.1177/1066480710372123

Vygotsky, L. S. (1976). Play and its role in the mental development of the child. In J. S. Bruner, A. Jolly, & K. Sylva (Eds.), *Play: Its role in development and evolution* (pp. 536-552). New York, NY: Basic Books.

CHAPTER 12

CHOICE REALITY PLAY THERAPY FOR CHILDREN INVOLVED IN BULLYING

Kimberly L. Mason

Findings on the impact of bullying on students and the school environment illustrate a need for improved anti-bullying efforts in schools (Finkelhor, Turner, Ormrod, & Hamby, 2009; Finkelhor, Turner, Ormrod, Hamby, & Kracke, 2009; Kosciw, Greytak, Diaz, & Bartkiewicz, 2010; O'Brennan, Bradshaw, & Sawyer, 2009; Swearer, Espelage, Vaillancourt, & Hymel, 2010). Recent legislative responses in the United States have focused on bullying prevention efforts with both federal and state mandates holding schools accountable to develop anti-bullying policies and evidenced-based programs (U.S. Department of Education, 2011). In March 2011, the Anti-Bullying and Harassment Act of 2011 was introduced in Congress, and, to date, 49 states have passed legislation related to harassment, intimidation, and bullying in schools (stopbullying.gov, 2012). In light of the increased attention to aggressive behaviors at school, bullying has been designated as the dominant type of school violence.

One result of increased attention to aggressive behaviors at school is that a wider range of victimization has come under the rubric of bullying (e.g., various forms of physical and relational aggression and violence,

Integrating Play Techniques in Comprehensive School Counseling Programs, pp. 227–261

acts of prejudice and discrimination, antisocial attacks, cyberspace attacks, physical and sexual harassment, etc.). Accordingly, the American School Counselor Association (ASCA) *National Model* (2012) asserts professional school counselors play a key role in designing responsive and preventive programs that promote safe schools, confront issues threatening school safety, and help remove barriers that may impede students' social/emotional, physical, academic, and behavioral functioning. Meta-analysis research indicated school-based anti-bullying programs are effective in reducing bullying (Farrington & Ttofi, 2009; Merrell, Gueldner, Ross, & Isava, 2008; Ttofi & Farrington, 2011).

This chapter provides a literature review of bullying and introduces a method school counselors can use, choice-reality play therapy (CRPT), when counseling children who bully through short-term directive play. By integrating expressive play therapy mediums such as puppets, art, music, and sandtray with CRPT interventions and techniques (Wubbolding, 2000, 2011), school counselors will gain a developmentally appropriate framework for addressing students' wants, needs, and behaviors as it relates to their bullying behaviors. At the conclusion of this chapter, a case study is used to demonstrate CRPT as well as an example of an 11-week girl's empowerment group which is based on the National Standards for School Counseling (ASCA, 2004).

Vignette 1

A middle school counselor in a school cafeteria observed a group of sixth and seventh grade girls at the lunch table. She heard one girl shout across the table to another girl that she is fat and needs to lose weight. She also yelled, "I can connect the dots on your face" and "your hair is so greasy I can fry an egg on it." She later calls her a loser and tells her to leave the table or she will be sorry. The girl receiving these comments begins to tear up and complies—leaving the table. The other girl has been a perpetrator of bullying for a number of years.

Vignette 2

A first grade teacher reported to the school counselor that one of the boys in her class continues to disrupt the class by his constant pushing and hitting other kids and talking back. She reports he usually exhibits these behaviors when he is placed in a group of kids or at free time.

These brief vignettes reveal bullying behaviors that occur in our schools. Often, for many children who are bullied, these aggressive negative behaviors like the ones noted above continue because school personnel and other children fail to respond to their need for help. In one study, 70% of teachers believed they intervene "almost always" in bullying situations; yet, only 25% of students agreed with this assessment (Charach, Pepler, & Ziegler, 1995). Furthermore, peers were present in 88% of childhood bullying episodes, but they intervened in less than one-fifth of these cases (Hawkins, Pepler, & Craig, 2001). Staff at all school levels (elementary, middle, and high) typically underestimates the number of students involved in frequent bullying (Bradshaw, Sawyer, & O'Brennan, 2007).

BULLYING BACKGROUND

Bullying is defined as an unwanted, aggressive behavior among school-aged children that involves (1) a real or perceived power imbalance; (2) the behavior is repeated, or has the potential to be repeated, over time; and (3) the behavior is intended to cause fear, distress, and/or harm to another person's body, feelings, self-esteem, or reputation (Farrington & Ttofi, 2009). Results from the 2009 School Crime Supplement to the National Crime Victimization Survey (National Center for Education Statistics, 2011) of students ages 12-18 indicated over seven million children reported being bullied at school and over 1.5 million children reported being cyberbullied on-or-off school grounds; thus, keeping over 141,300 children from attending school because they felt unsafe at school or traveling to and from school (DeVoe & Bauer, 2011). With the advent of technology, bullying has taken on a new form called *cyberbullying*. Cyberbullying is a form of psychological cruelty where an individual uses electronic devices, the Internet, mobile phone, or other social media platforms to intimidate, threaten or humiliate another individual or group of individuals (Mason, 2008).

Bullying can be overt, direct, or physical (i.e., tripping someone in the hallway or pushing a peer on the playground) or covert through subtle, verbal exchanges, intimidations, rumors, and excluding peers (Lamb, Pepler, & Craig, 2009; Olweus, 1992, 1993, Wang, Iannotti, & Nansel, 2009). A higher percentage of females (20%) than males (13%) ages 12-18 reported being the subject of rumors, while a lower percentage of females (8%) than males (10%) reported being pushed, shoved, tripped, or spit on (DeVoe & Bauer, 2011). More direct physical forms of bullying tend to escalate in elementary school, peak in middle school or between the ages of nine through fifteen, and decline as children reach high school. Whereas, verbal and indirect bullying, particularly cyberbullying, increases in high school (DeVoe & Bauer, 2011).

Children who exhibit bullying behaviors have a tendency to seek excitement through aggression, be easily frustrated, impulsive, have temper outbursts, be grandiose, psychologically defensive, react against rules and authority, and have positive attitudes toward violence (Conners-Burrow, Johnson, Whiteside-Mansell, McKelvey, & Gargus, 2009; Ragozzino & O'Brien, 2009; Swearer et al., 2010; Ungar, 2011). Conversely, children who are victimized by bullies are seen as quiet and withdrawn individuals, socially isolated, have few friends, and typically appear depressed and/or anxious (Cole, Maxwell, Dukewich, & Yosick, 2010; Conners-Burrow et al., 2009). Finally, bystanders (i.e., children who witness bullying) have several reasons for actively or passively participating in bullying situations such as they are afraid to get hurt, they do not want to become the next target, they are afraid that their interventions might make things worse, they believe the target deserves it, or they are not sure what to do (Gini, Pozzoli, Borghi, & Franzoni, 2008; Thornberg & Knutsen, 2010).

Research indicates that many children will experience psychological (e.g., lowered self-worth, higher rates of depression, anxiety, feelings of loneliness, psychological trauma, self-harm, and suicidal ideation), academic (e.g., lower grades, disliking school, absenteeism, and dropping out of school), interpersonal (e.g., increase in violence-related behaviors, decrease in friends, and being ostracized), physical (e.g., headaches, stomach aches), and long-term (e.g., greater and prolonged violence, later offending, and incarceration), issues as a consequence of their involvement in bullying (Bender & Losel, 2011; Cappadocia, Weiss, & Pepler, 2012; Farrington, Loeber, Stallings, & Ttofi, 2011; Fleming & Jacobsen, 2009; Golmaryami & Barry, 2010; Graham, Bellmore, Nishina, & Juvonen, 2009; Juvonen, Wang, & Espinoza, 2010; O'Brennan et al., 2009; Rubin, Coplan, & Bowker, 2009; Saylor, Twyman, & Saia 2008; Swearer et al., 2010; Ttofi, Farrington, Lösel, & Loeber, 2011; Wang, Iannotti, & Luk, 2010; Winsper, Lereya, Zanarini, & Wolke, 2012).

Prevalence Rates

Estimates of bullying prevalence rates vary considerably—from low estimates under 10 percent to estimates surpassing 70% (Centers for Disease Control, 2010; Cook, Kirk, Guerra, Kim, & Sadek, 2010; DeVoe & Bauer, 2011; Finkelhor et al., 2009; Finkelhor, Turner, Ormrod, Hamby, et al., 2009; Kosciw, Greytak, Diaz, & Bartkiewicz, 2010; Lamb et al., 2009; Robers, Zhang, & Truman, 2012; National Center for Education Statistics, 2011; Wang et al., 2009). On an average day, 3 out of 10 children in Grades 6-12 are involved in bullying, as perpetrators, targets, or both (DeVoe & Bauer, 2011), and one in five students ages 12-18 have been a target of cyberbullying (Robers et al., 2012). Although cyberbullying usually occurs off school grounds, schools are experiencing its repercussions and school personnel are forced to deal with its consequences (Mason, 2008; Robers et al., 2012); however, less than eight percent of the 115,000 public schools surveyed are aware of the extent of cyberbullying among students (Robers et al., 2012).

In the largest national study to date, Olweus and Limber (2010) surveyed 524,054 students in Grades 3-12 at 1,593 schools in 45 different states. Results indicated that 17% of students reported being bullied two to three times a month or more. Similarly, in a national sample of 16,410 students in Grades 9-12, the Centers for Disease Control (2010) found one out of five youth (over 20%) reported that that they experienced bullying at school during the past year and approximately 8% admitted to bulling others. Some youth—6.5%—had both bullied others and been bullied themselves. Unfortunately, several youth have resorted to violent means such as engaging in physical fights (11.1%), bringing a weapon (5.6%) to school, or threatening or injuring others with a weapon (7.7%) at school to protect themselves from being a target of bullying. For example, on Monday, February 28, 2012 in Chardon, Ohio, 17-year-old T. J. Lane walked into Chardon High School on a shooting rampage firing 10 shots at a group of students in the cafeteria, resulting in three dead and two wounded (cbsnews.com). Many students who witnessed the shootings describe T. J. as "an outcast who had been bullied." These sobering statistics illustrate why nationwide parents, schools, and students are concerned with the consequences of bullying behaviors that can lead to violence in our schools and engagement in at-risk behaviors.

Students of nonwhite ethnic origin experience more racial name-calling than White children of the same age and gender (Robers et al., 2012; National Center for Education Statistics, 2011). Lesbian, gay, bisexual, and transgender (LGBT) youth are at risk for being targets of severe bullying with nearly 9 out of 10 experiencing harassment at school (Kosciw et al., 2010). Additionally, children with learning disabilities, specific language impairment, social-emotional disorders, physical disabilities, weight-related issues, and who are gifted and talented are three times more likely to be targets of bullying, and are ostracized or purposely ignored more often than their nondisabled peers (Baumeister, Storch, & Geffken, 2008; Campbell & Missiuna, 2011; Hamiwka et al., 2009; Peterson & Ray, 2006; Taylor, Salor, Twyman, & Macias, 2010; Twyman et al., 2009; Twyman et al., 2010; Saia, Saylor, Allen, & Arnau, 2010; Van Cleave & Davis, 2006). In light of these findings, children who are bullied based on their differences attend school in a hostile environment which may impede their access to, participation in, or recipient of benefits, services, or opportunities at school (U.S. Department of Education, 2000); thus, school counselors and school personnel have a duty to take action and protect these children.

School Based Approaches for Reducing Bullying

The Olweus Bullying Prevention Program (OBPP) is the only evidence-based program deemed a Blueprints Model Program, Substance Abuse and Mental Health Service Administration (SAMHSA) model program, effective program for the Office of Juvenile Justice and Delinquency Prevention, and a Level 2 program for the U.S. Department of Education in the United States (Violence Prevention Works, n.d.). Designed for students in elementary, middle, and junior high schools (students ages 5 to 15 years old), the OBPP is a school-wide program that combines positive involvement from teachers and parents, firm limits to unacceptable behavior, and consistent use of nonhostile, noncorporal sanctions on rule violations with the purpose of improving peer relations and making the school a safer and more positive place for students to learn and develop (Olweus, Limber, & Mihalic, 1999). Other promising bullying and violence prevention programs include PATHS, the Good Behavior Game, FAST Track, Seattle Social Development Project, I Can Problem Solve, and LIFT (Center for the Study and Prevention of Violence (n.d.).

THE SCHOOL COUNSELOR'S ROLE IN BULLYING INTERVENTION

School counselors play a significant role in preparing all students to acquire the attitudes, skills, and knowledge necessary for successful academic achievement (ASCA, 2004; Campbell & Dahir, 1997; Roberts & Mills, 2009); therefore, they can work with students who are involved in bullying situations to help improve the school climate and encourage positive interactions so students can attend school in a safe, orderly, and caring environment (ASCA, 2012). Individual and small group counseling are two activities that are classified as responsive services of the ASCA *National Model* (ASCA, 2012). Responsive services prevent the escalation of problem areas and intervene to alleviate some of the immediate concerns of students. It provides special help to students who are facing problems that interfere with their personal-social, career, or educational development. Additionally, the goal of implementing counseling interventions is to promote students' personal and social growth and foster their educational progress; thus, these services help students resolve personal concerns that could potentially impede their academic achievement if left unattended. Although the ASCA *National Model* (2012) states, "professional school counselors do not provide traditional therapy" (p. 86) school counselors provide students with short-term counseling interventions (ASCA, 2009).

Two of the most effective and appropriate means for school counselors to work with students involved in bullying situations is through the use of play and choice theory/reality therapy (CT/RT) (Glasser, 1998; Nystul, 1995; Schaefer, 2011; Wubbolding, 2011). Play is a medium in which children's knowledge of the world, ability to navigate relationships, and comfort and skill in processing and expressing emotions is communicated (Landreth, 2012). Play is the universal and the natural language of children (Drewes & Schaefer, 2010; Landreth, 2012; Schaefer, 2011). Play provides a means through which conflict can be resolved and feelings can be communicated, and is a child's way of coping with his/her world. A child's play reveals the child's inner world: experiences, feelings or reactions about experiences, wishes, wants, or needs in life, and the child's self-concept (Landreth, 2012). Moreover, play can offer children the means to develop resolutions to specific issues and at the same time develop their emotional and social skills in more generic and transferable outcomes. Play therapy is developmentally appropriate for young children through high school age (O'Conner, 1991), effective in working with children who exhibit aggressive behaviors and conduct problems (Allan & Brown, 1993; Axline, 1947; Bratton, Ray, Rhine, & Jones, 2005; Cattanach, 1992; Fall, Balvanz, Johhson, & Nelson, 1999; Gil, 1991; Kottman, 1993; LeBlanc & Ritchie, 1999; Ray, Bratton, Rhine, & Jones, 2001; Willock, 1983) and known to raise children's self-efficacy and improve learning behaviors (Fall, 1994; Fall et al., 1999). Furthermore, short-term play therapy has been found to be effective with childhood issues such as school-related learning problems, behavioral problems, emotional adjustment, and issues with self-worth and self-esteem (Landreth, 2012; Nystul, 1995; Schaefer, 2011; Riviere, 2006). Short-term play therapy conducted in the schools can range from 4 to 32 sessions; with an average of 10.5 sessions, once a week, for 30-minutes (Drewes & Schaefer, 2010). Children can also benefit from an alternative, condensed format that includes 8 sessions, twice a week for 30 minutes (Ray, Henson, Schottelkorb, Brown, & Muro, 2008)..

According to Drewes, Bratton, and Schaefer (2011), theoretical integration takes "the best elements of two or more approaches to therapy and blends them with the expectation that the result will be more than the sum of the two separate therapies" (p. 23); thus, the aim is to integrate the underlying theory along with the integration of play therapy techniques. From a play therapy perspective, there is growing support for combining different theoretical models in a clinically grounded, integrated manner to address the needs of children, including those impacted by abuse and trauma (Gil, 2006; Kelly & Odenwalt, 2006; Kenney-Noziska, 2008); hence, by combining choice theory/reality therapy (CT/RT) with play therapy interventions and techniques, school counselors can attempt to help students address bullying issues with developmentally, culturally appropriate interventions. Consequently, CRPT is an integrative model of play therapy incorporating elements of cognitive-behavioral models (Knell, 1993) and child-centered models (Landreth, 2012) of play therapy along with choice/reality therapy (Glasser, 1998; Wubbolding, 2000, 2011). Both counseling approaches are well suited for short-term counseling while helping students discover how to make choices regarding their behavior, take responsibility, and use the techniques throughout life to meet their needs (Davis & Clark, 2012; Drewes et al., 2011; Landreth, 2012; Mason & Duba, 2009; Nystul, 1995; Wubbolding, 2011).

CHOICE REALITY PLAY THERAPY

William Glasser (1965, 1998) developed choice theory/reality therapy and CRPT takes its roots from his theory. CRPT is a structured, directive, yet empathic method for counselors to hold the child responsible for the child's choices about behaviors, thoughts, and feelings (Wubbolding, 2000, 2011). It is a brief method of treatment that is problem-focused and goal oriented with the purpose of facilitating adaptive behaviors, thoughts, and feelings. CRPT can be considered as a form of directive play therapy since it includes more structure and guidance by the counselor as children work through their emotional and behavioral difficulties through play. Schaefer (2011) indicated that structuring a child's play is necessary so that the child can reexperience through play, a stressful situation, thereby releasing emotions and hopefully, cognitively, and behaviorally restructuring the event. Furthermore, directive play therapy is more likely to be classified as a type of cognitive behavioral therapy (Ray et al., 2001); thus, it is reasonable to conclude that CRPT would incorporate cognitive-behavioral principles and interventions within the play paradigm.

CRPT Process and Role of the Counselor

CRPT asserts that children are motivated by five basic intrinsic needs including love and belonging, power and achievement, freedom and independence, fun, and survival, and they choose behaviors that best satisfy their own personal needs (Glasser, 1998; Wubbolding, 2011). Children satisfy their needs by satisfying their inner world of wants or pictures representing their ideal, quality world, which includes the type of life they would like to have, the people they want to be with, the possessions or experiences they would like to have, and the ideas and beliefs they value that control their behavior (Glasser, 1998).

CRPT contends the following may be sources of a child's unhappiness: (a) the child is unable to develop satisfying relationship and feels disconnected to others; (b) the child typically blames his or her difficulties on other people; (c) the child focuses and blame his or her unhappiness on things that happened in the past; and (d) the child avoids the fact that he or she is directly or indirectly choosing all that he or she is complaining about (Glasser, 1998; Wubbolding, 2000, 2011). Thus, a basic goal of CRPT is to help children match their inner world to the real world, help them reconnect, take responsibility for the choices they make, and learn better ways to fulfill their needs (Glasser; 1998; Wubbolding, 2011).

In CRPT, counselors implement a three-step process that focuses on the counseling environment and the procedures that lead to client change (Glasser, 2000; Wubbolding, 2011; Wubbolding & Brickell, 1999). The first step is to create an environment that is coercion free and conducive to self-exploration and change where the counselor exhibits an attitude of non-judgmental acceptance in order to help the child identify and clarify problems and opportunities and assess the child's resources (Wubbolding, 2000, 2011). To create a caring environment, counselors exhibit seven relationship-enhancing behaviors such as "supporting, encouraging, listening, accepting, trusting, respecting and negotiating differences" to strengthen the therapeutic alliance between the counselor and the child for effective outcomes (Glasser, 2005, p. 21).

The second step of CRPT, once trust is established, is to confront the child's unrealistic or irresponsible behavior with reality, discuss consequences of the child's actions, and encourage new behaviors that build the child's confidence (Wubbolding, 2000, 2011). Counselors communicate that they will be actively involved in the process by asking questions, listening for themes or behavior patterns, intervening, and having faith in the child to make positive changes in the child's life now if he or she is willing to work to make life enhancing changes. Furthermore, counselors never criticize, argue with, punish, encourage excuses, instill fear, or give up on the child; rather they set firm and appropriate boundaries where the child is required to take responsibility for himself inside and outside of counseling (Wubbolding, 2011; Wubbolding & Brickell, 1999). It is important to note that because children use metaphors in their play, counselors must be aware of what they are doing in the playroom in order to identify themes correctly. For example, children coming from chaotic families will often demonstrate a theme of disorder or messiness throughout their play (Boyd-Webb, 2007).

In the third step of CRPT, counselors guide a child's play by selecting materials and activities, provide interpretations to bring conflict into verbal expression for the child, act as a teacher of responsible behavior where the child is taught skills and alternative behaviors, and use praise to encourage, reinforce, and shape positive behaviors by emphasizing issues of control, mastery, and responsibility for one's own behavior change (Schaefer, 2011; Knell, 1998, 2008; Wubbolding, 2000, 2011). Because CRPT is a directive approach, this step should only be implemented once a positive therapeutic relationship is firmly established and the child is judged to possess sufficient strength to tolerate an emotional upheaval (Schaefer, 2011).

CRPT Procedures That Lead to Change

The WDEP system (i.e., W [wants], D [doing], E [evaluation], and P [plans]) is the procedure that explores tenets of choice theory by identifying children's basic needs, discovering their quality world, discussing how they choose their total behaviors (integrated components of doing, thinking, feeling, and physiology), and determining the direction their behaviors have taken them (Wubbolding, 2000, 2011). It is a system that provides a structure for implementing one of the most important environment establishing skills: listening for wants (quality world pictures), examining total behavior (core beliefs, ineffective and effective self-talk, and their actions), exploring self-evaluation, and attaining positive plans for improvement. These plans should be simple, attainable, measureable, and immediate, involved by the counselor, consistent, controlled by the child, and committed (SAMI^{2}C^3). Specifically, CRPT teaches children strategies to identify and clarify their wants and sharing their perceptions (**W**), describe what they are doing to get what they want and their current direction their behaviors take them (**D**), evaluate their wants and total behaviors (**E**), and to formulate specific plans about how to get their wants and needs met with appropriate choices and behaviors and commit to plans for change (**P**) (Wubbolding, 2011).

Implementing CRPT Model

There are eight steps in facilitating CRPT through the WDEP delivery system of choice theory helping children make better choices to meet their needs (Glasser, 1998; Wubbolding, 2011).

1. *Involvement*: The counselor builds a good, trusting relationship with the child.

2. *Current Behavior*: The child describes his current behavior.
3. *Evaluating Your Behavior*: The child evaluates what going on in his life and how he is helping himself. To help the child, the counselor can ask, "How does this behavior help you?" "How does this behavior hurt you?" "Is this behavior getting you what you want?"
4. *Planning Responsible Behavior*: The counselor and child brainstorm alternatives for helping the child get what he wants in life. The counselor assists the child if he is stuck, but ultimately, the child is responsible for coming up with ways to modify his behavior.
5. *Commitment*: The child selects alternatives for reaching his goals and commits to trying the choices and the new plan. The child chooses one behavior at a time and commits to trying the new behavior.
6. *Accept No Excuses*: The counselor and child examine and evaluate the results. The counselor evaluates the child's level of commitment. If the child reports being unsuccessful, the counselor does not focuses on why or allow the child to give excuses.
7. *No Punishment*: The counselor does not remove the child's logical and natural consequences.
8. *Never Give Up*: The counselor does not give up on the child and does not get discouraged. The counselor gives the child extra sessions, working with him longer than expected.

Because counseling often involves adjusting what is in a child's quality world, it is helpful for the counselor and child to explore what the child's quality world looks like. Intentional questioning is used to explore the purpose and meaning of the child's world before goals and plans are generated. Questions to help the child articulate the quality world include: "Who are the most important people in your life?" What is something that you have done that you are really proud of?" What does it mean to be a friend?" Once these aspects are identified, the counselor can help the child evaluate whether these aspects are realistic. In other words, do these aspects match the child's wants and basic needs? Five general questions are used to facilitate CRPT such as (1) What are you doing or what have you tried? (2) Is what you are doing helping you get what you want? (3) If not, what might be some other things you could try? (4) Which idea would you like to try first? and (5) When would you like to start?

Specific questions counselors could ask when counseling a young child who hits other children when the child does not get his or her way are: "What did you do?" "What is our rule about hitting?" "Is hitting against the rule?" "What were you supposed to do instead of hitting?" "What are you going to do next time?" "Do you want to write your plan for next time or do you want me to write it?" "Let's check tomorrow to see if your new plan is working." With younger children, the counselor is encouraged to change questions into to statements (i.e., I am wondering or I am curious).

Conversely, specific questions counselors could use to ask older children and adolescents who are exhibiting similar behaviors include: "Let's begin by talking about what you have been doing to solve the problem?" It would be helpful if you could give me an idea of how the actions you are doing are helping you? "Is your behavior in touch with *reality*?" "Is your behavior the *responsible* thing to do?" "Is your behavior the *right* thing to do?" "Is your behavior *cost-effective*?" "If your behavior is not getting you what you want, what would you like to do differently?" "What plan would you like to develop?" "When can we follow up on your plan?" As previously mentioned, counselors can use statements such as "I'm wondering about ...." or "I'm curious about..." rather than asking a serious of questions.

Although relevant questions "assist clients in gaining insights, seeing relationships, and arriving at plans and solutions" (Wubbolding, 2011, p. 104), the WDEP system consists of more than a series of questions. It is a listening system that involves "translating tales of woe into wants, goals, hopes and aspirations" and "provides a methodology for dealing with resistance and denial (p. 31). Thus, in addition to questions, counselors use tracking (stating what the child is doing), restatement (paraphrasing with empathy what the child has said), and reflection of feelings (clarifying verbal and nonverbal emotional cues).

Through the WDEP system, the counselor helps the child explore his or her basic needs and examines chosen behaviors that are and are not working as a process for therapeutic intervention (Wubbolding, 2000, 2011). CRPT is a process where the child learns how to solve problems, and counselors help the child to practice the transition from external control thinking to internal control thinking by learning to reframe language in an empowering way. Teaching the child the language of inner control includes recognizing the value of phrases such as "I chose to do it" rather than "He made me do it" so the child learns that he or she can empower himself or herself to regulate the child's life more effectively (Wubbolding, 2011, p. 101). One of the keys to CRPT is helping children to make judgments about what will happen if they do or do not do something, while simultaneously, providing opportunities for detecting and confronting excuses and considering consequences of actions.

CASE STUDY: TAYLOR

The following case example illustrates the use of CRPT conducted with an 11-year-old boy who has been defiant and aggressive toward others. The client was seen for eight sessions; each lasting approximately 40 minutes once a week.

Background Data

Taylor is an 11-year-old, White male, in the fifth grade. He attends school in an urban area. Taylor's parents have been married for 18 years, have recently separated, and are going through a divorce. He is the middle child with one older brother, Evan, age 16 and a younger brother, James, age nine. At the beginning of fourth grade, Taylor began acting aggressively toward other students and exhibited bullying behaviors. Teachers have reported that he has pushed, kicked, hit other students as well as verbally taunted them. They also report he has been disrespectful and has vandalized school property when he was angry. During his fourth grade year, Taylor's bullying behaviors continued and his grades dropped from As and Bs in his subjects to low Cs. Because of his bullying behaviors, Taylor was not allowed to try-out for the football, basketball, and track teams in fifth grade.

Taylor just transitioned into fifth grade where is now has to change classes. He continues to struggle academically. His teachers report that he talks back, does not participate in class, does not turn in his homework on a regular basis, has sudden outburst of anger, and is physically hitting other students. Taylor missed 5 days of school before the first report period in November. In addition to an increase in absences, Taylor is tardy to first period at least 2 out of the 5 days of the week. In consulting with Taylor's mother, she reports that she does not know why Taylor is skipping school because she drops him off in the front of school every morning. His father used to bring him to the school in the morning, but since the separation, she has been bringing him. She also reports her marriage has been "shaky" for the past 2 years and during that time, there has been a lot of screaming and arguing. She also reports that Taylor has been fighting with his brothers, and talking back and not listening to her. She is trying to adjust to being a single mother of three boys, but it has been difficult. Taylor has been referred to the counselor by his mother and teachers because of his declining grades and increase aggressive behaviors.

Taylor Receives Choice Reality Play Therapy

In their first counseling session, the counselor and Taylor established goals for counseling which included:

- *Goal One*—To explore Taylor's quality world.
- *Goal Two*—To help Taylor understand his wants and needs as it relates to his interactions with family, peers, and school staff.
- *Goal Three*—To help Taylor find better ways to meet his need for love, belonging, survival, power, freedom, and/or fun without infringing on other people's rights to meet theirs.
- *Goal Four*—To help Taylor make effective decisions to meet his needs in order to prevent problems before they happen.
- *Goal Five*—To help Taylor become connected or reconnected with people he has chosen to place in his quality world.
- *Goal Six*—To help Taylor gain psychological strength, accept personal responsibility, and regain control of his life.

Expressive art (Bruneau & Protivnak, 2012; Gladding, 2011) was used throughout the counseling process to help Taylor examine specific incidents related to his bullying behaviors, to clarify how he can best fulfill his needs, and evaluate his behaviors. Additionally, Taylor needs to learn how to make effective and need satisfying choices, both now and in the future and, importantly, without infringing the needs of others. Five specific expressive art directives were used during the counseling process to explore his quality world, total behavior, and WDEP process. The counselor recognized that the brief work accomplished in eight sessions with Taylor was only a small part of change that needed to happen in the larger family system. Consequently, it is important the counselor establishes an on-going partnership with Taylor's family so everyone can work together to help resolve Taylor's problem while helping the family finding solutions to theirs within their social context (ASCA, 2012).

DIRECTIVE 1: EXPLORING TAYLOR'S QUALITY WORLD THROUGH SANDPLAY

The use of the sandtray allowed Taylor to express his inner and outer world to his wants and needs (Homeyer & Sweeney, 2011). The counselor asked Taylor, "If you could change one thing in your world, show what it would be and place them in the sand; you may add as many items as you like to create a world in the sand." As he constructed his world in the sandtray, the counselor listened and attended more through body language and less through words and employed similar child-centered techniques of tracking, paraphrasing and reflections of content and feelings (DeJong & Berg, 2008; Homeyer & Sweeney, 2011; Vinturella & James, 1987). To establish the therapeutic relationship questions were minimal.

Using the sandtray and the miniatures Taylor created a picture of his family playing in the park. He placed two dog miniatures next to each other and three others directly across from them. Once he finished his picture, Taylor was invited to share it with the counselor. The counselor asked, "Tell me about your tray." "What is the title?" "Perhaps you could make up a story." As he began to speak, the story unfolded. To process his pictures the counselor asked, "Are you in the tray?" "Which figure represents you?" "Are there others in the tray?" "What (who) has the most power?" "What are you saying to the others?"

Through discussion, Taylor stated that he was playing baseball with his family and was having fun. His parents were not fighting, yelling or screaming at each other; rather they were laughing and smiling like a family should be. He described how he wanted his parents to stay together and not get a divorce. He was sad that he did not get to see his father often and missed him very much. The sandtray activity allowed the counselor to discover the source or motivation of Taylor's bullying behaviors. Themes derived from Taylor's play were powerlessness over his family's situation, disconnected from his father, lack of freedom to see his father, and lack of enjoyment as a family unit.

DIRECTIVE 2: EXPLORING TAYLOR'S QUALITY WORLD THROUGH MUSIC

Music is a central part of at least 90% of adolescents' lives (Kiefer, 2004) and may serve as a vehicle for self-expression and emotional release (Campbell, Connell, & Beegle, 2007). Music intervention is a strategy implemented by counselors who use some form of music application in their work with clients in a positive, constructive way but who lack a degree or special training in music therapy (Gallant & Holosko, 2001). Songs can bring vivid memories of persons, places, and events from an individual's past and serve to document ones thoughts, feelings, and emotions at a given time or place. Thus, the use of music can be used to explore a child's quality world. The "soundtrack of your life" activity is used to gather information on a child's life since for many students it is often easier to explain who they are through music and lyrics. The counselor asks the student "If your life was a movie or television show, what would the theme song be?" Other topics could include "Write about the most influential person in your life. Describe what this person has taught you about life and how their influence has shaped the person you are." "Write about the most challenging experience in your life. Explain the events leading up to the event, and what happened after these events. Describe how the experience affected or changed your life." "Write about a change you made in your life. Describe why and how the change occurred. Explain whether the change was positive or negative and how or if this impacted your life." "Write about how your upbringing helped to define the person you are today. Describe whether culture and environment had any influence in how your identity was shaped." "Write about the most memorable moment in your life. Explain how and why this moment is significant. Give a lot of description." The student chooses the most significant moments in his or her life and thinks about songs and lyrics that the student feels connect to these events. Once the autobiographical playlist is created, the counselor and student process the activity.

Through Taylor's autobiographical playlist, several need-satisfying bullying themes were presented: (a) He chose the song, "Second Chance" by The Shine Down to represent how he felt disconnected and unloved from his parents; (b) He chose the song "Fight For Your Right" by the Beastie Boys to represent how he had to fight for everything because he had no control over anything at home. He does not believe he has the freedom to do things or engage in activities that he would like to do. Taylor stated, "Mom is never home, so Evan is in charge. Basically, if I don't do what Evan wants me to do he either hits me or yells at me. So, I fight back to avoid getting hurt;" and (c) He chose the song, "Bohemian Rhapsody" by Queen because it was one of his dad's favorite songs and they used to sing it together. Taylor spoke about missing his father and the fun stuff they used to do together. He wished there was something he could do to get his parents back together (feeling powerless over his family situation).

DIRECTIVE 3: EXPLORING TAYLOR'S TOTAL BEHAVIOR THROUGH PUPPETS AND STORYTELLING

The use of puppetry and the mutual storytelling technique can be used to explore a child's total behavior. Using puppets or stuffed animals in CRPT can help a child communicate, both verbally and nonverbally, the child's personal issues in an impersonal way which makes it possible to indirectly address issues the child is experiencing such as bullying. Because the puppets indirectly do the talking rather than the child directly, this distance enables the child to step back to a "safe place" where the child can examine his or her behaviors, opinions, emotions, and reactions (Landreth, 2012). Playing with puppets may also provide a method for understanding the child's language, beliefs, and value systems, and for teaching social skills that could enhance self-control (Drewes, 2009). Furthermore, role-playing with puppets may also help the child learn theory of mind, which is the ability to use empathy, or to imagine what someone else is feeling or thinking. Thus, in puppet play, the counselor joins in the play, which provides a path for intervention with the goal of modifying or altering the child's thoughts, behaviors, and feelings.

Using the five steps to mutual storytelling, Taylor was able to share his inner conflicts, frustrations, wishes, and defenses (Gardner, 1993).

> *Step One*—Invite the child to volunteer to create a story. The counselor began their counseling session by stating, "We're going to play a storytelling game using puppets."
>
> *Step Two*—Turn on the recorder and narrate the instructions. The counselor explained to Taylor that the story should have a beginning, a middle, and an end. Then the counselor added, "Tell me what the people are doing, feeling, and thinking."
>
> *Step Three*—Record the child's story and listens for relevant themes. Taylor chose a recent situation in which he had been disciplined by the school principal for hitting another student. Taylor was able to tell his side of a story about this incident using different puppets to represent the people that were involved in the situation: Taylor, Taylor's teacher, the principal, and the other student. Taylor first used the puppet animals to tell the story as it actually happened.
>
> *Step Four*—Create a story that is similar to the child's story in characters and setting but has healthier resolutions and better behavioral adaptations. Taylor created a similar story, but this time he gave the story a more positive outcome. For instance, rather than hitting the student he "doodled" in his notebook to calm down. This prevented him from being disciplined by the teacher and principal.
>
> *Step Five*—Tell the new story and make sure that the child understands the message that the counselor conveyed. By reenacting the event, Taylor was able to explore the feelings he had experienced when the other student angered him and then he was able to devise alternative, positive solutions. When the story was over the counselor asked Taylor what the moral of the story was. Since he could not think of one the counselor asked him to make up a title for his story. He titled it, "Calm After the Storm" because he needed to remain calm after an unpleasant event.

Telling his story using the puppets gave Taylor a chance to visualize his thinking process, explore his behaviors and feelings surrounding the incident, and learn new behaviors and problem-solving methods for getting what he wanted. In the end, Taylor was able to identify the problem (i.e., he got mad when another student bumped him); the problem led to behavior (i.e., he hit the student); that in turn caused consequences (i.e., in-school suspension and punishment from mom); and, as a result, he was able to express his feelings (i.e., anger and frustration) and thoughts (i.e., I am tired of being pushed around) surrounding the incident. Subsequently, this led Taylor to develop new behaviors to cope with his thoughts and feelings (e.g., doodle in his notebook).

DIRECTIVE 4: EXPLORING TAYLOR'S WDEP THROUGH CARTOON STRIPS

Gray (1994) developed a cartooning strategy known as comic/cartoon strip conversations. A cartoon strip conversation is a technique in which cartoon sketches are used to enhance social understanding by making thoughts, perspectives, and verbalizations visible. For example, two characters in a social situation will appear along with "bubbles" which contain what each character was saying, thinking, or feeling. It also helps children learn how to behave in a socially acceptable manner, conform to social standards, and take into account the thoughts of other people in a given situation. "Children with limited verbal skills benefit from comic strip conversations because they rely on extensive use of visual materials" (Glaeser, Pierson, & Fritschmann, 2003, p. 15). Thus, cartoon strip conversations help children paint a picture of what they really want, how things could get better, and develop pro-social strategies. Based on an evidence-based practice called social stories, cartoon strip conversations help improve a child's social skills, on-task behavior, and appropriate play behaviors, and may help reduce disruptive behaviors (Attwood, 2011; Rogers & Myles, 2001; Whittingham, Sofronoff, Sheffield, & Sanders, 2009). In CRPT, the cartoon strip conversation technique can assist children in discovering what they want, examining their present behavior, establishing realistic goals to meet their needs, and planning for more adaptive behaviors. At the same time, the counselor encourages the child to take appropriate action by changing ways of relating and working through issues using problem solving or decision-making methods.

First, the counselor explained the purpose of the cartoon strip technique (e.g., to write or draw down things that happened—especially those that made him angry, upset or confused), and described the different elements to be included (Gray, 1994). Next, Taylor was asked to think of a situation where he became mad or upset because he felt like no one was listening or paying attention to him; thus, he physically hit another student. After, he was instructed to depict his thoughts, behaviors, and feelings surrounding the event in his cartoon strip. As Taylor created his cartoon strip, the counselor gathered information and helped guide him through the process while he was drawing by asking "Where are you? "

"Who is here with you?" "What are you doing?" "What happened?" "What did you say?" "What did others say? (speech bubbles)" "What did you think when you said that?" and "What did others think when they said that? (thought bubbles)." "What are you feeling?" "How is your relationship affected?" "What would a person who does not bully do in this situation?" Once Taylor completed his cartoon strip, he and the counselor brainstormed possible solutions or ways the situation could have been handled differently. Using the same strip, Taylor created an alternative ending where he replaced his previous thoughts and behaviors with more functional ones.

The goal of this directive was to have Taylor think about the many bullying incidents he was involved in so he could gain an understanding that he is in control over his behavior and reactions to events and his choice of negative consequences that result from his bullying behavior. Through processing, Taylor was able to understand how his bullying behavior and thinking were distorted by his feelings of being powerless to change his home situation, wanting to "fit-in" again since his grades have declined, and wanting to have fun at home and school. He also realized the harm he caused to numerous relationships due to his bullying behaviors. Subsequently, Taylor and the counselor developed a plan that would allow him to meet his needs in a healthy manner without infringing on the rights of others.

DIRECTIVE 5: EXPLORING TAYLOR'S WDEP THROUGH BRIDGE TECHNIQUE

The bridge drawing technique can assist children in understanding where their present behaviors are and where they would like their future behavior to be (Hays & Lyons, 1981). It is a visual aid used to assess how children view obstacles and how they choose to face them. Typically, this technique is used in the initial phase of counseling to establish counseling goals, express more adaptive behaviors, and determine how much progress is needed or desired by the client.

The counselor asked Taylor to "draw a picture of a bridge going from one place to another and draw a landscape on the side of the bridge you have come from and draw a landscape of the side you are going to." The counselor also reminded him to draw a picture of himself in the present and a picture of how he would like things to look in the future; plus, draw himself somewhere in the picture. Taylor used markers, colored pencils, and stickers to create his bridge scene. Questions the counselor asked about the drawing were: Where is the bridge?; What time of day is it?; Where is the bridge leading to?; Where is the bridge coming from?;

Where are you in relation to the bridge (coming, going, on the bridge, under the bridge ... etc.); What is the bridge crossing over? Is it dangerous? What is the bridge made out of? Is it sturdy or flimsy? How long is the bridge? How high is the bridge?

Taylor and the counselor examined his drawing. Taylor described it as "a battle of wills between two Pokémon's, Arceus, and Magakarp." He indicated that he was Arceus because he is the creator of all Pokémon; he can become any type of Pokémon; and he always wins. On the other hand, Magakarp is a much weaker Pokémon and really does not pose as a threat. Even though Magakarp was on the right side of the bridge blocking the entrance to the other side, Arceus had no problem going through him. Upon further examination, Taylor acknowledged that he acts aggressively toward others when his parents are fighting, but stated he could not help it. Although the counselor acknowledged that Taylor felt powerless in his family situation, she did not accept his excuse and challenged his faulty thinking. The purpose of this directive was to have Taylor think about choice in life, obstacles that may prevent him from reaching his goals, and to develop strategies that would remove the barriers that are blocking his success.

Since Taylor was experiencing issues with anger management, the counselor also had him draw a bridge spanning from his current behavior (e.g., hitting others, throwing objects, being disrespectful to teachers and parents, and receiving low grades) to the way he would like to behave. The drawing technique provided a springboard for discussing Taylor's coping skills, new patterns of behavior, and emotional responses to the changes being experienced, which over several sessions, created a bridge to Taylor discovering his own inner strength, reliance, and trust in himself.

The bridge technique was also used during the termination phase of counseling to compare the products of the two drawings (initial and final) and to discuss them in context of progress made and insights gained. In the final session, Taylor was able to summarize how his bullying behaviors played a role in school functioning and relationships with family, friends, and school staff. He related these insights by reviewing all expressive art creations made throughout counseling to assess his treatment progress and reinforce change. This allowed Taylor to see the similarities between his bullying behaviors and his parent's aggressive behaviors toward each other. In the last session, Taylor arrived at several conclusions: First, he recognized that his bullying behavior was an experience of loss (e.g., loss of his family as a unit). Second, he recognized that when he engaged in bullying behaviors this led to having (a) no feeling of safety, which meant no security; (b) loss of belonging, which led him to question who is my group? Who are my friends, and how do I fit in?; (c) loss of power which led to his belief that he was no good and could not do anything right; (d) loss of freedom which limited his choices and decrease sense of power and control to change his behavior; and (e) no fun. Consequently, Taylor and the counselor discussed ways he could use his new insights, behaviors, and resources to refrain from engaging in bullying behaviors so he could achieve personal and academic success.

Concluding CRPT With Taylor

Taylor was able to use CRPT to explore his behaviors, express his emotions, and deal with ongoing thoughts and feelings. Over the course of counseling, the following themes were prevalent in Taylor's play. He felt disconnected from and unloved by his parents. He felt powerless (i.e., lacked control) over his home situation. He felt different or inferior from his peers because of his declining grades, lack of participation in extracurricular activities, and his parents separation. In analyzing his work, the counselor and Taylor discovered a variety of feelings besides his anger such as fear, sadness, and love; consequently, Taylor demonstrated a strong desire to belong and be accepted by his family and peers. Although not all of his bullying behaviors had completely disappeared at the end of the eight weeks, a reduction of aggressive behaviors were noted at home, in the classroom, and in his expressive art work. His work even began to show concepts around safety, trust, and hope for the future. Throughout the year, the counselor continued to check-in with Taylor and met with him as needed.

Taylor was able to use CRPT to explore his behaviors, express his emotions, and deal with ongoing thoughts and feelings. Over the course of counseling, the following themes were prevalent in Taylor's play. He felt disconnected from and unloved by his parents. He felt powerless (i.e. lacked control) over his home situation. He felt different or inferior from his peers because of his declining grades, lack of participation in extracurricular activities, and his parents separation. In analyzing his work, we discovered a variety of feelings besides his anger such as fear, sadness, and love. Consequently, Taylor demonstrated a strong desire to belong and be accepted by his family and peers. Although not all of his bullying behaviors had completely disappeared at the end of the eight weeks, a reduction of aggressive behaviors was noted at home, in the classroom, and in his expressive art work. His work even began to show concepts around safety, trust and hope for the future. Throughout the year, the counselor continued to check-in with Taylor and met with him as needed.

GROUP COUNSELING AND CHOICE REALITY PLAY THERAPY

The responsive services component of the ASCA *National Model* (2012) provides for targeted assistance for those students who are not achieving their potential. Small group work with students is one strategy for helping students become more successful in their personal relationships, educational pursuits, and career aspirations. Students who would benefit from working in small groups are referred from guidance activities, self-referral, or referral by parents, teachers, and peers (Sink, Eppler, & Edwards, 2012). Additionally, because groups are a microcosm of the real world, small group settings are ideal places to conduct both preventive guidance work and remedial counseling. Group work can provide students with the opportunity to learn more about themselves and others, work through interpersonal issues, learn appropriate social skills, and develop strategies to positively impact their school climate. Group counseling can help group members learn effective and efficient ways of dealing with their academic, career, and personal-social issues, and allow them to practice and utilize these behaviors in a safe environment (Sink et al., 2012).

Group play therapy is a viable intervention for addressing the needs of children in a school setting who are experiencing adjustment difficulties. It is equally effective as individual play therapy because several children playing in a group can create a more relaxed (anxiety reduced) environment for children to express themselves (Ginott, 1994). Group play therapy has been correlated with young children's positive changes which include (a) externalizing behaviors such as aggression, impulsivity, and self-control; (b) internalizing behaviors such as depression, anxiety, and somatization; (c) academic performance; and (d) increases in self-esteem, self-concept, and self-confidence (Landreth, Homeyer, Glover, & Sweeney, 1996). The focus in group play therapy with children shifts from intrapersonal processes to interpersonal interactions and processes where children are able to learn and practice new relationship skills (Berg, Landreth, & Fall, 1998). For many children, a play therapy group may provide the closest experience to family structure and acceptance as possible (Sweeney & Homeyer, 1999).

Girl Empowerment Group

Problem-centered groups focus on meeting the needs of students who are exhibiting dysfunctional, unhealthy or self-defeating behaviors since these behaviors may interfere with or become a barrier to normal functioning, including academic growth (Sink et al., 2012). As noted previously, children who are victimized by bullies often experience confusion, anger, blame, shame, guilt, lowered self-esteem, sadness, and feelings of insecurity which affects their learning while at school (Olweus et al., 1999). As a result, a problem-focused group called, "Girl Power" was developed to help sixth and seventh grade girls who are targets of bullying. The purpose of the girl empowerment group was to (a) increase female students who have been victimized by bullies self-esteem and self-worth; (b) enhance their self-awareness and social-awareness; and (c) increase their problem-solving and decision-making skills so they can better cope. The following National Standards for School Counseling (ASCA, 2004) included under the personal-social domain were addressed by the "Girl Power" group:

Standard A: Students will acquire the attitudes, knowledge, and interpersonal skills to help them understand and respect self and others.

- Goal: Girls will learn to communicate effectively with peers in an appropriate manner.
- Outcome: After completion of group all girls will be able to express feelings more appropriately. They will learn necessary skills and techniques to stand up for themselves and others. As a result, they will have a more positive self-concept about themselves and the school.

Standard B: Students will make decisions, set goals, and take necessary action to achieve goals.

- Goal: Girls will learn effective problem solving skills.
- Outcome: After the termination of group, girls will have several coping methods to deal with conflicts involving children who bully. They will have multiple opportunities to hear other students' opinions on the subject as well as learn different strategies from how other girls have dealt with or will deal with children who bully in similar situations.

Standard C: Students will understand safety and survival skills.

- Goal: Girls will learn ways to reduce stress and tension caused by friends or children who bully.
- Outcome: After completion of group, girls will have different ways of dealing with the stressors related to being a target of bullying. Since stress is a barrier to academic success (i.e., studying and getting good grades) girls would now have ways to deal with children who bully instead of letting it bother them every day with no answer in sight.

Group Composition

Participants for the group were recruited from observations conducted by teachers and counselors in the school and from surveys that students filled out in their English class. For accountability purposes, the survey was used as the pretest and posttest for assessing changes and growth as a result of the group as well as to see what, if any, changes could be made to the group to make it even more successful (ASCA, 2012). Before the group officially started, the counselor conducted a prescreening assessment by meeting with each potential group member to see if her individual goals would fit within the goals for the group, inform her what the group would involve, and if she was agreeable to participating. An informed consent and disclosure statement was given to potential participants for parental approval for group participation. The girl's empowerment group consisted of five participants and was a closed group since the loss of a group member during the therapeutic process could have potential negative implications on other group members (Yalom, 1995).

The group met over an 11-week period, during their lunch period, anywhere from 40-50 minutes with each session focusing on a content area included within four phases of group work (Corey, Corey, & Corey, 2008). The 11-session girl empowerment group using CRPT is provided in Table 12.1. Overall, the girls' empowerment group helped girls gain information regarding female-bullying behaviors (e.g., relational aggression), empowered them to take action, and highlighted coping strategies to help alleviate the bullying. Group members were able to share their anxieties in a safe and secure environment and were able to encourage and empower each other to take action on their decisions by providing support, feedback, and unconditional acceptance. Studies have shown that counseling programs involving group activities have led to reducing bullying activity (Mouttappa, Gallaher, & Valentes, 2004).

SUMMARY

Bullying is an age-old problem that is widespread in our schools and communities. It is an unacceptable antisocial behavior that can undermine the quality of the school environment, affect students' academic and social outcomes, cause victims physical, emotional and psychological trauma, and, in extreme cases, lead to serious violence and suicide. Legislative responses in the U.S. have mirrored this concern, with both federal and state mandates holding schools accountable to develop active antibullying policies and programs (U.S. Department of Education, 2011). In response, many school

Table 12.1. Girl Power Group Using Choice-Reality Play Therapy

Session	*Description and Activity*
1	**Getting to Know You** • Rules of the group (developed by group members) and confidentiality • Icebreaker—Students will introduce themselves by playing a modified version of the game Don't Break the Ice (Milton Bradley). As the group members knock out a block of ice, they share something based upon the color sticker located on the bottom of the cube (Kenney-Noziska, 2008).
2	**Setting Group Goals, Exploring My World** • Welcome the group back, go over names, have the group summarize the previous session, and remind them of the ground rules. • Use the worksheet, "Red, Yellow, and Green Light Pictures" (see *My Quality World Workbook* by Carleen Glasser, 1996) to explore group members quality world. Invite each student to share the picture with the group, explain their picture, and tell about their current situation. As students share their stories, the counselor draws attention to similarities amongst stories and feelings.
3	**Understanding Bullying Behaviors and Reactions** • Using the book, *Mean, Mean Maureen Green* by Cox (2001) group members will learn various aspects of bullying. The goal of this session involves helping members understand the bullying, as well as increasing members' awareness of when bullying happens. • Incident drawing will be used to explore group members' reactions to being bullied and recognizing their triggers.
4	**Getting In Touch** • Counselor will lead a discussion about variety of feelings using the "Feelings Hide-and-Seek" game (Kenney-Noziska, 2008). A therapeutic version of the childhood game hide-and-seek, feelings are initially hidden, and through the course of hide-and-seek are found and discussed. Feelings are written on index cards that are hidden at varying levels of difficulty around the room. Players take turns finding the hidden feeling cards and processing a time they experienced the emotion written on the card. • At the end of the session, groups members can place their worries and fear in the "worry can" (Lowenstein, 2010). • Homework—next session they will be doing a story and activity about being a victim of bullying; thus, have them think of a time when they were bullied.

(Table continues on next page)

Table 12.1. Continued

Session	*Description and Activity*
5	**How Big is Your Hurt—Storytelling using Puppets** • Ask group members "how big is your hurt today?" As way of measuring, ask them to stretch out their arms as wide as their hurt is big. Then take a wide ribbon and measure the length of the child's arms (this equals the amount of hurt). Cut the ribbon. Then put the hurt ribbon in an envelope. Decide together where to keep the envelope. Tell group members that in a few weeks we will measure their hurt again. • Using a situation when they were the victim of bullying, group members will write a story on the incident and how they handled the situation. Group members will be asked to read their short story to other group members; puppets will be used to enact the scenarios. A CD-ROM version for the personal computer called, "The Mutual Storytelling Game" (Erford, 2000) helps students construct backgrounds and offers diverse character sets to facilitate storytelling. • Homework—group members will bring items that would describe who they are and how they see themselves and what they think others see in them.
6	**Who Am I?** • The "Bag Self Portrait" activity is used to explore how group members define themselves. Group members will create a self-portrait on the side of a brown paper bag. It can be made with paint, crayons, colored pencils, markers, hair, fabric, etc. Either side of the bag can be used to express certain things. For example, if they wanted to represent their fears and dreams or goals and aspirations. Another idea for this art activity is to have group members put things inside the paper bag that make them the person they are. It can be pictures of people who are important to them, personal items, favorite books, CDs, paintings...anything. At the end of the activity, group members will process the activity.
7	**Dear Me** • The "Erase the Place" technique (Goodyear-Brown, 2005) will be utilized for groups members to address cognitive distortions based on messages received from the child who bullies. This activity will help members increase their self-awareness, gain increased self-esteem and increase confidence by changing self-defeating thoughts. • The "Positive Posting" activity will be used to combat the negative messages received and replaced with positive qualities (Lowenstein, 2010). This positive approach will enhance their self-esteem. • Homework. To reinforce their learning, journaling will be introduced. Discuss why people keep journals, what people write in journals, and ask group members to write a journal entry pertaining to being a target of bullying. Each group member will get a notebook to keep. Ask them to write in it each day about a bullying incident or whatever else they want. Once students have completed writing, ask for volunteers to share some of what they wrote. • Letter writing activity will be used to encourage them to use the letter as a way for them to express how they hope to grow and change in the upcoming months (Riordan, 1996). The counselor will hand out writing paper and an envelope. Group members will be instructed to write a letter to themself answering the sentence starters from a list. Let them know that no one will see the letter except for them. Once they have written the letter and sealed it in an envelope have them address the envelope to themself. The counselor will mail the letter to them in 3 months.

(Table continues on next page)

Table 12.1. Continued

Session	*Description and Activity*
8	**I Will Survive** • Assertiveness training for effective reactions to bully. Group members will learn assertive strategies to help them survive a child who bullies. They will learn assertive communication skills, and introducing skills to help group members feel empowered in challenging situations. • Using a "Road Map" activity worksheet, group members will develop an action plan using the new assertive skills when presented with a challenging bullying situation.
9	**Weathering The Storm** • The "Weather the Storm" activity is a way to channel group members' inner strength and focus on the things that they can control (Knell, 2008). Sometimes staying inside during a storm (i.e., bullying situations) is not an option! The goal of this activity is to encourage group members to use positive self-talk, build their self-esteem and supply them with a technique for self-soothing. To achieve this goal group members will create a mantra (a coping self-statement), make a mantra print (a creative representation of the self-statement), and select a location for her mantra print. Each group member will share her creation, what the creation represents, and her positive strengths and qualities so she can weather the storm.
10	**Making Connection, Finding Supports** • This session allowed members to explore, identify, and discuss a place at school, home, or in the community where they would feel safe and where they could go to and who they can turn to for support. • Group members will complete the "Give Me A Hand" activity where groups members will trace their hand and on each finger group members will write a person or place they could go to. It is helpful to place a phone number next to the name. • Follow-up on "How Big is Your Hurt" activity. Ask group members how big (or little) is their hurt now by having them hold out their arms as wide as the hurt is now. With the wide ribbon, measure how big the hurt is now. Cut the ribbon. Take out the ribbon from the hurt envelope and compare the measurement of the two ribbons. Hopefully, group members hurt will be lessened and the ribbon will be smaller. If this is the case ask group members about how much less hurt they are feeling now, or reinforce that in time their hurt will get smaller, and even go away. Even if it takes a long time, remind them there are things they can do to stay safe and have fun.
11	**Grow With Me** • This session will give group members an opportunity to discuss what they have learned and to say good-bye. They will also discuss how they can transfer what they have learned in this group to other situation in and out of school. • Group members will decorate a cup and plant their seeds in their cup. The "Planting a Seed" activity will be used to reinforce that as they grow and change the flower/plant will be there to grow and change right along with them. The flower can serve as a reminder of what they learned from being in the group. Ask group members to take home their cups, place it in sunlight, water it often, and watch as it grow and change as they grow and change.

districts have embraced universal, schoolwide efforts such as the Olweus Bullying Prevention Program (Olweus, 1993), although the majority of antibullying programs have produced nonsignificant or weak effects (Farrington & Ttofi, 2009; Merrell et al., 2008; Ttofi & Farrington, 2011; Ttofi, Farrington, & Baldry, 2010).

To address bullying in the schools, school counselors are well suited for a central role in a school's antibullying efforts. As part of the responsive services in the ASCA *National Model* (2012), school counselors' work with students individually or in a small group to address issues surrounding bullying. In this chapter, CRPT was introduced as a method for working with children who are involved in bullying situations. This brief, problem-focused, and goal-oriented method of treatment can be used to help students explore and adapt their behaviors, thoughts, and feelings. Implementation procedures have been discussed and various techniques were employed using case studies. By combining expressive play therapy techniques with choice theory/reality therapy principles using the WDEP method (Wubbolding, 2000, 2011), it is hoped that the school counselors gained a developmentally appropriate framework for addressing students wants, needs, and behaviors in combating the adverse effects of bullying.

REFERENCES

Allan, J. & Brown, K. (1993). Jungian play therapy in elementary schools. *Elementary School Guidance & Counseling, 28,* 30-42.

American School Counselor Association. (2004). *ASCA National standards for students*. Alexandria, VA: Author.

American School Counselor Association. (2009). The professional school counselor and student mental health. *Position Statements*. Alexandria, VA: Author.

American School Counselor Association (2012). *The ASCA National Model: A framework for school counseling programs*. Alexandria, VA: Author.

Attwood, T. (2011, March 26). The links between social stories, comic strip conversations and cognitive models. Retrieved from http://www.tonyattwood.com.au/index

Axline, V. M. (1947). *Play therapy: The inner dynamics of childhood*. Boston, MA: Houghton Mifflin.

Baumeister, A. L., Storch, E. A., & Geffken, G. R. (2008). Peer victimization in children with learning disabilities. *Child and Adolescent Social Work, 25,* 11-23.

Bender, D., & Losel, F. (2011). Bullying at school as a predictor of delinquency, violence, and other antisocial behavior in adulthood. *Criminal Behaviour and Mental Health, 21,* 99-106.

Berg, R., Landreth, G., & Fall, K.A. (1998). *Group counseling: Concepts and procedures* (3rd ed.). Munice, IN: Accelerated Development.

Boyd-Webb, N. (2007). *Play therapy with children in crisis: Individual, group, and family treatment* (3rd ed.). New York, NY: Guilford Press.

Bradshaw, C. P., Sawyer, A. L., & O'Brennan. L. M. (2007). Bullying and peer victimization at school: Perceptual differences between students and school staff. *School Psychology Review, 36,* 361-382.

Bratton, S. C., Ray, D., Rhine, T., & Jones, L. (2005). The efficacy of play therapy with children: A meta-analytic review of treatment outcomes. *Professional Psychology, Research and Practice, 36,* 376-390. doi:10.1037/0735-7028.36.4.376

Bruneau, L., & Protivnak, J. J. (2012). Adding to the toolbox: Using creative interventions with high school students. *Journal of School Counseling, 10*(9). Retrieved from http://www.jsc.montana.edu/articles/v10n9.pdf

Campbell, P., Connell, C., & Beegle A. (2007). Adolescents' expressed meanings of music in and out of school. *Journal of Research in Music Education, 55*(3), 220–236. doi:10.1177/002242940705500304

Campbell, C. A., & Dahir, C. A. (1997). *Sharing the vision: The National standards for school counseling programs.* Alexandria, VA: American School Counseling Association.

Campbell, W., & Missiuna, C. (2011). Bullying risk in children with disabilities: A review of the literature. *CanChild Centre for Childhood Disability Research.* Retrieved from http://www.canchild.ca/en/canchildresources/bullying_risk_children_disabilities.asp

Cappadocia, M. C., Weiss, J. A., & Pepler, D. (2012). Bullying experiences among children and youth with autism spectrum disorders. *Journal of Autism and Developmental Disorders, 42*(2), 266-277.

Cattanach, A. (1992). *Play therapy with abused children.* London, England: Jessica Kingsley.

Conners-Burrow, N. A., Johnson, D. L., Whiteside-Mansell, L., McKelvey, L., & Gargus, R. A. (2009). Adults matter: Protecting children from the negative impacts of bullying. *Psychology in the Schools, 46*(7), 593-604. doi:10.1002/pits.20300

Centers for Disease Control. (2010). Youth Risk Behavior Surveillance Survey—United States, 2009. Surveillance summaries: Morbidity and mortality weekly report [MMWR] 2010; 59 (No. SS-5). Retrieved from http://www.cdc.gov/mmwr/pdf/ss/ss5905.pdf

Center for the Study and Prevention of Violence. (n.d). *Blueprints for violence prevention.* The Center for the Study and Prevention of Violence—a research program of the Institute of Behavioral Science (IBS) at the University of Colorado at Boulder. Retrieved from http://www.colorado.edu/cspv/blueprints/

Charach, A., Pepler, D., & Ziegler, S. (1995). Bullying at school: A Canadian perspective: A survey of problems and suggestions for intervention. *Education Canada, 35*(1), 12-18.

Cole, D. A., Maxwell, M. A., Dukewich, T. L., & Yosick, R. (2010) Targeted peer victimization and the construction of positive and negative self-cognitions: connections to depressive symptoms in children. *Journal of Clinical Child & Adolescent Psychology, 39*(3), 421-435.

Cook, C., Kirk, R. W., Guerra, N. G., Kim, T. E., & Sadek, S. (2010). Predictors of bullying and victimization in childhood and adolescence: A meta-analytic investigation. *School Psychology Quarterly, 25*(2), 65-83.

Corey, M., Corey, G., & Corey, C. (2008). *Groups: Process and practice* (8th ed.). Belmont, CA: Brook/Cole, Cengage Learning

Cox, J. (2001). *Mean, mean Maureen Green* (Illustrated by C. Fisher). New York, NY: Random House Children's Books.

Davis, E. S., & Clark, M. A. (2012). Elementary school counselors' perceptions of reality play counseling in students' relationship building and problem-solving skills. *Journal of School Counseling, 10*(11). Retrieved from http://www.jsc.montana.edu/articles/v10n11.pdf

DeJong, P., & Berg, I. K. (2008). *Interviewing for solutions* (3rd ed). Belmont, CA: Brooks/Cole.

DeVoe, J. F., & Bauer, L. (2011). *Student Victimization in U.S. Schools: Results From the 2009 School Crime Supplement to the National Crime Victimization Survey* (NCES 2012-314). U.S. Department of Education, National Center for Education Statistics. Washington, DC: U.S. Government Printing Office.

Drewes, A. A. (2009). *Blending play therapy with cognitive behavioral therapy: Evidence-based and other effective treatments and techniques*. Hoboken, NJ: John Wiley.

Drewes, A. A., & Schaefer, C. (2010). *School based play therapy* (2nd ed.). Hoboken, NJ: John Wiley.

Drewes, A. A., Bratton, S. C. & Schaefer, C. (2011). *Integrative play therapy*. Hoboken, NJ: John Wiley.

Erford, B. T. (2000). *Mutual storytelling game CD*. Shrewsbury, PA: Counseling Innovations.

Fall, M. (1994). Self efficacy: An additional dimension in play therapy. *International Journal of Play Therapy, 3*(2), 21-32.

Fall, M., Balvanz, J., Johnson, L., & Nelson, L. (1999). A play therapy intervention and its relationship to self-efficacy and learning behaviors. *Professional School Counselor, 2*, 194-204.

Farrington, D. P., & Ttofi, M. M. (2009). School-based programs to reduce bullying and victimization. *Campbell Systematic Reviews, 6*, 1-147. doi:10.4073/csr.2009.6

Farrington, D. P., Loeber, R., Stallings, R., & Ttofi, M. M. (2011). Bullying perpetration and victimization as predictors of delinquency and depression in the Pittsburgh Youth Study. *Journal of Aggression, Conflict and Peace Research, 3*(2), 74-81.

Finkelhor, D., Turner, H., Ormrod, S., & Hamby, S. L. (2009). Violence, abuse, and crime exposure in a national sample of children and youth. *Pediatrics, 124*(5), 1411-1423.

Finkelhor, D., Turner, H., Ormrod, R., Hamby, S., & Kracke, K. (2009) *Children's exposure to violence: A comprehensive national Survey*. Washington, DC: U.S. Department of Justice. Retrieved from http://www.ncjrs.gov/pdffiles1/ojjdp/227744.pdf

Fleming, L. C., & Jacobsen, K. H. (2009). Bullying and symptoms of depression in Chilean middle school students. *Journal of School Health, 79*(3), 130-137. doi:10.1111/j.1746-1561.2008.0397.x

Gallant, W., & Holosko, M. (2001). Music intervention in grief work with clients experiencing loss and bereavement. *Guidance & Counseling, 16*, 115-121.

Gardner, R. A. (1993). Mutual storytelling. In C .E. Schaefer & D. M. Cangelosi (Eds.), *Play therapy techniques* (pp. 177-189). Northvale, NJ: Jason Aronson.

Gil, E. (1991). *The healing power of play: Working with abused children*. New York, NY: The Guilford Press.

Gil, E. (2006). *Helping abused and traumatized children: Integrating directive and nondirective approaches*. New York, NY: The Guilford Press.

Gini, G., Pozzoli, T., Borghi, F., & Franzoni, F. (2008). The role of bystanders in students' perception of bullying and sense of safety. *Journal of School Psychology, 46*, 617-638.

Ginott, H. G. (1994). *Group psychotherapy with children. The theory and practice of play therapy.* Northvale, NJ: Aronson.

Gladding, S. T. (2011). *Counseling as an art: The creative arts in counseling* (4th ed.). Alexandria, VA: American Counseling Association

Glaeser, B. C., Pierson, M. R., & Fritschmann, N. (2003). Comic strip conversations: A positive behavioral support strategy. *Teaching Exceptional Children, 36*(2), 14-19. Retrieved from ERIC database.

Glasser, C. (1996). *My quality world workbook*. Chatsworth, CA: William Glasser institute.

Glasser, W. (1965). *Reality therapy.* New York, NY: Harper & Row.

Glasser, W. (1998). *Choice theory: A new psychology of personal freedom*. New York, NY: HarperCollins.

Glasser, W. (2000). *Counseling with choice theory.* New York, NY: HarperCollins.

Glasser, W. (2005). Defining mental health as a public health issue: A new leadership role for the helping and teaching professions. Los Angeles, CA: William Glasser Institute.

Goodyear-Brown, P. (2005). *Digging for Buried Treasure 2: Another 52 Prop-based Play Therapy Interventions for Treating the Problems of Childhood.* Nashville, TN: Paris Goodyear-Brown.

Golmaryami, F. N., & Barry, C. T. (2010). The associations of self-reported and peer-reported relational aggression with narcissism and self-esteem among adolescents in a residential setting. *Journal of Clinical Child and Adolescent Psychology, 39*, 128-133.

Graham, S., Bellmore, A., Nishina, A., & Juvonen, J. (2009). It must be me: Ethnic diversity and attributions for peer victimization in middle school. *Journal of Youth and Adolescence, 38*, 487-499. doi:10.1007/s10964-008-9386-4

Gray, C. (1994). *Comic strip conversations: Illustrated interactions that teach conversation skills to students with autism and related disorders.* Arlington, TX: Future Horizons.

Hamiwka, L. D., Yu, C. G., Hamiwka, L. A., Sherman, E. M. S., Anderson, B., & Wirrell, E. (2009). Are children with epilepsy at greater risk for bullying than their peers? *Epilepsy & Behavior, 15*, 500-505.

Hawkins, D. L., Pepler, D., & Craig, W. M. (2001). Naturalistic observations of peer interventions in bullying. *Social Development, 10*(4), 512-527.

Hays, R., & Lyons, S. (1981). The bridge drawing: A projective technique for assessment in art therapy. *Arts in Psychotherapy, 8*, 207-217.

Homeyer, L. E., & Sweeney, D. S. (2011). *Sandtray therapy: A practical manual* (2nd ed.). New York, NY: Taylor-Francis.

Juvonen, J., Wang, J., & Espinoza, G. (2011). Bullying experiences and compromised academic performance across middle school grades. *The Journal of Early Adolescence, 31*(1), 152-173.

Kelly, M. M., & Odenwalt, H. C. (2006). Treatment of sexually abused children. In C. E. Schaefer, & H. G. Kaduson (Eds.), *Contemporary play therapy: Theory, research, and practice* (pp. 186-211). New York, NY: Guilford Press.

Kenney-Noziska, S. (2008). *Techniques-techniques-techniques: Play-based activities for children, adolescents, and families*. West Conshohocken, PA: Infinity.

Kiefer, H. M. (2004, October 26). *Teens' leisure habits: TV on top*. Gallup. Retrieved from http://www.gallup.com/poll/13783/Teens-Leisure-Habits-Top.aspx

Knell, S. M. (1993). *Cognitive-behavioral play therapy*. Northvale, NJ: Jason Aronson.

Knell, S. M. (1998). Cognitive-behavioral play therapy. *Journal of Clinical Child Psychology, 27*(1), 28-33.

Knell, S. M. (2008). Cognitive behavioral play therapy. Theory and applications. In A. Drewes (Ed.), *Blending Play Therapy with Cognitive Behavioral Therapy. Evidence-based and other effective treatments and techniques* (pp. 117-138). New York, NY: Wiley & Sons.

Kosciw, J. G., Greytak, E. A., Diaz, E. M., & Bartkiewicz, M. J. (2010). *The 2009 National School Climate Survey: The experiences of lesbian, gay, bisexual and transgender youth in our nation's schools*. New York, NY: GLSEN.

Kottman, T. (1993). The king of rock and roll. In T. Kottman and C. Schaefer (Eds.), *Play therapy in action. A casebook for practitioners* (pp. 133-167). Northvale, NJ: Jason Aronson.

Lamb, J., Pepler, D. J., & Craig, W. (2009). Approach to bullying and victimization. *Canadian Family Physician, 55*, 356-360.

Landreth, G. L. (2012). *Play therapy: The art of the relationship* (3rd ed.). New York, NY: Taylor-Francis.

Landreth, G. L., Homeyer, L. E., Glover, G., & Sweeney, D. S. (1996). *Play therapy interventions with children's problems*. Northvale, NJ: Aronson.

LeBlanc, M., & Ritchie, M. (1999). Predictors of play therapy outcomes. International *Journal of Play Therapy, 8*(2), 19-34.

Lowenstein, L. (2010). *Creative family therapy techniques: Play, art, and expressive activities to engage children in family sessions*. Toronto, Canada: Champion Press.

Mason, C. P., & Duba, J. D. (2009). Using reality therapy in schools: Its potential impact on the effectiveness on the ASCA National Model. *International Journal of Reality Therapy, 29*, 5-12

Mason, K. L. (2008). Cyberbullying: A preliminary assessment for school personnel. *Psychology in the Schools, 45*(4), 323-348. doi:10.1002/pits.20301

Merrell, K., Gueldner, B., Ross, S., & Isava, D. (2008). How effective are school bullying intervention programs? A meta-analysis of intervention research. *School Psychology Quarterly, 23*(1), 26-42.

Mouttappa, M., Gallaher, P., & Valentes, T. (2004). Social network predictors of bullying and victimization. *Adolescence, 39*, 315-335.

National Center for Education Statistics. (2011). *Student Reports of Bullying and Cyber Bullying: Results From the 2009 School Crime Supplement to the National*

Crime Victimization Survey. Retrieved from http://nces.ed.gov/pubs2011/2011336.pdf

Nystul, M. S. (1995). A problem-solving approach to counseling: Integrating Adler's and Glasser's theories. *Elementary School Guidance and Counseling, 29,* 297-304.

O'Brennan, L. M., Bradshaw, C. P., & Sawyer, A. L. (2009). Social-emotional problems among bullies, victims, and bully/victims: Implications for prevention and intervention. *Psychology in the Schools, 46,*100-115.

O'Conner, K. J. (1991). *The play therapy primer: An integrating of theories and techniques*. New York, NY: John Wiley.

Olweus, D. (1992). Bullying among schoolchildren: Intervention and prevention. In R. Peters, R. McMahon and V. Quinsey (Eds.), *Aggression and violence throughout the life span*. Newbury Park, CA: SAGE.

Olweus, D. (1993). *Bullying at school: What we know and what we can do*. Williston, VT: Blackwell.

Olweus, D., & Limber, S. P. (2010). Bullying in school: Evaluation and dissemination of the Olweus Bullying Prevention Program. *American Journal of Orthopsychiatry, 80*, 124-134.

Olweus, D., Limber, S., & Mihalic, S. (1999). *The bullying prevention program. Blueprints for violence prevention*. Boulder, CO: Center for the Study and Prevention of Violence.

Peterson, J. S., & Ray, K. (2006). Bullying and the gifted: Victims, perpetrators, prevalence, and effects. *Gifted Child Quarterly, 50*(2), 148-168.

Ragozzino, K. & O'Brien, M.U. (2009). *Social and emotional learning and bullying prevention*. Chicago, IL: CASEL. Retrieved from http://www.casel.org/downloads/2009_bullyingbrief.pdf

Ray, D., Bratton, S., Rhine, T., & Jones, L. (2001). The effectiveness of play therapy: Responding to the critics. *International Journal of Play Therapy, 10*(1), 85-108.

Ray, D., Henson, R., Schottelkorb, A., Brown, A., & Muro, J. (2008). Effects of short-and long term play therapy services on teacher-child relationship stress. *Psychology in the Schools, 45*(10), 994-1009.

Riordan, R. J. (1996). Scriptotherapy: Therapeutic writing as a counseling adjunct. *Journal of Counseling and Development, 74,* 263-269.

Riviere, S. (2006). Short-term play therapy for children with disruptive behavior disorders. In H. G. Kaduson & C. E. Schaefer (Eds.) *Short-term play therapy for children* (pp. 51-70). New York, NY: Guilford Press.

Robers, S., Zhang, J., & Truman, J. (2012). *Indicators of School Crime and Safety: 2011* (NCES 2012-002/NCJ 236021). National Center for Education Statistics, U.S. Department of Education, and Bureau of Justice Statistics, Office of Justice Programs, U.S. Department of Justice. Washington, DC.

Roberts, L. C., & Mills, C. (2009). Meeting students' needs. *School Counselor, 46,* 12-17.

Rogers, M. F., & Myles, B. S. (2001). Using social stories and comic strip conversations to interpret social situations for an adolescent with Asperger Syndrome. *Intervention in School and Clinic, 36*(5), 310-313.

Rubin, K. H., Coplan, R. J., & Bowker, J. C. (2009). Social withdrawal in childhood. *Annual Review of Psychology, 60*, 141-171.

Saia, D. Saylor, C., Allen, R., & Arnau, P. (2010). Bullying experiences, anxiety about bullying, and special education placement. *Journal of the American Academy of Special Education Professionals*, 38-50.

Saylor, C. F., Twyman, K. A., & Saia, D. (2008, May). *Relationships between past and present bullying and victimization experiences.* Paper presented at the National Association of School Psychologists meeting, Boston, MA.

Schaefer, C. E. (2011). *Foundations of play therapy* (2nd ed.). Hoboken, NJ: John Wiley.

Sink, C. A., Eppler, C., & Edwards, C. (2012). *School based group counseling*. Belmont, CA: Brooks/Cole.

Stopbullying.gov. (2012). South Dakota is the 49th state to pass an antibullying law. stopbullying.gov. U.S. Department of Health & Human Services. Washington DC. Retrieved from http://www.stopbullying.gov/index.html

StopBullying.gov. (2012). U.S. Department of Health & Human Services. Washington: D.C. Retrieved from http://www.stopbullying.gov/index.html

Swearer, S. M., Espelage, D. L., Vaillancourt, T., & Hymel, S. (2010). What can be done about school bullying? Linking research to educational practice. *Educational Researcher, 1*, 38-47.

Sweeney, D. S., & Homeyer, L. E. (1999). Group play therapy. In D. S. Sweeney & L. E. Homeyer (Eds.), *The handbook of group play therapy: How to do it, how it works, whom it's best for* (pp. 3-14). San Francisco, CA: Jossey-Bass.

Taylor, L., Salor, C., Twyman, K., & Macias, M. (2010). Adding insult to injury: Bullying experiences of youth with attention deficit hyperactivity disorder. *Children's Health Care, 39,* 59-72. doi:10.1080/02739610903455152

Thornberg, R., & Knutsen, M.A. (2010). Teenagers' explanations of bullying. *Child and Youth Care Forum, 40*(3), 177-192. doi:10.1007/s10566-010-9129-z.

Ttofi, M. M., & Farrington, D. P. (2011). Effectiveness of school-based programs to reduce bullying: A systematic and meta-analytic review. *Journal of Experimental Criminology, 7,* 27–56. doi:10.10007/s11292-010-9109-1.

Ttofi, M. M., Farrington, D. P., & Lösel, F. (2011). Editorial: Health consequences of school bullying. *Journal of Aggression, Conflict and Peace Research, 3*(2), 60-62.

Ttofi, M. M., Farrington, D. P., Lösel, F., & Loeber, R. (2011). Do the victims of school bullies tend to become depressed later in life? A systematic review and meta-analysis of longitudinal studies. *Conflict and Peace Research, 3*(2), 63-73.

Twyman, K., Macias, M., Saia, D. Saylor, C. Spratt, E. & Taylor, L. (2009, May). *Bullying and ostracism in children with special healthcare needs*. Presented as a Platform Presentation, Pediatric Academic Society Meeting, Baltimore, MD.

Twyman, K., Saylor, C., Saia, D., Macias, M., Taylor, L., & Spratt, E. (2010). Bullying and Ostracism Experiences in Children with Special Health Care Needs. Journal of *Developmental & Behavioral Pediatrics, 31*(1), 1-8. doi:10.1097/DBP.0b013e3181c828c8

Ungar, M. (2011). The social ecology of resilience: Addressing contextual and cultural ambiguity of a nascent construct. *American Journal of Orthopsychiatry, 81*, 1-17.

U.S. Department of Education. (2000). *Prohibited disability harassment: Reminder of responsibilities under Section 504 of the Rehabilitation Act of 1973 and Title II of the Americans with Disabilities Act*. Washington, DC: Office for Civil Rights.

U.S. Department of Education. (2011). *Analysis of State Bullying Laws and Policies*. Washington, DC: Office of Planning, Evaluation and Policy Development. Policy and Program Studies Service.

Van Cleave, J., & Davis, M. (2006). Bullying and peer victimization among children with special health care needs. *Pediatrics, 118*(4), 1212-1219.

Violence Prevention Works (n.d.). *The Olweus Bullying Prevention Program*. Hazelden. Retrieved from http://www.violencepreventionworks.org/public/faqs.page_

Vinturella L., & Jones, R. (1987). Sandplay: A therapeutic medium with children. *Elementary School Guidance and Counseling, 21*(4), 263-275.

Wang, J., Iannotti, R. J., & Nansel, T. R. (2009). School bullying among adolescents in the United States: Physical, verbal, relational, and cyber. *Journal of Adolescent Health, 45*, 368-375.

Wang, J., Iannotti, R. J., & Luk, J. W. (2010). Bullying victimization among underweight and overweight U.S. youth: Differential associations for boys and girls. *Journal of Adolescent Health, 47*, 99-101.

Whittingham, K., Sofronoff, K., Sheffield, J., & Sanders, M. R. (2009), Behavioural family intervention with parents of children with ASD: what do they find useful in the parenting program stepping stones triple P? *Research in Autism Spectrum Disorders, 3*, 702-713.

Willock, B. (1983). Play therapy with the aggressive, acting-out child. In C.E. Schaefer & K.T. O'Connor. *Handbook of play therapy* (pp. 386-411). New York, NY: John Wiley & Sons.

Winsper, C., Lereya, T., Zanarini, M., & Wolke, D. (2012). Involvement in bullying and suicide-related behavior at 11 Years: A prospective birth cohort study. *Journal of the American Academy of Child & Adolescent Psychiatry, 51*(3), 271-282.

Wubbolding, R. (2000). *Reality therapy for the 21st century*. Philadelphia, PA: Brunner Routledge.

Wubbolding, R., & Brickell, J. (1999). *Counselling with reality therapy*. Milton Keynes, England: Speechmark.

Wubbolding, R. E. (2011). *Reality therapy: Theories of psychotherapy series*. Washington, DC: American Psychological Association.

Yalom, I. (1995). *The theory and practice of group psychotherapy*. (Rev. ed.). New York, NY: Basic Books.

CHAPTER 13

ANGER MANAGEMENT AND ADLERIAN PLAY THERAPY

M. Ann Shillingford and S. Kent Butler

Where there is anger, there is always pain underneath.

—Eckhart Tolle

Finding solace from emotional and physical pain is a difficult task to take on for even the most well adjusted person among us. Children, who are striving to find a sense of self and are still evolving in their identity development, may not be able to correctly manage the emotions and feelings that present themselves when harmful things surface. Negative externalizing behaviors fueled by anger often lead to detrimental consequences such as pain to self and/or others. Children who are angry might lack the cognitive capacity to understand and verbally express the cause of their anger; as a result, they retaliate in ways that impact them academically, socially, emotionally, and physically. Many individual and systemic factors significantly contribute to the development of feelings of anger and anger expressions including health issues or medical problems, learning difficulties, dysfunctional home life, and systemic factors such as racism and oppression. Unfortunately, there may be instances where the

Integrating Play Techniques in Comprehensive School Counseling Programs, pp. 263–279

root of children's anger is unknown at first glance and undetected. Even more distressing, adults may attribute anger to personal qualities of the child such as disposition or temperament; thus, imparting unfair judgment or bias toward the child.

Several evidenced-based approaches and best practices are noted in literature for interventions that support children with anger management concerns. These effective approaches (i.e., cognitive behavioral interventions, peer mediation opportunities, and conflict resolution techniques), may be the appropriate or best interventions based on the particular needs of clients. This chapter introduces the use of play therapy with school-aged children as a viable approach to supporting children struggling with anger management issues. Moreover, the techniques suggested herein are appropriate to a school setting within the context of a comprehensive school counseling program.

Vignette 1

Julie, a first grade student, was retained the previous academic year. Her teacher is concerned about her behaviors in class such as yelling at other students, being oppositional with the teacher, and refusing to complete classroom assignments. Julie was recently suspended from the school bus for cursing at the bus driver. Now, she has been sent to the principal's office because she threw a pencil at another student. When asked about her behavior, Julie responds that she hates school and just wants to go home.

Vignette 2

Rico is a new student at Springhill Elementary School and he is extremely disruptive in his second grade class. Today is Rico's first day of being brought to school by his foster parent. He lashes out at anyone who tries to speak with him and has already made several attempts to run off school grounds.

LITERATURE REVIEW

Anger Management

Anger management is a process of learning to recognize signs and symptoms of becoming angry, and taking action to calm down and deal with the situation in a positive manner. Anger management techniques are not designed to keep individuals from repressing anger or encouraging them to not express the anger they are feeling. Anger is a normal, healthy emotion, especially when individuals are knowledgeable of anger management strategies and can utilize positive coping strategies to express themselves appropriately (Mayo Clinic, 2011). However, maladaptive anger is a volatile emotion which may lead to aggressive, violent behaviors that may prove dangerous to self or others (Luutonen, 2007). Similar to other emotions, being in control of anger allows individuals to better understand their state of cognitive and affective processes. However, anger left uncontrolled can be damaging; in fact, repressed anger may lead to poor physical and mental health (Mabry & Kiecolt, 2005). For instance, hypertension and high cortisol levels are both physical conditions found to be related to internalized anger.

The display of unaddressed anger emotions is influenced by environmental factors such as previous exposure to violence including hearing or witnessing violence (at home or community) as well as previously being a victim of violence (Lines, 2007). For children, incidents of anger rooted in systemic factors are often carried into the educational environment and have been well noted as problematic. Anger in the classroom is not only detrimental to students involved, but it may also cause a significant distraction in the learning environment for other students and faculty.

Much has been done over the past decade to decrease the incidents of school violence fostered by student anger. However, school personnel still recognize threats and crimes committed in schools as challenging in spite of decreases in occurrences. Indeed, although incidents may have decreased, there is evidence that the severity of violent acts has actually increased. Specifically, according to the indicators of school crime as published by the Bureau of Justice Statistics (2012), between academic years 2009 and 2010, approximately 27% of public schools had reported incidents of student bullying; 9% reported students' verbal abuse to teachers; and 12% reported acts of disrespect against teachers in the classroom other than verbal abuse. According to teachers in the public school setting, at least 40% expressed that students misbehavior interfered with their ability to teach effectively.

Even more alarming, reports by school administrators for the 2009-2010 academic year revealed that at least 60% of public schools had reported crimes to the police. Of the crimes reported, 40% were violent crimes including incidents of rape, sexual battery other than rape, physical attacks or fights with or without weapons, threats of physical attack with or without weapons, and robberies with or without weapons. Additionally, 10% were serious violent crimes and included rape, sexual batteries other than rape, physical attack, or fight with weapons, threats of physical attack with weapons, and robberies with or without weapons (Bureau of Justice Statistics, 2012). These statistics suggest that although the number of students engaging in physical altercations has decreased, a significant number of young people are still exhibiting aggressive behaviors and experiencing negative anger outbursts.

Students are often fearful of aggression displayed by their peers and may seek safety elsewhere; unfortunately, many students seek safety outside of the school's periphery. Although the number of students who reported on the indicators of school crime (Bureau of Justice Statistics, 2012) of their fear of attack and harm (7%) and those who avoid certain places on school grounds (6%) may seem low, concern should still be expressed for the academic development of these students and those who are themselves deficient in appropriate management of their anger. Though this literature review highlights a few statistics related to school violence, it is neither comprehensive nor exhaustive. What is important is that the statistics underscore the need for appropriate interventions to support students.

In the following sections we examine manifestations of anger in the school environment including the impact on students' social, academic, and behavioral functioning to support the necessity for further intercession on behalf of students experiencing intense anger. A review of evidence-based interventions is also presented along with introduction and information to Adlerian play therapy.

IMPACT OF ANGER ON SOCIAL, ACADEMIC, AND BEHAVIORAL FUNCTIONING

Children's anger may significantly limit their developmental progress, in respect to their varied life functions, and more specifically within their academic and social pursuits (Sportsman, Carlson, & Guthries, 2010). Sportsman and colleagues suggested that uncontrolled anger may lead to negative social outcomes such as dysfunctional relationships, poor occupational functioning, mood disorders, and substance abuse. Anger and aggression has also been found to be associated with peer difficulties, problem-solving deficits, and psychosocial adjustment (Leff et al., 2010). Nichols, Mahadeo, Bryant, and Botvin (2008) found that a relationship exists between anger and substance abuse by school-aged children. Nichols and colleagues contended that aggression and levels of anger were predictive of drug use, inclusive of smoking, alcohol use, and marijuana among adolescents. These deficiencies in social and behavioral functioning suggest that children with uncontrolled anger may have the potential to experience advanced pathology and psychological dysfunction, especially when individuals lack necessary support for controlling anger.

Unfortunately, studies have shown that children who experience social and psychological concerns may be in danger of poor academic performance, academic disengagement, school failure, and school drop-out (Archambault, Janosz, Morizot, & Pagani, 2009; Henry, Knight, & Thornberry, 2012; Fowler, 2011). In light of the significant effects of anger on students (socially, academically, or behaviorally), several evidenced-based approaches have been tried to mitigate the negative outcomes.

EVIDENCED-BASED APPROACHES FOR TREATMENT

Sofronoff, Attwood, Hinton, and Levin (2007) reported on the usefulness of a cognitive behavioral approach with children diagnosed with Asperger's syndrome dealing with anger. The 6-week intervention included anger management related games and short activities. Sofronoff and colleagues found that both parents and teachers reported positive behavioral changes. For example, teachers indicated that students were better able to use strategies to manage their anger and were more open in discussing issues of anger and emotional outbursts. Parents also reported their children's willingness and ability to use behavioral strategies to handle their emotions. Overall, the researchers noted that the parents of participating children expressed decreases in anger episodes.

Similarly, Feindler and Engel (2011) promoted cognitive behavioral anger management training (AMT) as an effective tool for working with school-aged students. AMT, successful with individuals and in small groups, directs students to pinpoint their anger, label the intensity of the experience, and identify triggers or red flags. In addition, Feindler and Engel recommended inclusion of parental involvement in the intervention process for a more valuable experience.

The supporting tempers, emotions, and anger management (STEAM) program is another program that has been found to be effective in schools. STEAM is useful in helping children identify the emotions they are experiencing and developing skills that foster more positive emotional outcomes (Bidgood, Wilkie, & Katchaluba, 2010). The program focuses on teaching children how best to handle their anger, improve self-control, reduce temper outbursts, strengthen self-esteem, and increase social support through successfully developed interpersonal skills. Bidgood and colleagues noted that students, teachers, and parents expressed satisfaction in the positive behavioral and emotional changes fostered through utilization of the program.

These intervention programs have been valuable in reducing incidents and intensity of anger episodes while fostering more significantly optimistic changes in children. The following section introduces play therapy, another evidenced based approach to improving anger management skills within children. Play therapy has been well researched and demonstrates efficacy as a beneficial counseling strategy for working with children (Landreth, 2012). In the following section we highlight tenets of Adlerian play therapy and introduce an illustration for application with children displaying anger concerns.

ADLERIAN PLAY THERAPY

Adlerian play therapy consists of techniques that are instrumental in providing an open and accepting atmosphere for children. According to Thompson and Henderson (2007), an Adlerian approach suggests that ideally, upon using these techniques, the child will demonstrate: (a) respect for the rights of others, (b) tolerance of and cooperation with others, (c) courteousness, (d) strong positive self-concept, (e) increased sense of belonging, and (f) willingness to share with others. Furthermore, Adlerian theorists believe that behaviors are goal-oriented, individual perceptions are subjective to one's reality, individuals are constantly striving to overcome feelings of inferiority, and (d) social interests are improved through guidance and training (Archer & McCarthy, 2007). Following, we explore each of these Adlerian concepts in detail.

Goal oriented. The key concept of goal oriented behavior is that humans are driven by the desire for success towards a particular goal. Things do not occur by happenstance, but rather by intentionally motivated ideologies. In fact, Adlerian theory suggests that individuals are driven by the notion that there is always a purpose behind human action and that one should constantly strive towards betterment (Adler, 1969). Goals may be rational or irrational, especially with children. For example, if a goal is to get attention, there are myriad of positive and negative ways that a child may seek attention. Even if actions resulting in receiving negative attention seem illogical, for a child, the attention may be desired in any form. Therefore, children often require interventions and supports to help them change mistaken goals and beliefs. Adlerian theory also suggests that the cause of children's behaviors is not the issue but what they are hoping to accomplish (Thompson & Henderson, 2007); hence, observation of children's behaviors may help determine their unspoken goals. For example, in the case of Rico above (vignette 2), he may be striving for a sense of belonging but confused by his displacement (i.e., being in foster care). To determine the underlying goal of behavior, counselors can rely on behavioral assessment strategies.

Subjective perceptions. Subjectivity defines how an individual chooses to view and interpret events that may occur in their lives. Such interpretations certainly affect the decision-making process and influence how one chooses to move forward in society. Subjective reality further impacts one's determination of right and wrong, how to get wants fulfilled, and perceptions about other people (Morrison, 2009). Once again we look to Rico, who because of his maladaptive behavior and irrational thought process may be incorrectly interpreting the actions of others within the school community causing him to lash out when approached.

Striving to overcome feelings of inferiority. Adlerian theorists believe that individuals have an innate desire for self-improvement. There is always that need to be better and overcome identified limitations. These improvements may include physical organic limitations, such as an illness, or more socially related perceived limitations (i.e., feelings that one does not belong in a desired social group). Children may struggle with feelings of inferiority as they compare themselves to peers at school and in their communities, as well as comparing themselves to siblings at home. Indeed, Adlerian therapists believe that children who feel inferior within their social context (school, home) may react in ways that would improve their own self-worth. Unfortunately, these behaviors are often negative attempts to secure attention from a given group or system. In Rico's case, he may be striving to overcome feelings of inferiority brought on by being removed from his home whilst school friends are observed interacting with their loved ones.

Social interest. Adler emphasized the importance of social interest to humans. Social interest denotes the need to contribute positively to society; a desire for involvement with others. Adlerian therapists suggest that social interest does not occur naturally but must be trained and encouraged (Thompson & Henderson, 2007). Adlerian theorists also highlight the significance of an atmosphere of trust and safety. Therefore, when systemic structures are considered unsafe, trust is affected. This concept is especially important with children as trust, particularly within the family dynamics, promotes their sense of positive community. In our above example, we can say then that Rico may be feeling insecure because of the malfunctioning in his family structure.

ADLERIAN PLAY THERAPY TECHNIQUES

Kottman (2003) recommended a four-phase approach for the successful application with clients: (1) building an egalitarian relationship (especially when working with children), (2) investigating the client's lifestyle, (3) assisting the client with developing insight, and (4) reorienting and reeducating the client.

Phase 1: Building an Egalitarian Relationship: Using Reflection of Feelings, Tracking, Encouragement, and Setting Limits

To build such a relationship, the school counselor needs to be engaged in sessions with the child whereby both share responsibility in the relationship. In order to address and begin the process of establishing a relationship with children, the following techniques should be employed: reflection of feelings, tracking, encouragement, and setting limits. *Reflecting feelings* involves connecting with the child and identifying their feelings about their particular situations. Such statements as "You feel angry that your dad broke his promise," and "Sometimes you feel left out on the playground" may be helpful in enabling the child to understand his or her feelings. *Tracking* statements such as "you're tearing up the pages" and "you're staring at the doll" tells the child that the counselor sees what she is doing. Providing *encouragement* to the child bestows empowerment on her that she is recognized as being capable of accomplishing a desired goal. For example, consider a situation where a child is trying to figure out how best to dress a doll during a play session. When that task is accomplished, the counselor might say "Ohh!! You stuck with it until you got it done." This conveys to the child that she is capable of persevering, a verbal way of affirming the child's behavior and empowering the child to action.

Finally, in building the egalitarian relationship, *limit setting* is of vital importance. This requires the counselor to explain to the child appropriate and safe ways to conduct herself during the counseling session. The child is free to say whatever she desires during the session; however, behavior control is set by the counselor so as to avoid harm to the child and others. So, for example, in a play situation where a child is banging his head against a wall, the counselor might say "I see that you are angry but banging your head is harmful and it's against the rules in this play room to hurt yourself "As a follow-up, the counselor will need to provide alternative ways that the child can display her anger such as using a pillow or other non-threatening manner.

Investigating Lifestyle: Using Questioning and Art Expression

According to Kottman (2003) investigating the child's lifestyle gives the counselor insight as to the objectives of observed behaviors. Observations are used to answer the question: what is the goal or purpose behind what they child is doing and saying? Adlerian theorists believe that individual's negative behaviors stem from a need for revenge, power, attention, and/or withdrawal. Therefore, during the counseling session, the counselor focuses on examining these goals, exploring the family atmosphere (parental patterns adapted by the child), family constellations (child's position in the family), and the child's early recollections through the play medium. Early recollections, such as family events, and the child's perception of why these events occurred are helpful in further understanding the child's behaviors. Patterns of recollections are especially important.

Techniques such as questioning can be beneficial to clarifying and understanding what the child is trying to express. For example, a child might state something like this in counseling "my dad is always taking my younger brother to work with him and he never takes me." This child may be concerned about her place in the family constellation and may potentially feel that the younger child is more liked than she. The Adlerian approach would also encourage the use of such strategies as art expressions (i.e., the Kinetic family drawing) to explore with the child how family dynamics impact her behaviors.

Assisting in Developing Insight Into Life-Style: Using Tentative Hypotheses

To support the child in developing insight into her behavior, the counselor constructs tentative hypotheses (guesses or assumptions) for exploration using the child's words and actions during play sessions (Kottman, 2003). This approach is beneficial in allowing the child to investigate and discover her thoughts, attitudes, and behaviors. For example, using the illustration above, the child feels like the younger sibling is more liked than her. She may display this by pinching a small doll that she has identified as her brother during play. The counselor, who has already established that the child has feelings of inferiority, might say and of the following: "so you hit your brother even though it's your dad you're really mad at." "It looks like you get your dad's attention when you hit your brother." "Getting your dad's attention is important to you." In this instance, the counselor has hypothesized that the child is misbehaving in order to get attention from her parent. By voicing the assumptions or guesses, the counselor is allowing the child to see herself differently. When the child has begun to realize her patterns of thinking and behaving, the counselor then moves to the final phase of the Adlerian approach.

Reorienting and Reeducating: Using Role-Plays to Explore Alternative Behaviors

The counselor now focuses on introducing new ways of thinking and behaving. Alternative behaviors are suggested and practiced using problem solving, brainstorming, identifying possibilities, testing solutions, and evaluating decisions (Portrie-Bethke, Hill, & Bethke, 2009). By engaging the child in the problem solving process, it allows her to feel a sense of power and control over her actions. This results in efficacy for change. Some children may have difficulty developing ideas for alternative behaviors; therefore, the counselor can take a proactive role in introducing and teaching the child more appropriate actions (e.g., using puppets to act out different anger management strategies). Once alternative actions have been identified, the counselor can lead the child in active role-play in order to practice and solidify new behaviors.

So, using the child above who is seeking attention from her father, the counselor may choose to role-play alternative behaviors to gain her dad's attention. For example, it may be decided between the child and counselor that a more appropriate way of gaining attention might be to help her little brother with his reading and sharing their storybook with her father. That way, all three family members are involved and engaged. Identifying the child's strengths and efforts as well as recognizing her progress will promote her self-confidence and procure growth. Parental involvement and feedback on the child's behaviors will also be advantageous in fostering feelings of trust, safety, control, and success.

SAMPLE OUTLINES OF ADLERIAN PLAY IN THE SCHOOL ENVIRONMENT: MEETINGS 1-3

It is understood that in the school setting, time and resources are a key factor for consideration. These meetings should be scheduled in collaboration with the classroom teachers so as not to affect the academic experience. Resources may also be a factor due to budgetary constraints; therefore, a dollhouse with basic necessities of typical home life may be sufficient. The following section presents a sample outline of four Adlerian play therapy meetings in the school setting. These sample sessions provides school counselors with a framework for using play therapy within the confines of their school community.

Meeting 1

Goal: To introduce the child to the counselor and begin building the therapeutic/egalitarian relationship.

Materials Needed: Play area with relevant play materials (e.g. "furnished" dollhouse, dolls (different sizes, games, balls, books, puppets).

Procedure: Boundaries and limitations based on school policies as well as play area concerns are discussed before play begins. The school counselor allows the child to play freely with the dollhouse and available material and tracks actions and verbalizations. Feelings are reflected and the child is encouraged throughout the play process.

Closure: The school counselor lets the child know when her time is almost up and then reminds the child that they will meet again.

Note: This play meeting is unstructured and the child should be allowed to explore and engage in play.

Meeting 2: This Meeting Can Be Used for Further Exploration and Relationship Building Much as Meeting 1

Meeting 3

Goal: To begin the process of life-style exploration.

Materials Needed: Play area with relevant play materials (e.g. "furnished" dollhouse, dolls (different sizes, games, balls, books).

Procedure: As the child plays, the counselor begins to identify and address thematic patterns of behaviors (e.g., preoccupation with a particular object).

The school counselor uses questioning to explore these behaviors. Examples of questions might include:

- What does this ball remind you of?
- How would you be different?
- Who says you are too active?

Closure: The school counselor lets the child know when her time is almost up and then reminds the child that they will meet again.

Note: The counselor can also use this time to explore early recollections based on the child's responses to the above questions.

Meeting 4

Goal: To continue building the therapeutic relationship and also to further explore the life-style of the child.

Materials Needed: Play area with relevant play materials (e.g. "furnished" doll house, dolls (different sizes, games, balls, and books), paper, crayons, or markers.

Procedure: The child is allowed to play for a few minutes while the counselor begins the process of questioning. The counselor is continuing to observe patterns of behavior that may need to be addressed.

The school counselor then leads the child in constructing an art project. One activity for expressive art exploration is using *The Gingerbread Person Feelings Map* (Drewes, 2001). A large piece of construction paper is presented to the child. Due to time constraints, the counselor should already have the outline of a gingerbread person with eyes, nose, and a smile. Feeling words are listed next to the outline such as angry, sad, happy, and so forth. The child should be encouraged to think of some additional feelings words and write those on the list. The counselor then brings out a number of crayons and asks the child to choose a color for each feeling word and then proceeds to ask the child to color in the gingerbread outline areas on the body where they experience each of the feeling words. The counselor can then use the rest of the meeting time to process the Gingerbread Person with the child and also address any discrepancies (e.g., happy feet, sad face).

Closure: The school counselor lets the child know when her time is almost up and then reminds the child that they will meet again.

Note: Drewes (2001) mentioned that children may sometimes choose to use non traditional colors for particular feelings words. The important point is to observe for feelings related to behaviors and how the child perceives herself.

CASE STUDY

The following case study is presented as an illustration of the application of Adlerian play therapy a viable intervention option when working with children with anger concerns.

The Client and Presenting Problems

Rico is a 7-year-old Hispanic male who was brought to the school counselor because of extremely disruptive behaviors in his second grade class. Until recently, Rico resided with his mother and stepfather. However, due to domestic violence in the home, he was removed and placed in foster care. He has not seen his mother since being displaced. During his first meeting with the counselor Rico has a difficult time sitting still and refuses to talk about his behaviors. The school counselor, Jenni, who has included play therapy items in a small section of her office, encourages Rico to engage in play instead of trying to convince him to speak. Jenni explains to Rico that he can play with any item in the area but he cannot throw any items outside of the play area (setting limits). Rico continues to be quiet but appears to have a constant scowl on his face and seems to play aggressively with the toys. Jenni tracks Rico's actions and offers periodical reflections. One moment went as such:

Jenni: "You threw that doll on the floor"
Rico: "I hate girl dolls"
Jenni: "You are angry with the girl doll"

Jenni surmises that Rico may have issues with females in his life and continues to offer support and encouragement during their time together.

Setting Up the Techniques

Building the Relationship and Questioning

After the initial meeting with Rico, Jenni speaks with his teacher and caseworker and shares that she would like to continue working with him using a play therapy approach. She mentioned that her meetings with him should run for about 30 minutes each week for 6 weeks. All parties were in agreement with the plan that if Rico does not show any improvements he would be referred to the school's child study team.

In the second meeting with Rico, Jenni needed to gain a clearer picture of what was happening with him and the source of his aggression. As an Adlerian counselor, Jenni knew that there was a particular goal that Rico was endeavoring to meet through his negative behaviors (attention, power, revenge, withdrawal). During this session, she again reminded Rico of the boundaries of play and then led him to the play area. He immediately went to the dollhouse and picked up the smallest doll and began to play with it. He picked up a male doll and threw it to the floor, while he left a female doll in the dollhouse.

Rico: No, I don't want to play with her.
Jenni: What don't you like about the girl doll?
Rico: She never plays with me so I don't want to play with her.
Jenni: What would you have liked for her to play with you?
Rico: Anything. I don't care anymore. My mom never plays with me.
Jenni: You are angry at your mom.

Jenni uses questioning to help Rico understand how events in his life have impacted him. Jenni also recognizes that Rico may be seeking revenge on his mother for making him feel unsafe and for "going away".

Expressive Art Activity

During the next two meetings, Jenni decides to engage Rico in an art activity. At first, Rico is reluctant and doesn't seem to want to play. However, he relents and joins Jenni at her table. Jenni encourages him by recognizing his effort to join her. She leads Rico in *The Gingerbread Person Feelings Map* activity (Drewes, 2001). Jenni explains to Rico, "Here is a gingerbread man and we are going to see how he is feeling." Jenni already has several feelings words written beside the gingerbread man including happy, sad, angry, and afraid. She asks Rico if he would like to add more feelings words. He immediately said scared, lonely, and love. Jenni adds Rico's feeling words to her list. She then instructs Rico to choose any color crayon and draw a line through each feeling word according to the color he thinks represents that feeling. For example, on happy, Rico chose green, sad, he chose black, and so forth.

Jenni then asked Rico to think about a time at home with his mom that was troubling to him. He was then instructed to color inside the gingerbread man where he felt each feeling on the word list. Jenni then processed the picture with Rico. Together Jenni and Rico examined the drawing and observed the number of different feelings that he was experiencing. Jenni explored with Rico about his coloring the head area gray (the color he had chosen for angry) and the color he chose for the heart area, which was red, the color he chose to represent love.

In subsequent meetings, Jenni and Rico were able to talk more about his drawing and Rico discovered that although he was angry at his mom for not being there for him, he still loved her.

Termination of Play Therapy Sessions

Jenni and Rico spent the final three meetings exploring his thoughts, feelings, and behaviors through play. Jenni was determined to help Rico change his negative behaviors by reassessing the situation with his mom. By realizing that he still cared about his mom, Jenni and Rico were able to reconstruct what it would be like to express that love. Through play, Rico began "talking" to his mom and including her in more activities with him. Jenni explored with him how he was feeling when he and his mom were interacting positively together.

Jenni: You smile when you play with the girl doll.
Rico: I like when my mom plays with me.

Jenni and Rico also explored other ways that he can express his feelings in the classroom and at home. Together they determined that he could draw how he was feeling and also talk with an adult. The teacher was included in the last session and a plan was developed for Rico to use a cool down area whenever he felt that he was getting upset. In this area he could draw how he was feeling. Rico was also seeing a private outside counselor provided by social services who was able to consult with Jenni. It was decided that Rico would continue to share his feelings drawings with that counselor during their weekly sessions. In the meantime, Jenni would continue to check in with Rico and his teacher periodically.

SUMMARY

Adlerian play therapy is a useful tool for school counselors. It can be accomplished with minimal resources and time but would require some training in order for the meetings to be fully effective. The approach is practical and is evidence-based in its effectiveness with children. The tenets and strategies of this theoretical approach present a creative intervention modality for children with varied emotional concerns. Finally, it provides children with a safe and unrestricted atmosphere for activating more positive changes in attitudes and behavior. To learn more about Adlerian play therapy please see the reference list in Appendix A.

APPENDIX A

Adlerian Play Therapy Resource List

Association for Play Therapy:
http://www.utahplaytherapy.org/web/calendar/partners-play-adlerian-play-therapy-children-teens-and-families

Depression A to Z:
http://www.depressionatoz.com/depression-treatment/adlerian-therapy.html
DVD: Adlerian Play Therapy by: Terry Kottman:
http://www.psychotherapy.net/video/adlerian-play-therapy
Finding a Therapist: Psychology Today:
http://therapists.psychologytoday.com/rms/name/Makiko_Fujita_MEd,CAGS,LCMHC,RPT_Concord_New+Hampshire_82131
Play & Child Therapy: http://www.childtherapytoys.com/store/index.html?gclid=CI-7v_fhqq8CFcJM4AoduwvEYA
The Psychology Career Center. Adlerian Play Therapy: http://www.allpsychologycareers.com/topics/adlerian-play-therapy.html

REFERENCES

Adler, A. (1969). *Individual psychology.* Totowa, NJ: Littlefield & Adams

Archambault, I., Janosz, M., Morizot, J., & Pagani, L. (2009). Adolescent behavioral, affective, and cognitive engagement in school: Relationship to dropout. *Journal of School Health, 79*(9), 408-415

Archer, J., Jr.,& McCarthy, C. J. (2007). *Theories of counseling and psychotherapy: Contemporary applications.* Upper Saddle River, NJ: Pearson Prentice Hall.

Bidgood, B. A., Wilkie, H., & Katchaluba, A. (2010). Releasing the steam: An evaluation of the supporting tempers, emotions, and anger management (STEAM) program for elementary and adolescent-age children. *Social Work with Groups, 33*(2), 160-174

Bureau of Justice Statistics. (2012). Indicators of school crime and safety, 2011. Retrieved from http://bjs.ojp.usdoj.gov/index.cfm?ty=pbdetail&iid=2295

Drewes, A. A. (2001). *The gingerbread person feelings map.* In H. G. Kaduson & C. E. Schaefer's (Ed.), *101 more favorite play therapy techniques.* Northvale: NJ, Jason Aronson.

Feindler, E. L., & Engel, E. C. (2011). Assessment and intervention for adolescents with anger and aggression difficulties in school settings. *Psychology in Schools, 48*(3), 243-253

Fowler, D. (2011). School discipline feeds the "pipeline to prison". *Phi Delta Kappan, 93*(2), 14- 19

Henry, K., Knight, K., & Thornberry, T. (2012). School disengagement as a predictor of dropout, delinquency, and problem substance use during adolescence and early adulthood. *Journal of Youth & Adolescence, 41*(2), 156-166

Kottman, T. (2003). *Partners in play: Adlerian approach to play therapy* (2nd Ed.) Alexandria, VA: American Counseling Association

Landreth, G. L. (2012). *Play therapy: The art of the relationship.* New York, NY: Taylor & Francis

Leff, S. S., Waasdorp, T. E., Paskewich, B., Gullan, R., Lakin, A. F., MacEvoy, J. P., Feinberg, B. E., & Power, T. J. (2010). The preventing relational aggression in schools everyday program: A preliminary evaluation of acceptability and impact. *School Psychology Review, 39*(4), 569-587

Lines, D. (2007). Violence in schools: What can we do? *Pastoral Care in Education, 25*(2), 14-27

Luutonen, S. (2007). Anger and depression: Theoretical and clinical considerations. *Nordic Journal of Psychology, 61*(4), 246-251.

Mabry, J. B., & Kiecolt, K. J. (2005). Anger in black and white: Race, alienation and anger. *Journal of Health and Social Behavior, 46*, 85-101

Mayo Clinic (2011). Anger Management. Retrieved from http://www.mayoclinic.com/health/anger-management/MY00689

Morrison, M. O. (2009). Adlerian play therapy with a traumatized boy. *The Journal of Individual Psychology, 65*, 57-68

Nichols, T. R., Mahadeo, M., Bryant, K., & Botvin, G. J. (2008). Examining anger as a predictor of drug use among multiethnic middle school students. *Journal of School Health, 78*(9), 480-486

Portrie-Bethke, Hill, N. R., & Bethke, J. G. (2009). Strength-based mental health counseling for children with ADHD: An integrative model of adventure-based counseling and Adlerian play therapy. *Journal of Mental Health Counseling, 31*(4), 323- 339

Sofronoff, K., Attwood, T., Hinton, & S., Levin, I. (2007). A randomized controlled trial of a cognitive behavioural intervention for anger management in children diagnosed with Asperger Syndrome. *Journal of Autism & Developmental Disorders, 37*(7), 1203-1214

Sportsman, E. I., Carlson, K. S., & Guthrie, K. M. (2010). Lessons learned from leading and anger management group using the "seeing red" curriculum within an elementary school. *Journal of Applied School Psychology, 26*, 339- 350

Thompson, C. L. & Henderson, D. A. (2007). Counseling Children (7th ed.). Belmont, CA: Thomson Higher Education

Tolle, E. (n.d.). Joys of quotes: Anger quotes. Retrieved from from, http://www.joyofquotes.com/anger_quotes.html

CHAPTER 14

PLAY THERAPY

Interventions for Children With Asperger's Syndrome

Ashley Churbock

Play therapy has become an increasingly used modality with children and adolescents within the school setting. Since the early 20th century, play therapy has been the leading intervention utilized with children and has been used across most theoretical approaches (Schaefer, 2011). As children and adolescents face greater hardships within the school environment, school counselors seek innovative techniques to use with students to incorporate within comprehensive school counseling programs as a means to decrease emotional and behavioral disturbances (Drewes, & Schaefer, 2010). Because a child's inner world is best expressed through the act of play, this eliminates the child from having to use words to describe how they experience this world. One can argue that play therapy is the most beneficial approach for school counselors to use when seeking to understand a child's language, perspective, and reality (Landreth, Ray, & Bratton, 2009).

Play therapy has powerful change mechanisms that allow the child to overcome difficulties and achieve positive self-growth (Schaefer, 2011).

Integrating Play Techniques in Comprehensive School Counseling Programs, pp. 281–307

According to Schaefer (2011), "therapeutic powers can be classified into eight categories: communication, emotional regulation, relationship enhancement, moral judgment, stress management, ego boosting, preparation for life, and self-actualization" (p. 4). These therapeutic powers assist the child in mastering his or her world through creativity, development, and maintenance of self (Schaefer, 2011). The ultimate goal of counseling is to recognize and utilize these powerful change mechanisms to bring about healing for the child.

Students diagnosed on the autism spectrum may suffer greater hardships adjusting to the school environment and may have delayed social development due to their reluctance in forming close bonds with others and difficulties with language and communication. According to Landreth, Sweeney, Ray, Homeyer, and Glover (2005), it is often believed that children on the spectrum would not benefit from counseling because of limitations in language and symbolic thought. However, children diagnosed with Asperger's syndrome (AS) typically display higher levels of intellect and social interest than more pervasive forms of autism (Landreth et al., 2005). Thus, structured and traditional forms of play therapy may benefit children with AS because it allows for the child to have enough control of the sessions to build an emotional and therapeutic bond with the therapist (Landreth et al., 2005). This chapter seeks to address how a school counselor can benefit from using play therapy within their school counseling program to promote the emotional, social, and academic growth of students diagnosed with AS. The following vignettes will be used throughout the chapter to explore the relationship between AS and play therapy.

Vignette 1

Brandon is a 12-year-old sixth grader who was diagnosed with Asperger's at the age of 8. He attends a public middle school and is in an inclusion classroom with 24 other students. The classroom lacks the necessary structure for adequate acquisition of skills and learning necessary for Brandon. The classroom is devoid of visual aids and prompts, such as a schedule, that would help Brandon transition and prepare the necessary materials for the day's assignments.

Brandon has an updated individualized education plan (IEP) but it is not being effectively delivered due to a lack of accommodations for Brandon within each classroom. Brandon is frequently bullied and often avoids attending school. He enjoys the regular education science class with Mrs. Jones. However, Brandon does not deal well with transitions to his elective classrooms such as physical education and art. Brandon also has difficulties with sensory issues in physical education and art because the supplies used in the classroom tend to be adverse to him (e.g., paint, clay, and rubber balls.) He is failing his elective classes because he refuses to participate in certain activities which cause him sensory discomfort and he is often distracted within these particular classroom environments. Brandon's inability to cope with sensory issues, classmates, and changes within the classroom setting manifest by his acting out in maladaptive ways. Brandon often becomes easily angered, raises his voice, or becomes argumentative with others when he feels frustrated or misunderstood. When Brandon displays these behaviors, it is difficult for his teachers to de-escalate him and as a result, he is disruptive to other students.

Brandon has an older brother, Ben, who is patient, kind, and works well with Brandon. Brandon's father works full-time but Brandon's mother works part-time to ensure that she spends extra time helping Brandon when he arrives home from school. Brandon was referred to the school counselor by his science teacher, Mr. Jones. Mr. Jones noticed Brandon's difficulties with transitions in the classroom, which typically lead to outbursts of anger. Mr. Jones also believes Brandon's social skill deficits and eccentric and tangential verbiage make Brandon more vulnerable to bullying and teasing by classmates.

Vignette 2

Sarah is an 8-year-old student in second grade. She attends a private school that specializes in autism spectrum disorders and is in a classroom with one certified special education teacher, one paraprofessional, and seven students. The classroom is highly structured with scheduled activities, a visual board, and station work. Since the school is comprised solely of students on the spectrum, she does not regularly engage peers that do not have a diagnosis on the spectrum. She receives speech therapy and occupational therapy twice-per-week for 30-minute sessions. She is passing her classes but tends to have anxiety when any disruptions occur in their daily schedule (e.g., field trips, substitute teacher).

Sarah's mother wanted Sarah to have more engagement with neurotypical peers her age, as this is lacking in her present school environment. She registered Sarah for a recreational soccer team and Sarah is having difficulties making friends with her teammates. Although they do not overtly criticize or tease Sarah, Sarah's mother is concerned that Sarah is excluded and avoided by her teammates. Sarah does well with the structured exercises during practice but has difficulties with the disorganization and randomness of the games.

Sarah's mother contacted the school counselor to make a referral for counseling. Sarah's parents are very involved in her academic and social life and are a great support system. Sarah's parents were trained in applied behavioral analysis (ABA) techniques 5 years ago and use this model when working with Sarah on schoolwork, or any academic material. They have seen progress in Sarah's academics and behavior.

LITERATURE REVIEW

Asperger's Syndrome is a neurobiological disorder that is listed under the pervasive development disorders in the *Diagnostic and Statistical Manual of Mental Disorders IV* (DSM IV) along with autism and Rett's disorder (American Psychiatric Association, 2000). There has been a long standing debate about whether AS is a unique disorder with characteristics not found in another disorder, or simply a form of autism. The opinion of the authors of the DSM-IV-TR, was that "Asperger's syndrome could be differentiated from autism by an examination of the child's early development and the existence of some characteristics that were rare in children with autism" (Attwood, n.d., p. 1).

According to the American Psychiatric Association (2000), the following criteria must be met for diagnosis:

1. Qualitative impairment in social interaction, as manifested by at least two of the following:

    (a) marked impairments in the use of multiple nonverbal behaviors such as eye-to-eye gaze, facial expression, body posture, and gestures to regulate social interaction
    (b) failure to develop peer relationships appropriate to developmental level
    (c) a lack of spontaneous seeking to share enjoyment, interest or achievements with other people (e.g., by a lack of showing, bringing, or pointing out objects of interest to other people)
    (d) lack of social or emotional reciprocity

2. Restricted repetitive and stereotyped patterns of behavior, interests and activities, as manifested by at least one of the following:

    (a) encompassing preoccupation with one or more stereotyped and restricted patterns of interest that is abnormal either in intensity or focus

(b) apparently inflexible adherence to specific, nonfunctional routines or rituals
(c) stereotyped and repetitive motor mannerisms (e.g. hand or finger flapping or twisting, or complex whole-body movements)
(d) persistent preoccupation with parts of objects

3. The disturbance causes clinically significant impairments in social, occupational, or other important areas of functioning.
4. There is no clinically significant general delay in language (e.g., single words used by age 2 years, communicative phrases used by age 3 years)
5. There is no clinically significant delay in cognitive development or in the development of age-appropriate self help skills, adaptive behavior (other than in social interaction) and curiosity about the environment in childhood.
6. Criteria are not met for another specific pervasive developmental disorder or schizophrenia. (p. 84)

The diagnosis of AS and its classification is expected to change once the *Diagnostic and Statistical Manual of Mental Disorders V* is released in May 2013. It is proposed that AS would merge under autism spectrum disorders (ASD) and clinicians would rate the severity of presentation: mild, moderate, and severe (American Psychiatric Association, 2012).

The origin of AS is unknown but can result from genetics, brain disease, or other causes. But most researchers agree that is likely a combination of genetics and environmental factors (Moore, 2002; The National Autism Center, 2011). Frombonne (2003) notes that epidemiology rates for AS coupled with pervasive developmental disorder not otherwise specified, is approximately 0.3 to 4.84 per 1000. Furthermore, autism rates are higher at 1 per 150 and male to female ratio is 4:1 (Frombonne, 2003; Yeargin-Allsopp et al., 2003).

Children with AS show a broad range of cognitive profiles and typically have deficits in the areas of motor functioning, language development, social/emotional, cognitive processing and sensory integration. Since AS falls on a continuum symptoms can present in a multitude of ways: mild to severe and with or without sensory, motor, and language difficulties (Moore, 2002). Although AS presents differently in each individual, general findings have led researchers to underscore some salient characters. School counselors' awareness of the deficits and strengths of children diagnosed with AS will be crucial in providing the most appropriate and effective services within the school environment.

Asperger's Impact on Academic Functioning

The large variance in academic achievement in youth with AS has been one of the most widely discussed factors of this population (Myles, Barnhill, Hagiwara, Griswold, & Simpson, 2001). Youth with AS display IQs that range from "Very Superior" to "Intellectually Deficient" (Myles et al., 2001). Specifically,

> Current belief is that children and youth with AS have problems with the following academic areas: (a) abstractions; (b) comprehending metaphors, idioms, and other figures of speech; (c) discerning relevant from irrelevant stimuli; and (d) over application of literal interpretations. (Attwood, 1998; Myles & Simpson, 1998; Myles & Southwick, 1999, as cited in Myles et al., 2001, p. 305)

Although IQs can vary greatly, the majority of individuals with AS have average to above average intelligence (Myles & Adreon, 2001).

This discrepancy in the cognitive profile of children with AS can make preparing and implementing interventions challenging. In addition, children with AS are strong in rote-based material however this does not necessary lead to comprehension of material (Myles et al., 2001). Although individuals with AS are extremely verbal, Myles et al. (2001) found that they experienced "grave difficulties in interpreting the oral language of others and constructing solutions to routine problems and challenges that occur in the home, school, and community" (p. 306). School counselors may use student data to monitor progress and guide supports and services provided to a student with AS (American School Counselor Association, 2005). Guidance curriculum, individual student planning, responsive services, and systems support are the four fundamental components which comprise the delivery system element of the ASCA *National Model* (American School Counselor Association, 2005). These components help assist every student through the delivery of an appropriate and comprehensive program which targets all students through direct and indirect services.

The physical school environment may also affect a student's ability to concentrate. Movement and visual distractions can prove problematic for a student with AS to maintain focus and attention (Reitzel & Szatmari, 2003); this is particularly critical during transitions (i.e., moving from one classroom to another with minimal supervision and structure). Self-contained classrooms may help alleviate these problems, but at the expense of social interaction with typical peers. Myles and Adreon (2001) note that individuals with AS are often expected to perform academically due to their average to above average IQs. However, AS characteristics are often exacerbated within the school setting because of the expectations and demands of school such as homework, following multistep directions, and routine changes combined with a low tolerance for stress can lead to anxiety and low academic performance for this population (Myles & Adreon, 2001).

Asperger's Impact on Social Functioning

Social interactions and peer relations are often areas of difficulty for youth with AS. Myles et al. (2001) conducted a study in which parents of students with AS reported "significant problems in the areas of overall behavioral symptoms, externalizing behaviors, hyperactivity, and atypicality" (p. 307). Atypicality signifies unexpected developmental and behavioral features, given normal development or in children without developmental delay (Lyman, 2008). Furthermore, parents also perceived their children with AS to be at-risk for the following: depression, attention problems, isolation, poor adaptability, and delayed social skills (Myles et al., 2001). In comparison, teachers rated students similarly but less severe than did parents.

Students with AS often misread the social cues of their peers which is a crucial skill needed to make friends and "fit in" (Myles & Adreon, 2001). In addition, Myles and Adreon (2001) argue that maturity is often gauged by one's actions and abilities within social situations, therefore, students with AS are often labeled as "immature" and inept. Furthermore, these students lack the ability to conform to the social norms of their peers and lack awareness of body language, subtlety, and facial expressions (Moore, 2002).

Students with AS often monopolize conversations and have difficulties answering social questions appropriately. Further, when placed in stressful situations, students with AS have difficulty answering others' questions or engage in stereotypies such as repetitive and ritualistic movements, postures, or utterances (Moore, 2002). In particular, they lack the skills to initiate and maintain conversation with peers. Myles and Adreon (2001) note that as conversations become more complex, the social and conversational skills of students with AS begin to deteriorate due to excess stimuli, lack of awareness or understanding of others' perceptions or feelings, or the tendency to interpret phrases and words concretely. This limits their ability in adolescence to understand complex language structures such as intimation, social nuance, and sarcasm. Of critical importance, individuals with AS tend to display higher levels of motivation for socialization than those with autism but may be insensitive, overly eccentric, and longwinded in their interactions with others (Attwood, n.d.).

The social use of language, or pragmatic impairment, also disables individuals diagnosed with AS. "From school-age onward, individuals with AS report that their social language vulnerabilities give rise to anxiety, avoidance of some social situations, and self-image challenges and are a great source of concern for them" (Klin, Volkmar, & Sparrow, 2000, p. 125).

Asperger's Impact on Behavioral Functioning

Sensory issues plaguing students with AS may manifest as difficulties in behavioral functioning at school. Adverse reactions to stimuli are common in those with AS in all seven sensory areas: tactile, vestibular, auditory, olfactory, visual, proprioceptive, and gustatory (Myles & Adreon, 2001). Sensory experiences are often painful, disgusting, or unpleasant for students with AS which may cause anxiety, stress, avoidance, and isolation (Myles & Adreon, 2001).

Inconsistent and unpredictable reactions to stimuli can also cause behavioral issues for these students. Myles and Adreon (2001) found that students with AS may react adversely to a stimuli at one point in the school day but may have no, or an opposite reaction to the same stimuli at another point in time. This can potentially lead to high levels of anxiety due to students' expectations of randomly facing adverse sensory situations within the school setting. Tantrums, rage, emotional meltdowns, and shutdowns are common reactions to sensory overload in this population (Myles & Adreon, 2001).

In addition to sensory issues, the following situations can cause tantrums, and other behavioral issues within the school setting: (a) failure to understand rules and routines; (b) desire for friendships coupled with a lack of social skills to fulfill this wish; (c) disruptions from pursuing self-interests; (d) stress from sensory input that is overwhelming or undesired; and (e) teasing and bullying (Myles & Adreon, 2001, p. 20). According to Myles (2003), understanding the cycle of behavior and its function is crucial in providing the necessary intervention and resources for the student to extinguish unwanted behaviors. Behavioral cues from the student may help counselors and teachers become more aware of a potential tantrum or emotional meltdown and halt further agitation. In addition, Myles suggested teaching self-monitoring skills to the student for identification of triggers, increasing self-awareness, and preventing behavioral issues. This coping skill will be beneficial to increase behavioral functioning and efficacy in students with AS.

THEORETICAL FOUNDATION OF PLAY THERAPY

The Association for Play Therapy (2001) defined play therapy as "the systematic use of a theoretical model to establish an interpersonal process wherein trained play therapists use the therapeutic powers of play to help clients prevent or resolve psychosocial difficulties and achieve optimal growth and development" (as cited in Reddy, Files-Hall, & Schaefer, 2005, p. 4). Play is universal, spontaneous, symbolic, and need not to be taught to children. Moreover, it is the most appropriate and powerful medium for children to learn relationship building, critical thinking, and social skills (Drewes & Schaefer, 2010). According to Schaefer (2011), the counselor seeks to acknowledge, recognize, and utilize the therapeutic powers of play that will promote positive development and growth and assist a client in overcoming psychosocial hardships. Play therapists should also obtain particular characteristics that bode well for play therapy such as a genuine caring and support for the child, empathy, and unconditional positive regard.

Ginott (1994) notes that play is an age appropriate display of a child's concrete reality, life events, oneself, and the important people in one's life through the use of toys rather than words (as cited Landreth, 2002, p. 12). Play can foster the use of concrete objects to act as symbols for direct or indirect encounters that a child has experienced (Landreth, 2009). Landreth (2009) argues that play is a way children gain power and control through the organization of their thoughts and experiences. This sense of power and can help the child feel more secure and comfortable in their world. The counselor must use this medium to interpret emotions and foster therapeutic healing by engaging the child in their most comfortable form of communication. Play allows children with the inability or reluctance to adequately display feelings to openly express themselves (Drewes & Schaefer, 2010). It invites independence, autonomy, and self-selection as the child chooses toys and actions to express their inner feelings and attitudes (Landreth, 2009). Furthermore, Liles and Packman (2009) noted that children with AS are commonly labeled and these labels can become a source of negative feedback for children. However, the play therapy environment can promote unconditional positive regard, and ultimately, a sense of control over their world. Thus, play should be considered in the treatment of childhood mental health.

Although play therapy is not identified as "evidence-based," it does have sufficient empirical backing to support its use in schools (Drewes & Schaefer, 2010). The idea of play as a therapy is not a newly founded idea and has been around since as early as the 1930s and can be credited to individuals such as Anna Freud and Hermoine Hugh-Hellmuth. Schaefer (1999) conducted a meta-analysis of play therapy research which yielded

25 therapeutic factors (Drewes & Schaefer, 2010). According to Schaefer (1999), the following therapeutic powers of play were discovered: (a) self-expression; (b) access to the unconscious; (c) direct and indirect teaching; (d) abreaction; (e) stress inoculation; (f) counterconditioning of negative affect; (g) catharsis; (h) positive affect; (i) sublimation; (j) attachment and relationship enchantment; (k) moral judgment; (l) empathy; (m) power/ control; (n) competence and self-control; (o) sense of self; (p) accelerated development; (q) creative problem solving; (r) fantasy compensation; (s) reality testing; (t) behavioral rehearsal; and (u) rapport building (as cited in Drewes & Schaefer, 2010).

Ray, Bratton, Rhine, and Jones (2001) note that play has been effective in a wide variety of populations and found that play therapy has been proven effective in improving the following areas applicable to children with AS: social and emotional adjustment, self-concept, emotional and intellectual problems, correction of speech problems, academic performance, and aggressive and acting out behaviors (as cited in Moore, 2002). Although play therapy has been shown to be effective in a wide range of populations it is contraindicated for severe forms of autism and schizophrenia (Moore, 2002).

Even with an empirical foundation, there are still limitations within the research of play therapy and criticism of its use as a mental health intervention with children is still prevalent. According to Phillips (1985) a lack of rigorous research designs and data-analytic research methods contributes to ongoing criticism of play therapy (as cited in Reddy et al., 2005). However, a meta-analysis of 42 experimental studies was conducted within the past two decades and has yielded an overall positive effect size of .66 to .80, or in other words, a moderate to large treatment effect (LeBlanc & Ritchie, 1999, as cited in Reddy et al., 2005). This analysis revealed that play therapy treatment was effective across modalities, age groups, and theoretical orientations (Reddy et al., 2005).

In addition to criticism of empirically based findings, inadequate education and support from the school community hinders the growth of play therapy interventions with students. According to Drewes and Schaefer (2010), the lack of administrative "buy-in," financial resources, and professional training prohibits the growth of play therapy within the school setting. School counselors must actively educate administration, school board members, and stakeholders on the importance of play therapy and its role in the treatment of mental health disorders in children. It has become imperative that counselors vigorously advocate for change and essential resources needed to provide such interventions to students (Drewes & Schaefer, 2010). In addition, all mental health professionals: school counselors, school social workers, and school psychologists, should be trained in play therapy to adequately meet the mental health needs of the student body.

Developmental, Individual Difference, Relationship Model ("floor time")

According to Rye (2012), the developmental, individual difference, relationship (DIR) approach developed by Greenspan and Weider (1999) may be the most effective and appropriate form of play therapy for children with AS. This approach, better known as "floor time," is a nondirective approach that emphasizes "individual differences, child-centered interests, and affective interactions between child and an adult" (Simpson, 2005, p. 26).

Greenspan et al. (1998) outlined the following six goals of treatment in the DIR model:

1. The dual ability to take an interest in sights, sounds, and sensations of the world and to calm oneself down.
2. The ability to engage in relationships with other people.
3. The ability to engage in two-way communication.
4. The ability to create complex gestures and to string together a series of actions into an elaborate and deliberate problem-solving sequence.
5. The ability to create ideas.
6. The ability to build bridges between ideas and to make them reality based and logical (as cited in Simpson, 2005, p. 27).

Essentially, the DIR method seeks to enhance the child's interpersonal relationships, flexibility, problem-solving, communication, enjoyment of learning, self-initiative, self-soothing, and frustration tolerance (Simpson, 2005). It is crucial that the play should be initiated and directed by the child and the therapist take an active but non-commanding role. The DIR model was developed for younger children but can be used with older children and adolescents with the appropriate adjustments (Simpson, 2005).

PLAY THERAPY TECHNIQUES

Play therapy provides a safe environment for children to express feelings or issues that may be anxiety producing or threatening for the child. The play therapy room is an established place where the child may play out concerns and issues. The counselor's role is to get on the child's level and use reflection to foster a greater understanding of the child's issues and concerns (Drewes & Schaefer, 2010; Landreth, 2009). Since children with AS typically struggle around social settings, change or disruptions in routine, communication, and body language, the quick-paced nature of social situations may cause high levels of stress and anxiety (Moore, 2002). Programs and strategies have been developed to help improve social skills of those with AS, and play therapy is one noted example.

According to Moore (2002), it is essential that the counselor adequately understand the child's specific triggers, issues, and situations that cause heightened reactions or difficulties controlling behavior and emotions. Landreth et al. (2005) suggest shortened or brief sessions, approximately 15-minute sessions, at the beginning of counseling to build the therapeutic relationship and to ease the child's anxiety. Counselors use symbolism and interpretation of play to facilitate sessions. The counselor uses patience and cues from the child to guide the therapy sessions and foster therapeutic healing.

The use of toys can also help build the therapeutic relationship by removing the invasiveness of direct verbal interaction between child and counselor (Landreth et al., 2005). The toy becomes the medium through which the child communicates with the counselor and provides a level of control over the environment for the child; the child is in control of when, how, or what is communicated within the session. This process allows the child to build mastery and self-regulatory behavior.

Wilson and Ryan (2008) suggest using Axline's (1987) eight guidelines for nondirective play therapy for children with AS. The guidelines suggest the following:

1. The therapist must develop a warm, friendly relationship with the child, in which good rapport is established as soon as possible.
2. The therapist accepts the child exactly as he or she is.
3. The therapist establishes a feeling of permissiveness in the relationship so that the child feels free to express feelings completely.
4. The therapist is alert to recognize the feelings the child is expressing and reflects those feelings back in such a manner that the child gains insight into his or her behavior.
5. The therapist maintains a deep respect for the child's ability to solve problems if given the opportunity. The responsibility to make choices and institute change is the child's.
6. The therapist does not attempt to direct the child's actions or conversation in any manner. The child leads the way; the therapist follows.

7. The therapist does not attempt to hurry the therapy along. It is a gradual process, recognized as such by the therapist.
8. The therapist establishes only those limitations necessary to anchor the therapy to the world of reality and to make the child aware of his or her responsibility in the relationship (as cited in Wilson & Ryan, 2008, p. 73-74).

Although these guidelines were based on neurotypical children, these guidelines will also help promote unconditional positive regard, empathy, and warmth between therapist and a client with AS while allowing the child to feel empowered and in control. Once the therapeutic relationship is established, then specific play therapy techniques can be selected and implemented with the client. Kaduson and Schaefer (2003) note seven groups of play therapy techniques: expressive arts, puppet play, storytelling, group play, game play, toys and objects, and other techniques.

Expressive Arts Techniques

Clay, paint, sculptures, drawings, and other similar mediums would be classified as expressive art play therapy (Kaduson & Schaefer, 2003). This type of play therapy has been used extensively when working with children who have experienced trauma. One example of a specific expressive art technique may be a family collage which can be interpreted by the counselor examining how the child depicts the family members. The counselor will observe the colors and shapes used, the placement of family members, and the absence of family members within the drawing. This technique is a nonthreatening, culturally sensitive, and easy way for the child to express family dynamics.

The following is an example of an application of expressive arts play therapy via the vignette of Brandon:

Counselor: *"Brandon, what word would you use to describe your art class?"*

Brandon: *"Messy."*

Counselor: *"I would like for you draw me a picture of you in Art class. I would like for you to show me where in your body you feel those feelings."*

Brandon: Brandon draws a picture of himself and colors his stomach blue. "*I* guess it mostly feels weird in my stomach."

Counselor: *"Wow Brandon, I can see why you might not like going to art class. You also mentioned you do not like PE class. Is this how you feel in PE class too?"*

Additional examples of specific expressive arts techniques outlined by Kaduson and Schaefer (2003) include drawings, family collages, storyboards, problem-solving techniques through "hand-ling." "Hand-ling," or outlines of hands, is an art activity that allows students to brainstorm ways they may react to a presenting problem. The presenting problem is written on the palm and then the child must write five separate ways to handle the situation along each finger. These techniques help children express emotions, reassures them to use their own thoughts and abilities to problem solve, allows the therapist to give the child feedback about the options he has chosen, and encourages the child the say, "I can 'handle' this!" (Kaduson and Scahefer, 2003).

Puppet Play

Nondirective art, games, and play can be helpful techniques to use with children who are not ready or willing to discuss feelings. An exercise or game can help guide the conversation more quickly and without the pressure of direct questioning (Kaduson & Schaefer, 2003). "Some children are easily distracted by the external (the puppet), so you eliminate one element: the voice" (p. 160). The puppet may reinforce the idea that counseling is a safe environment for this child to express feelings through a nondirect expression of feelings and emotions and particularly helpful for children who are shy, shamed, or have difficulties with communicating. This technique may be particularly helpful with children with AS who struggle with communication and social skills by providing them with an indirect outlet for communication and expression of feelings.

The counselor can define the rules of the puppet play and guide the session that will be most appropriate and effective and this should be done at the beginning of this process. Kaduson and Schaefer (2003) recommend that the counselor explain to the child that the puppet will "talk" only to the therapist. The counselor will then convey the puppet's message to the child. This sets the dynamic which helps keep the therapeutic relationship in tact because the message comes from the puppet and not the therapist (Kaduson & Schaefer, 2003).

The following is an example of an application of puppet play via the vignette of Sarah:

Counselor: *"Sarah, I would like you to meet my friend* (Therapist pulls puppet out of her bag). *He told me he does not have a name, would you like to name him?"*

Sarah: *"Ok."* Sarah is silent for a minute. *"Sam."*

Counselor: *"Alright. Well Sam would like to talk to you, but he is kind of shy like you so he would like to tell me things and then I will tell them to you. Do you understand?"*

Sarah: Sarah nods her head.

Counselor: Therapist makes puppet whisper in her ear. *"Sam would like to know what school you go to."*

Sarah: *"Mason Academy."*

Counselor: Puppet is brought to therapists ear again. *"Sam goes to a private school just like you do. He wants to know if you like Mason Academy?"*

Sarah: *"Yes."*

Counselor: Puppet whispers. *"Sam loves school. What do you do after school is over?"*

Sarah: *"Sometimes I play soccer."*

Counselor: *"Sam loves soccer and plays too! How do you feel about soccer?"*

Sarah: Looks at the floor. *"It's ok."*

Counselor: *"Sam says you look sad."*

Sarah: *"Sam, the girls are mean to me. I cry sometimes."*

Counselor: *"Sam would like to help you make more friends. Is that ok?"*

Sarah: *"Ok."*

The puppet has allowed Sarah to express her difficulties making friends. The counselor set the guidelines from the beginning, which Sarah agreed to, and she began to open up to the puppet by disclosing that she cries sometimes about the way her team treats her. This provided the counselor with the opportunity to work on Sarah's social skill deficits and allows Sarah to voice her distress through the puppet.

Storytelling

The use of storytelling has been a tradition that dates back to early communities around the world. Native Americans used objects such as the "Talking Stick" for decision making and allowing all members to have a voice (Kaduson & Schaefer, 2003). This technique healed relationships through listening and honesty (Forest & Pearpoint, 2001, as cited in Kaudson & Schaefer, 2003). Sharing stories can help aid the connection between therapist and the child while still allowing the child to process, at a safe distance, emotions through the narrative (Kaduson & Schaefer, 2003).

Storytelling and narration can be just as therapeutic and helpful when working with children with AS. According to Wilson and Ryan (2008), storytelling is when a child tells a story and the counselor then tells a responding story. This responding story uses the same characters and events but with "healthier adaptations and conflict resolution; guided fantasy; the empty chair technique, to name a few" (p. 10). In addition, the breadth and flexibility of storytelling can allow the child to insert personally meaningful storylines, characters, events, and underlying issues.

The following is an example of storytelling via the vignette of Brandon:

Counselor: *"Brandon, I learned this fun game today. Would you like to play it with me?"*

Brandon: *"Ok."*

Counselor: *"We are going to work together to tell a story. This story can be about anything you want it to be about. What do you want our story to be about?"*

Brandon: *"Sharks."*

Counselor: *"Great! We are going to tell a story about sharks. First I am going to start the story off. Then when I point to you, you will continue the story. When you want me to go again, you point back at me. Do you understand?"*

Brandon: *"Yes."*

Counselor: *"It was a warm day and Shane the shark was swimming in the ocean."* Brandon watches the counselor as she pretends to swim around the room. The counselor points at Brandon to signal his turn.

Brandon: *"Shane is looking around for his friends but no one is there."* Brandon puts his hands up to his eyes pretending they are binoculars and searches around the room. He points back to the counselor.

Counselor: *"Shane feels really sad about being all alone."* Counselor slumps her shoulders and pretends to swim really slowly around the room and frowns. Points back to Brandon.

Brandon: *"Shane really hates not having any friends. He would like to make new friends."* Shane does not move around the room but looks down and away from the therapist.

Counselor: *"Shane wants to learn how to make friends so he asks his older brother, Ben."* Therapist inserts the older brother to model how Brandon can use his own older brother in social skill acquisition.

Brandon: *"Shane tells Ben he is sad. Ben tells him to throw a party to make new friends!"*

Storytelling and back and forth sharing shown in this example can help the therapist model appropriate social skills, problem solving techniques, change the subject or topic of the story, and incorporate positive messages or perspective (Kaduson & Schaefer, 2003).

Group Play

Social skills, anger management, and other support groups are common group play formats (Kaduson & Schaefer, 2003). The counselor can model appropriate skills while giving each child the opportunity to practice skills with peers. This allows children to generalize the skills learned in a more natural setting while still allowing the therapist control over the sessions. Furthermore, the structure and acceptance from the therapist and peers may provide close interpersonal relationships for the child and encourage uniqueness, originality, and creativity (Fall & Levitov, 2001).

The group setting allows the child to experience others, fosters communication, and promotes knowledge of self, others, and life (Fall & Levitov, 2001). The group setting is particularly effective at improving social skills and is a commonly cited reason for referral to the school counselor. "Play therapy groups provide the opportunities for children to master new behaviors, offer and receive assistance, and experiment with alternative expressions of emotions and behavior" (Sweeney, 1997, as cited in Fall & Levitov, 2001, p. 103). Imitation is common in group therapy because children are able to watch peers and attempt behavioral changes they wish to make (Fall & Levitov, 2001).

Forming the group is critical to its success and balance, screening, and selection must be carefully examined. Fall and Levitov (2001) warn against placing "developmentally egocentric" children within the group noting that if they must be removed, they are likely to internalize this message as a failure. When working with a child with AS, it is crucial to measure their "social hunger," or desire to be accepted by and maintain a sense of belongingness within the group, to ensure that a group setting is most appropriate (Fall & Levitov, 2001). As with any group, it is important to balance the group, strive for heterogeneity, and screen members before placement.

The following is an example of a group play therapy session via the vignette of Sarah:

Counselor: *"Sarah, John, Mary, Jimmy, and Katie, this is our playroom. You can play with anything you want in here."*

John: John runs to the trucks and starts pushing them around the room and making noises. "*Come here, Jimmy!*"

Jimmy: Still standing by the therapist, "*Can I go play with John?*"

Counselor: *"You can play with whomever or whatever you like in here."* Jimmy runs to John and picks up a toy car. Katie has sat down by a doll and Mary is walking around the room. Sarah is standing by the door.

"Katie, it looks like you have found a doll. Mary, it seems like you are looking at everything. Sarah, it seems like you're wondering about this place."

John: *"Come on, Sarah!"* John walks over to Sarah and grabs her hand and tries to guide her into the room. Sarah pulls her hand back and remains at the door.

Counselor: *"It seems like Sarah is not ready to come in yet, John. She did not seem to like that."* John returns to Jimmy and takes Jimmy's car.

Jimmy: *"Hey! That is my car."*

Counselor: *"Jimmy is telling you he did not like that you took his car away from him."* John drops the car and returns to the truck he was play with. Jimmy takes the car back.

Counselor: *"Jimmy has the car again and now John has decided to play with truck again."*

Sarah: Sarah goes to sit next to Katie and picks up a doll. *"My doll's name is Susie."*

Counselor: *Sarah has named her doll, Susie.*

The counselor is attuned to each child and shows understanding and respect of their choices. The therapist allows the children to take the lead, acknowledges emotions and behaviors, but sets appropriate limits. Children with AS are more likely to accept and follow rules of a group if structure is present and consistent. Fall and Levotiv (2001) recommend using the A.C.T. model in groups: A-*Acknowledge* the child's feelings (it is important to the setting of limits by continuing reflection and acceptance); C-*Communicating* the limit (in a neutral and nonpunitive manner); and T-*Targeting* an acceptable alternative (which recognizes that the child still has a need to express self and can do so within acceptable boundaries) (p. 111). By using this model, unacceptable behaviors (such as John's) will be ameliorated by the group and the counselor, the children receive verbal and nonverbal cues from the counselor and peers, and each child will eventually be drawn into the play process (Fall & Levitov, 2001).

Game Play

Game play is a type of directive play therapy technique that uses "store bought or self-created games to help children express psychological issues" (Kaduson & Schaefer, 2003). Hall, Kaduson, and Schaefer (2002) note games help facilitate affective expression in children and the technique is a fun way for children to pair affective states with environmental contexts of the game. As noted, this will allow for the child to express feelings and emotions at a safe distance. Game play is an easy and inexpensive technique that can be particularly helpful when working with a shy or resistant child (Hall, Kaduson, & Schaefe, 2002).

The structure and rules associated with games can be helpful for a child with AS who may be rigid and inflexible to free association and nonfigurative activities. Games have set limits, goal-directed, rules, and roles for players which restricts the scope of behavior as compared to nondirective play (Schaefer & Reid, 2001). In particular,

> Games tend to have more concrete objectives and the focus is typically apparent in board games, card games, street games, computer games, and fine and gross motor games. Not all types of games are adaptable to therapy; organized sports, recreational games, and arcade games, for example, are generally not utilized in child psychotherapy. (p. 2)

Game play fosters practicing and repetition of skills, learning and following rules, emotional control, problem-solving skills, self-discipline, and cooperation (Schaefer & Reid, 2001). Furthermore some researchers have stressed that games present a microcosm of society where the child must follow rules just as one must follow the power and hierarchies of society (Schaefer & Reid, 2001).

The following is an application of game play with Pick-Up-Sticks via the vignette of Brandon:

Counselor: *"Brandon, I would like to play Pick-Up-Sticks with you. Would you like to play Pick-Up-Sticks with me?"*

Brandon: *"Ok."*

Counselor: *"The sticks are red, yellow, blue, and green. We are going to make each color an emotion. Red is anger, yellow is happy, blue is sad, and green is lonely. I am going to let you drop the sticks on the table and then we will take turns picking them up. If you pick up a red stick you'll have to tell me about something that makes you angry. If you pick up a blue about something sad, and so on. Do you understand the rules?"*

Brandon: *"Yes."*

Counselor: *"Ok drop the sticks on the table."* Brandon drops the sticks and picks up a blue stick. *"Ok, you picked blue. Tell me about something that makes you sad."*

Brandon: *"When the kids at school make fun of me."*

Counselor: *"I can see why that would make you sad."* The therapist picks up a red stick. *"I picked a red stick, so I will tell you about something that makes me angry. I get angry when someone calls me stupid."*

Brandon: *"That makes me angry too."* Brandon picks a green stick.

Counselor: *"Green. What makes you feel lonely?"*

Brandon: *"Lunch. No one sits by me at my table."*
Counselor: *"Wow. That does sound lonely. What is that like for you?"*
Brandon: *"Not good. It makes me not want to go to school at all but my mom makes me go."*

The Pick-Up-Sticks game helped facilitate a conversation about affective states and process the emotions that Brandon feels in specific environments. This will allow the counselor to target identified social skill deficits, self-regulation, and problem-solving skills.

Toys and Objects

Toys and objects are the most commonly used manipulatives in play therapy and made more popular in 1980 by Dora Kalff. She singlehandedly created one of the major contributors to the play therapy movement known as sandtray therapy (Gil, 1994). Homeyer and Sweeney (1998) define sandtray therapy as "an expressive and projective mode of psychotherapy involving the unfolding and processing of intra- and inter-personal issues through the use of specific sandtray materials as a nonverbal medium of communication, led by the client(s) and facilitated by a trained therapist" (p. 6). Although sandtray is under the play therapy umbrella, it has its own theoretical approach and techniques (Gil, 1994).

Sandtray therapy is a client-centered approach where the counselor accepts, reflects, and occasionally comments (Kaduson & Schaefer, 2009). The child will select figures, assign meaning, and present the counselor with a view into their world. "Like the use of art, sandplay concretizes feelings, shifts internal events into the external arena, and produces a tangible product that holds the significance of the child's communication and reduces the need for verbalization" (p. 281).

Sandtray can help children who have difficulties with attention and impulsivity focus their energy. The objects used in the sand, or figurines, become the child's language of play and can be manipulated at will by the child (Gil, 1994). According to Kaduson and Schaefer (2009), the sand tray objects can be displayed according to the following categories: animals, vehicles, people, landscape, accessories, large shadow figures, power/ego protector figures, magic, treasure, and natural materials. The display can offer the child a familiar environment which helps engage the child in the sandtray (Kaduson & Schaefer, 2009).

The following is an example of sandtray therapy via the vignette of Sarah:

Sarah: *"Who is this?"* Sarah points to a female figurine.
Counselor: *"In here, she can be whoever you want her to be."*
Sarah: *"This is me."*
Counselor: *"Ok."*
Sarah: Sarah buries the figurine in the sand.
Counselor: *"You are burying Sarah in the sand."*
Sarah: Sarah picks up another female figure and manipulates the female figurine so that she is throwing sand on the buried figurine Sarah.
Counselor: *"Who is she?"*

Sarah: *"This is Michelle. Michelle doesn't like me."*
Counselor: *"So, Michelle does not like Sarah."*
Sarah: Sarah throws sand out of the tray.
Counselor: *"You would like to throw sand. You may throw sand in the tray."*
Sarah: Sarah continues to throw sand outside of the tray.
Counselor: *"Remember, the rules of the sandtray. If you choose to throw sand in the sandtray, you choose to continue playing."*
Sarah: Sarah stops throwing the sand and returns to burying the figurine.
Counselor: *"You chose to continue playing. You are burying Sarah again."*

The counselor set limits with Sarah but allowed Sarah to choose her actions and consequences. The counselor allows Sarah to take the lead and respects her choices and decisions within the sandtray using reflections to process the experience for Sarah. It is crucial that the choices of figures, placement, movement, and story are under the child's control and can be changed at any point by the child (Kaduson & Schaefer, 2009).

CASE STUDY: BRANDON

Case Formulation

When working with children, it is crucial to incorporate parents into the process. If possible, the school counselor should have an initial session or contact with Brandon's parents to build a relationship, gather information to conceptualize the family, and introduce the parents to play therapy and the therapeutic process (O'Connor & Braverman, 2009; Schaefer, 2011). When working with children with disabilities, the family can be a great asset in gathering information, supporting the therapeutic process, and providing crucial information to identify the presenting problem. Brandon's parents can provide an insight into the Brandon's perspective of self, others, and their world (O'Connor & Braverman, 2009). In addition, Brandon's parents offer information about him as it applies to the family. This information can help solidify and confirm the issues brought forth by the teachers or compartmentalize Brandon's issues to solely school-related.

Classroom observations provide another precounseling opportunity for the school counselor to assess Brandon's behavior, interpersonal relationships, and social skills. The school counselor received the referral for Brandon by Mr. Jones and asked him for permission to do a classroom observation on Brandon before initiating services. The school counselor sought to validate the observations made by Mr. Jones that confirm counseling services are, in fact, appropriate for Brandon (Schmidt, 2010). The school counselor and Mr. Jones agreed upon a set time and day for the school counselor to observe. After observing, the school counselor discussed her initial perceptions with Mr. Jones. This allowed for Mr. Jones to confirm if the observations made were typical of Brandon's behavior that prompted him to make the referral to the school counselor.

Treatment Description

Based on the meeting with Brandon's parents and classroom observation in Mr. Jones' classroom, the counselor determines that Brandon displays the following inappropriate classroom behaviors: (a) an aversive sensory experience; (b) teasing or bullying from classmates; and (c) unexpected changes in classroom routine. Brandon's inability to cope with these situations results in social skill deficits, lack of close interpersonal relationships, impulsivity, anger outbursts, and maladaptive coping skills. According to Klin et al. (2000), treatment should never solely be based on an individual's diagnosis; rather treatment should capitalize on the child's assets and address specific needs. In addition, the counselor should be careful to not push the therapeutic process or the therapeutic relationship, but rather allow Brandon to express feelings and make changes when he feels ready and willing to do so (Harris & Landreth, 2001).

The school counselor prioritizes Brandon's presenting problems and would initially like to address his maladaptive coping skills which often results in impulsivity and anger outbursts. This is the most pressing issue noted by his teachers and parents and would be improved through self-monitoring skills. The counselor will later address Brandon's social skill deficits, as this would be a more complex issue for Brandon to master. However, the therapeutic relationship allows for the counselor to model appropriate social skills through turn-taking activities, verbal and nonverbal communication, and reciprocal play.

Session one. In the first session with Brandon, the counselor seeks to build the therapeutic relationship and introduce Brandon to play therapy. The counselor provides Brandon with an age and developmentally appropriate explanation of the counseling process and the play room. The counselor mentions to Brandon, "You can play with whatever you like in here! If there is anything you can't do in here, I will let you know" (Schaefer, 2011, p. 8). The counselor allowed Brandon to explore the play room at his own pace and did not direct Brandon on which materials or objects to use. Brandon plays with the miniature figurines and the sandtray. The counselor is surprised that Brandon is not averse to the sand, due to the unique sensory (tactile) experience it presents, and watches him play. She awaits Brandon's invitation to join the play. Brandon uses a snake to dig a hole in the sand in which he buries a male figure that he names "Brandon." The snake repeatedly dumps sand on top of "Brandon." Brandon notes "the snake is mean to Brandon," and the counselor states, "the snake seems to dislike Brandon." The counselor focused on building a warm, inviting, safe, and welcoming environment for Brandon. The counselor gave Brandon a five-minute warning to signal the end of the therapy session so he could mentally prepare to leave the space.

Sessions two and three. In sessions two and three, the counselor continued to build rapport and trust with Brandon since they were still in the "rapport building" stage of therapy (Schaefer, 2011). The counselor sought to be supportive in nature and wanted to build the most comfortable and safe environment for Brandon since he struggled with this in his normal day-to-day interactions at school. The counselor was sensitive to the idiosyncratic characteristics of AS and knew that counseling was a change in his routine, thus, took extra care to ensure the rapport building stage was thoroughly implemented. During these sessions, the counselor was gathering information about Brandon and his school and home life experiences while allowing him to further explore the play room and therapy process. Brandon repeated the process of the snake burying the male figure (i.e., "Brandon") and the counselor began to form themes around Brandon's play.

Sessions four and five. The counselor and Brandon moved into the "working through" stage which brought about the most therapeutic change and where the counselor and Brandon spent the majority of their time (Schaefer, 2011). The counselor began to pick up on themes of play and recognized that aggression and control was often exhibited. For instance, the snake was consistently mean to "Brandon" and the snake controlled "Brandon." Brandon also used the snake to pick up new objects to go in the sand and the snake seemed to control what went in and out of the sandtray. The counselor used these contextual cues to recognize themes and then addressed them within the sessions.

Brandon felt that he lacked control of the symptoms associated with having AS and when he experienced bullying and teasing. The counselor believed this lack of control was represented by the snake. These experiences and feelings lead to anger outbursts and arguments at school. Through play, the counselor helped Brandon better understand and connect his play within the session with his feelings and his behaviors outside of the sessions.

CONCLUSION

Play is a fun, yet educational, way for children to relieve stress, express creativity, and increase positive social interactions and communication. In addition, play allows children to practice task completion, new skills, and how to regulate emotions and frustrations (Schaefer, 2011). Play therapy is a natural and developmentally appropriate means for children to express their inner world. Therefore, children with AS who have complications with communication and social interactions may greatly benefit from play therapy as an intervention for identified psychosocial difficulties. The positive outcomes of play therapy may help alleviate the aversive symptoms associated with AS if applied appropriately and consistently. Although debates still remain around the lack of depth in play therapy research, studies have shown play therapy to be effective across age, gender, and presenting issues (Bratton, Ray, Rhine, & Jones, 2005).

Play therapy is flexible in nature and most theoretical approaches have dabbled in its methods. In addition, the numerous types of play therapy techniques allow this modality of therapy to be particularly comprehensive, widespread, and coveted. School counselors can adapt techniques to the various populations in which they serve in the school environment while remaining authentic to their theoretical foundation. Most counselors would agree that regardless of theoretical approach and techniques, the relationship between the counselor and the child is the most crucial element that determines the success of therapy. Interpersonal relationships are typically a weak area for children with AS; therefore, the therapist must create an environment that is welcoming and safe. The play therapist sets the climate of the playroom through behavior and attitude towards the child (Harris & Landreth, 2001). According to Harris and Landreth (2001), the dimension of self is the key; the counselor is more important than any skills the therapist possesses. Regardless of age, gender, race, or ethnicity, play is a form of self-expression and when coupled with a positive, working therapeutic relationship, can be quite beneficial for a child.

REFERENCES

American Psychiatric Association. (2000). *Diagnostic and statistical manual of mental disorders* (4th ed., text rev.). Washington, DC: Author.

American Psychiatric Association (2012). Proposed revisions: 299.80 asperger's disorder. Retrieved from http://www.dsm5.org/ProposedRevisions/Pages/proposedrevision.aspx?rid=97

American School Counselor Association. (2005). *The ASCA National Model: A Framework for school counseling programs* (2nd ed.). Alexandria, VA: Author.

Attwood, T. (1998). *Asperger's syndrome.* London, England: Jessica Kingsley.

Attwood, T. (n.d.). Is there a difference between asperger's syndrome and high-functioning autism? Retrieved from http://www.tonyattwood.com.au/articles/newpapers3.html

Axline, V. (1987). *Play therapy.* London, England: Ballantine Books.

Bratton, S., Ray, D., Rhine, T., & Jones, L. (2005). The efficacy of play therapy with children: A meta-analytic review of treatment outcomes. *Professional Psychology: Research and Practice, 36*(4), 376-390.

Drewes, A., & Schaefer, C. (2010). *School based play therapy* (2nd ed.). Hoboken, NJ: John Wiley.

Fall, K., & Levitov, J. (2001). *Modern applications to group work.* Huntington, NY: Nova Science.

Frombonne, E. (2003). The prevalence of autism. *The Journal of American Medical Association, 289*(1), 87-89. doi:10.1001/jama.289.1.87

Gil, E. (1994). *Play in family therapy.* New York, NY: Guilford.

Greenspan, S., Wieder, S., & Simons, R. (1998). *The child with special needs.*New York, NY: Perseus.

Hall, T., Kaduson, H., & Schaefer, C. (2002). Fifteen effective play therapy techniques. *Professional Psychology: Research and Practice, 33*(6), 515-522.

Harris, T., & Landreth, G. (2001). Essential personality characteristics of play therapists. In G. Landreth (Ed.), *Innovations in play therapy: Issues, process, and special populations* (pp. 23-30). New York, NY: Brunner-Routledge.

Homeyer, L. E., & Sweeney, D. S. (1998). *Sandtray: A practical manual.* Royal Oak, MI: Self-Esteem Shop.

Kaduson, H., & Schaefer, C. (2003). *One hundred and one play therapy techniques* (Vol. 3). Lanham, MD: Rowman & Littlefield.

Kaduson, H., & Schaefer, C. (2009). *Short-term play therapy for children.* New York, NY: Guilford Press.

Klin, A., Volkmar, F., & Sparrow, S. (2000). *Asperger syndrome.* New York, NY: The Guilford Press.

Landreth, G. (2002). *Play therapy: The art of the relationship* (2nd ed.). New York, NY: Brunner-Routledge.

Landreth, G. (2009). *Play therapy: The art of the relationship* (2nd ed.). New York, New York, NY: Brunner-Routledge.

Landreth, G., Ray, D., & Bratton, S. (2009). Play therapy in elementary schools. *Psychology in the Schools, 46(3), 281-289.* doi: 10.1002/pits.20374

Landreth, G., Sweeney, S., Ray, D., Homeyer, L., & Glover, G. (2005). *Play therapy interventions with children's problems*. Lanham, MD: Rowan & Littlefield Publishing, Inc.

Liles, E. E., & Packman J. (2009). Play therapy for children with fetal alcohol syndrome. *International Journal of Play Therapy, 18*(4), 192-206. doi:10.1037/a0015664

Lyman, J. A. (2008). *Qualitative study of male asperger's syndrome students : Transition from high school to college. (Doctoral dissertation.* Retrieved from PCOM Psychology Dissertations (Paper 86).

Moore, S. (2002). *Asperger syndrome and the elementary school experience: Practical solutions for academic and social difficulties*. Shawnee Mission, KS: Autism Aspergers.

Myles, B., Barnhill, G., Hagiwara, T., Griswold, D., & Simpson, R. (2001). Education and Training in Mental Retardation and Developmental Disabilities. Retrieved from http://www.cs.cmu.edu

Myles, B. (2003) Behavioral forms of stress management for individuals with asperger syndrome. *Child and Adolescent Psychiatric Clinics of North America, 12*(1), 123-141. doi:10.1016/S1056-4993(02)00048-2

Myles, B., & Adreon, D. (2001). *Asperger syndrome and adolescence: Practical solution for school success*. Shawnee Mission, KS: Autism Asperger Publishing Co.

Myles, B., & Simpson, R. (1998). *Asperger syndrome: A guide for educators and parents*. Austin, TX: Pro-Ed.

The National Autism Center. (2011). Evidence-based practice autism in the schools: A guide to providing appropriate interventions to students with autism spectrum disorders. Retrieved from http://www.nationalautismcenter.org/pdf/NAC%20Ed%20Manual_FINAL.pdf

O'Connor, K., & Braverman, L. (2009). *Play therapy theory and practice: Comparing theories and techniques*. Hoboken, NJ: John Wiley.

Reddy, L., Files-Hall, T., & Schaefer, C. (Eds.). (2005). Announcing empirically based play therapy interventions for children. In *Empirically based interventions for children* (Chapter 1). Retrieved from http://www.apa.org/pubs/books/4317066s.pdf

Reitzel, J., & Szatmari, P. (2003). Cognitive and Academic Problems. In M. Prior (Ed.), *Learning and behavior problems in apserger syndrome* (pp. 35-54). New York, NY: Guildford Press.

Rye, N. (2012). Child-Centred Play Therapy. In: JH Stone, M Blouin, editors. *International Encyclopedia of Rehabilitation*. Retrieved from http://cirrie.buffalo.edu/encyclopedia/en/article/275/

Schaefer, C. (1999). Curative factors in play therapy. *Journal for the Professional Counselor, 14*(1), 7-16.

Schaefer, C. (2011). *Foundations of play therapy*. Hoboken, NJ: John Wiley.

Schaefer, C., & Reid, S. (2001). *Game play: Therapeutic use of childhood games*. New York, NY: Wiley.

Schmidt, J. (2010). *The elementary/middle school counselor's survival guide* (3rd ed.). San Fransisco, CA: Jossey-Bass.

Simpson. R. L. (2005). *Autism spectrum disorders: Interventions and treatments for children and youth*. Thousand Oaks, CA: Corwin Press.

Wilson, K., & Ryan, V. (2008). *Play therapy: A non-directive approach for children and adolescents* (2nd ed.). London, England: Bailliere Tindall.

Yeargin-Allsop, M., Rice, C., Karapurkar, T., Doernberg, N., Boyle, C., & Murphy, C. (2003). Prevalence of autism is us metropolitan area. *The Journal of American Medical Association, 289*(1), 49-55. doi:10.1001/jama.289.1.49

CHAPTER 15

REACTIVE ATTACHMENT DISORDER

Play Therapy Interventions for School Settings

Julie A. Ritchie

Reactive attachment disorder (RAD) has received increasing attention as a possible explanation of severe behavioral disturbances in children and adolescents (Kemph & Voeller, 2008). RAD is a childhood disorder characterized by markedly disturbed and developmentally inappropriate social relatedness in most contexts that begins before the age of 5 years (American Psychiatric Association [APA], 2000). RAD is one of the more difficult disorders for teachers and school counselors to work with due to the behavioral problems displayed by children with RAD. These challenges are often exacerbated by dysfunctional family processes, such as parental abuse, neglect, or lack of a consistent caregiver, and limited coping resources (Davis, Kruczek, & McIntosh, 2006). Students with RAD require far-reaching support including individual counseling, therapy, and classroom guidance. Unfortunately, many students with attachment

Integrating Play Techniques in Comprehensive School Counseling Programs, pp. 309–323

disorders leave school without any recognition of their need for counseling (Hayes, 1997).

Vignette 1

Penelope was an 8-year-old, Caucasian female in the third grade. She had recently been sent to the school counselor's office after hitting a teacher who tried to move her desk from the back corner of the room to another location. Penelope was being moved after students next to her complained about receiving threats from Penelope. Additionally, she was caught cheating on a test. This was her third new school since she began kindergarten. Penelope had lived in four different foster homes since she was removed from her mother's care at age four by the Department of Children and Family Services. She was emotionally and verbally abused by her mother and was profoundly neglected. As an infant, Penelope was left unattended in her bed for hours at a time while her mother was intoxicated. Moreover, she was molested as a child by one of her mother's boyfriends. She was found by a neighbor in deplorable condition: her hair was matted; she was unbathed, and severely underweight. The neighbor reported Penelope's condition to the police. Penelope's mother surrendered her parental rights after being taken to prison. Penelope has been removed from foster homes for uncontrollable rages and destructive behavior. Her last foster parent took her to a psychiatrist and she received a RAD diagnosis. She struggled with maintaining positive relationships with foster parents and other foster children. She was reported to be mild mannered unless she gets upset in which she responds quickly with outbursts of anger and aggression. In school, she remains isolated from classmates and acts out aggressively to her classmates and teachers. She often disrupts class and refuses to cooperate in group projects. Penelope is quick to act tough by cursing, acting like she does not care, ignoring teachers and other students, and being physically aggressive. When foster parents or teachers in the past have tried to work with Penelope in a soft nurturing way; she would back away and not respond.

Vignette 2

Carly was a 6-year-old, African American female in the first grade referred to the school counselor by her teacher. The teacher reported that Carly was a good student but acted out behaviorally in class and struggled to interact with peers. She was impulsive, aggressive at times, and refused to listen to directions. The teacher reported that Carly would also be very loving and overly affectionate towards her but would also act out at times in order to prompt receiving the teacher's immediate attention. Carly lived with her mother and a 2-year-old brother in a one bedroom apartment. Her father left before her brother was born. Her mother worked two jobs to support the family. Carly and her brother were often left with an elderly neighbor when her mother worked, which mostly consisted of watching TV alone in a room. Carly did not discuss her mother and showed a disrespectful lack of interest when the class would create school projects about family. Carly had no other family beyond her mother and brother. Although she was a good student, her maladaptive behaviors, limited interpersonal skills, and dysfunctional affect regulation kept Carly from being successful academically and personally.

LITERATURE REVIEW

Reactive attachment disorder (RAD) is a childhood disorder characterized by markedly disturbed and developmentally inappropriate social relatedness in most contexts that begins before the age of 5 years (APA, 2000). Observed disturbances in social interactions must be attributable to pathogenic care, defined as the failure to meet the basic emotional and/or physical needs of the child/or an absence of a stable caregiver to whom the child can form an attachment (Buckner, Lopez, Dunkel, & Joiner, 2008). Grossly pathogenic care is characterized by: (a) a persistent disregard for the child's emotional needs for comfort, stimulation, and affection; (b) persistent disregard for the child's physical needs; and (c) repeated changes in primary caregivers (APA, 2000). This definition of RAD places the direct cause of behavioral issues on the primary caregiver.

According to the *Diagnostic and Statistical Manual for of Mental Disorders* (APA, 2000), RAD is divided into two subtypes: inhibited and disinhibited. The *inhibited* subtype refers to children who persistently and pervasively fail to initiate and to respond to social interactions in a developmentally acceptable way. Erikson (1963) noted that within the first year of life, an infant gains trust when a caregiver is warm and responsive. Conversely, an infant may come to mistrust others when his or her basic needs are not met, particularly needs for shelter, comfort, food, and consistent love and support. Erikson furthered stated that autonomy is fostered when parents permit reasonable free choice and do not forcibly control or shame the child. Between the ages of 6 and 11, Erikson emphasized that at school, children develop the capacity to work and cooperate with others, but inferiority develops when negative experiences at home, at school, or with peers lead to feelings of incompetence. Erikson's developmental theory emphasizes the impact of positive, social interactions on a child's development.

Children displaying the *inhibited* subtype of RAD tend to be emotionally withdrawn and are unlikely to seek comfort or attention, even from familiar adults. Children with this subtype are indiscriminately sociable or demonstrate a lack of selectivity in their attachments; such as being overly assertive in social interactions or demanding attention or affection from any adult in their proximity (Buckner et al., 2008; Schwartz & Davis, 2006). Both subtypes are considered equally problematic for the child or adolescent.

The theoretical framework of RAD is based in the work of John Bowlby and Mary Ainsworth (Ainsworth & Bowlby, 1991). John Bowbly's (1969) attachment theory can be defined as the biological functioning of humans to bond with a caregiver for the sake of their protection and preservation (Robinson, 2002). Bowlby believed that attachment had four characteristics: (1) proximity maintenance, (2) safe haven, (3) secure base, and (4) separation distress. Proximity maintenance is the desire to be near the person the child is attached to. Safe haven is when a child returns to the attachment figure for safety when faced with fear. Secure base is when the child uses the attachment figure as a base of security from which the child can explore his or her surroundings. Lastly, separation distress describes anxiety that occurs in the absence of the attached caregiver. Bowlby suggested that infants are primed by evolution to form a close, enduring, dependent bond with a primary caregiver beginning in the first moments of life (Hardy, 2007). Bowlby further contended a young child's early experiences of coping with caregiver unavailability may create, cognitively, a template or set of rules and expectations about the availability and emotional supportiveness of others, including peers, teachers, and therapist (Langevin, 2001). Ainsworth and colleague (1978) expanded Bowlby's attachment theory and identified three levels of attachment patterns as exhibited in her *Strange Situation* study: secure attachment, avoidant attachment, and resistant attachment. *Securely* attached children exhibit little avoidance or resistance to contact with the caregiver and use the caregiver as a base of exploration. An *avoidant (dismissive)* attachment is when the child seems unresponsive to the parent when he or she is present and is not distressed when the parent leaves. The child reacts in the same way to a stranger as he or she does the parent. When the parent returns, the child is slow to greet the parent. A *resistant* attachment is characterized by a child that seeks closeness to the parents and fails to explore his or her environment. Upon the parent's return, the child combines the following behaviors: clingy, angry, and resistive behavior, struggling when held, and sometimes hitting and pushing. A child that forms this style of attachment cannot be comforted easily. Lastly, the disorganized or disoriented style of attachment presents the greatest insecurity. When the child is reunited with the parent, the child may show a confused expression, contradictory behaviors, flat depressed emotions, and may cry out. Thus, the theoretical base of RAD, attachment theory (Bowlby, Ainsworth) and psychosocial development theory (Erikson), helps to explain the breakdown of the natural bonding process of an infant or child with their caregiver (Marshall, 2010).

Children diagnosed with RAD appear to demonstrate significantly more behavioral problems and psychosocial problems than children without RAD (Buckner et al., 2008). Many clinicians have described numerous behaviors that indicate the presence of RAD, such as superficial charm, severe tantrums, low intelligence, intentional destruction of property, age-inappropriate sexual acting out, physical aggression toward adults, profanity, difficulty adjusting to change, running away, sociopathic tendencies, and toileting accidents (Kay Hall & Geher, 2003; Zeanah, 1996). Additionally, many children with RAD exhibit developmental delays. Richters and Volkmar (1994) reported that most children in their study of RAD had developmental delays that included unusual patterns of language and motor delays, failed acquisition of age appropriate self-care skills, poor attention and concentration, emotional liability, aggression, impulsivity, and oppositionality. Of concern to school counselors, children with RAD may present with a host of difficulties that are exacerbated by the school environment. Specifically, children with RAD consistently exhibit more teacher-attention seeking behaviors such as: overdependence upon a teacher, significantly more emotional dependence, and they are more likely to engage in proximity-seeking behaviors (Floyd, Hester, Griffin, Golden, & Smith Canter, 2008). RAD places children at risk for other psychopathology as they grow older, so that by the time a child with RAD moves into adolescence other diagnoses have been added, such as attention deficit hyperactivity disorder (ADHD), oppositional defiant disorder (ODD), posttraumatic stress disorder (PTSD), mood disorder or conduct disorder (Kemph & Voeller, 2008).

It is important to note that RAD significantly differs, and should be distinguished, from mental retardation, autistic disorder, and other pervasive developmental disorders (APA, 2000). Clearly, children with RAD show many characteristics of other psychiatric and behavior disorders. However, the obvious difference is the inability to form healthy, consistent patterns of attachment coupled with a history of pathological care (Shaw & Paez, 2007). One of the challenges with the identification of RAD is the lack of effective assessment instruments or protocols to diagnosis RAD and distinguish RAD from other diagnoses. Some of the assessment instruments that may be useful for diagnosis of RAD include the Child Behavioral Checklist (CBCL), Randolph Attachment Questionnaire, Sutter-Eyeberg Student

Behavior Inventory Revised, and Eyeberg Child Inventory (Floyd et al., 2008). Sheperis et al. (2003) concluded that any assessment protocol should include the following key components: (a) distinguishing cognitive and lingual characteristics of RAD from other developmental disorders; (b) noting behavioral portions even though they overlap with other conduct disorders; (c) specifically addressing the origin of the disorders; and (d) placing emphasis on all of this areas listed when making the diagnosis.

The exact prevalence or incidence of RAD is unknown (Richters & Volkmar, 1994). The DSM-IV-TR states that reactive attachment disorder is relatively uncommon; however, the number of reported cases is on the rise (Marshall, 2010). Zeanah et al. (2004) identified the prevalence among high-risk toddlers in foster care as 38-40%. Reber (1996) reported that 80% of abused or neglect children show some symptoms of RAD.

RAD treatment protocol varies greatly. There is little research and empirical evidence of the efficacy of any of the treatments. This is due in part to the individualized nature of RAD. Each child presents with varying causes and experiences, (i.e., neglect, abuse, lack of a consistent caregiver) that trigger the child's individual characteristics that constitute a diagnosis of RAD, so treatment variances must be taken into account (Marshall, 2010). Treatment of RAD requires many repetitions of appropriate thoughts and behaviors over a prolonged period of time to foster the changes necessary to form new neuronal patterns that might enable the child to develop socially acceptable relationships with other people (Kemph & Voeller, 2008). Treatment of disordered attachment and related behaviors tends to be focused in several areas: enhancing current attachment relationships, creating new attachment relationships, and reducing problematic symptoms and behaviors (Hardy, 2007). Research shows that the most effective intervention to prevent the diagnosis of RAD is prevention and includes a stable and nurturing home; however, that is not always possible (Shaw & Paez, 2007).

INTERVENTIONS FOR REACTIVE ATTACHMENT DISORDER

School counselors use a variety of interventions to address the specific needs of students diagnosed with RAD. Play therapy is an attachment-based intervention that utilizes a balance of structure, engagement, and nurturance as a way to form healthy attachments (Weir, 2007). Play is used in therapy as a means of helping children deal with emotional and behavioral issues. It is an age appropriate medium for expressing feelings, exploring relationships, describing experiences, disclosing wishes, and self-fulfillment (Landreth & Bratton, 1999). In the safe, emotionally supportive setting of the counseling room, the child can play out concerns and issues, which may be too horrific or anxiety producing to directly talk about. In the counseling setting, the school counselor can help the child to feel heard and understood (Schaefer & Drewes, 2009). Play therapy helps children develop confidence and self-efficacy; this is accomplished through mastery of fears, skill acquisition, and learning new tasks. Children release emotion through action, use creative thinking to solve problems, learn about themselves, and gain clarity regarding their lives feelings, and abilities (Pehrsson & Aguilera, 2007).

Play therapy is considered best practice for counselors working with children and is evidenced-based as its efficacy is supported by research (Bratton, Ray, Whine, Jones, 2005). This therapeutic approach meets the goals and standards set by the American School Counselor Association's *National Model* (2012) and meets students' developmental needs. The ASCA *National Model* ensures that school counselors keep holistic development of students at the forefront of education reform (ASCA, 2012). According to the ASCA *National Model,* school counselors provide direct and indirect services in response to the immediate needs of students (Bowers & Hatch, 2005) which may include individual counseling sessions or small group play sessions. The ASCA *National Model* (2012) outlines school counselors' work with students in three development domains: academic, career, and personal/social. School counselors need to look at each student's developmental level to choose the appropriate play therapy interventions. Elementary school counselors are more likely to use toy based and playroom oriented interventions. Middle and high school counselors may utilize more expressive arts, games, role plays, sand tray, and other techniques in their work with students (Wynne, 2008). Indirectly, the counselor may integrate play therapy principles and techniques with parent consultations, teacher consultations, and school programs.

One approach that is appropriate for working with students with RAD is for the school counselor to use child centered play therapy (CCPT). CCPT is defined as a dynamic interpersonal relationship between a child and a counselor trained in play therapy. It provides selected play therapy materials and facilitates the development of a safe relationship for the child to fully express and explore self through child's natural medium of expression-play (Landreth, 2002). In this approach the toys are viewed as the child's words and the play as the child's language (Landreth & Bratton, 1999). Axline (1947) developed eight guidelines to use in non-directed play therapy. These principles include: (a) the establishment of a caring relationship between the therapist and the child; (b) full acceptance of the child for who he or she is; (c) creation of a free atmosphere in which the child feels capable of expressing a range of emotions; (d) recognition and reflection of the child's feelings; (e) respect for the child's ability to internally solve difficulties and provision of opportunities to establish responsibility; (f) allowance of the child's leadership in play sessions; (g) understanding of the gradual process of therapeutic change; and, finally, (h) provision of therapeutic boundaries only when necessary (Blanco & Ray, 2011). The focus in CCPT is on the child's innate capability to move towards growth and maturity as well as the child's ability to self-direct.

CCPT is not a completely permissive counseling relationship because children do not feel safe, valued, or accepted in a relationship without boundaries. Boundaries provide predictability. A prescribed structure provides parameters for the relationship though play therapy has minimal limits: messiness is accepted, exploration is encouraged, neatness or doing play activities in a prescribed way is not required, and persistent patience is the guiding principle (Landreth & Bratton, 1999). Some limits that are set in the playroom may include not leaving the room until session is completed, not hitting the counselor, and not removing toys from the playroom. Landreth (2002) suggested that because of the unique relationship established in CCPT, the child perceives the playroom and the counselor as safe; the counselor in the playroom will accept and reflect the child's emotional expressions, thereby allowing the child to become more empowered and accepting of him- or herself. As children feel free to accept themselves, they will hypothetically be open to accept others, including knowledge from others, such as teachers.

Another approach utilized by school counselors that incorporates play therapy techniques for students diagnosed with RAD is CBT. CBT is based on the premise that cognitions determine how people feel and act, and that faulty cognitions can contribute to psychological disturbances (Knell, 2009). CBPT allows the counselor to bring components from both theoretical styles. The components of traditional non-directive play that are blended with CBT are: reliance on a positive therapeutic relationship, using play as a means of communication, and therapy as safe place for the child (Knell, 2009). Differences from traditional play therapy include directions and goals of treatment, such as teaching relaxation techniques; choice of play materials and activities by both the counselor and child, play being psycho-educational and the importance of having the school counselor make the connection between the child's behavior and thoughts. Blending play therapy with CBT has been successful in addressing issues connected with sexual abuse, trauma, domestic violence, social skill development, emotional/affect regulation, anxiety, depression, and aggression (Knell, 2009).

Additionally, CBPT can be used to address affect regulation. Children diagnosed with RAD need more specific and targeted interventions to improve their self-regulation because of persistent and serious interpersonal deficits (Floyd et al., 2008).CBPT can be a highly effective and efficient means of producing improvement in children's ability to manage their emotions. By working through play, the therapist also has a potentially greater impact on the child's functioning and deregulation (Paula, 2009). CBPT interventions can be divided into two parts: (1) affect identification and (2) building coping skills. Before children can effectively cope with their feelings, they must recognize the emotion and the physical manifestations (i.e., identifying feelings of anxiety in their chest or back muscles). Playing a game with children helps connect emotional frustration with its physical manifestation. The school counselor can talk about his or her own physical reactions to the therapeutic games. Children may then be asked to pay attention to their bodily reactions during the game. The next stage is building coping skills. Learning relaxation techniques helps children reduce tension in their bodies and distract from any physical and cognitive distress they may be experiencing when they are feeling overwhelmed by their emotions (Paula, 2009). Teaching children relaxation techniques such as muscle relaxation or imagery in the session allows them to develop skills which they can then practice outside of counseling sessions. By practicing these techniques in and out of sessions, children are able to use the skills more readily when needed. The school counselor can educate caregivers about the techniques while conducting a family session, through parent consultation; or by allowing children to teach their parents these techniques.

Another intervention that a school counselor may use with children diagnosed with RAD is the *Coping Power Program* (Lochman, Boxmeyer, & Powell, 2009). This program is an empirically supported, cognitive behavioral intervention for late elementary and early middle school age children who demonstrate aggressive behavior problems, which can be exhibited in children diagnosed with RAD (Lochman, Boxmeyer, & Powell, 2009). This school based counseling program is delivered in a group setting of four to six students that meets on a weekly basis for an 18-month period. The program has a parenting component that is designed to run concurrent to the group intervention. The *Coping Power Program* is an intervention for at-risk aggressive children. The student component is designed to improve children's social cognitions and their positive social and academic oriented behaviors. The parenting component is designed to enhance parenting skills, such as parental involvement, child monitoring, setting clear expectations, and providing rewards and consequences (Lochman, Boxmeyer, & Powell, 2009). The intervention mediums include puppets, role-playing, games, and activities. These interventions help foster emotional awareness, practice anger management strategies, learn problem-solving skills, discuss personal issues, learn social skills, and increase self-efficacy. The parental component allows parents to learn to play more productively with their children. By enhancing parents' abilities to more competently play with their children, the counselor is enhancing the parent-child bond (Lochman, Boxmeyer, & Powell, 2009).

CASE STUDY: CARLY

At the beginning of this chapter, the second vignette describes a young girls' attachment behaviors that are concerning to her classroom teacher. The purpose of this section is to further explore the case of Carly and the interventions chosen by her school counselor.

Session 1

Carly was referred to the school counselor by her teacher due to verbal outburst and aggressive behavior toward other students in class. The counselor met with Carly for thirty 30 minutes and introduced Carly to the playroom. Carly was quiet and did not respond to anything the counselor asked or said. She finally sat on a chair in the corner of the room after looking and touching different items around the room. The counselor tracked and reflected Carly's movements in a safe, nonjudgmental tone. The counselor used this time to begin building rapport with Carly. The goal of this session was for Carly to recognize that this is a nonthreatening environment in which she can be secure and to allow Carly to begin to explore the toys in the room. By allowing her to explore and show interest in the toys on her own; the counselor was using a non-directive play therapy method of building rapport with the Carly. Though the counselor knew Carly from classroom guidance, this was the beginning of the counseling relationship. Therefore, the school counselor used counseling skills, including reflecting and tracking, to allow Carly to know that the counselor was working with Carly but was not instructing her on what to do in the room. At the end of the session, the counselor thanked Carly for coming and sat up a counseling session for the following week.

Second Session

In the second session, the school counselor continued to build rapport with Carly through play. The goal of the second session was to help Carly recognize her feelings and how her feelings relate to her behavior. The counselor began by helping Carly reflect on her thoughts and feelings about the last session. The counselor then provided Carly with a blank sheet of paper, markers and crayons. She then asked Carly to sketch facial expressions on the piece of paper; specifically, the counselor asked Carly to draw a face for each feeling that the counselor named. Then the counselor asked what her body felt like when Carly felt that emotion. For example, the counselor asked Carly to draw a mad face. After Carly drew the face, the counselor asked Carly to consider in which ways she feels the emotion, mad, in her body. Carly stated that when she is mad her face gets red; her fists tighten; and she feels like she is going to explode. The counselor connected Carly's feelings with physical manifestations by processing more feelings and asking Carly to reflect about the feelings and actions she experiences with each emotion. The counselor did this with many of the emotions that Carly appeared to be experiencing (i.e., happy, confused, scared, sad). Following this, the counselor had Carly use a puppet to act out each emotion. The counselor read the story, *"Alexander and the terrible, horrible, no good, very bad day,"* written by Judith Viorst. The counselor would read a couple of pages and then have Carly, using a puppet, act out how Carly thought the main character in the story, Alexander, was feeling. At the end of the session, the counselor asked Carly to be aware of her feelings until they meet next time and to recognize how her body was reacting.

Third Session

In the third session the counselor's goal was to begin helping Carly work on coping skills. By learning coping skills, Carly could start to change the behaviors that had manifested as a result of her emotions. The counselor began by teaching Carly deep breathing. This technique can be very effective for managing strong emotional reactions, especially those that involve a physiological response (Paula, 2009). Blowing bubbles is a useful tool for teaching children to breathe in deep and let it out very slowly. To make it into a game, the counselor and the client can see who can use their breathing skills to make the biggest bubbles without bursting. In this session the counselor, using store bought bubble liquid and bubble wands, taught Carly to breathe in for four counts and to slowly blow the bubble for four counts. The counselor and Carly practiced deep breathing without the bubbles and talked through how to use these skills in school and outside of school.

Fourth Session

To continue to build rapport with Carly, her school counselor implemented a play therapy technique, *Holding You in My Mind* (Langevin, 2001). *Holding You in My Mind is* a simple technique and to do the activity the counselor and Carly each created their own containers. The counselor provided small containers (empty peanut butter jars), glue, glitter, markers, stickers, magazines, scissors, construction paper, and so forth. They each decorated and placed their names on their containers. The counselor used this time to chat with Carly and continue building a relationship with her. The act of creating the containers appeared to give Carly a sense of ownership and accomplishment.

Next, the counselor explained how they would use the containers by stating, "In these containers, we're going to write and collect the special things that we hear each other say during counseling sessions. For instance, I'm often told that I say, "Can you think of a time when something different happened?" Carly wrote that phrase down and placed it in her box. Next Carly would speak and the counselor would then write down Carly's words on a small slip of paper and place it in the counselor's box. The counselor and Carly would choose important words or phrases that the other stated during their conversations in session to place in their containers. At the end of each session, Carly would bring her container home to be able to review phrases and words.

The process of collecting and writing messages began in the next session. The counselor and Carly wrote down messages on small strips of paper. This helped to provide a nurturing experience through dialogue. The counselor focused on making statements that allowed Carly to recognize the counselor was paying close attention to her. Some statements might include reflections of facial expressions, body movements, likes and dislikes, and other statements that provided the kind of attention a caregiver might give a child during bonding. To help Carly listen to the counselor, the counselor would often provide a cue: "Let's put that down on paper for your container." The importance of bringing the container back for each session was stressed. Each session began with a review of how *Holding You in My Mind* works. During subsequent sessions, if the school counselor heard Carly repeat a phrase that was already documented, the school counselor searched it out and would make special reference to it. The same process was repeated if the counselor said something that was already captured in Carly's container. The process was incorporated into every session as other work was also implemented in the sessions, such as with behavioral interventions, relaxation techniques, and expressive arts. This intervention provided cohesion, continuity, and a repetitive review of positive messages that Carly had often lacked. Carly remained in counseling with the school counselor for a total of 14 sessions and demonstrated improved emotional regulation, a decrease in outbursts, and a reduction in clinging behaviors.

CONCLUSION

Although RAD is diagnosed in early childhood, its impact can last long into adolescence and adulthood. It has been well documented that children with this disorder have had a history of parenting characterized by grossly pathogenic care. Children with RAD may present in school with a variety of behavioral, academic, and social-emotional challenges and problems (Schwartz & Davis, 2006). School counselors should be aware of the many challenges that RAD may present in the school setting. The counselor should also be aware that RAD requires work on the guardian or parents' part outside of the school for the best results. By working with the child and guardian to produce a stable, safe environment along with working with the child on emotional regulation, behaviors, and relationships; the child's chances of success can be enhanced. The school counselor can implement play therapy techniques mentioned in this chapter to reach the goals for student in a developmental appropriate way in counseling a student diagnosed with RAD to help the child meet academic, career, and personal and social development within the school setting.

REFERENCES

Ainsworth, M. D., Blehar, M. C., Waters, E., & Wall, 5. (1978). *Patterns of attachment: A psychological study of the Strange Situation.* Hillsdale, NJ: Erlbaum.

Ainsworth, M. D. S., & Bowlby, J. (1991), An ethological approach to personality development.*American Psychologist, 46,* 331-341.

American Psychiatric Association. (2000). *Diagnostic & statistical manual of mental disorders* (4 ed., text revision).Washington, DC: Author.

American School Counseling Association. (2012). *ASCA National Standards for Students.* Alexandria, VA: Author. Retrieved from http://static.pdesas.org/content/documents/ASCA_National_Standards_for_Students.pdf

American School Counseling Association. (2012) The ASCA national model: A framework for school counseling programs. Retrieved from http://www.schoolcounselor.org/files/Natl%20Model%20Exec%20Summary_final.pdf

Axline, V. (1947). *Play therapy.* New York, NY:Ballantine Books.

Blanco, P. J., & Ray, D. C. (2011). Play therapy in elementary schools: A best practice for improving academic achievement. *Journal of Counseling and Development, 89*(2), 235-243. doi:10.1002/j.1556-6678.2011.tb00083.x

Bowers, S., & Hatch, T. (2005). The ASCA National Model: A framework for school counseling programs (2nd ed.). Alexandria, VA: American School Counselor Association.

Bowlby, J. (1969). *Attachment & loss* (Vol 1, attachment). New York, NY: Basic Books.

Bratton, S., Ray, D. Rhine, T., & Jones, L. (2005). The efficacy of play therapy with children: A meta-analytic review of the outcome research. *Professional Psychology: Research and Practice, 36*(4), 375-390. doi:10.1037/0735-7028.36.4.376

Buckner, J. D., Lopez, C., Dunkel, D., & Joiner, T., Jr. (2008). Behavior management training for the treatment of reactive attachment disorder. *Child Maltreatment, 13*(3), 289-297. doi:10.1177/1077559508318396

Davis, A. S., Kruczek, T., & McIntosh, D. (2006). Understanding and treating psychopathology in schools: Introduction to the special issues. *Psychology in the Schools, 34*(4), 413-417.doi:10.1002/pits.20155

Erikson, E.H. (1963). *Childhood and Society* (2nd ed.). New York, NY: Norton.

Floyd, K. K., Hester, P., Griffin, H. C., Golden, J., & Smith Canter, L. L. (2008). Reactive attachment disorder: Challenges for early identification and intervention within the schools. *International Journal of Special Education, 23*(2), 47-55. Retrieved from http://www.eric.ed.gov/PDFS/EJ814399.pdf

Hardy, L. (2007). Attachment theory and reactive attachment disorder: Theoretical perspectives and treatment implications. *Journal of Child and Adolescent Psychiatric Nursing, 20*(1), 27-39. doi:10.1111/j.1744-6171.2007.00077.x

Hayes, S. H. (1997). Reactive attachment disorder: Recommendations for school counselors. *School Counselor, 44*(5), 353-361. Retrieved from http://www.eric.ed.gov/PDFS/EJ553583.pdf

Kay Hall, S. E., & Geher, G. (2003). Behavioral and personality characteristics of children with reactive attachment disorder. *The Journal of Psychology, 137*(2), 145-163. Retrieved from http://web.ebscohost.com/ehost/results?sid=20cd5398-4808-45eb-a589-1f6dbca9c40b%40sessionmgr4&vid=3&hid=17&bquery=AN+9909059&bdata=JmRiPXBiaCZ0eXBlPTAmc2l0ZT1laG9zdC1saXZl#1

Kemph, J., & Voeller, K. (2008). Reactive attachment disorder in adolescence. In L. Flaherty (Ed.), *Adolescent psychiatry* (Vol. 30, pp. 159-178). New York, NY: The Analytic Press/Taylor & Francis Group.

Knell, S. (2009). Cognitive behavioral play therapy. Theory and applications. In A. Drewes (Ed.), *Blending Play therapy with cognitive behavioral therapy: Evidenced-based and other effective treatments and techniques* (pp. 117-138). New York, NY: John Wiley.

Langevin, C. A. (2001). Holding you in my mind: An approach for working with traumatized and attachment-disordered children. In Kaduson, H.G., & Schaefer, C.E. (Eds.), *101 more favorite play therapy techniques* (p. 208). Northvale, NJ: Jason Aronson.

Landreth, G.L. (2002). *Play therapy: The art of the relationship* (2nd ed). New York, NY: Brunner-Routledge.

Landreth, G.L. & Bratton, S. (1999). *Play Therapy* (report no. EDO-CG-99-01). Retrieved from http://www.counseling.org/Resources/Library/ERIC%20Digests/99-01.pdf

Lochman, J. E., Boxmeyer, C., & Powell, N. (2009). The role of play with cognitive behavioral therapy in aggressive children. In A. Drewes (Ed.), *Blending play therapy with cognitive behavioral therapy: Evidenced-based and other effective treatments and techniques* (pp. 179-197). NY: John Wiley.

Marshall, A. (2010). Effective therapies and interventions for foster care children with reactive attachment disorder. *Lewis-Clark State College Research Excellence Journal, 3*(5). Retrieved from http://www.lcsc.edu/bchristenson/LCSCREJ.5.2010.pdf

Paula, S. T. (2009). Play therapy techniques for affect regulation. In A. Drewes (Ed.), *Blending play therapy with cognitive behavioral therapy: Evidenced-based and other effective treatments and techniques* (pp. 353-371). NY: John Wiley.

Pehrsson, D. E., & Aguilera, M. E. (2007). *Play therapy: Overview and implications for counselors* (ACAPCD-12). Alexandria, VA: American Counseling Association.

Reber, K. (1996). Children at risk for reactive attachment disorder: Assessment, diagnosis, and treatment. *Progress: Family Systems Research and Therapy, 5*, 83-98.

Richters, M. M., & Volkmar, F. R. (1994). Reactive attachment disorder of infancy or early childhood. *Journal of the American Academy of Child and Adolescent Psychiatry, 33*(3), 328-332. doi:10.1097/00004583-199403000-00005

Robinson, J.R. (2002). Attachment problems and disorders in infants and young children: Identification, assessment, and intervention. *Infants & Young Children, 14*(4), 6-18. Retrieved from http://www.eric.ed.gov/PDFS/EJ645016.pdf

Schaefer, C. E., & Drewes, A. (2009). The therapeutic powers of play and play therapy. In A. Drewes (Ed.)., *Blending play therapy with cognitive behavioral therapy: Evidenced-based and other effective treatments and techniques* (pp. 3-15). New York, NY: John Wiley.

Schwartz, E., & Davis, A. (2006). Reactive attachment disorder: Implications for school readiness and school functioning. *Psychology in Schools, 43*(4), 471-479. doi:10.1002/pits.20161

Shaw, R. S., & Paez, D. (2007). Reactive attachment disorder: Recognition, action, and considerations for school social workers. *Children & Schools, 29*(2), 69-74. doi:10.1093/cs/29.2.69

Sheperis, C. J., Doggett, R. A., Hoda, N. E., Blanchard, T., Renfo-Michel, E. L., Holdiness, S. H., & Schlagheck, R. (2003). The development of an assessment protocol for Reactive Attachment Disorder. *Journal of Mental Health Counseling, 25*(4), 291-479. Retrieved from http://www.eric.ed.gov/PDFS/EJ675856.pdf

Weir, P. K. (2007). Using integrative play therapy with adoptive families to treat reactive attachment disorder: A case study. *Journal of Family Psychotherapy, 18*(4), 1-16. doi:10.1300/J085v18n04.01

Wynne, L.S. (2008). Play therapy in school settings. Mining Report. Retrieved from the Association of Play Therapy website, http://www.a4pt.org/download.cfm?ID=26654

Zeanah, C. H. (1996). Beyond insecurity: A reconceptualization of attachment disorders of infancy. *Journal of Counseling and Clinical Psychology, 64*, 42-52. doi:10.1037/0022-006x.64.1.42

Zeanah, C. H., Scheering, M., Boris, N. W., Heller, S. S., Smyke, A. T., & Trapani, J. (2004). Reactive attachment disorder in maltreated toddlers. *Child Abuse & Neglect, 28*, 877-888. doi:10.1016/j.chiabu.2004.01.010

CHAPTER 16

SCHOOL-BASED PLAY THERAPY FOR STUDENTS WITH SEPARATION ANXIETY

Vanessa Bowles

It is reported that 6 to 9 million children in the United States (U.S.) have serious mental health problems (Post, 2001). Specifically, incidents of childhood anxiety are increasing. Separation anxiety affects approximately 4%-5% of children in the U.S. ages 7 to 11 years old, and appears to affect boys and girls equally. Therefore, given the prevalence, there is a great need for children to receive counseling services and schools provide an ideal setting for providing counseling services to students (Drewes, 2001).

Elementary school children require specific counseling interventions based on their unique developmental needs (Shen & Sink, 2002). Conventional verbal or "talk" therapy does not always work with children; thus, it is necessary for school counselors to enter the world of children by adapting strategies that broaden communication in the counseling relationship (Landreth, Baggerly, & Tyndall-Lind, 1999). One such strategy is to integrate play therapy techniques within the school counseling program's responsive services (American School Counselor Association [ASCA], 2012).

Integrating Play Techniques in Comprehensive School Counseling Programs, pp. 325–341

Play therapy has grown over the past 100 years and has become a widely accepted approach to helping children, and child centered play therapy (CCPT) has strong research support and the longest history of use of all play therapy approaches (Landreth, Ray, & Bratton, 2009). The purpose of this chapter is to describe brief, school-based child-centered play therapy interventions with two children with Separation Anxiety Disorder. This chapter is designed to highlight details and a definition of separation anxiety disorder (SAD), and provides an overview of play therapy and specific techniques of CCPT.

Vignette 1

Matt is a 5-year old boy who alternates living with his mother 1 week and his father the following week due to a recent divorce (6 months). Matt just began kindergarten at a rural primary school. Matt attended day care and pre-K prior to his entry into Kindergarten. Since the second week of school, Matt has either refused to attend school or refused to enter the school building. He is suffering from distress as demonstrated by crying, tantrum behavior, screaming, and somatic complaints such as headaches and stomachaches. Both of Matt's parents reported that he had sleeping problems at both of their homes and he "worries about going to school most nights." Matt's mother and teacher have both referred him to the school counselor. Matt's mother and grandmother both disclosed to the school counselor that they each have a history of generalized anxiety disorder.

Vignette 2

Hope was referred to the school counselor by her grandmother who is her primary caregiver. Hope's mother has been absent from her life since she was a baby and her father, the grandmother's son, is in and out of her life but has no caregiver responsibilities. Her grandfather was recently diagnosed with cancer and the grandmother had to leave for a month to tend to him while he was being treated at a hospital in a neighboring state. Hope was left with extended family members during her grandparents' travel. Hope struggled academically in third grade and her separation anxiety began almost the first day of the current school year. Hope's grandmother struggles with her school refusal and has to tell her that she is at the nearby park walking so Hope will go to school. Hope is an avid softball player and practices and plays a few days a week. Her grandmother expressed concerns about Hope's social awkwardness, her anxiety, and her lack of coping skills.

LITERATURE REVIEW

In the following literature review, separation anxiety disorder (SAD) is discussed, as well as types of attachment and the impact SAD has on children's academic, behavioral, social, and family functioning. An overview of play therapy is provided, focusing on child-centered play therapy.

Definition and Scope

Anxiety disorders comprise the most common mental health issue experienced by children and adolescents and 20% of U.S. youth are affected by these disorders. Untreated anxiety disorders may lead to more severe long-term consequences such as substance abuse and educational underachievement (Velting, Setzer, & Albano, 2004). One of the most common anxiety disorders in children is SAD (Perwien & Bernstein, 2004), with an estimated occurrence between 3% and 13% (Eisen & Schaefer, 2005). Separation anxiety has been defined as a developmentally appropriate distress reaction to separation situations from significant others shown by infants between the ages of 6 and 20 months. For most children, the symptoms decrease after age 2, but for other children separation anxiety continues into childhood (Kearney, Sims, Pursell, & Tillotson, 2003).

According to the *Diagnostic and Statistical Manual of Mental Disorders* (DSM-IV-TR), the diagnostic definition and criteria for 309.21 separation anxiety disorder (American Psychiatric Association [APA], 2000) is developmentally inappropriate and excessive anxiety concerning separation from home or from those to whom the individual is attached, as evidenced by a minimum of three of the following:

1. Recurrent excessive distress when separation from home or major attachment figures occurs or is anticipated
2. Persistent and excessive worry about losing, or about possible harm befalling, major attachment figures
3. Persistent and excessive worry that an untoward event will lead to separation from a major attachment figure (e.g., getting lost or kidnapped)
4. Reluctance or refusal to go to school or elsewhere because of fear of separation

5. Persistent and excessive fear or reluctance to be alone or without major attachment figures at home or without significant adults in other settings
6. Persistent reluctance or refusal to go to sleep without being near a major attachment figure or fear of sleeping away from home
7. Repeated nightmares involving the theme of separation
8. Repeated complaints of physical symptoms (such as headaches, stomachaches, nausea, or vomiting) when separation from major attachment figures occurs or is anticipated
9. The duration of the disturbance(s) is at least 4 weeks
10. The onset is before age 18 years
11. The disturbance causes clinically significant distress or impairment in social, academic, or other important areas of functioning
12. The disturbance does not occur exclusively during the course of a pervasive developmental disorder, schizophrenia, or other psychotic disorder and, in adolescents and adults, is not better accounted for by panic disorder with agoraphobia

Primary symptoms of separation anxiety include excessive worry about possible harm to self and/or other attachment figures, nightmares about separation, somatic problems (stomach ache, headaches, heart palpitations), and an extreme need to return or contact parents/guardians during separation (APA, 2000).

Impact of SAD on Children's Academic, Social, Behavioral Functioning, Family

The presence of SAD can effect a child's school progress, social interaction with others, family system, and daily functioning. School refusal is the most frequent characteristic behavior associated with SAD and greatly impacts learning. Each year, school districts are challenged with students who have difficulty attending school or those who experience grave difficulty when asked to go to school (Brand & O'Conner, 2004; Kearney & Bates, 2005). Approximately 30% to 38% of children who refuse to go to school meet the criteria for SAD (Heyne, King, & Tonge, 2004). Due to their attendance issues, students become further behind academically which only perpetuates their anxiety. In addition, students become embarrassed about their absences and find it increasingly challenging to interact with teachers and peers (Elliot, 1999). Other consequences associated with school refusal include family problems, lower academic achievement, legal problems, and lack of adult supervision especially when caregivers must go to work (Kearney, 2001). Additionally, one study showed that children with SAD and school refusal behavior have more likelihood of psychiatric consultation and a decreased rate of parenthood as adults, suggesting limited social skills (Doobay, 2008).

Toren and colleagues (2000) discovered that children with anxiety disorders, such as separation anxiety, had more difficulty learning than children without anxiety. In addition, 79% of children with SAD also had at least one comorbid disorder (Kendall, Brady, & Verduin, 2001). These comorbid disorders include: (1) generalized anxiety disorder, (2) panic disorder, (3) depressive disorder, (4) attention deficit hyperactivity disorder, (5) oppositional defiant disorder, and (6) obsessive-compulsive disorder (Kendall et al., 2001). Furthermore, research has shown that SAD may be a precursor to anxiety disorders in adulthood, such as panic disorder and agoraphobia (Battaglia et al., 2009; Perwien & Bernstein, 2004). "Despite its high prevalence and unfavorable long-term prognosis, SAD remains neglected and under researched with respect to etiology and treatment" (Kossowsky, Wilhelm, Roth, & Schneider, 2012, p. 178).

EVIDENCED BASED APPROACHES FOR TREATMENT OF SEPARATION ANXIETY DISORDER

Cognitive-Behavioral Interventions

Research continues to support cognitive-behavioral therapy (CBT) and behavioral therapy as effective treatments for children with separation anxiety disorder. CBT is considered an evidenced based therapeutic technique for the treatment of anxiety disorders with 68.9% of children completing CBT no longer meeting the diagnostic criteria for anxiety disorder (Silverman, Pina, & Viswesvaran, 2008). Overall, CBT reduces anxiety and emotional disturbances, while also increasing children's adaptive, positive coping skills (Perwien & Bernstein, 2004). Cognitive techniques have also been utilized to reduce the symptoms of SAD. *Cognitive restructuring* is a technique that helps children become aware of irrational beliefs about separation and promotes learning ways to change their faulty belief system (Ellis, 1963; Gosch, Flannery-Schroeder, Mauro, & Compton, 2006). For example, the counselor may help a child change his or her self-talk from "If I sleep alone something bad will happen to me and my parents" to "My parents are in the next room and I am okay" (Doobay, 2008).

Another cognitive technique that is effective in helping children with SAD in reducing their anxiety is relaxation techniques. Children are taught guided imagery, breathing exercises, and progressive muscle relaxation.

Relaxation techniques are most effective when children and parents are both trained (Doobay, 2008), which may be a complication of this approach in the school setting as parents are not often present during the course of counseling.

Velting et al. (2004) suggested that CBT is most effective with children with SAD when combined with psychoeducation, cognitive restructuring, problem-solving, somatic management, and exposure as part of a cohesive program. One such program, *The Coping Cat Program*, was designed for use with 7- to 16-year old youth with SAD, generalized anxiety disorder, or social phobia (Kendall, Kane, Howard, & Siqueland, 1990). The program involves modeling and teaching relaxation techniques and training to help children establish coping skills, set goals, and evaluate their performance (Barrett, Dadds, & Rapee, 1996). Additionally, Schneider and colleagues (2011) studied 43 children with SAD and concluded that 76.19% of children assigned to the treatment group no longer met the DSM criteria for SAD after cognitive behavioral therapy.

Behavioral Interventions

Gosschalk (2004) found that the use of behavioral interventions with a 5-year old child diagnosed with SAD improved her school attendance, and after 5 weeks, she no longer met the criteria for SAD. Likewise, Weems and Carrion (2003) combined cognitive-behavioral interventions with an attachment theory framework. The 9-year-old boy in their study showed improvement in school attendance, bedtime routine, and being alone for periods of time. Several behavioral techniques are used with students with SAD: (a) counterconditioning, (b) extinction, (c) modeling, and (d) contingency management. *Counterconditioning,* also referred to as systematic desensitization, occurs when a client practices a new behavior while utilizing behavioral strategies for managing anxiety. For example, in the case of SAD, a child may be asked to sleep in his or her room without the parent while practicing relaxation techniques (Farris & Jouriles, 1993). *Extinction* is a technique that involves increasing a child's understanding that even with separation from his or her parents at night, the child and parents will remain safe. This is reinforced every morning when the child interacts with the parents and has evidence that everything is fine. *Modeling* is a technique used to teach children proper responses and improve coping skills during separation. This may involve a child with SAD observing a peer or sibling prepare for school, saying goodbye to the parent, and calmly entering the school/classroom while the child with SAD simultaneously engages in the same behaviors (Doobay, 2008). *Contingency management* occurs when teachers, school personnel, and parents are trained to provide positive reinforcement, such as praise and rewards, to the child when the child demonstrates desired behaviors (Farris & Jouriles, 1993).

THEORETICAL FOUNDATIONS OF PLAY THERAPY

Attachment Theory

Bowlby (1959) built on other researchers' observations and work (Robertson, 1953) and began to research separation anxiety. Bowlby's theory of attachment provides a framework for understanding separation anxiety (Bowlby, 1969/1982). According to attachment theory, infants learn how to adjust their emotions and emotional expressions through strategies (adaptive or maladaptive) that maintain their closeness to an attachment figure. Once infants develop an attachment with their primary caregivers, specific behaviors serve to maintain a close, intimate connection to the caregiver. Infants who are securely attached to their caregivers are more confident that their caregiver will be available when needed and that their primary needs (food, shelter, emotional soothing) will be met. Conversely, insecure-ambivalent infants lack this confidence. School age children who are securely attached as infants to their caregivers are more socially successful and less anxious. Children with insecure-ambivalent attachments are afraid of being alone because their caregivers were perceived as unreliable and did not meet their needs. Furthermore, attachment theory supports that infants with ambivalent-insecure attachments are prone to develop chronic levels of anxiety later in life (Mofrad, Abdullah, & Uba, 2010).

Bowlby believed that infants and children experience separation anxiety when a situation triggers escape and attachment behavior, but an attachment figure—such as a primary caregiver—is not accessible (Bretherton, 1992). He believed that extreme separation anxiety was due to unfavorable family problems or possibly to an illness or death in the immediate family where the child felt responsible. His ideas were later expanded by Ainsworth's classification of three major attachment styles: ambivalent, avoidant, and secure patterns of mother-infant attachment (for more, please see Ainsworth, Blehar, Waters, & Wall, 1978).

Later in his book *Separation,* Bowlby (1973) elaborated on his previous work and stated that two sets of stimuli cause fear in children: (1) the presence of danger and/or (2) the absence of an attachment figure. In particular, according to Bowlby,

> If the attachment figure has acknowledged the infant's need for comfort and protection while simultaneously respecting the infant's need for inde-

> pendent exploration of the environment, the child is likely to develop an internal working model of self as valued and self-reliant. (p. 34)

"Conversely, if the parent has frequently rejected the infant's bids for comfort or for exploration, the child is likely to construct an internal working model of self as unworthy or incompetent" (Bretherton, 1992, p. 767).

Winnicott (1971) researched the relationship between mother and infant and published works related to the "holding environment" and the importance of a mother nurturing and holding her infant to create long-lasting bonds. A central theme running through Winnicott's work was the idea of play. He first introduced the concept of the transitional object or a "security blanket" to help children cope with separation and move towards independence.

PLAY THERAPY

Play is a child's primary method of communication and expression (Landreth, 2002). Play therapy is an empirically studied, innovative counseling process that is considerate of children's social and academic development (Bratton & Ray, 2000; Landreth, 2002). Play therapy has been used in elementary schools as a responsive service to help decrease problematic behaviors (Bratton & Ray, 2000; Green & McCollum, 2004). Studies have shown that play therapy can improve self-efficacy (Fall, Balvantz, Johnson, & Nelson, 1999) and self-concept (Post, 1999), while decreasing behavior problems (Raman & Kapur, 1999); anxiety (Baggerly, 2004); depression (Baggerly, 2004) and attention deficit hyperactivity disorder symptomology in children (Ray, Schottelkorb, & Tsai, 2007). Furthermore, Green and Christensen (2006) found that elementary school children who participated in play therapy reported decreased anxiety, increased empathy, improved self-confidence, and made better choices. "Play is the child's most natural way of communicating this internal awareness of self and others" (Landreth, Ray, & Bratton, 2009, p. 281). Additionally, children can work through their separation anxiety by using objects symbolically in their play (Cheah, Nelson, & Rubin, 2001).

Milos and Reiss (1982) describe two justifications for proposing that play therapy can reduce anxiety. One is that play provides a safe place in which children can express problems and find solutions without fearing immediate consequences. Additionally, play therapy provides children with exposure to problems and situations and allows them to desensitize to these dilemmas. Milos and Reiss's findings provide support that play and working with a nonjudgmental adult were acceptable methods in lowering participants' levels of separation anxiety.

Moreover, Danger (2003) conducted a study using five sessions of adaptive doll play with a 5-year-old child suffering from separation anxiety. The child's crying, clinging behaviors, and requests by the child to call home were all reportedly reduced after five weeks. Lastly, Jalali and Molavi's (2011) used an experimental design to study 30 children diagnosed with separation anxiety. The experimental group received group play therapy for 6 weeks while the control group received no intervention. The Child Abnormal Symptoms Inventory (CSI-4) was administered as a pre- and posttest. The experimental group scored less than the control group in separation anxiety in the posttest.

Child-Centered Play Therapy

Child-centered play therapy (CCPT) was developed by Virginia Axline (1947) and is a nondirective approach based on the premise that children communicate mainly through play (Landreth, 2002). In this approach, toys and games are used to help children express their emotions and to allow children to make their own choices (Axline, 1947). In CCPT the child, not the counselor, directs the play therapy sessions and decides when and how he or she should play. This approach focuses on the child, not the child's presenting problem, as the center of therapy (Landreth et al., 1999).Further, CCPT empowers children to command their own environment and increases internal locus of control.

In CCPT, limits on behavior are set only when necessary to keep the child, therapist, and toys safe and unharmed (Guerney, 2001). The counselor uses empathy and acceptance to reflect the child's feelings in the sessions. In the initial sessions, the counselor explains that the playroom is a safe place where the child can say anything and do almost anything they want (Landreth, 2002). Most play therapy sessions are approximately 45 minutes in length and can be shortened as needed for the school environment (for example, 25-30 minutes may be a maximum length for sessions in a school setting).

Axline (1969) proposed eight basic principles for the play therapist: (1) develop a sincere relationship with the child; (2) accept the child completely; (3) help to create a feeling of safety so that the child may express self to the fullest; (4) understand the child's feelings and reflect those feelings to the child; (5) believe the child can act responsibly; (6) trust the child's intuition; (7) value the therapeutic process; and (8) respect therapeutic limits. All of these principles can be easily utilized by a school counselor in a school setting. Landreth (1987) stated that "it is not a question of whether the elementary school counselor should use play therapy but, instead, of how play therapy should be used in the schools" (p. 255).

Specific CCPT Techniques

The following section summarizes common CCPT techniques and how they are utilized in counseling sessions by the school counselor. These techniques do not require a large amount of supplies or space and can be easily implemented by a school counselor in a school setting. School counselors often have many of these supplies readily available and the techniques require little preparation.

Art techniques. The school counselor may learn about the child's own perceptions, as well as family dynamics, using the draw-a-person and/or draw-your-family exercises (Dileo, 1973). The squiggle technique (Winnicott, 1971) can be used in an initial session as an ice breaker with the child. The technique helps establish trust and rapport, as both the school counselor and child are interacting and taking turns making pictures from each of their scribbles. It can also be used as a projective tool later when the school counselor asks the child to choose his or her favorite squiggle and create a story about it.

Play-dough/clay. This technique involves allowing the student to create and sculpt images from play-dough or clay to represent a problem or situation occurring in his or her world. This technique is a great tool to build self-esteem because students can independently create and feel proud of the end result. Moreover, the use of play-dough is sensory and often the student will open up more to the school counselor while shaping and molding the dough. A directive technique using Play-Doh is for the school counselor to ask the student to create themselves or create their family out of the Play-Doh. For students with anger problems, the Play-Doh can be smashed or thrown until the student releases feelings of anger (Webb, 1991).

Doll/Puppet play. This play therapy technique allows a child to use dolls to create solutions to problems rather than solely focusing on the child and provides emotional distance. This separation helps children identify with the dolls and puppets and helps lessen their anxiety and fear because they can project their issues outward (James, 1989). Puppets serve a similar role in play therapy. Children often project their own thoughts and feelings onto the puppets. The use of the symbolic play removes the focus from the child and increases the child's level of comfort and safety (Webb, 1991).

Board games. This play therapy technique requires a child to have more self-control and reasoning skills. Games provide a way for students to learn appropriate social skills by interacting with others. The student learns to deal with anger and frustration in an acceptable manner because the student has to follow the rules of the game. Games can also help students learn to control impulses (Landreth, 2001). Games are familiar to students and may make them feel safe in the counseling setting (Reid, 1993).

Sand play. This technique allows students to arrange miniature figures in a sandbox to create a world consistent with their reality (Dale & Wagner, 2003). The school counselor will provide trays or bins with sand, both dry and wet. School counselors may also choose to vary the color of the sand. The counseling room should have a large variety of miniatures such as people (military, fantasy, nationalities, races), animals (domestic pets, wild, prehistoric, zoo, farm), buildings (churches, schools, castles, houses), foliage (bushes, trees, flowers, plants), vehicles (land, air, water), structures (fences, borders, bridges, gates), natural objects (rocks, shells, feathers, bones, eggs, stones), and symbolic objects (wells, jewelry, treasure chests, marbles). Students are allowed to construct their problems, their families, and resolutions to personal issues.

PLAY THERAPY SESSIONS

The following section presents a sample outline of three school counseling session with Matt and Hope whose cases were presented in vignettes at the beginning of this chapter. Counseling themes are presented at the end of their sessions with a summarization of future sessions, as well as counseling outcomes.

The Case of Matt

Session 1: Matt entered the play therapy room and looked around. He walked around the kitchen set and then spotted the puppets. He walked across the room to the basket of puppets and picked up the dragon and the sock puppet. The school counselor tracked him and reflected his actions with the puppets. Matt took both of the puppets to the puppet theater and began to talk for both the puppets. He named the dragon "Fred" and used a gruff voice for this character. Matt named the sock monkey "Baby" and began to use a gentle voice for that puppet. Matt continued the dialogue between Fred and Baby while Fred spoke angrily to Baby stating, "Stop crying, and stop whining now!" Later in the session, Matt instructed the school counselor to play the role of the baby.

Session 2: Matt entered the counseling room and pointed to the bin of army men and tanks. The school counselor reflected that Matt wanted the bin down from the shelves and pointed to the stepping stool. Matt easily climbed the stool to pull the bin off the shelf. Matt lined up the red army men on one side of the table and the black army men on the other side of the table. He was the leader of the red army and declared war on the black army. Step-by-step, the school counselor reflected Matt's actions and allowed him to destroy the black army until all the men were down. Matt continued his 'war' on the black army leading the red team to victory every time.

Session 3: Matt entered the counseling room and approached the drilling tool set on the shelf. He swiftly opened the tool set and began to use the tools to repair the tables, shelves, chairs, and desks in the playroom. As he played, Matt spoke about his father and how he always "fixed" items in his home when his parents were together. The school counselor reflected his safe feelings about his father's nurturing nature and his need to imitate his father now that he no longer lived with him.

The school counselor and Matt met for 3 more sessions. The themes that arose from these sessions included Matt's identification with his father and his role in the home, his anger towards his mother about the divorce, and his guilt about the demise of his parent's relationship. The school counselor allowed Matt to play out each of these scenarios and refrained from offering advice, correcting Matt's thoughts or feelings, or judging him because in CCPT, the goals is to allow the child to come to resolution through the medium of play. After the counseling sessions came to an end, his teacher reported that Matt was calmer in the classroom with fewer disruptions and both his parents reported that school refusal and major sleeping issues were no longer an issue.

The Case of Hope

Session 1: Hope entered the play room appearing nervous as exhibited by giggling and rubbing her hands together. She immediately walked to the colors and crayons on the table and began drawing a picture. As Hope drew, she began talking to the school counselor about her worries and her fears. She expressed fears of "something bad happening to grandma." She stated that she becomes so upset that she often experiences stomach aches and this occasionally leads to vomiting. The school counselor reflected her feelings and validated that her fears were normal, but the time they spent together would be used to teach her skills to help her lessen her anxiety and cope with negative feelings. The school counselor introduced an activity called, "Butterflies in my Stomach" (Lowenstein, 2002). The school counselor encouraged Hope to lie down on bulletin board paper and traced the outline of her body. Hope was asked to draw her features such as her eyes, hair, and clothing onto her outline. The school counselor gave Hope assorted sizes of paper butterflies and asked her to write her worries on them. The larger butterflies represented big worries and the small butterflies represented smaller worries. As Hope identified her worries, the counselor prompted her with questions such as, "Tell me more about the worry" and "Where do you notice this worry in your body?" The butterflies are then placed on the outline of Hope's body by her stomach. The school counselor allowed Hope to color the butterflies. She informed Hope when five minutes remained in their session and closed the session by telling her she will see her in a week for their next session.

Session 2: Hope entered the playroom with a smile on her face. She talked about her weekend and her softball game. The school counselor reflected that being home on the weekend with her family and playing her favorite sport made her happy. The school counselor showed Hope a picture of a thermometer with three levels: low, medium, and high. Hope was asked to rate her separation anxiety on the thermometer by coloring it in to the anxiety level experienced that day. Hope colored to the "low" section of the thermometer. The school counselor discussed her low anxiety and the difference between her anxiety today than from a day(s) she experiences high anxiety. Hope verbalized that she saw her father over the weekend and was able to spend time with her teammates. The school counselor reflected that seeing her father and friends brought her relief, joy, and a sense of calmness.

Session 3: Hope entered the playroom with her head down and immediately walked to the play dough box and pulled out several cans of play dough. She said nothing to the school counselor and began to pound the play dough with her hands on the table. The school counselor reflected that Hope was quiet and was feeling frustrated. As Hope pounded more and more on the play dough, the school counselor's tracking became more specific, "You want to beat the play dough into the table." The school counselor asked Hope if she would like to use the play dough to sculpt her troubles. Hope spent the next 10 minutes creating figures with the play dough. She created herself, her grandmother, her grandfather, and her father. She put the grandfather figure on the table as if he was lying down. The "Hope figure" and the "grandmother figure" stood next to each other while the "father figure" was moved to the other end of the table away from the others. The school counselor reflected that Hope and her grandmother stand together while Hope's father is separated from them. Hope began to cry and shared that her father left again and she did not know when he would return. Hope remained tearful in silence for several minutes. As the session came to a close, the school counselor reminded her that she would see her again the following week and they would be able to process more at that time.

Hope and the school counselor met for four more sessions. Hope dealt with abandonment issues related to both her mother and father. These intense feelings, and lack of parental support, seemed to exacerbate her fear of abandonment related to her grandmother. Hope's future sessions involved dealing with her social issues, angry feelings towards her mother and father, and her need to be accepted. Although Hope at times struggled while in school, her school refusal ceased and she was able to enter school without her grandmother's support.

SUMMARY

Identifying early counseling interventions that are effective for children and that can be delivered in settings such as schools is a crucial need for the 21st century (U.S. Public Health Service, 2000). One in eight children ages 9-17 has some sort of anxiety disorder and it is known that SAD plagues 4-5% of children in the United States (Post, 2001). The effects of SAD are often debilitating to a student's academic and emotional learning. CCPT is a highly researched and efficient therapeutic approach that helps students overcome a multitude of factors. School counselors are called to utilize CCPT with students diagnosed with SAD. The importance of play is essential in assisting students to overcome their fears and move forward in their healing.

REFERENCES

Ainsworth, M., Blehar, M., Waters, E., & Wall, S. (1978). *Patterns of attachment: A psychological study of the strange situation.* Hillsdale, NJ: Erlbaum.

American Psychiatric Association. (2000). *Diagnostic and statistical manual of mental-disorders,* (4th ed., text revision). Washington, DC: American Psychiatric Association.

American School Counselor Association. (2012). *The ASCA National Model: A Framework for School Counseling Programs* (3rd ed.). Alexandria, VA: Author.

Axline, V. (1947). *Play therapy: The inner dynamics of childhood.* Boston, MA: Houghton Mifflin.

Axline V. (1969). *Play therapy.* New York, NY: Ballantine Books.

Baggerly, J. (2004). The effects of child-centered play therapy on self-concept, depression, and anxiety of children who are homeless. *International Journal of Play Therapy, 13*(2), 31-51.

Barrett, P., Dadds, M., & Rapee, R. (1996). Family treatment of childhood anxiety: A controlled trial. *Journal of Consultation & Clinical Psychology, 64*(2), 333-342.

Battaglia, M., Pesenti-Gritti, P., Medland, S., Oglersi, A. Tambs, K., & Spataloa, C. (2009). A genetically informed study of the association between childhood separation anxiety, sensitivity to CO2, panic disorder, and the effect of childhood parental loss. *Archives of General Psychiatry, 66,* 64-71.

Bowlby, J. (1959). Separation anxiety. *International Journal of Psycho-Analysts, XLI,* 1-25.

Bowlby, J. (1982). *Attachment and loss: Attachment* (Vol. 1., 2nd ed.). New York, NY: Basic Books. (Original work published 1969).

Bowlby, J. (1973). *Attachment and loss: Separation* (Vol. 2). New York, NY: Basic Books.

Brand, C., & O'Connor, L. (2004). School refusal: It takes a team. *Children & Schools, 26*(1), 54-64.

Bratton, S., & Ray, D. (2000). What the research shows about play therapy. *International Journal of Play Therapy, 9*(1), 47-88.

Bretherton, I. (1992). The origins of attachment theory: John Bowlby and Mary Ainsworth. *Developmental Psychology, 28,* 759-775.

Cheah, C., Nelson, L., & Rubin, K. (2001). Nonsocial play as a risk factor in social and emotional development. In A. Goncu & E. Klein (Eds.), *Children in play, story, and school* (pp. 39-71). New York, NY: Guilford Press.

Dale, M., & Wagner, W. (2003). Sandplay: An investigation into a child's meaning system by the self-confrontation method for children. *Journal of Constructivist Psychology, 16,* 17-36.

Danger, S. (2003). Adaptive doll play: Helping children cope with change. *International Journal of Play Therapy, 12*(1), 105-116.

Dileo, J. (1973). *Children's drawings as diagnostic aids.* New York, NY: Brunner/Maze.

Doobay, A. (2008). School refusal behavior associated with separation anxiety disorder: Cognitive-behavioral approach to treatment. *Psychology in the Schools, 45*(4), 261-272.

Drewes, A. A. (2001). The possibilities and challenges using play therapy in schools. In A. A. Drewes, L., Carey, & C. Schaefer (Eds.), *School-based play therapy* (pp. 41-60). New York, NY: John Wiley.

Eisen, A., & Schaefer, C. (2005). *Separation anxiety in children and adolescents: An individualized approach to assessment.* New York, NY: Guilford Press.

Elliot, J. (1999). Practitioner review: School refusal- issues of conceptualization, assessment, and treatment. *Journal of Child Psychology and Psychiatry and Allied Disciplines, 40*(7), 1001-1012.

Ellis, A. (1963). *Rational-emotive psychotherapy.* New York, NY: Institute for Rational-Emotive Therapy.

Fall, M., Balvantz, J., Johnson, L., & Nelson, L. (1999). A play therapy intervention and its relationship to self-efficacy and learning behaviors. *Professional School Counseling, 2,* 194-204.

Farris, A., & Jouriles, E. (1993). Separation anxiety disorder. In M. Hersen & A. Bellack (Eds.), *Handbook of behavior therapy in a psychiatric setting* (pp. 407-426). New York, NY: Plenum Press.

Gosch, E., Flannery-Schroeder, E., Mauro, C., & Compton, S. (2006). Principles of cognitive-behavioral therapy for anxiety disorders in children. *Journal of Cognitive Psychotherapy, 20,* 247-262.

Gosschalks, P. (2004). Behavioral treatment of acute onset school refusal in a 5-year old girl with separation anxiety disorder. *Education and Treatment of Children, 27*(2), 150-160.

Green, E., & Christensen, T. (2006). Elementary school children's perceptions of play therapy in school settings. *International Journal of Play Therapy, 15*(1), 65-85.

Green, E., & McCollum, V. (2004). Empowerment through compassion: Training school counselors to become effective child advocates. *School Counselor, 42*(1), 40-46.

Guerney, L. (2001). Child-centered play therapy. *International Journal of Play Therapy, 10*(2), 13-31.

Heyne, D., King, N., & Tonge, B. (2004). School refusal. In T. Ollendick & J. March (Eds.), *Phobic and anxiety disorders in children and adolescents: A clinician's guide to effective psychosocial and pharmacological interventions* (pp. 236-271). Oxford, England: Oxford University.

Jalali, S., & Molavi, H. (2011). The effect of play therapy on separation anxiety disorder in Children. *Journal of Psychology, 14*(4), 370-382.

James, L. (1989). *Treating traumatized children: New insights and creative interventions.* Lexington, MA: Lexington Books.

Kearney, C. (2001). *School refusal behavior in youth: A functional approach to assessment and treatment.* Washington DC: American Psychology Association.

Kearney, C., & Bates, M. (2005). Addressing school refusal behaviors: Suggestions-for frontline professionals. *Children & School. 27*(4), 207-216.

Kearney, C., Sims, K., Pursell, C., & Tillotson, C. (2003). Separation anxiety disorder in young children:A longitudinal and family analysis. *Journal of Clinical Child & Adolescent Psychology, 32*(4), 593-598.

Kendall, P., Brady, E., & Verduin, T. (2001). Comorbidity in childhood anxiety and treatment outcome. *Journal of the American Academy of Child & Adolescent Psychiatry, 40*(7), 787-794.

Kendall, P., Kane, M., Howard, B., & Siqueland, L. (1990). *Cognitive behavioral treatment of anxious children: Therapist manual* (Unpublished treatment manual). Temple University, Philadelphia: PA.

Kossowsky, J., Wilhelm, F., Roth, W., & Schneider, S. (2012). Separation anxiety disorder in children: Disorder specific responses to experimental separation from the mother. *Journal of Child Psychology and Psychiatry, 53,* 178-87

Landreth, G. (1987). Play therapy: Facilitative use of child's play in elementary school counseling. *Elementary School Guidance & Counseling, 21,* 253-261.

Landreth, G. (2001). *Innovations in play therapy: Issues, process, and special populations.* Philadelphia, PA: Brunner-Routledge.

Landreth, G. (2002). *Play therapy the art of the relationship.* New York, NY: Brunner-Rutledge.

Landreth, G., Baggerly, J., & Tyndall-Lind. (1999). Beyond adapting adult counseling skills for use with children: The paradigm shift to child-centered play therapy. *Journal of Individual Psychology, 55*(3), 272-287.

Landreth, G., Ray, D., & Bratton, S. (2009). Play therapy in elementary schools. *Psychology in the School, 46*(3), 281-289.

Lowenstein, L. (2002). *More creative interventions for troubled children & youth.* Toronto: Champion Press.

Milos, M., & Reiss, S. (1982). Effects of three play conditions on separation anxiety in young children. *Journal of Counseling and Consulting Psychology, 50*(3), 389-395.

Mofrad, S., Abdullah, R., & Uba, I. (2010). Attachment patterns and separation anxiety symptom. *Asian Social Science, 6*(11), 148-153.

Perwien, A., & Bernstein, G. (2004). Separation anxiety disorder. In T. Ollendick & J. March (Eds.), *Phobic and anxiety disorders in children and adolescents: A clinician's guide to effective psychosocial and pharmacological interventions* (pp. 272-305). New York, NY: Oxford University

Post, P. (1999). Impact of child-centered play therapy on self-esteem, locus of control, and anxiety of at risk 4th, 5th, and 6th grade students. *International Journal of Play Therapy, 8,* 1-18.

Post, P. (2001). Child-centered play therapy for at risk elementary school children. In A. A. Drewes, L., Carey, & C. Schaefer (Eds.), *School-based play therapy* (pp. 105-122). New York: John Wiley .

Raman, V., & Kapur, M. (1999). A study of play therapy in children with emotional disorders. *NIMHANS Journal, 17,* 93-98.

Ray, D., Schottelkorb, A., & Tsai, M. (2007). Play therapy with children exhibiting symptoms of attention deficit hyperactivity disorder. *International Journal of Play Therapy, 16*(2), 95-111.

Reid, S. (1993). Game play. In C. E. Schaefer (Ed.), *The therapeutic powers of play* (pp. 323-348). Northvale, NJ: Jason Aronson.

Robertson, J. (1953). Some responses of young children to loss of maternal care. *Nursing Care, 49,* 382-386.

Schneider, S., Blatter-Meunier, J., Herren, C., Adornetto, C., In-Albon, T., & Lavallee, K. (2011). Disorder specific cognitive behavioral therapy for separation anxiety disorder in young children: A randomized waiting list controlled trial. *Psychotherapy and Psychosomatics, 80,* 206-215.

Shen, Y., & Sink, C. A. (2002). Helping elementary-age children cope with disasters. *Professional School Counseling, 5,* 322-330.

Silverman, W., Pina, A., & Viswesvaran, C. (2008). Evidence based psychosocial treatments for phobic and anxiety disorders in children & adolescents. *Journal of Clinical Child and Adolescent Psychology,* 37(1), 105-130.

Toren, P., Sadeh, M., Wolmer, L., Eldar, S., Koren, S., Weizman, R., & Labor, N. (2000). Neurocognitive correlates of anxiety disorders in children: A preliminary report. *Journal of Anxiety Disorders, 14*(3), 239-247.

U.S. Public Health Service. (2000). *Report on the Surgeon General's conference on children's mental health: A national action agenda.* Washington, DC: Department of Health & Human Services.

Velting, O., Setzer, N., & Albano, A. (2004), Update on and advances in assessment and cognitive-behavioral treatment of anxiety disorder in children and adolescents. *Professional Psychology: Research and Practice, 35,* 42-54.

Webb, N. (1991). *Play therapy with children in crisis: A casebook for practitioners.* New York, NY: Guilford Press.

Weems, C., & Carrion, V. (2003). The treatment of separation anxiety disorder employing attachment theory and cognitive behavior therapy techniques. *Clinical Case Studies, 2,* 188-196.

Winnicott, D. (1971). *Playing and reality.* London, England: Tavistock.

CHAPTER 17

SOCIAL SKILLS DEVELOPMENT AND SCHOOL BASED PLAY TECHNIQUES

Engaging and Empowering Students

Laura J. Fazio-Griffith

Children's play is not mere sport. It is full of meaning and import.

—F. Froebel

The universal importance of play to the natural development and wholeness of children has been underscored by the United Nations (UN) proclamation of play as a universal and inalienable right of childhood. Play is the singular central activity of childhood, occurring at all times and at all places, including the school environment (Landreth, 2012).

School counselors are tasked with working with children that lack substantial social skills on a daily basis. The daily challenge faced by school counselors when working with children is to enhance their academic, social, and emotional development. Social skills are essential to the devel-

Integrating Play Techniques in Comprehensive School Counseling Programs, pp. 343–365

opment of children's academic and social functioning in the school environment. The following two vignettes detail common presentations of social skills deficits in the school setting that might contribute to inadequate academic and social development.

Vignette 1

Greg is a 9-year-old Caucasian male. He was referred to the school counselor, Ms. Grey, by his third grade teacher who has noticed a continued disruption in class. Greg is unable to focus in class, does not listen to the teacher, and is having difficulty communicating with his classmates. Greg's mother, Shannon is a 45-year-old Caucasian female who is divorced and has three other children. Shannon has told Greg's teacher that she has also noticed his inappropriate behaviors at home. Greg is unable to play with the neighborhood children without conflict. Greg does not take any responsibility for his behavior. Greg has a twin sister, Chelsea, who is also in third grade. Shannon's ex-husband lives in another state and occasionally sends child support. The twins spend the summer months with their father. Greg has a diagnosis of attention deficit hyperactivity disorder (ADHD) and is prescribed the medication Concerta but Shannon only administers it to him during the week and not on the weekends or during the summer.

Today, the students in Greg's class are working on a math worksheet. Greg finishes the worksheet rather quickly and the teacher instructs him to quietly read a book. Greg turns to the student behind him, who is still working on the math worksheet, and begins to discuss the book he is reading. The student asks Greg to be quiet, but Greg continues to engage the student in conversation about his book.

Vignette 2

During a parent-teacher conference, Carol's mother tearfully tells her daughter's teacher, Ms. Snow, that she is at wit's end with her 7-year old. Carol is in the first grade and has been diagnosed with ADHD. She stubbornly refuses to do even minor tasks at home such as dress or eat breakfast. She erupts into a rage at the slightest provocation and screams obscenities at her mother in public. Carol's rage is intensified when any attempts are made to apply consequences. Her mother is completely unable to manage Carol's behaviors. Ms. Snow reported fewer displays of rage, and added that she does not work well with the other children at her table during class activities. Ms. Snow reports that she often observes

Carol alone at recess. The other children have invited her to play on occasion, but Carol seems to want to control every aspect of the playground games. The other students have tired of her behavior; and consequently she often plays alone during recess. Ms. Snow describes Carol as immature and anxious when she has to interact with the other students. Ms. Snow refers Carol to the school counselor, Ms. Bright, for services. Today, Ms. Bright was observing Carol on the playground and noticed her playing with a group of first grade girls. The girls are playing a game of tag. The girls decide they are tired of tag and want to play hide and seek; however, Carol informs the girls that she wants to continue to play tag and proceeds to explain to them the benefits of continuing the game of tag. The girls walk away from Carol and leave her standing there alone and crying.

PLAY AS AN INTERVENTION IN SCHOOLS

Play therapy and interventions in the school setting are encouraged to meet a broad range of developmental needs of children including social and emotional needs. Dimick and Huff (1970) believed that the use of play media is mandatory if significant communication is to occur between the child and the counselor. The main question for these authors is not whether the elementary school counselor should use play therapy, but rather how play therapy should be used in elementary schools (p. 35).

Recent school counseling literature encourages the use of play therapy as a counseling medium for elementary school counselors (Baker & Gerler, 2004; Newsome & Gladding, 2003; Ray, Muro, & Schumann, 2004; Schmidt, 2003; White & Flynt, 1999). Studies have demonstrated the efficacy of play therapy with elementary school students suffering from conduct disorders (Cochran & Cochran, 1999), autism, obsessive-compulsive disorder, attention deficit/hyperactivity disorder, cerebral palsy (Johnson, McLeod, & Fall, 1997), posttraumatic stress disorder (PTSD) (Shen & Sink, 2002), attention and hyperactivity issues (Ray, Schottelkorb, & Tsai, 2007), aggressive behavior (Ray, Blanco, Sullivan, & Holliman, 2009), and children at risk (Post, 1999). All these issues can highly impact the development of prosocial skills.

Play therapy is not only a remediation process for children experiencing developmental, social, and behavioral problems, but can also be viewed as a preventive, consulting, and appraising model (Ray, Muro, & Schumann, 2004). The school counselor can take play therapy skills and integrate these skills and interventions into existing school guidance programs. Play therapy can become an integrated part of the responsive services indicated for school counselors by the American School Counselor Association's *National Model* (ASCA, 2012).

Gysbers and Henderson (2011) identified four components of a comprehensive school guidance program in conjunction with the ASCA model (2012). The components include: guidance curriculum, responsive services, individual planning, and systems support. At the elementary school level, the majority of the school counselors' time (75%) should be spent developing and facilitating guidance curriculum and responsive services. Individual planning and systems support should comprise only 25% of the school counselors' time.

Guidance curriculum is designed to address the needs of students' basic skills. These skills can include life skills, social skills, and academic skills. Guidance, while promoting awareness is rooted in prevention to assist in skills development, and improve application of these skills to everyday life. Guidance is preventive rather than remedial, like responsive services, and focuses on the prevention of future issues. Elementary school counselors should view guidance as the highest priority.

Elementary school counselors need to employ a solid developmental understanding of children. With this understanding, it would seem natural to utilize play therapy interventions with their students. Landreth (2002) promotes the facilitation of play therapy in schools by explaining that the objective of play therapy in a school is to assist children in readiness to profit from what teachers can offer in the classroom. Play therapy is an approach that can help elementary school counselors to effectively assist children to grow and enhance their successful achievement of developmental tasks. The development of prosocial skills is vital for the enhancement of academic functioning for elementary school students.

SOCIAL SKILLS DEVELOPMENT

According to a survey by the U.S. Department of Health and Human Services the three most common mental health problems for elementary school students are social, interpersonal, or familial in nature. These types of mental health problems for elementary school aged children can lead to aggressive and disruptive behaviors in the classroom and thus can have negative effects on the learning environment for all children (Ebrahim, Steen, & Paradise, 2012). A critical component of children's learning is their mental health and ability to develop prosocial skills during the school day. The American School Counselor Association (2012) acknowledges that schools are increasingly playing a larger role in providing services to children. These responsive services provided by the school counselor can focus on the social and interpersonal development of children. Social skills can be developed and enhanced in the school environment and contribute to academic success.

Perhaps more than any other single indicator, according to Landreth, Homeyer, Glover, and Sweeney (2005), social interactions, or lack thereof, provides essential clues to a child's emotional growth and adjustments. When children exhibit poor social skills and relationships it is important to provide play therapy techniques and interventions to enhance self-concept, impulse control and healthy growth and development. For children who perceive themselves as different from their peers, or who have poor social interactions, group play therapy provides an especially effective modality for them to learn new social skills, to discover that they are capable of peer acceptance, self-control, and self-acceptance (p. 213). Many children lack the skills needed to survive in the world. One method of teaching children social skills, including problem solving skills, negotiation skills, and assertiveness skills, is to use toys, art, play materials and direct instruction to provide them with a fun way that optimizes their learning (Kottman, 2011).

Albert Bandura's (1973) social learning theory highlights the techniques of modeling, behavioral rehearsal, and social reinforcement as integral components in teaching social skills to children in the group setting. Bandura believed that social skills were essential to a positive experience in the learning environment. Children learn by observing adult interactions, hence, when teaching social skills in the classroom or in a small group setting, modeling the appropriate social skills will promote academic and social success.

Children's' competencies developed during elementary and middle school years (ages 6-12), can be applied directly to social skills that need to be honed and developed for academic and personal development. This is a time when parent-child relationships, peer friendships, and participation in meaningful interpersonal communication provide children with social skills that are extremely important if they are to cope with the trials and tribulations of adolescence (Feldman, 2008). Most children begin to explore complex social relationships with their peers and other significant adults, and use these relationships as a model to develop prosocial skills (Galbo, 1983). For some children suffering social skills deficits, the result is peer rejection, academic failure, and disruption in the classroom.

Recent attention has been given to the social and cultural context in which many skills, especially school-related social skills, emerge (Eccles, 1995). Children progress in skill development based on parental and school expectations regarding their level of performance both academically and socially. Social skills development can be influenced by children's motivation to want to achieve new skill levels. Children need to direct their attention and energy to practice social skills such as: problem solving, appropriate communication with peers, and development of effective interactions in the classroom. Social skills development may be enriched by interactions with skillful peers as well as appropriate interventions by teachers and school counselors. Social skills development can enhance and promote children's interpersonal understanding of their behaviors that lead to social skills deficits. According to Karcher and Lewis (2002), interpersonal understanding is one social dimension of cognitive development. It includes self-understanding, social reasoning, social problem solving, and behavior regulation (Feffer, 1960; Flavell, 1992; Selman, 1980). Interpersonal understanding reflects the ability to coordinate social perspectives in a way that allows individuals to understand norms, expectations of acceptable behavior, and consequences of misbehavior. Past research on cognitive development consistently found that the maturity of children's interpersonal understanding is directly related to their social skills (Yeates, Schultz, & Selman, 1991). For this reason, it is imperative to address social skills deficits in the school setting through the modality of play. The school counselor should conceptualize and view "play as a window on cognitive development" (Belsky, cited in Schaefer & Kaduson, 2006, p. 9). Play therapy interventions and techniques are sustainable in the school setting, especially when promoting both social and cognitive development through guidance or responsive services.

Selecting Social Skills

What constitutes social skills? A definition that has been frequently used throughout the literature is that of Combs and Slaby (1977), "the ability to interact with others in a given social context in specific ways that are socially acceptable or valued and at the same time personally beneficial, mutually beneficial, or beneficial primarily to others" (p. 162). Generally, social skills are defined as socially acceptable learned behaviors that enable children in a school environment to interact with their peers and teachers in ways that elicit positive responses and assist in avoiding negative responses as a result of these interactions.

Researchers in the area of social skills training (Gresham, 2002; Gresham, Sugai, & Horner, 2001; Gresham, Van, &Cook, 2006) advocate that counselors and practitioners need to consider the difference between a skill deficit of the student (i.e., he or she cannot perform the skill), and a performance deficit of the student (i.e., he or she won't perform the skill consistently). School counselors need to determine the difference between a student who lacks the knowledge of how to perform a skill or how to select a skill that is appropriate in any given situation versus a student who may know how to perform the skill but lack the fluency in skill use necessary to perform the skill.

School counselors will need to decide which social skills should be taught to children in an elementary school setting. It is possible to apply both a general set of norms and specific criterion for selecting the behaviors that are needed by individual children to be viewed as competent. In selecting specific social skills for play therapy techniques, school counselors need to look at such characteristics as the child's age, developmental level, specific skill deficits, and social and cultural factors (Cartledge & Milburn, 1995).

Teaching social skills to elementary school children can be both challenging and rewarding for school counselors. Gresham and Elliot (1993) outlined specific goals when developing a curriculum for teaching social skills in the school setting. These goals include: (a) to assist children in acquiring social skills by working with their irrational belief system, (b) to enhance the performance of social skills through cognitive behavior and play therapy techniques such as role playing, homework assignments, videos, lecture, behavior rehearsal, handouts, and modeling, (c) to remove interfering problem behaviors such as fighting, inappropriate social interaction and receiving suspensions in the school setting, and (d) facilitating generalization of their new belief system and socially skilled behaviors (p. 137). Elliott and Gresham (2007) identified the top 10 skills that elementary school students need to succeed based on surveys of over 8,000 teachers and over 20 years of research in classrooms across the country. They are: (1) listen to others, (2) follow the steps, (3) follow the rules, (4) ignore distractions, (5) ask for help, (6) take turns when you talk, (7) get along with others, (8) stay calm with others, (9) be responsible for your behavior, (10) do nice things for others.

Additionally, social skills can also be grouped into four major categories targeting specific behaviors using a task analysis model. These categories of behaviors, according to Stephens (1978) who published a social skills curriculum for classroom guidance, consist of: self-related behaviors, environmental behaviors, task-related behaviors, and interpersonal behaviors (p. 15). These behaviors are then analyzed into 30 subcategories and 136 specific skills (pp. 34-38). Examples of these behaviors can include: expressing feelings, completing tasks, following directions, positive attitude towards others, and self care. However, attempting to develop a guidance curriculum that addresses all 136 skills may not be feasible for an elementary school counselor working in a medium to large school.

In selecting the specific social skills to focus on in the elementary school setting, the literature discusses different programs with developed curricula that can be modified to enhance individual or group work in schools. McGinnis and Goldstein (1997a) developed a Skillstreaming program for elementary school children. This program targets five global groups of categories each of which has several specific social skills that pertain to academic and social functioning. Group I is designated as *Classroom Survival Skills* and includes the following specific social skills: listening, asking for help, saying thank you, bringing materials to class, following instructions, completing assignments, contributing to discussions, offering help to and adult, asking questions, ignoring distractions, making corrections, deciding on something to do, and setting a goal. Group II is designated as *Friendship-Making Skills* and are comprised of the following: introducing yourself, beginning a conversation, ending a conversation, joining in, playing a game, asking a favor, offering help to a classmate, giving a compliment, suggesting an activity, sharing, and apologizing. Group III is labeled as *Skills Dealing with Feelings*, and the specific social skills include: knowing your feelings, expressing your feelings, recognizing another's feelings, showing understanding of another's feelings, expressing concern for another, dealing with your anger, dealing with another's anger, expressing affection, dealing with fear, and rewarding yourself. Group IV skills, labeled *Skill Alternatives to Aggression* include: using self-control, asking permission, responding to teasing, avoiding trouble, staying out of fights, problem solving, accepting consequences, dealing with accusations, and negotiating. Group V, *Skills for Dealing with Stress*, include: dealing with boredom, deciding what caused a problem, making a complaint, answering a complaint, dealing with losing, being a good sport, dealing with being left out, dealing with embarrassment, reacting to failure, accepting no, saying no, relaxing, dealing with group pressure, dealing with wanting something that is not yours, making a decision, and being honest (pp. 29-32). These skills are the most prevalent and common for elementary school children when developing their social interactions. The selection of social skills should be based on the skill deficiency of the students, the skills that are transferable beyond the school environment, and the skills that will assist the students in improving their academic and social functioning during the school day.

SOCIAL SKILLS GROUPS AND COGNITIVE-BEHAVIORAL PLAY THERAPY

Social Skills Groups

Gould as cited in Landreth (2001), suggested that "all children could profit or benefit from engaging in play therapy as an opportunity to exercise social skills within a controlled setting" (p. 229). Specifically, group play therapy, offers children a chance to hone new skills, recognize their social competencies, gain peer acceptance, and build and practice self-control (Landreth et al., 2005). Group work has become a major model by which children are helped (Bowman, 1987; Shechtman, 2004). This type of work concentrates on promoting life skills such as social skills, and correcting faulty assumptions. In elementary schools, psychoeduational and counseling groups are used to help children learn new skills and become aware of their values, priorities, and communities (Gladding, 2011). The research shows that approximately 70% of children's groups take place in school settings (Shechtman & Pastor, 2005). Small groups give students the opportunity to "explore and work through their social and emotional challenges with others who are experiencing similar feelings" (Campbell & Bowman, 1993, p. 173).

Small groups or guidance lessons are the most effective way to assist elementary school children in developing social skills. According to Gladding (2011), groups of all kinds can be helpful to children and adolescents in making a successful transition from childhood to adulthood. They are valuable because they allow members to experience a sense of belonging, share common problems, find and provide support, facilitate new learning, help ease internal and external pressures, and offer hope and models for change (p. 266). ASCA (2012) has endorsed group work as an important component in a comprehensive school counseling program. A small group counseling intervention can strengthen the development of social skills and promote school counselor visibility and improving school counselor relationships with parents, teachers, and other stakeholders (Kayler & Sherman, 2009). Group work is efficient, effective, and multifaceted (Akos & Milsom, 2007), an ideal method to meet the needs of at-risk students. Group counseling allows students to develop and maintain connections to others while exploring factors that influence achievement. ASCA's (2012) national standards for school counseling programs provided specific academic, career, and personal/social objectives for the groups.

Many psychoeducational groups, such as social skills development, revolve around activities and are subsequently called activity group guidance (AGG) (Hillman & Reunion, 1978 as cited in Gladding, 2011). These activities are developmental in nature and typically include coordinated guidance topics. For example, in promoting self-understanding and understanding of others, puppets, drawings, and music are often used (DeLucia-Waack, 2001b; Egge, Marks, & McEvers, 1987; Gladding, 2004; Harper, 1985, as cited in Gladding, 2011, p. 249). These expressive arts activities are beneficial for enhancing interaction and motivation in ways that language alone cannot do. It is important for children to be able to express feelings, handle aggression, deal with group pressure and develop friendship making skills through the use of music and art activities.

Cognitive-Behavioral Play Therapy

Cognitive behavior therapy (CBT) is a structured, goal-oriented therapy with a strong rationale for its use with children and adolescents (Knell, 2009). The focus of CBT is deficits or distortions in thinking, which are postulated to interfere with appropriate social skills. CBT emphasizes teaching skills that directly link assessment, intervention, and evaluation. Increasingly, CBT interventions are also being adapted for delivery to adolescent groups in school setting (Flanagan, Allen, & Henry, 2010). CBT used with adolescents in the group setting can have beneficial effects such as peer modeling, interpersonal learning, or group cohesiveness (Yalom, 2005). Knell emphasized that behavior is mediated through verbal and cognitive processes. The three key ideas in cognitive therapy are (a) thoughts influence emotions and behaviors; (b) beliefs and assumptions influence perceptions and interpretations of events; and, (c) most individuals who are having psychological problems have errors in logic, irrational thinking, or cognitive distortions (Beck, 1976; Knell, 2009). Several global goals exist for CBT interventions in relation to social skills. These goals may include increasing the adolescent's ability to express feelings, decreasing maladaptive thoughts, and perceptions, increasing adaptive and realistic assessment of relationships, increasing positive self-talk, increasing appropriate use of problem-solving skills (Kottman, 2011). CBT can be an integral piece for improving adolescent's social skills in a psychoeducational group setting. The CBT approach has been empirically proven to work effectively with adolescents in honing social skills.

Elementary school children require an adaptation of CBT. Adapting CBT for elementary school aged children is complicated, as the cognitive interventions must be more developmentally appropriate and accessible. Children need to be viewed as active and involved participants in change, which can have a direct impact on their social, emotional, and academic development. Cognitive-behavioral play therapy (CBPT) is a theoretical framework based on cognitive-behavioral principles and integrates these principles in a developmentally appropriate manner (Knell, 2009).

CBPT, developed by Susan Knell (1993a, 1994, 2000, 2009a, 2009b, as cited in Kottman, 2011), incorporates cognitive and behavioral interventions within a play therapy paradigm. CBPT integrates ideas from behavior therapy, cognitive therapy, and cognitive-behavioral therapy, which was the impetus for formulating the concepts and theoretical basis for

CBPT. Play activities, verbal, and nonverbal forms of communication are used to resolve problems. In CBPT, there are some global goals in addition to individual and specific goals of each child (Knell, 2009a, 2009b, as cited in Kottman, 2011). The general goal is to increase the child's ability to cope with problem situations and stressors; help the child master tasks that have been difficult; decrease the child's faulty thinking patterns; or assist the child in meeting developmental milestones that have been delayed for some reason.

CBPT places a very strong emphasis on the child's involvement in the process of developing appropriate social skills. According to Knell (2009), CBPT has six specific properties, or tenets, that provide the foundation for positive outcomes. The tenets are as follows:

1. CBPT involves the child in treatment via play.
2. CBPT focuses on the child's thoughts, feelings, fantasies, and environment.
3. CBPT provides a strategy or strategies for developing more adaptive thoughts and behaviors.
4. CBPT is structured, directive, and goal-oriented, rather than open-ended.
5. CBPT incorporates empirically demonstrated techniques such as modeling, and role playing.
6. CBPT allows for empirical evaluation of treatment which can enhance the involvement of parents and stakeholders in the school environment (pp. 44-45).

Although CBPT is very different from traditional play therapy approaches, the development of the relationship and communication via play are important tenets for this approach. CBPT has several properties that can be used in the group setting for working with children to develop and implement daily social skills. CBPT establishes concrete and objective goals and movement towards these goals is an important part of the group process. It is acceptable for the school counselor to introduce themes based on parent or teacher report of behavior in the school setting. In CBPT, the students and the school counselor will play a role in the choice of play materials and activities. School counselors can use CBPT to educate students by using play techniques to teach social skills or alternative behaviors. For example, puppets can be used to model certain appropriate social skills for students. Positive reinforcement is another component of CBPT that is important when working with the development and enhancement of social skills. Positive reinforcement from the school counselor and the teacher can communicate to the student which behaviors are appropriate and which ones are not. Additionally, positive reinforcement helps students feel better about themselves. All of these components may be applied individually or in small group settings in the school environment.

CBPT TECHNIQUES

The interventions used in CBPT can be facilitated by school counselors individually or in a group setting. When helping students develop and hone social skills, several cognitive-behavioral techniques are utilized. Some of the techniques outlined below can be used by school counselors to facilitate the integration of play therapy skills into preventive and responsive services indicated by ASCA (2012).

Modeling

Most of the techniques in CBPT are delivered by modeling, for example, using a puppet, doll, or stuffed animal to demonstrate the appropriate social skills to children. Several other examples of modeling with puppets can include shaping/ positive reinforcement during the social skills group (Knell, 2009). The school counselor selects two puppets along with a social skill to introduce to the small group and may say, *"Mr. Dragon is going to practice his listening skills with Ms. Butterfly."* The dragon puppet listens to the butterfly puppet and exhibits appropriate listening skills and is provided with encouragement and positive feedback as the dragon puppet exhibits the steps for appropriate listening skills.

Behavioral Rehearsal

Behavioral rehearsal provides an opportunity for school counselors to help children master difficult situations and learn more adaptive or social skills. By rehearsing, new more functional behaviors are observed and practiced by the students. The goal of behavioral rehearsal is for the students to learn to modify social skills deficiencies and ways of responding by role-playing a variety of appropriate responses. When using behavioral rehearsal, school counselors can provide immediate and concrete feedback, followed by continued rehearsal of problem situations (Knell, 2009). School counselors can use dolls or puppets to coach more adaptive responses. In this way social skills are modeled for the students, and the students can rehearse the new skills. School counselors will be providing students with the opportunity to practice new social skills in a group setting, and develop more functional ways of responding to peers and teachers.

For example, school counselors may choose to focus on dealing with anger and recognizing others anger as the targeted social skills. The selected puppets are having a dialogue about a situation at school that has made them angry. Schools counselors coach the puppets on the appropriate responses regarding expressing anger in appropriate ways. The students are then given the opportunity to practice with the puppets. School counselors provide immediate and concrete feedback regarding the interaction of the puppets and the appropriate responses. The students continue rehearsals and develop appropriate responses to expressing anger in the school environment.

Behavioral Contingencies

Behavioral contingencies can be used by school counselors to provide rewards in the group setting for acquiring new skills. For example, school counselors can ask the students in the group to pick three rewards they would like to earn during the group. Once the students have mastered the skills, rewards will be given. A chart can be displayed during the group that would indicate the social skills that need to be mastered with each students name by the specific skills and the rewards once the students master the specific skills. Examples of rewards include: stickers, homework passes, line leaders, and star group members.

Coping Self-Statements

The way in which children interpret events, and not the events themselves, affects their ability to cope and function effectively, both socially and academically. Children's perception of events and not the actual events can greatly impact their social development, hence hindering social skills (Knell, 2009). Negative thoughts lead to negative self-statements, which can lead to poor decision making and interactions with peers and adults. For example, a child who predicts no one will want to play hide and seek with her at recess, supported by her negative self-statements, *"I cannot run very well or hide as well as my friends,"* which leads to poor social interactions and social skills. School counselors can work with students in the group setting to teach them coping self-statements. Students need to learn simple statements about themselves, such as: *"I can hide as well as my peers."* These positive affirmations can be written down during the group and the students can apply these affirmations to learning the different social skills.

School counselors can model positive self-statements. These positive self-statements can be utilized to promote the development of healthy social skills.

Bibliotherapy

Bibliotherapy is used to provide a story telling approach for children in a group setting. Children's stories have an abundance of messages regarding specific problems or traumatic events such as: divorce, death, moving, anger management, and coping or social skills (Knell, 2009). School counselors may use these stories to convey a message indirectly, with the hope that the students will learn something through the main character(s) in the book. The story models for the children ways of coping with life events such as aggression, bullying, anger, and friendship. Examples of books specific to children developing appropriate social skills can be found in Appendix A.

The above techniques are specific for guidance and small group settings in the school environment. Several techniques can be used individually by school counselors to promote healthy social skills. Some of these techniques include: self-monitoring, activity scheduling, recording dysfunctional thoughts, and cognitive change strategies.

A SCHOOL BASED SOCIAL SKILLS GROUP: ENGAGING AND EMPOWERING STUDENTS

Emma Callahan is a school counselor in an inner city elementary school. She has had several teachers approach her concerning some students who they have observed are having difficulty completing assignments, building rapport, expressing and identifying feelings, choosing appropriate options, displaying negative and self-defeating behaviors, difficulty managing stress, and developing a negative self image which is causing a disruption in the classroom and on the playground. Ms. Callahan decides it may be beneficial to facilitate some groups to address the teacher's concerns about the student's lack of social skills.

Ms. Callahan asks each teacher to complete the Teacher/Staff Skillstreaming Checklist (McGinnis & Goldstein, 1997b, pp. 1-11). This checklist will be part of Ms. Callahan's assessment process to gather information about the children's current level of functioning, and social skills deficits. Ms. Callahan worked with the teachers, based on the data from the checklist, to identify six students who would benefit from a small group to assist them with their social skills deficits. She designed a group that would meet for 8 weeks, with 40 minute sessions, focused on assisting with social skills development using a CBPT approach. The six selected students are in the second and third grade and are grouped by skill deficit. The group is comprised of three boys and three girls, two Black males, one Hispanic male, two Caucasian females, and one Black female. Ms. Callahan meets with each student prior to the inception of the group. She explains the purpose of the group will be to assist the student in developing a positive self-image, expressing their feelings, dealing with stress, and making friends. Ms. Callahan was able to secure parental consent for all 6 students prior to her individual meetings with each student. Each session demonstrates CBPT techniques to foster skill development to further academic and social success in school.

Social skills group session 1. The first group session was spent developing rapport and building trust, which is an essential skill for friendships and classroom relationships. Ms. Callahan spent some time discussing the group rules prior to introducing the new skill that would be learned in that session. The group rules consisted of: being respectful, talking one at a time, listening to others, staying in your seat, and participating when asked.

Ms. Callahan introduced the skill by saying, "*We are going to learn how to introduce ourselves and build relationships in our group.*" Ms. Callahan provided the group members with a box of crayons and sheets of white paper. She asked each student to select a crayon and take a piece of paper. She then said, "*Please read the color on your crayon.*" "*If you were this color, how would you describe yourself? Please write words on your paper that describe how you are similar to the color crayon you selected.*" Each group member discussed the color they selected and described qualities they share with their choice of color. Ms. Callahan, modeled how to introduce the color and discussed the qualities by using her color; midnight sky. Ms. Callahan says, "*I have selected the color midnight sky. I am like midnight sky because I am hopeful, I am open and free, and I am calm, yet I can be stormy sometimes.* Each group member followed her example. The group ended with Ms. Callahan asking each group member to remember their qualities when they are having some difficulties at in school or at home.

Social skills group session 2. Ms. Callahan welcomed the group members back and checked in with each group member, by asking each member to state," *one thing that was positive about your week.*" Ms. Callahan reminded the members of the group rules and praised each member for following the rules. Ms. Callahan introduced the skill for the week, "*We are going to focus on learning how to identify and express our feelings can you give me some feeling words?*" "*This week we are going to play a game called feeling charades, which is going to help us learn how to express our feelings in class and on the play ground appropriately.*" Ms. Callahan introduced a game called feeling charades. Ms. Callahan passed out envelopes that contained feeling words and each paired group member selected a feeling word. The group member had to act out the feeling and his or her partner had to guess the feeling. The team that guessed the most feeling words correctly won homework passes for one subject to use that week. Once the game was over, Ms. Callahan and the group members process the feelings and how each of these feelings can affect their thoughts and behaviors in the classroom and on the playground. Ms. Callahan asked each group member to select a feeling and close the group with a time when this feeling was bothersome to them.

Social skills group session 3. Ms. Callahan welcomed the students back to group. She introduced the skill for the week, *"This week we are going to learn how to make appropriate choices and handling our own problems." She tells the group members that today," you are going to be able to create your own story and chose how your story ends."* Ms. Callahan began by having a puppet discuss a scenario that required making appropriate choices. She had another puppet choose the appropriate option at the end of the story. Then, after the puppets modeled the activity and made appropriate choices, each group member added their own story to the scenario. The group member who added last was able to choose the appropriate option or how the story ended. Group members discussed the appropriate options or outcome for the main character of the story. Each group member chose how the story ended. The group discussed the appropriate versus inappropriate endings to each story. Ms. Callahan then asked the group members to continue to rehearse the endings to the story until each group member was able to develop their own appropriate ending. Ms. Callahan ended the group session by giving each member a reward for following the group rules and providing appropriate responses to end each story.

Social skills group session 4. Ms. Callahan began the group by reviewing the skills that were discussed over the past three sessions. She reminded the students in the group that the group only had four more sessions left. The goal of session 4 was to help the students replace negative self-defeating behaviors. Ms. Callahan introduced the skill for the week, *"Today we are going to learn how to be positive about ourselves and present a positive self-image."* She then gives each group member a piece of poster board, glue stick, glitter, markers, crayons, yarn, and so forth, along with appropriate magazines. Ms. Callahan instructed each group member to cut out pictures and words in the magazines that represent his or her self. Ms. Callahan, stated, *"The goal of the activity is to develop your own collage that is a picture of you."* Once the collages were completed, Ms. Callahan said, *"Each of you is invited to share your collage and discuss the pictures and words that are representative of you."* Each group member discussed why they chose the pictures and words and how these pictures and words created a positive self-image for their collage. Ms. Callahan assisted the group members with negative pictures and words by replacing and reframing them into positive thoughts, feelings, or behaviors. Ms. Callahan closed the group by asking the members to share one positive thought they had about the group.

Social skills group session 5. Ms. Callahan welcomed the students to session # 5 of the group. The skill the group focused on was stress management. Ms. Callahan asked the group, *"What is stress?" "What happens when you feel stress?"* Ms. Callahan talked to the group about how stress can interfere with being productive in the classroom and on the playground. She introduced the activity, with the purpose of assisting the group members in dealing with stress in a positive manner instead of focusing on the stressor. *"Our activity for this session is called Welcome to my World. I am passing out a piece of paper and markers. You will notice a big circle on your paper. Please write your name and the word world at the top."* The group members divided their paper into four quadrants and marked them North, South, East, and West. Each group member drew in each specific quadrant a source of stress for them at home, in school, with their friends, and alone. Ms. Callahan encouraged each group member to share their four quadrants. The group discussed some positive things they could do to manage stress and how they can apply these strategies to the different environments. Ms. Callahan closed the session by asking each group member to state which stress technique would work best for them. Ms. Callahan gave each group member a coupon to check out one extra book in the library that week.

Social skills group session 6. Ms. Callahan began session # 6 by reminding the students that only two group sessions remained. Ms. Callahan praised the group members for coming to the group each week and being active participants. She then introduced the skill for the week, *"We are going to work on building our self-esteem by creating a positive self-image. Sometimes we thing negative things about our selves and these negative things can make us feel poorly about ourselves."* Each group member was asked to draw how he or she perceived him or herself on one side of the paper and on the other side of the paper the student drew how he or she think others perceive him or her. Once the group members completed their drawings, Ms. Callahan asked group members to share their pictures and discuss the differences and similarities between the two pictures. Ms. Callahan had the group members conceptualize how their perception is usually very different from how others perceive them (Fazio-Griffith, as cited in Lowenstein, 2011, p. 160). Ms. Callahan stated, *"These perceptions can interfere with our ability to learn and make friends, how you think your pictures will influence your behavior in class and with your friends on the play ground?"* Ms. Callahan closed the group by asking each group member to share one thought about their self-perception that would help them have a positive interaction when they went back to class or at recess.

Social skills session 7. Ms. Callahan welcomed the group back and explained that the group would end the next week. She talked with the group members about how to end the group and celebrate the work that the members had done collectively and individually. The group members decided they would like to show their appreciation for each other by creating a keepsake for each group member.

Ms. Callahan introduced the skill for the week. *"Our focus today will be on expressing your anger in appropriate ways, by having each of you create your own anger box."* Each group member was given a shoe box and construction paper. Glitter, yarn, paint, and markers were made available for use as well. Ms. Callahan asked each group member to decorate the outside of their box and then draw three things that have made them angry over the past week and place these three things inside their box. Once the boxes were completed, Ms. Callahan said, *"Who would like to begin and tell the group what is in your anger box? After you explain to us what is in your box, please tell us what you did when you got angry, and what you could have done instead.* The group members and Ms. Callahan discussed how to choose appropriate options to manage anger. The group members were asked to leave their issues in the box with Ms. Callahan at the close of the session so they would not carry them outside the group. Ms. Callahan ended the session by reading the book *"When Sophie Gets Angry—Really, Really Angry"* by Molly Bang (1996). Ms. Callahan closed the group by asking each group member what else Sophie can do when she gets angry.

Social skills session 8. Ms. Callahan began the final session by thanking all of the members for being such active participants in the group and adhering to the group rules for the past 8 weeks. Ms. Callahan told the group what she appreciated about them and how she had enjoyed watching each of them grow and develop their own set of social skills over the past eight weeks. Ms. Callahan introduced the final skills: interpersonal relationships and saying goodbye. Ms. Callahan informed the group members that each would leave with a keepsake from the group. *"We are going to make appreciation booklets for each other. I am going to pass out construction paper and markers for each of you. Fold your paper in half and write your name on the front cover of the paper. You may decorate the front cover any way you would like. I want you to open your booklets and inside your booklet write a word or two to answer the following:*

My proudest moment in this group was:
My greatest accomplishment was:
One goal I have for the future is:
The skill I have mastered in this group is:

Close your booklet and pass it to the person on your right. Do not open the booklet, please write one positive statement or word about the person whose booklet you have." The booklets were passed around until everyone had written a positive statement in every booklet. The group members received their own booklet back and were instructed by Ms. Callahan to read the positive statements from their peers. Group members were given the chance to reflect upon their work and to have closure by learning appropriate ways to end relationships with each group member.

Ms. Callahan closed the group by asking each member to reflect upon one skill that they had learned and utilized in the classroom or on the play ground. To show her appreciation for the group members, Ms. Callahan gives each member a coupon for a free ice cream in the cafeteria.

Social Skills Group Follow Up

Three weeks after the last group session Ms. Callahan asked the teachers to complete the same checklist that they completed on each student before the group sessions began. Ms. Callahan compared the results of the post checklist to the pre checklist to determine the students' progress during the duration of the group and the application of appropriate social skills beyond the group. Ms. Callahan worked with the teachers to encourage students' continued progress in displaying appropriate social skills to increase academic, social and emotional growth in the school environment.

CONCLUSION

Many elementary school children have maladaptive social skills. These skills include: poor interpersonal relationships, inability to make friends, issues with controlling emotions, and stress management. These deficiencies can have a great impact on their academic, social and emotional functioning in the classroom. It is imperative that school counselors and teachers recognize these maladaptive skills and provide responsive services in the form of individual or group counseling. School counselors can adapt the CBPT approach for use in the group setting. This approach will teach children varying social skills and how to apply these social skills to relationships in the classroom. In this chapter, CBPT was demonstrated in a series of eight group sessions to improve social skills. School counselors should be flexible when examining how to improve student's social skills. Individual counseling as well as group guidance can be beneficial when using this approach.

APPENDIX A: BIBLIOTHERAPY RESOURCES FOR SOCIAL SKILLS DEVELOPMENT

Double-Dip Feelings: A Book to Help Children Understand Emotions by Barbara Cain 1990. Grades K-4.

I Like Me by Nancy Carlson 1988. Grades K-4.

When Sophie Gets Angry--- Really, Really Angry by Molly Bang 1996. Grades K-4.

I'm Gonna like Me: Letting off a Little Self-Esteem by Jamie Lee Curtis. Illus. by Laura Cornell 1998. Grades K-3.

Today I Feel Silly & Other Moods That Make My Day by Jamie Lee Curtis. Illus. by Laura Cornell 1998. Grades K-3.

Where Do Balloons Go? An Uplifting Mystery by Jamie Lee Curtis. Illus. by Laura Cornell 1998. Grades K-3.

Whoever You Are by Mem Fox. Illus by Leslie Staub 1997. Grades K-5.

Go Away, Big Green Monster! by Ed Emberley 1992. Grades K-2.

Hands Are Not For Hitting by Martine Agassi. Illus. by Marieka Heinlen 2006. Grades K-2.

Words Are Not For Hurting by Elizabeth Verdick Illus. by Marieka Heinlen 2003. Grades K-3.

Alexander and the Terrible, Horrible, No Good, Very Bad Day by Judith Viorst. Illus. by Ray Cruz 1972. Grades K-5

REFERENCES

Akos, P., & Milsom, A. (2007). Introduction to special issue: Group work in K-12 schools. *Journal for Specialists in Group Work, 32,* 5-7.

American School Counselor Association. (2012). *The ASCA national model: A framework for school counseling programs* (3rd ed.). Alexandria, VA: Author.

Baker, S., & Gerler, E. (2004). *School counseling for the twenty-first century* (4th ed.). Upper Saddle River, NJ: Merrill Prentice Hall.

Bandura, A. (1973). *Aggression: A social learning analysis.* Englewood Cliffs, NJ: Prentice Hall.

Beck, A. T. (1976). *Cognitive therapy and the emotional disorders.* New York, NY: International University Press.

Bowman, R. P. (1987). Small-group guidance and counseling in schools: A national survey of school counselors. *School Counselor, 34,* 256-262.

Campbell, C., & Bowman, R. P. (1993). The "fresh start" support club: small group counseling for academically retained children. *Elementary School Guidance & Counseling, 27,* 172-185.

Cartledge, G., & Milburn, J. F. (Ed) (1995). *Teaching social skills to children.* New York, NY: Pergamon Press.

Cochran, J. & Cochran, N. (1999). Using the counseling relationship to facilitate change in students with conduct disorders. *Professional School Counseling, 2,* 395-403. Retrieved from http://www.schoolcounselor.org/content.asp?contentid=235.

Combs, M. L., & Slaby, D. A. (1977). Social skills training with children. In B. B. Lahey & A. E. Kazdin (Eds.), *Advances in clinical child psychology* (Vol. 1). New York, NY: Pienum Press.

Dimick, K., & Huff, V. (1970). *Child counseling*. Dubuque, IA: William C. Brown.

Ebrahim, C., Steen, R. L., & Paradise, L. (2012). Overcoming school counselors' barriers to play therapy. *International Journal of Play Therapy, 21,* 202-214.

Eccles, J. S. (1995). School and family effects on the ontogeny of children's interactions, self-perceptions, and activity choices. In J. E. Jacobs (Ed.*), Nebraska symposium on motivation* (Vol. 40, pp. 145-208), Lincoln, NE: University of Nebraska Press.

Elliot, S. N., & Gresham, F. (2007). *Social skills improvement system (SSIS): Classwide intervention program.* Upper Saddle River, NJ: Pearson Assessments.

Feffer, M. H. (1960). Cognitive aspects of role-taking in children. *Journal of Personality, 28,* 383-396.

Feldman, R. S. (2008). *Development across the life span* (5th ed.). Upper Saddle River, NJ: Prentice Hall.

Flanagan, R., Allen, K., & Henry, D. J. (2010). The impact of anger management treatment and rational emotive behavior therapy in a public school setting on social skills, anger management, and depression. *Journal of Rational-Emotive & Cognitive Behavior Therapy, 28,* 87-99.

Flavell, J. H. (1992). Perspectives on perspective taking. In H. Beilin (Ed.), *Piaget's theory: Prospects and possibilities.* The Jean Piaget symposium series (pp. 107-139). Hillsdale, NJ: Erlbaum.

Galbo, J. J. (1983). Adolescents' perceptions of significant adults. *Adolescence, 18,* 417-428.

Gladding, S. T. (2011). *Counseling a group specialty (6th edition).* Upper Saddle River, NJ: Pearson.

Gresham, F. M. (2002). Social skills assessment and instruction for students with emotional and behavioral disorders. In K. L. Lane, F. M. Gresham, & T. E. O' Shaughnessy (Eds.), *Interventions for children with or at risk for emotional and behavioral disorders*. Boston, MA: Allyn & Bacon.

Gresham, F. M., & Elliot, S. N. (1993). Social skills intervention guide: Systematic approaches to social skills training. *Special Services in the Schools, 9,* 137-158.

Gresham, F. M., Sugai, G., & Horner, R. H. (2001). Interpreting outcomes of social skills training for students with high-incidence disabilities. *Exceptional Children, 67,* 331-337.

Gresham, F. M., Van, M. B., & Cook, C. R. (2006). Social skills training for teaching replacement behaviors: Remediating acquisition deficits in at-risk students. *Behavioral Disorders, 31*(4), 363-377.

Gysbers, N., & Henderson, P. (2011). *Developing &managing your school guidance program* (5th ed.). Alexandria, VA: American Counseling Association.

Johnson, L., Mc Leod, E., & Fall, M. (1997). Play therapy with labeled children in schools. *Professional School Counseling, 1,* 31-34. Retrieved from http://www.schoolcounselor.org/content.asp?contentid=235

Karcher, M. J., & Lewis, S. S. (2002). Pair counseling: The effects of a dyadic developmental play therapy on interpersonal understanding and externalizing behaviors. *International Journal of Play Therapy, 10,* 19-41.

Kayler, H., & Sherman, J. (2009). At-risk ninth grade students: A psychoeducational group approach to increase study skills and grade point averages. *Professional School Counseling, 12,* 434-439.

Knell, S. M. (2009). *Cognitive-behavioral play therapy.* New Jersey: Jason Aronson Inc.

Kottman, T. (2011). *Play therapy basics and beyond* (2nd ed.). Alexandria, VA: American Counseling Association.

Landreth, G. (2001). *Innovations in play therapy: Issues, process, and special population*: New York, NY: Taylor Francis.

Landreth, G. (2002). *Play therapy: the art of the relationship.* London, England: Routledge.

Landreth, G. (2012). *Play therapy: the art of the relationship* (3rd ed.). London, England: Routledge.

Landreth, G., Homeyer, L., Glover, G., & Sweeney, D. (2005). Play *therapy interventions with children's problems* (2nd ed.). Northvale, NJ: Jason Aronson.

Lowenstein, L. (2011). *Assessment and treatment activities for children, adolescents and families: Practitioners share their most effective techniques.* Ontario, Canada: Champion Press.

McGinnis, E., & Goldstein, A. P. (1997a). *Skillstreaming the elementary school child: New strategies and perspectives for teaching prosocial skills.* Champaign, IL: Research Press.

McGinnis, E., & Goldstein, A. P. (1997b). *Skillstreaming the elementary school child: Program forms.* Champaign, IL: Research Press.

Newsome, D., & Gladding, S. (2003). Counseling individuals and groups in school. In B. Erford (Ed.), *Transforming the school counseling profession* (pp. 209-229). Upper Saddle River, NJ: Brunner-Routledge.

Post, P. (1999). Impact of child-centered play therapy on the self-esteem, locus of control, and anxiety of at-risk 4th, 5th, and 6th grade students. *International Journal of Play Therapy, 8* 1-18. Retrieved from http://www.apa.org/pubs/journals/pla/Index.aspx. doi: 101037/h0089428

Ray, D. C., Blanco, P. J., Sullivan, J. M., & Holliman, R. (2009). An exploratory study of child-centered play therapy with aggressive children. *International Journal of Play Therapy, 18,* 162-175. doi: 10.1037/a0014742

Ray, D., Muro, J., & Schumann, B. (2004). Implementing play therapy in the schools: Lessons learned. *International Journal of Play Therapy, 13*(1), 79-100.

Ray, D. C., Schottelkorb, A., & Tsai, M. (2007). Play therapy with children exhibiting symptoms of attention deficit hyperactivity disorder. *International Journal of Play Therapy, 16,* 95-111. doi: 10.1037/1555-6824.16.2.95

Schaefer, C., & Kaduson, H. (2006). *Short-term play therapy for children* (2nd ed.). New York, NY: Guilford Press.

Shechtman, Z. (2004). Group counseling and psychotherapy with children and adolescents: Curren practice and research. In J. L. Delucia-Waack, D. A. Gerity, C. R. Kaldoner, & M. T. Rica (Eds.), *Hanbook of group counseling and psychotherapy* (pp. 429-444). Thousand Oak, CA: SAGE.

Shechtman, Z., & Pastor, R., (2005). Cognitive-behavioral and humanistic group treatment for children with disabilities: A comparison of outcome and process. *Journal of Counseling Psychology, 52*(3), 322-326.

Schmidt, J. (2003). *Counseling in schools: Essential services and comprehensive programs* (4th ed.). Boston, IL: Allyn & Bacon.

Selman, R. (1980). *The growth of interpersonal understanding: Developmental and clinical ananlysis.* New York, IL: Academic Press.

Shen,Y., & Sink, C. (2002). Helping elementary-aged children cope with disasters, *Professional School Counseling, 5,* 322-330. Retrieved from http://www.schoolcounselor.org/content.asp?contentid=235.

Stephens, T. M. (1978*). Social skills in the classroom.* Columbus, OH: Cedars Press.

White, J., & Flynt, M. (1999). Play groups in elementary school. In D. S. Sweeney & L. E. Homeyer (Eds.), *Group play therapy: How to do it, how it works, and whom it's best for* (pp. 336-338). San Francisco, CA: Jossey-Bass.

Yalom, I. D. (2005). *The theory and practice of group psychotherapy* (5th ed.). New York, NY: Basic Books.

Yeates, K. O., Schultz, L. H., & Selman, R. L. (1991). The development of interpersonal negotiation strategies in thought and action: A social-cognitive link to behavioral adjustment and social status. *Merrill-Palmer Quarterly, 37,* 369-405.

CHAPTER 18

HELPING HOMELESS CHILDREN IN SCHOOLS

Play Therapy Interventions

Erin M. Dugan

Although school counselors have been challenged with the presenting issues of homeless children in their school environments, according to Sutton (2010), "homelessness is a relatively new social problem" (p. 435). Many presenting issues and challenges arise due to homelessness, most specifically dealing with the loss of a secure and safe environment in their lives, a sense of belonging, and self-esteem related concerns (Maslow, 1968). The lack of adequate support for homeless children leads to the development of insecurity, particularly in regard to socializing with peers. Current and past literature focuses on the impact of homelessness on children and their academic, behavioral, emotional, social, and psychological challenges leading to negative implications in their overall physical and mental health (Baggerly, 2006; Biggar, 2002; Buckner, Bassuk, Weinreb, & Brooks, 1999; Masten, Sesma, Si-Asar, Lawrence, Miliotis, & Dionne, 1997; Rubin, Erickson, Agustin, Cleary, Allen, & Cohen, 1996). Additionally, research reflects an array of treatment modalities and approaches that have been published on working with children who have been trau-

Integrating Play Techniques in Comprehensive School Counseling Programs, pp. 367–380

matized by homelessness. The focus of this chapter will be on the issues homeless children face; including an overview of statistics, prevalence rates, manifestations in the school environment, effective techniques and approaches based on solution-focused treatment in play therapy. Additionally, outlined sessions for school counselors are presented in a detailed manner that may be easily incorporated into both guidance curriculum as well as individual and small group counseling.

Vignette 1

Joe enters his kindergarten classroom and appears to be withdrawn and resistant to engaging with the children and toys in the learning centers. He looks around, takes note of the classroom, and stands motionless in the back by the cubbies. The teacher notices a faint odor of soiled underwear. Earlier that day the school counselor approached the teacher to inform her that Joe often soils his underwear as he is unable to use the bathroom at the appropriate times and has recently been placed on medication to help regulate his bowel movements. She informed the teacher that Joe has been recently diagnosed with encopresis. The teacher notices that although Joe remains standing, he begins to slowly manipulate some of the objects in his reach by one of the shelves. He turns his head around to the teacher and inquires, "Are all of these your toys?" The teacher responds, "You are curious about those toys. In here these are all of our toys to play with." Joe smiles with caution in his face as he is unsure of whether the teacher's response is truthful. He continues to manipulate the toys. The teacher notices that he is apparently having a hard time knowing exactly what to do with some of the toys.

Vignette 2

Germain enters the school counseling playroom. He goes over to the kitchen area and begins cooking – placing all the pots on the stove, stirring, and turning them over to set the table with dishes, bowls, forks, knives, spoons, cups and paper to serve as napkins. The school counselor perceives his play as a holiday dinner feast with all the trimming and place settings laid out perfectly! He turns to the school counselor and invites her over to sit down in one of the chairs and begins to eat. He has repeated this play pattern across several play therapy sessions. His grandmother is his guardian due to his mother's inability to afford housing and food. His grandmother reported in the initial meeting that Germain and his two brothers were evicted from their home and have moved in and out of shelters for the past several months as his mother tries to find a job. She additionally reports that every night Germain does everything he can to be included in the cooking, place setting, and serving of food just like in his school-based play sessions with the school counselor.

DEFINITION OF HOMELESSNESS

As mentioned, homeless children face an array of presenting challenges including health, academic, emotional well-being, and behavioral, cognitive, and developmental implications. Baggerly (2003) notes multiple causes of homelessness including lack of adequate and affordable health care, exposure to familial violence, mental illness, as well as substance use (including addictions). According to Kolos, Green, and Crenshaw (2009), additional challenges are negative effects on the parent-child relationship that impact the child's overall "development and functioning" (p. 367). Children need safety, love and belonging, and self-esteem in order to self-actualize (Maslow, 1968). These factors, as indicated by Maslow, are often neglected as a result of homelessness.

Homeless children are not just those living on the streets per se; they are children of all ages and races. According to the National Coalition for the Homeless (1999), as cited in Baggerly (2003), "families and children are homeless if they lack a fixed, regular, and adequate nighttime residence and if they have a primary nighttime residence that is a shelter or place not ordinarily designed for residence such as a car, abandoned building, or public park" (p. 88). Guarino and Volk (2010) additionally report that homelessness is "caused by the combined effects of lack of affordable housing, extreme poverty, decreasing government supports, changing family demographics, the challenges of raising children alone, domestic violence, and fractured social supports" (p. 10). School attendance can be a challenge for homeless children as some attend school regularly, some sporadically, others very inconsistently. Sutton (2007) reports "not only do homeless students face the daunting task of keeping up academically despite extended absences, lack of learning materials, and multiple school transfers, but they face the challenges of these difficult transitions without any emotional support" (p. 12). Additionally, she notes "homeless children have deep-rooted emotional problems due to a lack of stability in their living conditions, and their educational setting" (p. 12).

PREVALENCE OF HOMELESS CHILDREN

Homelessness has become a widespread phenomenon affecting not only adults, but children and adolescents as well. Baggerly and Jenkins (2009) report, as evidenced by the National Coalition for the Homeless (2007), that "there are 1.35 million children who are homeless each year in the United States, which is approximately 1% of the general population" (p. 45). Waxman and Reyes (1987), as cited in Timberlake and Sabatino (1994), state the "U. S. Conference of Mayors estimated that families with children constitute 35 percent of the homeless population" (p. 9). Additionally, Baggerly and Jenkins report, as stated in the Institute for Children and Poverty (ICP, 2001), "the average age of a homeless child is 6 years old" (p. 45). According to Cibrowski (1990), as cited in Timberlake and Sabatino (1994), "30% to 57%, or as many as 750,000 homeless children and youths, do not regularly attend school" (p. 9) and "approximately 50% of children who are homeless attend three different schools in 1 year (ICP, 2001)" (Baggerly & Jenkins, 2009, p. 45). These statistics provide an overwhelming sense of disparity homeless children and their families face.

MANIFESTATIONS OF HOMELESSNESS IN THE SCHOOL ENVIRONMENT

All environments, including the school environment are impacted by the fact that a child is homeless. Researchers, as previously mentioned, have discussed the impact of homelessness linked to behavioral, social, emotional, psychological, and academic challenges. Unlike other presenting issues and disorders, homelessness is not alleviated or lessened in a particular environment, but can manifest itself more in others For instance, children diagnosed with Attention deficit hyperactivity disorder (ADHD) excel in certain environments and fail in others due to heightened expectations to perform or master goals. Overstimulation and distractions exacerbate ADHD symptomology including hyperactivity or impulsivity, whereas, in an individual situation without overstimulation and/or distractions, the same child would be able to maintain attention and focus. Likewise, children with anxiety tend to become more anxious in particular environments and less anxious due to external and internal factors.

Homeless children remain clinically impaired in many environments. These environments are temporary stop gaps and provide places of learning and socialization for them. Homeless children "look on themselves and the world as being shaped by insecurity, fear, and isolation" (Oe, 1999, p. 324). This insecurity, fear, and isolation can become major obstacles for academic, social, and emotional growth in the school environment. According to Buckner et al. (1999), as cited in Baggerly and Borkowski (2004),

> Approximately 47% of children who were homeless were found to have clinically significant internalizing problems, such as depression and anxiety,

> compared to only 21% of children who were housed and behaviorally, children who are homeless tend to exhibit more externalizing problems, such as delinquent and aggressive behavior, then the normative sample. (p. 118)

Research has shown a correlation to childhood homelessness and the following presenting issues: lowered self-concept, neurodevelopmental problems, trauma, emotional and psychological developmental problems, behavioral problems, social problems, cognitive problems, self-control, low self-esteem, academic problems, achievement problems, depression, and anxiety (Baggerly, 2003, 2004; Baggerly & Jenkins, 2009, Masten et al., 1997). This is indicative of maladaptive factors associated with being homeless "place homeless children at risk for ongoing mental health problems" (Baggerly & Jenkins, 2009, p. 45).

Children manifest the effects of homelessness in multiple ways: academically, behaviorally, cognitively, and socially. Academically, the attention and focus required of students is often too intense to withstand for those who lack security of a home environment. Behaviorally, without adequate structure, homeless children act out more frequently; as noted by Landreth (2012), children who do not have limits and boundaries have ongoing relationship problems and issues with respecting others. Cognitively, homeless children may struggle due to lack of nutrition, adequate cognitive stimulation (such as learning toys and enrichment activities like going to museums) and the inaccessibility of materials for learning such as books, art supplies, and so forth. Lastly, homeless children are often teased when they display unkempt hygiene. Children in the school system often taunt and tease children who are different. For homeless children, there is a continued lack of adequate support, resources for learning, positive peer relationships, security, and acceptance.

REVIEW OF EVIDENCED BASED APPROACHES FOR TREATMENT

According to Sutton (2007), there was not a single intervention that showed effectiveness in treating homeless children's health nor their academic, behavioral, cognitive, emotional, psychological, or developmental functioning. However, over the past 11 years, play therapy has risen in its provision of meta-analyses with two noteworthy studies (Bratton, Ray, Rhine, & Jones, 2005; LeBlanc & Ritchie, 2001). In 1999, the Nana's Children Mental Health Foundation (MHF), was founded to provide no-cost play therapy services to homeless and impoverished children to decrease maladaptive functioning and increase adaptive functioning (Sutton, 2010). According to Baggerly, Ray, and Bratton (2010), "play therapy research continues to show strong evidence to support its use among a variation of populations and presenting problems" (p. 29). Evidenced-based treatment approaches continue to be needed to produce research on play therapy effectiveness with randomized and controlled studies for homeless children.

THEORETICAL UNDERPINNINGS OF PLAY THERAPY

The research has shown that play therapy is an effective treatment modality for children in both community and school settings (Baggerly, 2003; Baggerly, 2004; Baggerly & Jenkins, 2009; Sutton, 2007; Kolos, Green, & Crenshaw, 2009). According to Baggerly (2003), "play therapy has been proven to be effective in improving the mental health and self-concept of children residing in temporary shelters" (p. 91). Play therapy provides children with a safe, non-threatening environment to play out their life experiences, their reactions to life experiences and events, the way they would like for their life experiences to be, and their self-perception (Landreth, 2012). The following approaches have been demonstrated to be effective treatment modalities for homeless children: filial therapy, child-centered play therapy (CCPT), and child-centered group play therapy. According to Schaefer (2011), "Play therapy has been the leading psychotherapeutic intervention with children since the beginning of the 20th century" (p. ix). For the purpose of this chapter, solution-focused play therapy (SFPT) will be presented in the school environment as an intervention for working with homeless children.

Filial Therapy/Kinder Therapy

In filial/kinder therapy, caregivers/teachers are taught basic play therapy and filial therapy techniques and approaches that would allow them to become the therapeutic change agent in the home/classroom environment(s). Kolos, Green, and Crenshaw (2009) report filial therapy provides children with the opportunity to "experience unconditional acceptance and positive regard" (p. 366). More so, caregivers/teachers can implement basic play therapy techniques, while acting as agents of change to enhance and improve self-esteem and the relationship between homeless children and the caregivers/teachers.

Child Centered Play Therapy

Child-Centered Play Therapy (CCPT), also termed a nondirective approach, allows homeless children to experience freedom as noted in

Baggerly (2003, 2004) and Hunter (1993). According to Axline (1974), as cited in Hunter (1993, p. 4) "play is the natural medium of self-expression, supplying the opportunity to release fears and anxieties, frustration and aggression, and to make sense of and feel in control of their environment" (p. 40). According to Hunter, "nondirective play therapy gives children the experience of being completely accepted as they freely play in any way they choose; additionally, it allows nonverbal, indirect communication, and the building of a strong personal relationship with the therapist" (p. 40). Baggerly and Jenkins (2009), in a study on CCPT, found decreased negative and attachment avoidant behaviors. Behaviors that decreased included disengagement and self-negating which lead to more functional behaviors at home and school. Additionally, Baggerly and Jenkins found increased adaptive choice making behaviors both at home and school, higher levels of confidence, increased levels of empathy, toward self and others, and increased engagement in the learning process at school for children receiving CCPT interventions.

Child Centered Group Play Therapy

Homeless children respond positively to child-centered group play therapy according to a study by Baggerly (2004). Results indicated that CCPT group play therapy had positive effects on childrens' self-perception of perceived levels of competence, increased self-esteem, decreased negative mood, and decreased levels of physiological anxiety. The play therapy techniques utilized in this study consisted of returning responsibility to the child, encouragement, and self-esteem building. Baggerly reported CCPT group play therapy provided children freedom to play out their presenting challenges. Additional results indicated children communicate their challenges in relation to being homeless.

Solution-Focused Play Therapy

Several play therapy techniques are found to be effective by providing an array of play therapy approaches (child-centered play therapy, child-centered group play therapy, and filial/kinder therapy) when working with homeless children. More specific skills such as tracking, restating content, reflecting feeling, returning responsibility to the child, encouraging the child's effort, self-esteem building, and setting limits are utilized when providing interventions for these approaches (please see Baggerly, 2003; and Baggerly, 2004 for more information). According to Baggerly (2003), "play therapy provides many benefits for children who are homeless; it helps fulfill their needs for physiological survival, psychological safety, love and belonging, self-esteem, and self-actualization" (p. 103). SFPT includes the following techniques that have been found to be useful with homeless children: goal setting, The Miracle Question, exceptions, scaling, solution message, follow-up sessions (please see Nims, 2007 for more information). According to DeJong and Berg, as cited in Nims, 2007, "in solution-focused brief therapy (SFBT), the client is seen as competent and in charge, able to visualize desired changes and build on the positive aspects of what the client is already doing" (p. 54). He concludes the overall goal of SFBT is for clients to direct themselves toward adaptive behaviors, emotions, and thoughts that will accommodate new thinking patterns. More specifically, "the child wants this goal to happen" (p. 56). The American School Counselor Association's (ASCA) *National Model* (2012) suggests that goals for students in a learning environments are concrete, easily managed, and can be used for accountability purposes. SFPT has several of these tenets in common with the ASCA *National Model*. Solution-Focused Play Therapy offers school counselors a framework for incorporating counseling services for homeless children into the context of a planned, ASCA model program.

Solution-Focused Play Therapy Skills

Examples of each of the following skills are given in the case study at the end of this chapter.

Goal setting. As indicated earlier, goal setting with children should be done clearly and concretely (Nims, 2011). Given the academic, behavioral, cognitive, and social manifestations of homeless children, goal setting may need to be done in sequential order based on intensity and frequency levels of the desired need for change. The school counselor and teacher may need to consult about concrete goals prior to bringing the child in for counseling.

Miracle Question. To experience life without the challenges presented, children must visualize and create a solution to their presenting issue(s). According to Nims (2011), the miracle question allows for children to "experience what life would be like if the problem that brought them to therapy were magically solved" (p. 300).

Exceptions. Exceptions occur when presenting issues or challenges are not present because the child has adapted or used postitive coping skills in any given situation related to being homeless (Nims, 2011). In other words, there will be times when the child is successful or when the child is adapting, with positive coping skills, to difficult situations.

Scaling. Scaling allows the child to rate his progress, stagnation, and/or regression related to the goal set in the initial stages of the therapeutic intervention (Nims, 2011). As mentioned earlier, homeless children suffer from the impact of insecurity and fear in an array of environments in which they engage. Scaling allows the child to identify the intensity of emotions or experiences at a specific moment

Solution Message. The solution message is an expressive symbolism of the child's work in therapy (Nims, 2011). Solution messages can be utilized in an array of expressive arts and other mediums in the playroom.

SAMPLE SESSION OUTLINE IN THE SCHOOL ENVIRONMENT

Jessica is 8 years old. She has moved four times over the past year from one relative's house to the next with her mother and siblings due to her mother's inability to afford housing for Jessica and her family. Jessica and her family have recently moved into a community housing shelter for women and their children in the inner-city. Jessica attends public school and is in the second grade; since beginning at her new school she has struggled academically. Additionally, she has become disruptive and engages in misbehavior during class. Over the past year, her father has been incarcerated numerous times due to substance abuse and distribution. The recent moves have impacted Jessica in her academic, social, and familial environments. She has been referred to the school counselor, Ms. Smith, by her teacher, Ms. Ryan. Ms. Smith, the school counselor, enters her office while Jessica is waiting patiently for her on the bean bags outside of the playroom. When Jessica makes eye contact with Ms. Smith, she lowers her head down in shame and embarrassment. Her teacher, Ms. Ryan, sent her down to Ms. Smith's office when she stuck her tongue out at Johnny in class. Jessica reported that he laughed at her when she reported for the third day in a row that she did not do her homework and had to place a check by her name on the white board.

Ms. Smith eagerly invited Jessica into her playroom and inquired as to why she was sent to the office today. Jessica quickly responds, "I got into trouble with Ms. Ryan when I stuck my tongue out at Johnny. But he made fun of me for not turning my homework in and I had to go place a check by my name—he was rude!" Ms. Smith acknowledges Jessica's frustration with Johnny and invites her into a further conversation about why she has missed homework so often. Ms. Smith then asks Jessica "what has to change so that Jessica can stay in her classroom?" Jessica responds, "I need to do my homework and not let Johnny bother me, but it's really hard to do either." (Completing homework becomes a goal of the school counselor's work with Jessica). Jessica and Ms. Smith talk a bit longer about why Jessica has had such recent difficulty doing her homework and Jessica reports that sometimes it is just too loud at the shelter for her to concentrate because of the noises, kids running around, and the mothers yelling at their kids late at night. Ms. Smith asks Jessica if she thinks ear plugs might help. Jessica responds with a resounding "yes!" Ms. Smith pulls some ear plugs in a little plastic bag out of her desk and gives them to Jessica. She asks if Jessica "can set a daily goal of finding a quiet space to do her homework and ignoring Johnny when he makes fun of her?" Jessica responds positively to Ms. Smith and states that she "will tell the teacher instead of sticking her tongue out at Johnny." Ms. Smith encourages Jessica to go back to class but to come back in 2 days to meet again. Jessica agrees.

During the second session, Ms. Smith asks Jessica about the past 2 days and requests a report about both her homework and Johnny. Jessica is able to report positive successes in both areas. Ms. Smith then asks Jessica to "Imagine you woke up this morning and a miracle happened over night and your life was the way you want it to be. What would be going on?" "The miracle question helps children transition to experiencing what life would be like if the problem that brought them to therapy were magically solved" (Nims, 2011, p. 300). Jessica responds, "My dad would live with us again and we would be back in our old house." Ms. Smith invites Jessica to play with the sand tray. She asks Jessica to make a sand tray of a world where your dad was home again and you were all together in your old house. Jessica takes her time and constructs what appears to be a living room scene with all of her siblings and parents watching T.V. together while her dad was drinking what appears to be a beer. Ms. Smith continues with some clarification and expansion questions such as "What would you and your dad be doing right now? What would your siblings be doing? What would you and your mom be doing?" At this point Ms. Smith is trying to help Jessica visualize what it would feel like to be her old self again with her family together in her old house. More specifically, Ms. Smith is attempting for Jessica to remember the safety and security of the past. Ms. Smith gives Jessica a scale with faces ranging from 1-10 with the one face being very sad and the 10 face being very happy. She asks Jessica to circle a face with the number that shows the way she used to feel and then asks Jessica to circle on a picture face scale where she feels right now This technique, scaling, "elicits levels of feeling in child" (Nims, 2007, p.301) and helps the child recognize that there are times when they feel better and times when they feel worse. Jessica chooses a 7 for the way she used to feel and a 3 for the way she feels right now. Ms. Smith then asks Jessica "what has to happen over or the next few days for you to return to counseling and circle a 4?" Jessica responds, "I will continue to do my homework and not get into trouble."

In her third session, Ms. Smith talks about exceptions with Jessica. As noted by Nims, exceptions

> are little pieces of the miracle or times in the past when the problem that brought the child to therapy did not occur. Nims notes that exceptions are also used to describe past occasions when the child experienced some of the goal. (p. 301)

Ms. Smith and Jessica talk about times before Jessica's dad was incarcerated and before the family lost their house. Jessica recognized that during that time she was doing her homework and getting along well with others. Ms. Smith asks Jessica to "draw a picture of a time when she felt successful at turning in her homework or successful at not paying attention to Johnny."

In the fourth session Ms. Smith invited Jessica into the playroom and asked her to play with the puppets. They talked about goal setting and what Jessica feels she has accomplished based on the last session. Ms. Smith invites Jessica to use a puppet to play herself and Ms. Smith, along with some other puppets, acted out the roles of children being noisy at the shelter and trying to distract the Jessica puppet from doing her homework. Jessica practices, through the puppet, finding a quiet space and concentrating on completing math problems.

In the fifth session Ms. Smith invites Jessica to explore a solution message. According to Nims (2007), the solution message offers the child "a concrete, written summary of the session that the child can take home as a visual representation of the child's efforts toward finding his or her own solution" (p. 302). Because Jessica had shown improvement in her studies and turning in homework, she reported during a scaling question feeling like a 5. So, Ms. Smith asked Jessica to concentrate on drawing pictures of possible solutions that would help Jessica move from feeling like a 5 to feeling like a 7. Jessica draws several pictures including a picture of her playing with a few friends at recess, visiting her grandparents, and a picture of herself and another child at the shelter playing together. Ms. Smith's goal is directly related to Jessica feeling more positive and discovering solutions to her identified problems.

In follow up sessions, Ms. Smith and Jessica continue to work on ways for Jessica to feel safe and secure, by using school as her "home base." Ms. Smith continues to discuss Jessica's goals and assists her in developing solutions for improving her situation. Jessica continues to visit Ms. Smith once a week. Ms. Smith finds out over the summer Jessica's mother finds a job and permanent housing with Jessica's grandparents. Jessica still came to "visit" Ms. Smith often to check on her face scale, participate in some puppet shows, and complete some drawings which became her favorite activities. She would quietly stage the puppets together and Ms. Smith would often hear, "If a miracle was to happen..." as well as some solution messages.

CASE STUDY WITH APPLICATION OF TREATMENT RECOMMENDATIONS

As previously stated, there are many effective play therapy approaches for working with homeless children. Developing play therapy interventions can enhance homeless students' overall awareness of their problems, knowledge about change, goal setting capabilities, and actions toward change. Lastly, individual and/or group counseling can provide children with the freedom to express themselves metaphorically and symbolically as well as developing curative factors known to occur in group counseling such as universality, altruism, and catharsis.

CONCLUSION

As Baggerly (2003) states, the playroom is a place "where children can re-enact and resolve traumatic experiences and develop skills and confidence to face future challenges" (p. 103). Children possess an inner resiliency to withstand adversity. Play therapy has become a widespread intervention that encourages children to play out their presenting issues and challenges in a space that is unlike any other, a place where they will be accepted for who they are, and a place where they can express themselves without judgment. SFPT offers school counselors an opportunity to develop relationships while focusing on concrete and attainable solutions with homeless students who may lack the skills and supports necessary for succeeding academically and socially in a school environment.

REFERENCES

Axline, V. (1974). *Play therapy.* New York, NY: Ballantine Books.

Baggerly, J. (2003). Child-centered play therapy with children who are homeless: Perspective and procedures. *International Journal of Play Therapy, 12*(2), 87-106. doi:10.1037/h0088880

Baggerly, J. (2004). The effects of child-centered group play therapy on self-concept, depression, and anxiety of children who are homeless. *International Journal of Play Therapy, 13*(2), 31-51. doi:10.1037/h0088889

Baggerly, J. (2006). "I'm rich": Play therapy with children who are homeless. In C. E. Schaefer & H. G. Kaduson (Eds.), *Contemporary play therapy: Theory, research, and practice* (pp. 161-185). New York, NY: The Guilford Press.

Baggerly, J., & Borkowski, T. (2004). Applying the ASCA national model to elementary school students who are homeless: A case study. *Professional School Counseling, 8*(2), 116-123.

Baggerly, J., & Jenkins, W. (2009). The effectiveness of child-centered play therapy on developmental and diagnostic factors in children who are homeless. *International Journal of Play Therapy, 18*(1), 45-55. doi:10.1037/a0013878

Baggerly, J., Ray, D., & Bratton, S. (2010). *Child-centered play therapy research: The evidence base for effective practice*. Hoboken, NJ: John Wiley.

Biggar, H. A. (2002). Homeless children's self-report of experiences and the role of age, history of homelessness, and current resident in academic performance. *Dissertation Abstracts International, 63*(1-B), 563.

Bratton, S., Ray, D., Rhine, T., & Jones, L. (2005). The efficacy of play therapy with children: A meta-analytic review of treatment outcomes. *Professional Psychology: Research and Practice, 36*(4), 367-390. doi:10.1037/0735-7028.36.4.376

Buckner, J., Bassuk, E., Weinreb, L., & Brooks, M. (1999) Homelessness and its relation to the mental health and behavior of low-income school-age children. *Developmental Psychology, 35*(1), 246-257. doi:10.1037/0012-1649.35.1.246

Guarino, K., & Volk, K. (2010). Child homelessness: Minimizing the impact, ending the epidemic. *Communities & Banking, 21*(1), 10-12.

Hunter, L. (1993). Sibling play therapy with homeless children: An opportunity in the crisis. *Child Welfare, 72*(1), 65-75.

Institute for Children and Poverty. (2001). *Back to the future: The brownstone and future link afterschool programs for homeless children.* Retrieved http://www.icphusa.org/PDF/reports/BackToTheFuture.pdf

Kolos, A., Green, E., & Crenshaw, D. (2009). Conducting filial therapy with homeless parents. *American Journal of Orthopsychiatry, 79*(3), 366-374.

Landreth, G. (2012). *Play therapy: The art of the relationship* (3rd ed.). New York, NY: Taylor & Francis Group.

LeBlanc, M., & Ritchie, M. (1999). Predictors of play therapy outcomes. *International Journalof Play Therapy, 8*(2), 19-34. doi:10.1037/h0089429

LeBlanc, M., & Ritchie, M. (2001). A meta-analysis of play therapy outcomes. *Counseling Psychology Quarterly, 14*, 149-163.

Maslow, A. H. (1968). *Toward a psychology of being* (2nd ed.). Princeton, NJ: Van Nostrand.

Masten, A. S., Sesman, A., Si-Asar, R., Lawrence, C., Niliotis, D., & Dionne, J.A. (1997). Educational risks for children experiencing homelessness. *Journal of School Psychology, 35*(1), 27-46. doi:10.1016/S0022-4405(96)00032-5

National Coalition for the Homeless. (1999). Who is homeless? Retrieved from http://www.nationalhomeless.org/facts.html

National Coalition for the Homeless. (2007). How many people experience homelessness? *NHC Fact Sheet #2.* Retrieved from http://www.nationalhomeless.org/publications.facts/How_Many.pdf

Nims, D. (2007). Integrating play therapy techniques into solution-focused brief therapy. *International Journal of Play Therapy, 16*(1), 54-68. doi:10.1037/1555-6824.16.1.54

Nims, D. R. (2011). Solution-focused play therapy: Helping children and families find solutions. In C. E. Schaefer (Ed.), *Foundations of play therapy*. Hoboken, NJ: John Wiley.

Oe, E. (1999). Sibling group play therapy. In D. S. Sweeney & L. E. Homeyer (Eds.), *The handbook of group play therapy: How to do it, how it works, whom it's best for* (pp. 319-335). San Francisco, CA: Jossey-Bass.

Rubin, D. H., Erickson, C. J., Agustin, M. S., Cleary, S. D., Allen, J. K., & Cohen, P. (1996). Cognitive and academic functioning of homeless children compared with housed children. *Pediatrics, 97*, 289-294.

Schaefer, C. (2011). *Foundations of play therapy*. Hoboken, NJ: John Wiley.

Sutton, A. M. (2010). The nana's model: School-based play therapy with children who are homeless or severely impoverished. In A. Drewes & C. Schaefer (Eds.), *School-based play therapy* (2nd ed., pp. 435-466). Hoboken, NJ: John Wiley. doi:10.1002/9781118269701.ch20

Sutton, M. (2007). Play therapy and children who are homeless. *Play Therapy Magazine*, 12-13.

Timberlake, E., & Sabatino, C. (1994). Homeless children: Impact of school attendance on self-esteem and loneliness. *Social Work in Education, 16*(1), 9-20.

Waxman, L., & Reyes, L. (1987). *A status report on homeless families in American's cities: A 29-city survey*. Washington, DC: U.S. Conference of Mayors.

ABOUT THE AUTHORS

Jennifer N. Baggerly, PhD, LMHC-S, RPT-S, is an associate professor and chair of the Division of Counseling and Human Services at the University of North Texas-Dallas. She is on the board of directors of the Association for Play Therapy (APT) and the former chair of the APT research committee. Dr. Baggerly is a licensed mental health counselor supervisor, a registered play therapist supervisor and a field traumatologist. A recipient of the Outstanding Play Therapist Award from the Florida Association for Play Therapy, she has provided child mental health services locally and disaster relief services internationally, including victims of the tsunami in Sri Lanka and Hurricane Katrina. Dr. Baggerly's multiple research projects have led to her being recognized as one of the lead play therapy researchers in the world. She has numerous publications, including many juried articles; multiple books chapters and several videos. She is also the lead editor of the recently published book *Child-Centered Play Therapy Research: The Evidence Base for Effective Practice*. Dr. Baggerly is a recognized authority on play therapy and has presented papers on play therapy intervention with children who are homeless and tsunami victims in Argentina, Canada, England and Taiwan.

Vanessa Bowles, PhD, has served as a professional school counselor at Duplessis Primary (pre-K-5) in Ascension Parish, Louisiana for 8 years. Additionally, she has worked as an adjunct instructor for the Counselor Education Department at Louisiana State University (LSU) teaching group counseling, practicum, and internship since 2010. She has acted as an on-site supervisor for LSU master's student interns. Her educational background includes a bachelor of science degree from LSU, a master's of education in counselor education from Southeastern University, and a doctorate in counselor education from Virginia Tech. She is registered as a licensed professional counselor in the state of Louisiana. Dr. Bowles work experience includes working with court appointed special advocates (CASA) and The Children's Advocacy Center counseling children and families victimized by abuse, counseling children with emotional and behavioral disorders, counseling youth in the state's custody, and providing services to children and adults with mental illnesses including evaluation and assessment. Her research interests include compassion fatigue, counselor wellness, counselor supervision, school counseling and positive behavior support (PBIS). She has presented at local, state, and national conferences and has served as past-president of the Ascension School Counseling Association.

S. Kent Butler, Jr. holds a PhD and is an associate professor at the University of Central Florida in Orlando, Florida. During the 2012-2013 academic year he is a visiting associate professor at the College of William & Mary. He is the coauthor of a book for doctoral students on obtaining an academic post and has authored several book chapters and articles on counseling written from a multicultural perspective. His dedication and service to the Association for Multicultural Counseling and Development afforded him the opportunity to serve as the organization's 2011-2012 President. He continues to work closely with colleagues, students, and clients surrounding issues of diversity and social justice in counseling.

Peggy L. Ceballos, PhD, received her MEd in counseling from Southeastern Louisiana University in 2002 and her doctoral degree as a counselor educator in May of 2008 from the University of North Texas, where she received formal training in play therapy interventions for young children. She has work experience as an elementary school counselor and as a community counselor. Currently, she is an assistant professor at the University of North Carolina at Charlotte (UNCC) in the counseling department. In this position, Dr. Ceballos serves as associate director for the Multicultural Play Therapy Center at UNCC and as coordinator of the school counseling program. Her research agenda focuses on investigating the effectiveness of school counseling interventions with minority children identified as at-risk for academic success, with a special interest in Latino children and their parents.

Ashley Churbock, MA, graduated from the Ohio State University in 2008 with a bachelor of arts degree in psychology. She worked as an applied behavior analysis tutor from 2008 until 2012 under a board certified behavior anaylst. From 2009-2010, Ashley worked at nonprofit school, Greater Baton Rouge Hope Academy, that specialized in education for children with varying degrees of learning disabilities. In 2011, Ashley graduated from Louisiana State University with a master's degree in community counseling. She currently works for communities in schools and serves as a site coordinator at Capitol Middle School in Baton Rouge, Louisiana providing counseling, behavior interventions, and other psychosocial needs.

Kelly Cowart, EdS, NCC, is an elementary school counselor in Gwinnett County, Georgia. She has been an elementary school counselor for 13 years and was named the 2006 National Elementary School Counselor of the Year by the American School Counselor Association. She is a frequent presenter on school counseling issues at state and national conferences. Prior to becoming a school counselor, Ms. Cowart was a community counselor providing play therapy to sexually abused children and adolescents at a child advocacy center. She is presently a doctoral student in the P-16 Counseling and Student Personnel Services Program at the University of Georgia.

Jennifer R. Curry, PhD, is an assistant professor of counselor education at Louisiana State University where she is the coordinator of the school counseling program. Her education background includes a bachelors of science degree from Western Kentucky University, a master's of education in human development counseling from Vanderbilt University, and a doctorate in counselor education from University of Central Florida. She has served as a professional school counselor in elementary, middle, and high school. She has presented her work at over 50 national, and 20 international conferences, and has published over 30 peer reviewed articles in refereed national and international counseling journals. She has served as guest editor of American School Counselor Association's *Professional School Counseling* journal and the *Journal of Lesbian, Gay, Bisexual and Transgender Issues in Counseling*. In addition, she is the recipient of Vanderbilt's Roger Aubrey Northstar award for the counselor most likely to change the field of counseling, the American Counseling Association's Ross Trust Award for school counseling, the Biggs Pine Award for excellence in scholarship, and the Association for Spiritual, Ethical, and Religious Values in Counseling's national service award.

Erin M. Dugan, PhD, is a licensed professional counselor-supervisor and a registered play therapist supervisor. In addition to her clinical work, Dr. Dugan is an associate professor at Louisiana State University Health Sciences Center in the Rehabilitation Counseling Department. She has worked both in the schools and community and specializes in her work with children (ages 2-12), attachment disorders, and child-parent relationship therapy. She also provides counseling services to adolescents and families, offering parent training and child-parent relationship therapy classes. Dr. Dugan conducts workshops and training seminars to promote play therapy to students, professionals, and the community. She has presented nationally at professional conferences. She is the recent recipient of the Association for Play Therapy's Professional Education and Training Award.

Laura J. Fazio-Griffith received her PhD from the University of New Orleans in May of 2002 in counselor education. She is a national certified counselor, licensed professional counselor-supervisor, a licensed marriage and family therapist, and a registered play therapist-supervisor. Dr. Fazio-Griffith was the clinical director for the Counseling and Training Center of Families Helping Families of Greater New Orleans for approximately 5 years. She provided individual, group, and family counseling, as well as supervision for master's level counseling interns. She has been an adjunct assistant professor at the University of New Orleans, Southeastern Louisiana University, and Louisiana State University. She is currently an assistant professor at Southeastern Louisiana University in the counseling program since August of 2010, where she coordinates the play therapy program. She was the president of Louisiana Association of Counselor Educators and Supervisors from 2004-06. She was the counselor education representative on the LACES board until July, 2011. She serves as treasurer on the Louisiana Association for Play Therapy executive board. She is currently serving as president-elect for the Louisiana Association for Career Development. She has presented nationally and statewide on various topics related to supervision, play therapy, and group work. Her research interests include group work, personality disorders, supervision, and play therapy.

Eric J. Green, PhD, LPC-S, RPT-S, earned his doctorate in counselor education from the University of New Orleans in 2005. Previously, he was a professor and coordinated the Play Therapy Graduate Certificate Program at the Johns Hopkins University in Baltimore, Maryland. Currently, he is a full-time faculty member in the counselor education program at the University of North Texas at Dallas, as well as the director of the school counseling program.

Barbara B. Hebert, PhD, is the director of the University Counseling Center at Southeastern Louisiana University. She holds a doctorate in counselor education from the University of New Orleans and is a licensed professional counselor-supervisor and a registered play therapist-supervisor. Dr. Hebert has served as assistant professor and coordinator of school counseling at Northwestern State University in Natchitoches, Louisiana. She has also been an adjunct instructor at the University of New Orleans and Southeastern Louisiana University, a private mental health practitioner, and a secondary school counselor. In addition, Dr. Hebert supervises LPC-interns and volunteers as a play therapist at the Children's Advocacy Center in Covington, Louisiana. She has presented at state, regional, national, and international professional conferences and has published in both state and national professional journals.

Dodie Limberg, MA, is a doctoral candidate at the University of Central Florida in the counselor education program. She is a certified K-12 school counselor and has training as a mental health counselor with a focus on adolescent and couples counseling. She has experience as a school and mental health counselor in Florida, Switzerland, and Israel. Miss Limberg has used play therapy techniques with her clients and students, and has taught play therapy courses. Her research interests include school counseling, wellness, international counseling, and the development of altruism.

Kimberly L. Mason, PhD, is an assistant professor and practicum and internship coordinator in the counselor education program at the University of New Orleans. She earned her doctorate in counselor education and supervision, with a minor in school and child/adolescent counseling, and a master's in community agency counseling from the University of New Orleans. Prior to joining the faculty at UNO, she was an assistant professor and practicum coordinator at Cleveland State University. Her research focuses on bullying and cyberbullying, adolescents' use of social media and digital citizenship and its influence on psychosocial development, establishing best practices for school counselors, and the responsive nature school counselors serve in the school system. Currently, Dr. Mason is authoring a bullying book titled, *Bullying No More: A Guide to Protecting Your Child from Bullying*, which is under contract by Barron's Publishing Company. She was a contributing member of the Ohio Department of Education's Anti-Harassment, Anti-Intimidation, and Anti-Bullying Model Policy. She developed a remedial bullying intervention program for students titled, *Building Buddies, Not Bullies Program* for the Safe and Drug Free Schools Program and two instructional online courses on bullying and cyberbullying for counselors, educators, and other treatment and prevention professionals. Dr. Mason has experience working with a variety of diverse populations as a school counselor in pre-K-12 schools for 4½, as well as a clinical mental health and substance abuse counselor in urban and suburban settings for 9 years.

Jonathan H. Ohrt, PhD, is an assistant professor and chair of school counseling in the Department of Counseling and Higher Education at the University of North Texas. He is a certified K-12 school counselor and has experience counseling individuals and groups in high school, residential, and community settings. His research includes professional school counseling, group counselor training and effectiveness, and wellness.

Julie A. Ritchie has a bachelor of science degree in family studies concentrating in child development from Southeastern Louisiana University. She received her master's of education in counselor education concentrating in clinical mental health counseling from Southeastern Louisiana University. Her undergraduate experience includes working with children and families in a hospital setting with child life specialists. Her clinical experience includes completing her practicum experience at Southeastern University's Counseling Center. She completed her internship with child advocacy services in which she worked with children and families of alleged abuse. Julie is currently working towards licensure. Julie would like to continue counseling children and families utilizing play therapy interventions.

Angela I. Sheely-Moore, PhD, NCC, is an assistant professor at Montclair State University located in Montclair, New Jersey. A former school counselor, Dr. Sheely-Moore also served in a variety of research studies as lead and coinvestigator in grant supported, school-university collaborations in the area of play-based counseling services and strengths-based parenting programs. Her research interests include school-based mental health services for at-risk students and their families, play therapy, and multicultural competencies for school counselors.

M. Ann Shillingford, PhD, is an assistant professor of counselor education at the College of William & Mary. She has several years of experience as a professional school counselor prior to completing her doctorate at the University of Central Florida. Dr. Shillingford-Butler has a keen interest in factors that affect children and has written on topics such as children diagnosed with attention deficit hyperactivity disorder (ADHD) and children being raised by single parents.

Jacqueline M. Swank, PhD, LMHC, LCSW, RPT-S is an assistant professor of counselor education in the School of Human Development and Organizational Studies in Education at the University of Florida. She is a licensed mental health counselor, licensed clinical social worker and a registered play therapist-supervisor. Dr. Swank has clinical experience working with children, adolescents and their families in residential, inpatient, day treatment, and outpatient settings. Her research interests include play, adventure, and nature-based interventions with at-risk children and adolescents, counselor development, and assessment.

Shannon Trice-Black, PhD, is an assistant professor of counselor education at the College of William and Mary. She has over 10 years of experience working in schools and in private practice with children and adolescents. Her passion is training future school counselors to strive to meet the needs of every child.

Jenifer N, Ware is a LPC-S in a group private practice and a doctoral student at the University of North Texas. She has worked with children in a variety of settings, including agencies, schools, and private practice. Jenifer has extensive clinical experience with play therapy, both as a play therapist and a supervisor. She also advocates for the field and is active in leadership for the North Texas chapter of the Association for Play Therapy.

M. Whitfield-Williams has a wealth of counseling experience in multiple settings including private practice, therapeutic foster care, residential settings, intensive in-home, day treatment, and outpatient therapy among individuals, families, and groups. She is an assistant professor at Slippery Rock University in the department of counseling and development. Her credentials include national certified counselor, approved clinical supervisor, certified clinical mental health counselor, and licensed professional counselor.

June M. Williams, PhD, LPC-S, is the interim department head of the Department of Counseling and Human Development at Southeastern Louisiana University and an associate professor of counseling. She earned her doctorate from the University of New Orleans in 1997. Prior to joining the counseling faculty full-time in 2000, Dr. Williams served as the assistant director of the University Counseling Center and as the assistant dean of Student Life at Southeastern. She has served as president of several state and national professional associations including Chi Sigma Iota, International Counseling Honor Society, Louisiana College Counseling Association, American College Counseling Association, and Louisiana Counseling Association, and she has served on the editorial boards for the *Journal of College Counseling* and *Adultspan.* She served two terms (8 years) on the Louisiana LPC Board of Examiners. She has taught a variety of counseling courses including counseling techniques, group counseling, human growth and development, and grief and loss counseling. Her research interests include grief and loss, gratitude, and resilience.

Jolie Ziomek-Daigle, PhD, LPC is an associate professor at the University of Georgia and coordinator of the school counseling program. She received a PhD from the University of New Orleans in 2005. Prior to graduation, Dr. Daigle worked as a school counselor at both the elementary and high school levels in New Orleans Public Schools. She also worked in a private practice and counseled children, adolescents, and families. Her research interests include the development of clinical skills for school counselors, gatekeeping issues in counselor education, play therapy in the school setting, and research-based school counseling interventions that promote the academic and social development of K-12 youth. Dr. Daigle has presented at the international and national levels and has publications in referred journals such as the *Journal of Counseling and Development, Professional School Counseling, The Family Journal,* and the *Middle School Journal,* among others.

CPSIA information can be obtained at www.ICGtesting.com
Printed in the USA
BVOW08s2103250215

389229BV00004B/111/P